White Mountain

By Robert Twigger

Angry White Pyjamas: An Oxford Poet Trains with the
Tokyo Riot Police

Big Snake: The Hunt for the World's Longest Python

The Extinction Club

Being a Man

Voyageur: Across the Rocky Mountains in a Birchbark Canoe

Lost Oasis: A Desert Adventure: In Search of Paradise

Real Men Eat Puffer Fish

Dr Ragab's Universal Language (*a novel*)

Red Nile: A Biography of the World's Greatest River

White Mountain

Real and Imagined Journeys
in the Himalayas

Robert Twigger

WEIDENFELD & NICOLSON

First published in Great Britain in 2016 by Weidenfeld & Nicolson
an imprint of The Orion Publishing Group Ltd
Carmelite House, 50 Victoria Embankment
London EC4Y 0DZ

An Hachette UK Company

1 3 5 7 9 10 8 6 4 2

A CIP catalogue record for this book is
available from the British Library.

ISBN (hardback) 978 0 297 60871 4
ISBN (trade paperback) 978 1 474 60436 9
ISBN (eBook) 978 0 297 60872 1

Typeset by Input Data Services Ltd, Bridgwater, Somerset

Printed and bound by CPI Group (UK) Ltd, Croydon, CR0 4YY

www.orionbooks.co.uk

To Nonaka Iku Sensei
To all Mothers of Invention and Mothers of inventors

Contents

Maps

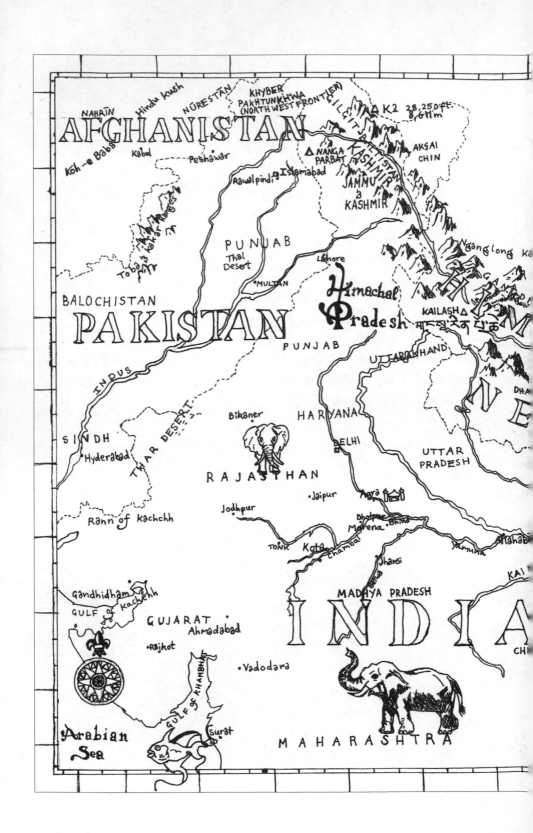

In your country you may be a great lord, a tax collector or a substantial landowner. Here, you are nothing. Even I, the ruler of this whole province, am nothing. *Only the gods rule here.*

Tibetan Garpon or Viceroy, Western Tibet, 1936

All India is full of holy men stammering gospels in strange tongues, shaken and consumed in the fires of their own zeal; dreamers, babblers and visionaries, as it has been from the beginning and will continue to the end.

Rudyard Kipling

Only much later on, when I had already journeyed to all the continents, did I sense that adventure is not made up of distant lands and mountain tops, rather it lies in one's readiness to exchange the domestic hearth for an uncertain resting-place.

Reinhold Messner

Watch out for the yak without horns, since he butts hardest.

Ladakhi proverb

PART I

Demons

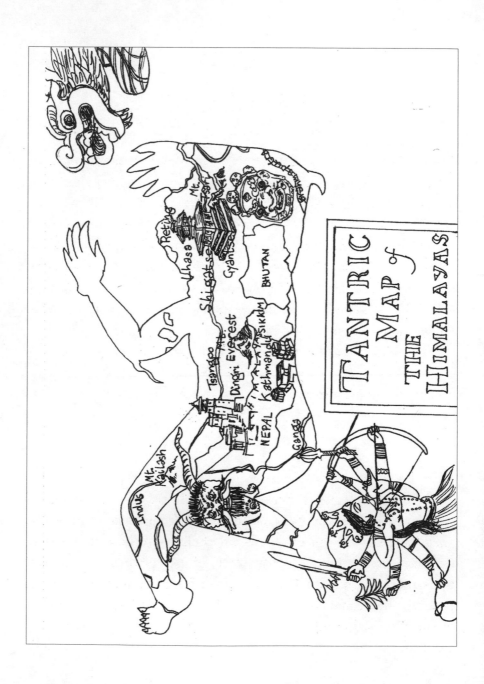

I

Magic Mountain

There is no really compelling geological argument to show clearly where to divide the Himalaya from adjoining mountain ranges. They are all part of a huge knot of mountains that is hard to fully disentangle. Consequently the placement of boundaries to shape the region is a problem of geographical interpretation. Some measurements of the Himalayas include Afghanistan's Koh-i-Baba range in the west and the highlands of northern Burma in the east, making the Himalaya over 4,000 km long . . . The northern and southern boundaries of the Himalaya likewise are not firmly fixed.

Professor David Zurick, author of Himalaya, Life on the Edge of the World

Neighbours living near are better than relatives living far away.

Balti proverb

The Anglo-Afghan Sufi writer Idries Shah was born in the Himalayas, in the hill town of Simla. In his many books he often retells ancient tales with an emphasis on their usefulness rather than their folkloric value. One story tells of a river that finds herself weaving through a dry sandy desert in front of a mountain range, perhaps the Himalayas. The river throws herself against the foot of the mountain and forms . . . a puddle in the sand. What can I do? she thinks miserably. A voice, the voice of the wind, tells

---

* Baltistan is to be found between Pakistan and Ladakh.

It's always further, always higher

the river, 'You must give yourself up to the winds, become clouds that will blow over the mountains. There you will fall as rain on the other side and find yourself rushing down to the sea.' The river was nervous and especially disliked the idea of giving up her individuality to the winds and then the sea, but the winds told her, 'Even if you throw yourself for a thousand years against the mountain foot the most you will become is a vile swamp. Instead, trust that your essence will survive even if your outer form changes – and finally you will find yourself home, with the ocean.' The river used all her courage and gave herself up to the winds and flew into the sky and over the mountains and finally down to the sea. There she at last understood how to be both a drop of water and an ocean at the same time and yet not lose sight of either; truly it was worth the journey.

I had been planning a journey to the Himalayas, the place of my father's birth (Mussoorie, another hill resort), for many years. As a young lad he had been carried in a sedan chair through the snow to his first school high in the hills. Such snippets of family history can act like a small demon, driving you on. Sir Richard Burton, an explorer I particularly admired, explained that he had to roam around endlessly because 'the devil drives'. While in India he also studied Sufism, along with falconry, and was tireless in his acquisition of local languages and dialects. Yet once I arrived I spent months not going near the mountains. For many weeks I lacked even the oomph to get out of Delhi.

We are so bombarded with images of the mountains, great photographs and YouTube documentaries featuring people squirrel-suiting* down canyons at 27,000 feet that, long before I'd been there, I felt I'd done that. Oddly enough, the weird and clunky end to *A Passage to India* (the movie) is very similar to the effect the Himalayas have on you when you finally get among them. Pristine angled mountains, often glimpsed from a road that is carved into a damp shale-collapsing hillside. But all that would come later.

In the meantime I was revelling in just being in India, the epicentre of all backpacker action, where the hippy traveller cliché is a daily reality and yet seems to dent the lives of Indians hardly a bit. Though in the fifteen years since I'd last been there the tent cities of semi-homeless people had grown bigger, and the smell of buffalo dung had given way to the more pervasive smell of diesel exhaust.

Amid displays of limes pyramiding in the harsh sunlight, endless tooting and underpowered revving, fewer people seemed interested in me as a foreigner. I had experienced the same in Cairo, my home for the last ten years: the falling off of interest in foreigners. Life the world over takes more out of you, or makes you more self-centred – why, I wasn't sure; maybe on this trip I would find out.

I was in the modern part of Delhi, out near the airport, not so distinguishable from the part of Cairo where my apartment was; it felt as if I had exchanged one dusty polluted madhouse

---

* A kind of flying suit used in freefall parachuting – halfway between hang glider and falling stone.

5

for another. Ring roads spanned and spasmed across dry rubbish-filled canals and fields stacked with bricks and other indications of their future. Wind down the cab window: a smell of burning – part straw on fire, part sweet reek of garbage. Still, there was always the curry. I became a considerable glutton, surprising myself at the extent to which I loved Indian food. I also became a connoisseur of Indian lagers – especially Kingfisher Super Strong and Godfather – surely a unique name for a beer in any language. I was sort of searching for traces of my grandfather – he'd been an engineer in the Indian army – when I wasn't searching for my next . . . Godfather. I also loitered in chain coffee shops such as Costa or Starbucks, which abroad have more caché than they have at home, owing, I imagine, to the relatively huge price of coffee.

The Costas I went to entailed going through a micro-park, every leaf grey with the daily downfall of airborne soot. There were monkeys in the trees and cowardly stray dogs that got bolder at night, even menacing me when I was crossing said park with a few cans of Godfather from the late-night liquor store. I was living free of charge at a friend's house, sleeping on his office floor; it was a beguiling combination of ease and discomfort.

My plan, such as it was, was to try and work out what was 'special' about the Himalayas. This would require both historical research and some tramping around. By 'special' I meant specifically some kind of meaning off the usual utilitarian/hedonistic scale, somewhere in the batsqueak-inaudible zone, the muted emissions of spirit and soma. I was loath to use the normal words: spirituality, numinous (no, actually I quite liked numinous), religion, prayer, worship, faith, because they seemed to take me in the wrong direction, back into abstraction. India is more about distraction than abstraction, for sure, as everyday reality and cosmic coincidence get rubbed in your face till you can't stop blinking. If I ignored the heartfelt urgency that piled-up coincidences bring on, then I'd be lying about the attraction of India; the trick was to try and broaden this out, roll it up to the mountains, their history, and why for centuries man had hurled himself at this huge rocky spine.

The book I would write would end up skewed around, skewered upon, the years 1903–05, which is when Kipling suddenly was proved wrong and East and West really did start to meet, cross over, intermingle or at least show some interest in each other after long centuries of semi-cocooned isolation. It would also begin and end with Nagas of one sort or another: gods or demons of Hindu mythology, depending on your perspective, but also a hill tribe in north-east India.

I have mentioned the reading and the tramping. Another tool in my formidable bag of writer's tricks was a tireless psychogeographical exploration/explanation of the Himalayan region using the tried-and-tested formulas of derive and détournement. Derive meant wandering, circling, drifting – usually through a city, though I saw no reason not to apply that to the whole of the region (mainly India) that bordered the Himalayas. My reasoning was that 'drift' became meaningful when incidents occurred that related to earlier incidents in this or previous journeys. Though 'drifting', which entailed obeying one's intuition rather than mere randomness (drifting was not rolling a dice to get directions), might be less daunting within the limits and confines of a city, India, as I have mentioned, had long ago proved to me to be a kind of coincidence generator i.e. merely travelling there produced the kind of meaningful incident that linked back and forward both in that journey and others. Many times I have travelled in India on a journey sparkling with details that I barely later recall, save that so many seemed to link up, and so many encounters seemed to channel one forward to some kind of destiny, maybe only in a small sense, but still an overwhelming sense of meaning that sadly seems to evaporate on my return to Blighty.

The bare facts of such a journey, the places visited, the trains ridden, the meals eaten – that would be 'real'. And yet what one made of it, the sense of magic that grew up around these mundane details, that would be the incomparably more powerful and influential imaginary journey. Being fairly bored by now with my own true-life adventures – which, if truth be told, were a little meagre alongside the great climbers, explorers and adventurers of the past – my imaginary journey around the Himalayas would therefore be a journey round the real exploits of others. But therein lay a side problem, also interesting.

For almost as long as I had been planning my trip to the Himalayas I had been observing with some relish the quantity and quality of the lies told by the great explorers. Some I had been able to check up on myself. I found that Scottish explorer Alexander Mackenzie had exaggerated the ferocity of Rocky Mountain rivers. Gerhard Rohlfs had reported certain dunes in the Sahara as fifty metres high and almost impossible to cross; these same dunes, which have barely shifted in 5,000 years (we know this from the evidence of prehistoric hearths found partly covered by slow-moving sands), I discovered were a mere 10 metres high and took no more than a couple of hours to cross. I liked these little lies because they showed the great explorers were human after all, regardless of their heroic exploits and travails.

Not for a minute am I impugning the psychological courage of Mackenzie or Rohlfs. To go where no man (or at least no European) has gone before, without a satphone or GPS – that is the real test; the physical one is merely a footnote. Several explorers, including Richard Burton, completed their major journeys while being carried by natives, having become too sick to travel under their own steam. And, thus, while I am properly amazed and impressed by such modern exploits as walking the Nile and the Amazon, I can't help feeling it is facing psychological unknowns rather than physical ones that sorts out the sheep from the goats. Not that goats are everyone's cup of tea; here is a proverb from the Himalayas that failed to make the collection I have dispersed under every chapter heading: 'If you have no problems, buy a goat.'

A cyclist with purpose

So, I would drift.

Drifting would, I theorised, generate the right connecting material for the reports of the visible and invisible worlds made by others more daring and ambitious than myself. By drifting I would allow my intuition to find the way; a fallible guide, but no more so than any other.

The invisible world includes the magical world, the world of demons – which is where I start. As I have almost hinted, any book about mountains has to be, inter alia, also . . . and, inevitably, about some forms of magic, even if it is just the snow-crunching magic of walking on a glacier in the blue light of dawn. Let us not be so limited! Here we must look at, and deal with, the magic endowed by, conjured up by, associated with, every aspect of the world's vastest range – the Himalayas.

In this way I hope to avoid the requirement to be either

credulous or metro-sceptical. And yet we *are* sceptical. We live in the scientific age, despite Wittgenstein's caveat that 'too little is made of the fact that we include the words "soul" and "spirit" in our own civilised vocabulary. Compared with this, the fact that we do not believe that our soul eats and drinks is a minor detail.'*

I have travelled in lands where souls do eat and drink – and I hope to take you there with me.

Do I eschew the scientific? I couldn't if I wanted to. It is the *given* of our age. Which means that it allows people the luxury of believing anything . . . as long as it is peer-reviewed and appears in *Nature*.

Magic hovers over the inexplicable. We seek it out because we love it. We adore mystery and we don't mind being conned, provided it is done well. Magic starts where we cease to believe an explanation will add anything. Of course we all want to know 'how the trick is done', but the reason magicians refuse to tell us is not just about self-aggrandisement; we do not really want to know. This may look like a wish to be fooled, but in reality it is about reaching a place where explanation in words adds nothing – in fact, it detracts. Magic is analogous to the next stage of our evolutionary journey, where we enter a region in which experiences are beyond words. It's about leaving the leaden prosaic world behind and flying. Is it any wonder that in all the Himalayan countries the shaman/sorcerer is portrayed as a flying man?

I once asked the writer Roger Clarke what Bruce Chatwin was like; 'he was a magician' was his answer. I knew instantly what he meant (though I never met Chatwin): he was the kind of person who could make something out of nothing, who would take coincidences and everyday occurrences and turn them into something significant. (Everything is meaningful, everything is a

---

* Ludwig Wittgenstein, *The Mythology in Our Language: Remarks on Frazer's Golden Bough*

sign to the paranoid and also to those living under the rule of the local shaman.)

I would define magic as that instance when imagination and reality seem linked. When the world takes a personal interest in you. It is a 'live version' of the central problem/situation of religion: how to square being a grain of dust in the universe with being the centre of the universe? It is hinted at in the story related above, of the river that must learn how to be happy as both a drop of water and as part of an ocean.

So, I would employ drifting to find all these different kinds of magic.

I also planned a little détournement. This more or less translates as 'hijacking' – as in hijacking an idea or image that has one official use and twisting it to suit another purpose that, to one's own mind, is truer. There were plenty of worthy biographies of willing mountaineers and endless tales told by explorers and climbers and men and women of the mountains – 'Because it is there' is both the most absurd and truest reason for climbing a mountain, but the blank-eyed prosaic duplicity of such answers would no longer be tolerated. I would hijack their yarns and turn them to my purpose: to better reveal the magic.

Back to magic. Here's another kind: if you perform certain breathing exercises and visualise a flame roaring inside you, it's possible to raise your base body temperature. It's an old Tibetan trick called gTum-mo – and Western scientists have managed to replicate it with people who are almost complete beginners. The esoteric literature claims it took 'years' to achieve the power to do this – probably because it looked impossible. When Westerners first saw Inuit doing Eskimo rolls, it was ponderously agreed that no European could ever do such a thing, you had to be born into it; nowadays you can learn how to roll on YouTube in about three minutes . . .

Magic promises shortcuts, it attracts the greedy and those who seek power. It's got a bad name. Yet look at these mountains, their incredible beauty, the way they create a kind of inner silence that is in the 'imagination' yet coincides with a reality . . .

Magic comes in two parts: the imagination, the image, the idea; and the context, the props, the setting, the result, the hard reality. You can't have one without the other. And the hard reality of the Himalayas is hard – rock and ice, millions of years old. But even considering that period when the mountains were formed becomes an exercise in pure imagination. How do you imagine a million years? I cannot imagine the passing of ten with any claim to accuracy.

Perhaps before we look at the hard rocks and geographical features of the Himalayas, we should decide how to pronounce it. I came up against this dilemma very early on in my research; when speaking to others, should I pronounce it English-style, as my father and grandfather did, i.e. 'Him-a-layer' to rhyme with prayer? Or should it be the Indian way: 'Him-marl-ee-a' to rhyme with . . . er, gnarlier? And no 's' on the end. I did not call Paris 'Paree', or Cairo 'El Kahira' (though I did call Marseilles 'Marsay' rather than 'Marsails'), so I was not entirely logical. But then again, no one seemed to mind that Everest was pronounced Ever-rest (the irony of it! – more like Never-rest, as mountaineer Stephen Venables would later call it) rather than Eve-rest which was how George Everest, the mountain's namesake, insisted his name be pronounced. Known as the 'most cantankerous sahib in India', he probably enforced that pronunciation too. But, no longer. Seek reason in such things and you are lost, so: Him-marl-ee-a when speaking to Indians, Nepalis, Bhutanese – otherwise I would stick to my old ways and rhyme it with prayer and hope that both would be sufficient. Though it did surprise me how many people were hung-up or irked by the way the name was pronounced; for some it seemed an issue almost overshadowing the place itself . . .

George Everest rested, coincidentally, in the hill town of

Mussoorie when he wasn't surveying India. His dilapidated house is still there. My dad's school has closed, turned into a hotel. I went there in winter. The air was so clear you could actually see Everest hundreds of miles away.

2

The Barrier

You cannot send a kiss by messenger.
Proverb widespread in the Himalayas

Silk flows through your hands. It is a flow from East to West. Gold one way, silk the other. Is it any surprise that the underground economy of the virtual world should be called Silk Road? Bitcoins replace gold, drugs replace silk. Drugs promise imaginary journeys every bit as enticing as real ones to the land of the Himalayas.

Long before Marco Polo, two Nestorian Christian monks returned from India, where they had either been studying or proselytising; they brought with them the secret of silk. It was the reign of the Eastern Roman Emperor Justinian (AD 527–65) who had long exercised his mind on how to obtain better access to the luxurious fabric. Sea journeys had failed; now it seemed the monks had the answer. They revealed that silk came from China and not India as had been supposed. They spoke of the mulberry tree, which far from producing silk was merely the food for an insect that produced silk. Their mission was to return and steal some eggs and larvae and break the Chinese monopoly. In this they succeeded – silk production became the cornerstone of the Byzantine Empire for the next six hundred years. It is as if the energy needed to cross the barrier of the Himalayas – the most awe-inspiring barrier on the planet – somehow becomes transmuted into a very real momentum for any ideas or products that successfully make that journey.

Nestorian Christians were officially heretics, convinced of the bipartite nature of Christ, putting more emphasis on his human than his divine attributes. To the secular Western mind it seems odd that mere descriptions of a deity should be the cause of friction and war, but look at the controversy that rages over the exact causes of climate change, the wording of sustainability and conservation agreements. Perhaps future generations will see such punctilious argument over the phrasing of important matters as equally misguided . . .

Nestorius (AD 386–450) and his followers were possibly influenced by the earlier movement of Buddhism within the Greek-speaking empire set up by Alexander. Certainly the invention of Western Monasticism in third-century Egypt occurred after Buddhism had arrived in Alexandria. There are remains of Buddhist graves in the town. Clement of Alexandria wrote: 'Among the Indians are those philosophers also who follow the precepts of Boutta, whom they honour as a god on account of his extraordinary sagacity.' He added:

> Thus philosophy, a thing of the highest utility, flourished in antiquity among the barbarians, shedding its light over the nations. And afterwards it came to Greece. First in its ranks were the prophets of the Egyptians; and the Chaldeans among the Assyrians; and the Druids among the Gauls; and the Sramanas among the Bactrians; and the philosophies of the Celts and the Magi of the Persians, who foretold the Saviour's birth . . .

It was in Persia that the Nestorian Church established its strongest foothold, a launch pad for travel over the Hindu Kush into India. Zoroastrians mistrusted the early Christians, but under Muslim rule in Persia (AD 633–54 onwards) Nestorians, as 'people of the book', were accorded the protection of a dhimmi* community. Monks went back and forth, setting up communities in China (from where they were eventually evicted by the Ming dynasty), Central Asia and India – where they survive as the Nasrani of Kerala – one of the oldest Christian congregations in the world, dating from the first century AD. Though it was a boat journey and not a mountain journey that brought St Thomas, the Keralan divine, to India, many Nestorians would enter India using the trade routes over the Himalayas of the Ancient Greek and Buddhist empires of what is now Afghanistan.

Alexander the Great had crossed the ranges of the Himalayas via the Khyber Pass in 323 BC, leaving behind Greek currency and buildings with Doric symmetry. This incredible incursion demanded a counterflow of some kind. It came in the form of Buddhism. Intriguingly, you may note the easy similarity between the words 'Boutta' and the land of 'Bot' (Tibet),† though at that time Buddhism had yet to enter the high heartlands of the Himalayas and merely existed along its foothills. It is almost as if Boutta had, through the imaginary journey of his name, begun already the spiritual conquest of the country that in some sense still bears his name. Buddha means 'enlightened' in Sanskrit. Is there any more powerful imaginary journey than the path higher, the one upwards to enlightenment? And what an odd coincidence

---

* Dhimmi refers to non-Muslims living as taxable 'protected persons' in Islamic lands.

† Geographical 'Tibet' refers to the land of the people known as Bod, the Tibetan term of national identity. Roman-era Ptolemy talks of the Baut people – who were mountain not boat people – though perhaps again there was already a confusion between early Buddhists and Tibetans. The Chinese added a T'u when talking about the T'u Fa, T'u Fan, T'u Fod, and the northern region of modern Tibet became known as Tuppet. Muslim writers since the ninth century referred to Tibet as Tubbet or Tibbet, and from here it entered Western languages as Tibet.

that in the Puranic and other Indian scriptures *Thibet* is the word for heaven.

The barrier of the Himalayas is their first fact. We will later try to uncover the geological facts, the real and imaginary forces that keep the tectonic plates spinning, but to start with we will focus on their sheer ability to *get in the way*. One of the most curious aspects of human vitality or energy is that it rises to meet an imagined occasion. We can psych ourselves up for something – and the bigger the thing the more psyched we can become. I once made a canoe journey across half of Canada; I knew at the time, a shorter trip – paradoxically – would have been harder; I would have been less motivated. People thrive on big goals and great ambitions. And great mountains demand precisely this.

It is excusable to believe that the Himalayas simply provide a north–south barrier. This is true, though less significant than the more formidable east–west barrier they provide.

Studying maps laid out in the common but illusionary Mercator projection, the Himalayas appear like a crown set upon the triangular head of India, blocking her off from Tibet. But when you study satellite photographs adjusted for the curvature of the Earth it becomes starkly apparent that the Himalayas are simply the heaviest part of a backbone of mountains that stretch up into the Steppes past the Altai and into the Arctic; and down through the Pamirs, Karakoram and the main Himalayas before snaking further south through Arunachal Pradesh, Nagaland and Burma until the hills drop into the Indian Ocean. It is the most formidable land barrier across any continent and a natural division since most ancient times.

The only way through is over. There are many high passes but only one lowish gap: the Dzungarian Gate, which has been equated with Herodotus's description of the home of Boreas, the north wind. It was through this six-mile-wide pass in north-west China that the Silk Road flowed and all the hordes of the steppes passed. It is to be found north of the main barrier of the Himalayas, more or less at a point known as the continental pole of inaccessibility. This is the furthest place from any ocean or sea in the continental mass of Eurasia. Later we will see that it coincides with the geopolitical notion of the 'heartland', control of which is key to the control of the largest land mass on Earth.

3

In the Beginning when the Demons Shook the Earth

Without seeing the ice you will not have sympathy for the water.

Nepali proverb

I was walking between villages in western Nepal when a huge rock detached itself high up the cliffside above the narrow path. Most Himalayan paths are narrow, with a precipice one side, which, even if wooded, is barely climbable, certainly not in a hurry. The noise a rock makes – this one was as big as a transit van – when it detaches from the cliff face is not that loud but it is distinct, like gunshot, and then it falls. I did nothing to save myself. I watched the giant sharp-edged boulder make random twists and turns, detaching a stream of small rocks, bruising and cutting the cliff; an arm-thick deodar branch was scythed in two, hardly splintering and offering no resistance. Then it was over my head and gone. I looked down. On the path below me, red-capped men with goats leisurely pulled in closer to the cliff; they were missed by what looked like inches. Apart from the devastation of earthquakes (I left shortly before the terrible earthquake in Lamjung in 2015 which killed over 8,000 Nepalis) it is only in such instances of quotidian rockfall that the mountain hints at the live forces that constitute its own reality.

For centuries, and still in many rural Himalayan areas,

earthquakes were believed to be caused by the Nagas, a race of demons or gods – it is hard to tell which, but their propensity for destruction is more in keeping with our idea of the demonic. The snakelike Nagas were part of the old chthonic religions that worshipped animal gods. They were displaced by the light religions – the sun religions and the monotheistic Middle Eastern religions. The demons were demoted to . . . mere demons. Then the great monotheisms were displaced by science. Science, too, has sought to eradicate the demons, unearth them and reveal the empty grave. But the demons simply burrow deeper. Now they inhabit our subconscious, influencing what we think in a shadowy way, even as we make the daily commute to the science lab and the hi-tech firm in the business park.

One of my favourite films is *Cosmic Zoom*; made in 1968, it is a short film of a boy rowing on the Ottawa River. I saw it when I was at school, projected during an 'integrated studies' lesson with the school's 16 mm projector, which had its own secret cavity in a square pillar in the middle of the room. Most of the films were documentaries about remote places. I loved them. Sitting with my back to the pillar was my preferred spot for viewing; hearing the humming and clicking of the projector and smelling the hot dead air tinged with the faint sweet smell of evaporating celluloid was all part of the ritual, a way of entering more fully into the reality of what I was seeing. The remarkable thing – and you will now recognise the film – is that nothing 'happens' except that the camera zooms ever outward to view the river, then Canada, then Earth and finally the solar system, before zooming back in, back to the boy. We see a mosquito on his hand and then the blood of the boy pumping through the mosquito, zooming further, right down to cellular and atomic level, before pulling back until we see the boy again, still rowing with his pet dog on the river. We've been on a journey through neither time nor space but rather a journey of perspective. Of course, you could argue that we've been on a spatial journey in the sense of height rather than along and across; the latter alters perspective too – but uniquely, I think, the perspective changes that occur as we go higher and higher change the *meaning* of what we see. All relationships are changed when we go higher, or get higher.

Science tries to explain things in terms of laws but it relies first on accurate descriptions of visible reality – journeys that everyone can make themselves and agree upon. Once science discovered tools that allowed macro and microscopic inspection, it began to provide information and theories about the invisible as well as the visible world. The telescope and the microscope are the tools that really changed science, turned it from being an exercise in gentlemanly curiosity to a branch of the occult. For the first time it could lay serious claim to knowing what was hidden.

Telescopes and microscopes change our perspective in a very radical way. If you spend all day looking down one or the other, you may start to think in different terms than someone always at ground level with normal eyesight.

The attraction of altitude, which we'll look at in later chapters, is that it offers this radical perspective change. Before telescopes were available, and before balloons existed, men had to climb mountains to get a change of perspective. People look antlike from on high and the stars seem closer.

Telescopes are for physicists; biologists prefer the microscope. Einstein's thought experiments involved planets and space, Darwin's involved animals and plants; both effected revolutions in their particular science. Today Einstein's and Darwin's ideas permeate the sciences they worked in. But earth sciences, which experienced a similar revolution in the form of plate tectonics and continental drift theory, have nothing like the same public interest or awareness. Wegener, the originator of continental drift as a testable hypothesis (and it's a lot easier to test than evolution; continents may be slow-moving but they are *reliably* slow), remains relatively uncelebrated, despite being the equal of Darwin and Einstein in terms of the audacity of his thinking. Perhaps rocks are just more boring than our own origin and the very fabric of the universe. Or is it that continental drift, though it took seventy years to become orthodoxy, didn't come up against a violent, vocal opposition? In any case, what lies deep beneath the Earth's surface is as hidden as the subatomic level or the furthest reaches of the solar system. We can get glimpses and make infer-ences, but that's about it. We can drill a little way into the Earth's crust (a few kilometres) but that leaves thousands of kilometres that we can merely speculate about. The inner Earth remains something we can only know second hand from refracted radio and magnetic waves. There is masses of disagreement among geologists about the details of plate tectonics (about the only thing they unequivocally seem to agree upon is plate movement itself), so here I will try to keep to the less controversial elements of the theory. As Dr Mike Searle writes, 'Every model that has been proposed for the Himalayas, Karakoram and Tibet is almost certainly wrong; some may be slightly useful, many are wildly inaccurate.'

We have seen how there is a natural barrier north–south, formed by the mega-Himalayas stretching up the left-hand side of the Tibetan Plateau towards the Altai Mountains and beyond, a tract of mountainous terrain that ends in stable Siberia – so called because, unlike the Indian tectonic plate, it remains resolutely in the same spot despite taking a pounding all along its southern borders. These northerly-running mountains are the result of earlier collisions and mountain-building impulses as the giant plates of the Earth's crust gradually shift.

But there is also an east–west line of mountains – from the Alps to the Himalayas via the Balkans and the Zagros Mountains of Turkey and Iran that marks the much later, though still ancient, collision boundary between two continental plates – the supercontinent of Gondwanaland – Africa, Arabia, India – with Laurasia (Europe and Asia). Squeezed between them was the old Tethys Ocean, the last remnants of which form the Mediterranean. The impact of these cruising supercontinents colliding led to massive crustal shortening some way inland – just as pushing a carpet back can result in a bump some distance from where the pressure was applied. From the Pyrenees across the Alps and the Balkans, all the way to the Zagros and the mega-Himalayas, there formed an uprising mountain belt that really separates cold climates from warm.

Both the north–south chain and the east–west chain meet in that vast area of high altitude around the Karakoram, where the tightest congregation of 8,000+ metre peaks meet. It really is the mountainous centre of the world and you feel it.

What evidence had I seen for myself? The enormous fault lines, curved and bent; the seashells fossilised and way up on the tops of mountains; and the rockfalls.

Rockfall – collapse of the mountain on which you are walking – is a sign of erosion, destruction, entropy. It doesn't show how the mountains were formed, but it gives a good indication of how they were shaped.

But before we discuss the end of a mountain as it is ground down into dust (imitating in a much slower way what happens to the river in the opening story), we need to go back 50 million years to when the vast Tethys Ocean separated the two super continents of Laurasia and Gondwanaland. These continents began to break up in the vast space of Deep Time between 140 and 50 million years ago. India separated from Madagascar and southern Africa and continued its way north, travelling maybe 20 centimetres a year. Then BANG: 50–55 million years ago it hits what will become the Tibetan Plateau. The demons have joined combat.

When two continental plates collide it is like a fight between gigantic equals – two Nagas. Neither will give up, so the collision is greater than when oceanic and continental crusts meet. This is what happens when the ancient continental plate of Gondwanaland closes in on the equally ancient plate of Laurasia.

In a sense, both Darwin and Wegener seek to replace gods and demons with Time – Deep Time; a length of time so huge that it functions as the infinite does, making all things possible. When Einstein showed that Time and Space were part of a continuum he provided us with a majestic vision of the infinite that works to awe us into humility – not unlike the written and spoken descriptions of the gods.

So, 50.5 million years ago the current version of the Himalayas begins to form; 10 million years go by as if in a blink and at 40 million years ago it appears that the mountains are in place as we see evidence in seawater that erosion is occurring – this is bona fide evidence of topographic elevation. How do we know? Strontium ratios in seawater rise, which we can measure.

Rocks from the summit of Everest contain the preserved

Sacred river junction in the upper Ganges

fossilised stems of sea-lilies that grew in the shallow tropical seas of 400 million years ago. On the Tibet Plateau the fossil record includes miniature primitive horses, hippopotami and palm trees – all set in stone 5 kilometres above sea level where modern man must gasp for breath.

Another 5 or 10 million years fly by. From 35 to 30 million years ago we see the peak metamorphism of the peaks. We see crustal thickening and ever-higher elevation.

Another cool 10 million pass. Cool, because this is the time of maximum rates of cooling, exhumation and elevation – this is when Everest is at its highest (a thousand feet higher than now and probably unclimbable without oxygen – had climbers, humans or even yetis been alive to climb it).

Around this time, 16–20 million years ago, we see major faunal changes in the Indian subcontinent. We begin to see rapid cooling of the climate, accompanied by erosion of the highest mountains on a major scale.

A few more million years of erosion and a general drying out of life. Northern Pakistan and India go from being entirely covered in jungle to being grassy places. Then, another million years go by and we see the emergence of a new Naga, a weather phenomenon that will dominate the entire region: the arrival and strengthening of the Indian monsoon season.

At 7.4 million years ago the summer monsoon grows in strength. We see increased weathering; a lot more sediment is being carried down the mountains.

Another 4 million years go by and the monsoon is getting more intense. Further cooling leads to the start, 2.5 million years ago, of the Quaternary glaciations of the Everest area. There is increased dust in the atmosphere, which gets deposited in China. The world cools further despite the increase of CO_2 in the atmosphere. The monsoon becomes more variable.

At 2 million years ago, glaciation is leading to the rapid erosion of those Himalayan giants. Everest is wearing down.

Now, as Tibet's population venture south we see the maximum advance of glaciers south of Mount Everest. Twenty thousand years ago and it's cold!

And now, from about 18,000 years ago, we see both cooling and gradual global warming, the retreat of major glaciers (though, anomalously, some extend while others shrink just as they do today). The weather gets more polarised. In Tibet and Ladakh, it becomes desert-like. The rest of the Himalayas sees increased rainfall. As recently as this the Karakoram rapidly uplifts compared to the rest of the Himalayas.

As more detailed studies were done in the Himalayas it became clearer that the basic theory of plate tectonics with its model of rigid, undeforming plates – somewhat like the slabs of bone that make up the infant skull – was deficient in explaining the truly immense distortions of these mountains. While it appeared true that ocean beds were rigid with large plates of dense basaltic crust, with brittle faulting and fracturing or gentle buckling being the ways in which a collision would be resolved, it was not at all clear that this was happening in Tibet and the Himalayas. Earthquakes occur all over the Tibetan Plateau, not just at its bending and buckling margins.

Destructive plate margins are where one plate dives, or 'subducts' under another. This is usually after a prolonged collision of some kind which causes crustal shortening; this sounds temptingly like a cooking process, but is in fact the horizontal collapsing of a plate which is then forced upwards into a mountain range.

One might reasonably ask why the rate of crustal formation is balanced by the rate of crustal destruction. It seems remarkable that it should be so, yet the world would very quickly cease to be an orb if it did not. One answer is that the gravitational and centripetal forces of a spinning planet are so huge that these serve to constrain any untoward growth. Think of the yin-yang image: it's as good a picture of this balance as any other. What is remarkable is the fact that, at the core of a 'hard science' like geology, there lies something esoteric, hidden, imaginary – a world miraculously in balance, gods and demons working it out. The Nagas are there, in the shadows, but they are still there.

4

The Rivers

———

On a spring day there are three colds and three warmths.

Ladakhi proverb

I saw the raft and had to have a go. It seemed like sacrilege. It *was* sacrilege. This was the mighty Ganges, after all. White-water rafting in holy water – a definite sign of something. Commerce erodes or consumes everything and leaves behind an experience, or pollution. The Ganges, the most sacred river in India, is polluted from various sources – agricultural run-off, industry, sewage, wildcat stone- and gravel-harvesting from the banks, dam-building and the floating dead. Floating down through Rishikesh, the smell of the river was rather pleasant; I've smelt worse on certain weedy backwaters of the Thames.

In 2015 over a hundred bodies were found in a Ganges backwater being devoured by crows and other scavengers. These were 'water burials' reserved for unwed girls and the very poor. Most dead people enter the Ganges as ashes after a cremation, which costs more than simply tipping them into the stream.

The living cause problems too. Over seventy million people perform their ablutions in the Ganges. According to a 2015 report, faecal contamination has spread a superbug resistant to antibiotics. Ashrams in the holy cities of Haridwar and Rishikesh are blamed for much of the untreated sewage discharge, with 17 out of 22 major ashrams reported dumping untreated sewage into the

8

Almost alone on the Ganges

river. In May and June, when thousands of devotees dip themselves in the sacred river, superbug levels were found to be sixty times higher than the rest of the year. It's regularly reported as the fifth most polluted river in the world: though I suspect there are many smaller dead rivers in ex-Soviet republics and rogue gold-mining operations in Latin America. At least there isn't three feet of detergent foam all across the river as I once saw on the La Brague, a charming little river in the South of France pretty close to Nice. And there are still fish in the Ganges; all I saw in the La Brague were nasty-looking black water snakes. That said, industrial effluents form 12 per cent of all the waste water entering the Ganges.

To a Western mind, pollution and white-water rafting simply don't fit with the religious significance of the Ganges. But attend any of the riverside ceremonies (pretty much every night) at Rishikesh or Haridwar and you'll change your notion of what constitutes religious significance. Unlike northern Europeans, Indians don't do pious in that joyless, rather stiff-arsed way. For one thing, there are too many people. And for another, there is just too much craziness going on . . . like people rushing to get some luck from the sacred fire that is being passed around.

Light/light: this may be a happy accident, but I don't think it is any accident that light plays a huge part in all religious iconography. I suspect it is lightness, in all its forms, which leads us closer to that which is significant. Heavy things sink, light things rise up, they go higher.

They also float, like the corpses jettisoned into the River Ganges. Or tourists in an Avon inflatable raft.

Going downstream, the river is an easy journey. Like a moving path, it takes you to your destination. But to get anything extra in life you have to go against the grain. Pilgrims travel upriver to the source, they go against the natural journey, the easy path. Pilgrims on the roads of Himachal Pradesh, some riding Enfield

Rishikesh, a good place to venerate the river gods

Bullet motorbikes that gasp for air even at moderate altitude, some in buses, others walking with Sadhu sticks and tin pots, nothing else, heading along the muddy, potholed, collapsing roads that line each gorge of the Ganges and its tributaries. Some of the pilgrims head to Haridwar or Rishikesh, others keep going to the sacred lake of Roopkund. The pilgrims can be Hindus or Sikhs or Jains or Buddhists. Buddhists and Hindus and Jains continue further, as far as the source of all sources – Lake Manasarovar, at the foot of Mount Kailash. It is a strange and obviously central fact for all real and imagined journeys in the Himalayas that all the rivers rise in the same place, around Mount Kailash and its environs.

It is rather wonderful that such a coincidence should be: five great rivers (the Indus, Sutlej, Karnali, Ganges and Tsangpo-Brahmaputra) rising in the same part of the Himalayas. Four rise not so very far from Mount Kailash (and the Ganges rises only forty miles away), a strange dome-shaped peak of 6,638 metres on the Tibetan side of the range. Kailash, perhaps derived from the Sanskrit *kelasa*, meaning crystal, is the most revered religious peak in the entire Himalayan zone. The Chinese asked a

Tyrolean alpinist to summit this most holy of peaks. Reinhold Messner – one of the world's top mountaineers – sensibly turned down the chance. Once, when asked who were the greatest climbers, Messner memorably answered, 'Those who are still alive'. He is aware that you cannot play at such things. Not in the long run.

Kailash, though, is the alibi, the marker stone – it is the place which is important. Rivers give life to wherever they pass through – in a banal sense, but also in a more refined sense. There is a quickening of the air, there is life of all kinds, movement and sustenance. The strangest thing is that the Indus, Tsangpo and Ganges define the main extent of the Himalayas by encircling them. The Tsangpo, after an incredible journey along the back of the Himalayas, punches a hole through this impregnable wall of mountains to become the Brahmaputra, a river that weaves back and under India, eventually merging with the Ganges. The whole of the Himalayas is encircled in their grip; the strictest definition of the Himalayas stretches from the source region of the Ganges to the Tsangpo gorge in Arunachal Pradesh. The mountains give birth to the rivers, which cradle the mountains. It is such thoughts as these that trundle through a pilgrim's mind watching Sadhu after Sadhu trudge up the roads in the Garwhal Himalaya, getting ever higher, ever nearer to the source.

The Oxus doesn't quite make the same source zone as the others but it is fairly close. Flowing west along the intriguing Wakhan corridor, it marks the northern boundary of Afghanistan. Flowing south is the Indus, which at various times has marked the boundary between Afghanistan and India – the Kishan kingdom, for example. In these troubled times, some insist on making a Pashtun realm between Helmand and the Indus, and a Tajik–Uzbek realm between the Oxus and the Helmand.

People follow rivers. The Tsangpo-Brahmaputra defines the eastern extent of India. The Ganges divides Himalayan India from its southern extremities. The Tsangpo is the main artery through Tibet, though right in the south of the country is its centre of gravity.

Mountains constitute a different kind of dividing line because they are never really lines in the way a river is. Crossing a river is an act of transformation, 'a fording / To dry, different clothes',* but crossing a mountain range is an act of defiance and a boost to the ego. Crossing over a high pass, one does not feel that one is entering a new country; one feels, with it all laid out below, that one has already conquered it – only the mopping-up remains. Both Tibet and Nepal have claimed each other's lands from the high vantage point of a mountain pass. China still claims parts of India below the highest parts of the natural backbone of the Himalayas. Rivers provide a less disputable boundary; the earliest kingdom, Mesopotamia, was literally the land between two rivers, not the land between two mountain ranges.

The dividing line between Tibet and India usually follows the line of highest peaks, but it is still far from settled. China claims most of Arunachal Pradesh and tried to take it in 1962. They continue to make regular incursions just inside the border – most recently in 2013 – but always back down when Indian soldiers appear in force. The Himalayas feel as if they are a kingdom in their own right; dividing them down the middle seems counter-intuitive. No wonder each side thinks it should have access to the foothills of the opposing side too. Nomads and mountain dwellers have traditionally criss-crossed mountain borders, finding them permeable. Rivers are less amenable. Unless there is a bridge you can't cross. And even with a bridge there tends to be a town on each side – like the Rio Grande towns in America and Mexico. Much of the sad stripping of territory happens because rivers have not been made the border. I envisage a new world map where new

---

* Philip Larkin, 'Water' in *Whitsun Weddings*

countries are defined by patches of land between rivers, every country a kind of Mesopotamia. We let nature dictate: countries with few rivers can remain large, otherwise they should be made small. It is perhaps the case that every country should be viewed as a series of inland islands, divided inexorably and without possible remonstrance by the rivers that criss-cross the land.

The Sutlej is the easternmost tributary of the Indus. It is a great long river in its own right, the longest flowing through the Punjab where some still call it the Satadree. It rises in Tibet, near enough to Kailash at Lake Rakshastal. It is called the elephant river in Tibetan and crosses into India through the Shipki La, a pass 5,669 metres high. It flows through the Punjab and into the Indus and Pakistan before reaching the Arabian Sea. Geologists believe that five million years or so ago it flowed the other way and joined the Ganges. In an attempt to reverse time there is a proposal afoot to build a canal linking the Sutlej again to the Ganges, allowing ships to cross India without going around the southern tip. Like all big canal projects, it relies on images with mythical force, ideas buried in the ancient brain of ancient waterways; such a canal, in its seemingly modern attempt to save money and time, is really a reversal, a reuniting of Pliocene water systems, another feeble attempt by man to challenge the gods and reverse the effects of time. The ecological cost of such a project, would, of course, be huge.

The Indus River, the watering place of one of the world's oldest civilisations, the Indus Valley Civilisation, gives its name to the language and religion and people of India – the Hindus. So named by the Persians as the land of the people of the Indus – Hindustan.

Ancient Egypt, Mesopotamia and the Indus Valley are all gifts of their great rivers; only through the sheer excess of regular water could man begin to build large cities and grope towards the current urban-dominated culture. But it is not the effect of the river we seek, but the mysteries of its source. One of the oddest things for science to explain is the exact coincidence in size between the Moon and the Sun when viewed from the Earth. It is rather like those trick photos where a giant distant boulder can be 'held' by someone posing in the foreground. The moon is 400 times smaller, but the sun is 400 times further away. It is a rare coincidence. According to Dr Myles Standish – formerly of Caltech and Yale University, and the author of over 300 papers on celestial mechanics – the similarity in size is unique among the planets and moons that form our solar system. I am reminded of the previous odd balance between the rate of crust formation and destruction; the tiniest imbalance here would result in the Earth having imploded or exploded billions of years ago . . .

There is another twist to this coincidence in the Himalayas, in that the Indus predates the current rise of the Himalayas but the Tsangpo came millions of years later – yet both rise in the Kailash region.

One way in is to study the Indus suture zone – the place where the actual collision took place. This suture zone runs across southern Tibet and right across the northern end of 'Little Tibet', Ladakh. Leh, the capital of Ladakh, was a significant crossing point for caravan routes bound for Central Asia, and a receiving point for goods from Khotan and Yarkand. That the ancient boundaries of geological events beyond human time should affect our existence is rather fascinating to contemplate. The very areas of plate destruction, no doubt due to the huge environmental effect they have, leave areas of great human difference too.

The Indus River predates the rise of the Himalayas – at least the present incarnation of the Himalayas. There seems to be some consensus that there were mountains before the present steroidal upthrust of fifty million years ago. The rivers were then 'captured' by the fault lines, in some places changing their route.

The major collision line is the Indus suture, which merges into the Tsangpo suture, which curves round at the top of Nagaland and interlinks with the line of hills running down the spine of the Burmese–Indian border.

That the Indus and the Tsangpo both rise very close to Mount Kailash and encircle the Himalayas is, as we have already noted, an extraordinary fact. That the Sutlej and the Ganges rise within a further 40 kilometres makes this the source pipe of the entire Himalayas and much of the Indian subcontinent. How did the ancients know that this spot was the key point in the formation of this epic mountain range? Until the nineteenth century, no one knew that the Brahmaputra was actually a continuation of the Tsangpo. Most thought it simply arose in the Himalayas, not that it cut right through them. Just as traditional knowledge in the Sahara suggests an understanding of geological processes that formed the sands, so, too, we find in the mythological foundations of humanity here in the Himalayas a form of understanding that operates, albeit in a very different idiom, to explain the significance of the landscape and yet is confirmed by the latest scientific findings. It is yet another mystery of the Himalayas.

The evidence of ancient wisdom resides in the scattered texts and art of previous civilisations, tailored though it was to previous peoples and eras. That these ancients also had an elevated knowledge of the planet's structure, accessed through dreams and hypnotic states, is not so far-fetched.* The act of pilgrimage to a river's source could be the simple checking of the life-source, making sure the river is running and hasn't any problems. Man has a tendency to ritualise everything he does, render it empty, mere spectacle. The pilgrimage may become something else, even if it has its roots in something as prosaic as river maintenance. One thing the ancients managed far better than us was finding

* Dr Jeremy Narby's 1999 book *The Cosmic Serpent* documents such activity.

activities that had synergy, that had multiple uses and benefits. Such activities radiate out and harmonise with the planet. Pilgrimage is one such activity.

5

The Mountains and the Weather

To catch fish you must not mind getting wet.
Lepcha proverb*

The day began to deteriorate around lunchtime. We were all sitting on rocks in misty rain, the fine misty rain you get in Scotland in the hills any time of the year. On a short multi-day walk in the Garwhal in 2014 we had no knowledge of what was happening in Nepal across the border. It would develop into the worst storm in years.

We had cleared the high pass and seen a distant view of 7,000-metre peaks; now the wind set in and the driving rain turned to hail. The guide was soon lost in the fog. I put on my overtrousers – or overshorts; they were cut-down heavy plastic overtrousers, the kind worn by road workers, but they extended just over the knee. I was wearing gaiters and making cut-offs saved weight and increased airflow; overtrousers can get very hot otherwise. We all had rainwear – some fancy and breathable, other stuff baggy and unbreathable but 100 per cent waterproof. No lightweight breathable gear will keep out driving rain after four or five hours, not unless it has been recently reproofed. Our faces were raw, revived then frozen by wet hail, large lumps, not golf balls but still painful to the face. I noticed we'd walked past the same ruined sheepfolds

---

* Lepchas are the original inhabitants of Sikkim.

for a second time. I was torn between elation that we were off the high parts, devoid of people and animals, but troubled by knowing we were now going round in circles. The guide said that in ten years of travelling in this part of the Himalayas he'd never known weather like this in late autumn; in the monsoon season, perhaps, but not now. None of us knew that just over the border the same storm would cause forty-three deaths in Nepal – twenty-one of whom were trekkers like us. It would be the worst trekking disaster in Nepal's history. Though over 1.5 metres of snow fell in a day in some areas, it was the poorly equipped who suffered most. Many were killed on the production-line trek known as the Annapurna Circuit. This is a high-level trek but the accommodation is all in hostels and tea houses. Not needing to carry tents, tour companies encourage people to hike in light boots and shoes and minimal waterproof and insulating clothing. When a group of such lightly clad people were trapped at a snow-filled pass, they started to freeze to death.

A hundred miles away, we finally found the path. It took us down through the deserted ski resort of Auli, all wet mud now, the carcass of a dead cow blocking one of the black runs. The rain-soaked concrete buildings were empty; the resort would open the following month. We dried off in a watchman's hut, our wet clothes steaming around his burning stove.

Out of doors all day and night in the mountains, some develop a nose for the weather. It is certainly one of the key skills of the advanced mountaineer. To hang back and then strike when a weather window appears, and be confident that it will last, or turn back when that confidence goes, all this comes with spending days and nights outdoors. Some never acquire this intuitive sense of what the weather will do. And many Himalayans, who live in houses, do not have any better a sense of the weather than a visiting climber or trekker. We will see later that the local weather advice given to trekker James Scott was crucial in encouraging him to try and make a perilous hike in Nepal that resulted in him being lost for forty-three days in the wilderness.

Though forecasters have become better at predicting the weather, any forecast that aspires to provide weather information more than two weeks in advance will be relying on statistical likelihoods rather than actually perceived conditions. Even in this day of satellite coverage and complicated technological mumbo jumbo the weather remains in the realm of the invisible and the imaginary.

High mountains make big weather; indigenous people, fearful of thunder and lightning, colossal downpours and rivers of ice, conclude that the mountains are where the Nagas make the weather. It is hard, when caught out at higher altitudes in a storm, to disagree. The Himalayas, being the world's highest mountains, also endure some of the most extreme weather in the world. K2 is famous for winds well over a hundred miles an hour, wind that will rip a climber and his ropes right off a snowfield. Rain and snow may be dumped by the monsoon, especially in the more easterly parts of the Himalayas; around Ladakh, however, it is a virtual desert with less than 7.5 centimetres of rain a year. High up, blizzards may rage with arctic intensity, while people viewing the same scene from Camel Back Road in Mussoorie may only see blue skies and scudding clouds. No one can accurately predict weather more than sixteen days in advance* whatever model they use, and this unpredictability is higher for the high mountains.

The prevailing winds in the higher altitudes of the Himalayas and Tibet are strong westerlies, often gusting at gale force. Above 7,000 metres, as we have mentioned, such winds may be well over a hundred miles an hour, destroying tents and making forward progress impossible.

The mountains create the weather in one sense, but they are fed by the monsoons. There are two monsoons that affect India – a south-west monsoon and a north-east monsoon. The eastern

---

* Michael Fish, 'The Ultimate Weapon of Mass Destruction' lecture, 2013

Himalayas, Nagaland and Burma act as a barrier to the north-east monsoon, which has little effect on India and skips over the northern parts completely. In this area there are three seasons (as opposed to the two seasons in the lower parts of India). Cold weather from early or mid October to about the end of February, hot weather from March to mid June, and the rainy season – from mid June to the end of September.

The heavily humid monsoon comes off the ocean and strikes India in late May or early June. Rain is dumped all across India. The eastern Himalayas of Sikkim, Bhutan and Assam receive the full impact. In the monsoon, Darjeeling gets 259 centimetres of the 310 centimetres it receives each year, with forty-five wet days (i.e. very wet) in July and August. Mussoorie has around twenty and Murree about fourteen. Rain is heavier and the days are less clear in the east than in the western parts of the Himalayas. The vale of Kashmir Srinagar only has about five wet days in August, receiving only 5–8 centimetres of rain.

In the Hunza, where the summer rains make valleys impass-able, in winter they allow exploration. Though it is too cold to go really high. In Ladakh there is almost no rainfall and summer is the best time to visit, unless you fancy walking along frozen rivers.

Around 15 June the monsoon bursts over Delhi and sweeps north into Nepal and the Garwhal. Tibet is not seriously affected by the monsoon. Approaching the Himalayas from the north can be deceptive. The northern slopes can be affected by the mon-soon rise in temperatures, even though the monsoon itself may not be apparent. Everest is traditionally climbed in the window of three or four weeks in May where the high westerly winds are checked by the approaching monsoon which has yet to burst.

The 'burst' of the monsoon is like no other rainstorm. However, in the high mountains, the *chhoti barsat*, which occurs about three weeks usually before the monsoon bursts, can be felt. It is a period of unsettled weather that can give the inexperienced climber or

The place where the gods make the weather

traveller the impression that the monsoon has arrived early. The onset of the monsoon on the plains is sudden; in the higher mountains it may be sudden or gradual, but unlike the *chhoti barsat** it does not clear up after a day or two – it is continuous.

The ending of the monsoon is much more gradual. Periods of bad weather in the Himalayas get shorter and periods of fine weather increase. By October it is over; October and November are usually freer of rain and cloud than any other months in the mountains. This is the traditional time for trekking and seeing the high peaks when they're not veiled in cloud. For climbers, however, there are drawbacks. As the monsoon air current lessens in strength, the high westerly winds start up again. In November they can easily reach gale force – far more deadly at high altitude than cloud; not only are you likely to be blown over, it is also

---

* Literally 'little rain', a precursor to the great rains of the monsoon.

very much colder than pre-monsoon in May. The days are getting shorter, too, and the sun is lower and has less warming power. The one good thing is that streams, previously swollen with meltwater or monsoon rain, are easily fordable.

From December to February it is too cold for most climbers, though in the 1970s a hardy breed of Polish mountaineers started to make winter ascents in the Himalayas; this trend continues today with a broader range of nationalities. The mountains are not affected by the north-east monsoon off the China Seas, but the bitterly cold winter air settles in the valleys and then is sucked out on to the warmer plains below. This causes northerly winds in the Himalayas. There are also cyclonic disturbances felt from Iran and as far away as Iraq, bringing snow and rain.

The high passes can be affected at any time through to May. Former mountain surveyor and climber Kenneth Mason wrote:

> On a cloudless night in April or May after two fine days the Zoji La offers an absolutely safe passage to a large caravan; by dawn or soon afterwards it may be dangerous. I warned a small party of Ladakhis not to cross by daylight on 17 May 1926; they took no heed and were swept away by an avalanche and killed, though two nights earlier I had taken over a party of 160 laden porters. Much the same applies to the Burzil, Kamri and other passes.

In the Karakoram the monsoon has less effect. North-westerly and westerly winds predominate in Gilgit and the Pamirs from May to August; only occasionally does a monsoon-inspired reversal make itself felt. In the Hunza and Nagir the old travellers believed that fine weather, unaffected by the monsoon that far west, was to be had between July and August.

In winter, going above 3,000 metres it is cold but worth it for the dry clarity of the air. At 2,000 metres it is often sunny, day after day. I spent a week in the 1990s teaching aikido to Indian soldiers at a training camp above Dehradun. In a great barnlike structure with soft judo mats to fall on, wearing only judo pyjamas, we worked on locks and throws with the double doors open to the clear cold air and blue sky, Everest visible in the very far distance. At night the hotel room was below freezing and I slept in a fur hat.

6

Mythical Origins

Everything that enters a salt mine becomes salt.
Proverb common in the Himalayas

Himavant was the ancient ruler of Himalayan India. He was the father of Ganga, the river goddess. His wife was the daughter of Mount Meru, the sacred mythical Hindu mountain (not to be confused with the Garwhal Himalayan Meru Peak, scene of some of the world's highest BASE jumping). T. S. Eliot captivated me as a young reader of poetry with:

> Ganga was sunken, and the limp leaves
> Waited for rain, while the black clouds
> Gathered far distant over Himavant.

There seems to be a continuum from sign to symbol to myth. That we have magic words, whose meaning is the way we use them; that we can freight public words with our own meaning – and maybe convey some of the excitement of that semi-private meaning to others – makes us doubt the bland scepticism of de Saussure that assures us that there is no essential connection between the thing itself and how we depict it. The inference we are meant to draw is that the words we use are just random signs, any word would do just as well. In theory, yes. But evolutionary etiolation prefers some words to others. The common occurrence of onomatopoeic words from Japan to Britain suggests they have a high survival rate. It is the words *we like saying* that survive. The latest neuroscientific research into multisensory neurons suggests that synaesthesia is not rare at all; in fact, it is part of the human condition. The words we use suggest colours, sounds, images. To be sure, much poetry depends on it. Who can ignore the suggestive imagery and undeniable effect of Eliot's next line:

> The jungle crouched, humped in silence.

Once you get used to the fact that a symbol is a highly potent thing, at least as powerful as a line of poetry or a certain set of musical notes, you understand the way the Himalayas can worm their way into the consciousness of even the most prosaic-minded of walkers and climbers. Though, to be honest, most trekkers I have met were not prosaic at all except in their choice of foul-weather gear or boots; most are quite open to, if not full-on mysticism, at least Buddhism lite and all its confusing symbology.

The people of Tibet call the place Bod. The bods of Bod are called Bod-pa. The higher places of the plateau are known as high-bod, or Tu-bod – hence Tibet. But once Tu-bod was actually a bed not a bod, not bad if you like alliteration.

The bed of the Tethys Ocean, or part of it, which once encompassed all of the Mediterranean as well as the Indian Ocean, was forced up to become the tableland of Tibet. This modern geological fact, explained elsewhere, the ancients knew too: Tibet was mythologically once an undersea world which soared upwards, drained and dripping and new. Wild animals such as the *drong*** proliferated and lived alongside unspeakable apes and mythical ogresses. At long last, after many aeons, a very meditative monkey

---

* Wild yak

– indeed, an incarnation of Avalokitesvara himself – became the progenitor of the Tibetan people (thousands of years before Darwin suggested similar ideas). The monkey, after long thought, searched out an ogress in order to have the strongest progeny possible. The union brought forth the first 'red-faced' humans, which is how the early Tibetans thought of themselves. With a true lack of reverence for chronology, this is all supposed to have happened *after* the historical life of the Buddha. A verse from the Buddhist text *Manjusri-mula-tantra* is often cited to show how the Buddha predicted the draining away of the sea and the tenacious growth of the *sal* tree into great verdant forests. Tibet was not exactly at the centre of the Buddha's compassion, however, which is why he neglected the place in favour of India and Nepal; nevertheless, it is held that he deputed the wise monkey Avalokitesvara to tame the country and populate it with monkey-derived progeny, including the great emperor Songtsen Gampo of the seventh century AD and the current Dalai Lama (which may, in part, account for his admirable humility). To this day, traditional Tibetan historians – who tread a fascinating line between myth, textual history and oral tradition – still uphold the primeval primatological origins of the country.

The Bon religion of Tibet existed before the introduction of Buddhism. It was not the only religion but it may have been the most prevalent. The Bonpo chronicles refer to the earliest people of Tibet as Bon instead of Bod. If this is accurate, then the earliest Tibetans were Bonpos, the people who welcomed the first King of Tibet down from the sky. There are still Bon monasteries in Tibet, but their difference from Buddhist monasteries is not so great. Monasticism as a concept may well have originated in Tibet, spreading into Buddhism and then via the Greco-Buddhist world back to Egypt, influencing the early hermits and anchorites in the desert. It isn't an obvious connection to make – if you want to get away from the community, why try and build a community in the wilderness? Unless the monastic community contains something that can be taught to its members: secrets.

If monasticism is a Tibetan/Himalayan invention, it makes sense that the monasteries in the Himalayas should look rather similar, as they do. But this doesn't mean they haven't a history of trying to do each other down.

The first histories – written accounts of the past – were accounts of this religious feuding. The battle between the original Bon religion and the newer arrival, Buddhism, becomes the subject of the first histories of Tibet, the first myths of the country. This battle is such a key event in Tibetan history – albeit plainly exaggerated to a great degree or even mythological – that it deserves to be recounted in some detail. There are elements within the story that, when drawn out, provide considerable insights into the nature of Tibet and its magic mountain, Kailash. Another name for Mount Kailash is Kang Rinpoche or 'Precious Snow Mountain' – the white mountain of all white mountains.* Kailash was recognised throughout the Himalayas, by Jain and Hindu and Bon alike, as the holiest and most magical place.

Mount Kailash was presided over by a supremely powerful Bon magician called Naro Bon-Chung. His Buddhist opponent in battle was Milarepa, one of the most important Tibetan Buddhist poet-mystics.

Milarepa lived in the late eleventh century and was a disciple of Marpa the Translator, leader of the Buddhist Karma Kagyu school, which Milarepa – a respected teacher in his own right – eventually headed. He is often depicted with one hand to his ear as if straining to hear the right note, and in paintings his body is always an odd shade of green, a symbolic (or perhaps literal) reference to having lived exclusively on nettle stew for long periods of his life.

When Milarepa went to the mountain he was met by the local

---

* It is also known as Mount Tise.

deities; recognising his advanced mystical powers, they welcomed him. He then travelled the short distance to the sacred Lake Manasarovar, where he encountered Naro Bon-Chung who was not at all polite. In fact, he laughed at Milarepa and told him he would have to convert to the Bon religion if he wanted to meditate there. 'This is a Bon Po place,' said Naro Bon-Chung. Milarepa could not accept this, for the Buddha himself had prophesied that one day Kailash would be a Buddhist place, and Marpa the Translator also spoken of the mountain. 'Are you to take away my teacher's words from me?' asked Milarepa, and then he counter-suggested that Naro renounce the faith of Bon and become a follower of the Dharma and a Buddhist. Naro was so confident in his magical abilities he believed he could settle the dispute that way. He suggested that the winner of this magical contest would win the mountain and the loser must slink away.

Like an egoistic rapper, Naro Bon-Chung started by trying to freak out Milarepa by singing his own praises, boasting his prowess in a decidedly inflammatory and intentional manner, throwing in some rude verses about Milarepa along the way. As he did so, he showed off by straddling the holy lake of Manasarovar. Milarepa's reply was to sing a sweet refrain while covering the lake with his own body, but magically *without enlarging himself* one bit. Then, because he could sense the boastful Naro Bon-Chung needed to be totally dominated rather than subtly beaten, he balanced the entire lake on his fingertip, naturally without hurting any living thing.

Naro had to concede defeat, but he insisted that another con-test should be staged, this time at the mountain – after all, it was the mountain they were contesting and not the lake. Naro Bon-Chung started to circumambulate the mountain anticlock-wise – which Bon-po (and Jains) do to this day. And Milarepa went clockwise, which remains the current Buddhist practice. When they met at a large rock on the north-east side, they locked like a pair of wrestlers and each tried to move the other in the direction that his faith bade him. Naro struggled and skidded and used every trick he could, but Milarepa could not be budged an inch. He was like the very rock they were next to, rooted to the very centre of the earth. Then, as Naro weakened, Milarepa moved first one foot and then the other, faster and faster, shoving the Bon priest along in the clockwise direction Buddhists favour.

He kept pushing Naro until the desperate priest managed to manoeuvre himself into the path of a large rock, which momentarily stopped Milarepa's progress. Straight away Naro suggested a 'real trial of strength' and lifted the rock, which was bigger than a yak, above his head. Milarepa laughed and lifted Naro *and* the rock he was holding high above his head. But still the stubborn Bon priest would not concede defeat. He went off to meditate in a cave on the side of the mountain and Milarepa did likewise in a cave on the opposite side. Then Milarepa could not resist extending his leg all the way into Naro's cave to wiggle his toes and distract the Bon priest in his serious meditations. And Naro could not retaliate.

By this time all the local deities watching from the skies above were hooting with laughter at Naro's constant losses. But though his face and large ears burned with embarrassment, Naro resolved to fight on. He began again to trudge round Mount Kailash in order to build up his power. Milarepa met him on the south side just as it began to rain. The Buddhist was conciliatory. 'Let's build a shelter together to get out of this rain,' he suggested. 'Would you prefer to lay the foundations, build the floor or the walls, or put on the roof?' Naro thought it best to go last – that way he couldn't be trounced by Milarepa. So he said, 'I'll put on the roof.' In a trice, amid a whirlwind of activity, Milarepa began to split rocks to fashion the hut. Naro joined in. For a brief moment they worked together but it soon turned into a bitter competition to see who could split the biggest rocks. There was only one more needed at this point – for the roof – and the cunning Milarepa had planned it so that the remaining rock was so huge poor Naro had no hope of lifting it or splitting it. Laughing, Milarepa picked up the gigantic rock roof as if it were a bag of feathers. He tossed it into the air several times, imprinting his hand and footprints into the rock. Eventually, he threw it up and caught it on the top of his head, leaving a headprint which is still there. Milarepa finished the shelter just as the rain started to get even heavier. He invited Naro into the hut – which is still there and is known as Milarepa's Miracle Cave – and offered him a conciliatory cup of tea. Naro conceded defeat – but not ultimate defeat.

The next day there were more contests and, though Naro did a little better, he was still bested. He suggested that there should be one final test to decide everything. And Milarepa simply laughed, as one would to a child who couldn't accept losing, and agreed. Naro said it should take place on the fifteenth day of the month so that he could get into proper training. He was convinced that with the right preparation he could use his best and so far unsurpassed skills of moving fast to get to the mountain's summit first. Milarepa spent his time relaxing and walking about and enjoying nature and talking to people, while Naro furiously fasted and meditated and chanted to improve his strength.

As dawn broke on the fifteenth day, Milarepa's disciples, who'd been keeping an eye on Naro even if Milarepa hadn't, reported back in great excitement that they'd seen Naro playing a drum and flying through the air in a green cloak (which is blue in some accounts – I prefer green as it links to the green man/green cloak theme common in many mystical traditions, East and West). Despite the agitation of his followers, Milarepa wouldn't get out of bed. He joked, 'You fear me losing because it is YOU who will look bad!'

Then, as Naro soared triumphantly to within metres of the top of the mountain, Milarepa stood up and clicked his fingers. By some strange spell, Naro was frozen in time and space, lodged with a shocked look on his face. Milarepa now flew to the summit and landed, soft as a bird, just as the first rays of the sun struck the mountaintop with glorious light. The light broke the spell holding Naro frozen in mid-air; he crashed to the slope below and tumbled all the way down the mountain, his broken drum bouncing and clattering over rocks behind him.

Some time later, his arrogance now departed, Naro Bon-Chung humbly asked if it would be all right for his disciples to keep circumambulating Mount Kailash in their old way. He added, without much hope of his wish being granted, that it would be nice, too, for the Bonpo to have a place of their own where they could catch a glimpse of the mountain each day. Milarepa said yes to both requests. He took up a fistful of snow and blew on it, sending it flying to the top of a nearby hill, which grew upwards to meet the snow and became the mountain known as Bonri. To this day, Bonri remains a sacred place for the Bonpo.

The story may tell of a battle, and it works as a story, but the esoteric explanation goes deeper. Both sides may be in opposition – but look for a level in which they are working together. (Governments today lack such sophistication, not understanding that many apparent conflicts actually mask people working together – for good or bad ends. Up to a point, the current terrorism that had its origin in the Himalayas – the invasion of Afghanistan by the former Soviet Union – works with the countries it preys upon. Governments of democracies increase their legitimacy by defending their countries while aiding terror groups in the relentless publicising of their acts.)

Milarepa is the 'victor' in that he employs shamanic, mystical techniques that are a dramatic symbolisation of the flexible use of the mind as opposed to the mechanical working of tradition and ritual. But habitual activity has its place, hence the final accommodation with Naro Bon, allowing the traditional circumnavigation to remain.

After the battle, Buddhism under Milarepa becomes dominant in Tibet – but Buddhism did not seek to extinguish the Bon religion. Even today 10 per cent of Tibetans are Bon worshippers, though both Bonism and Buddhism have come to resemble each other since that first historic battle on Mount Kailash.

7

The Ancient Rulers of Tibet

Even the highest mountain cannot block the sun.
Tibetan proverb

It is said that the ancient rulers of Tibet, before the Bon and the
Buddhists, were divided into three groups: the storytellers, the
magicians and the singers of songs. These three worked wisely together to rule the people justly; this was before the time of kings
and other worldly things gradually dragged the Tibetans down to
the present age.

Each in their own way, the magicians and village storytellers
and musicians and singers all worked with enchantment. The enchantment of a story, our interest in hearing what will happen; the
enchantment of a song, the magical effect of words working with
musical effect, the sublime rising of emotion, the hairs prickling
on the back of one's neck – a sure sign that emotion is flowing; it
is said to be the first sign of arousal in the hunt and in fleeing from
enemies. That fear and interest should be so closely wired helps
to explain why magic can so easily serve black as well as white,
darkness and evil as well as enlightened and benign. The magician knows the art of hypnosis and the use of magical objects and
signs whose sole purpose is to raise to a certain and defined pitch
the emotion of the magician, who can then, like a spark shooting
from a Tesla machine, enchant the participants. Flags also affect
the emotions – that is why you will see hundreds fluttering on the

steps up to a monastery in the Himalayas; flags were one of the tools of the old magicians for creating a carrier wave of emotion for their teachings and insights.

All forms of enchantment capture and raise our interest. The story enchants by seizing our interest and making us listen to what happens next. The story is one of the most subtle and ubiquitous forms of magic available. Songs are more powerful. Magic (by which I mean simply the symbols and incantations used to set up a kind of emotional oscillation and amplification between the audience and the witch doctor) is more powerful again – among those who have come prepared in the right way. Just as a stage magician requires some suspension of disbelief (we must sit in front of him, not grab at his cloak or wander the stage randomly, etc.) so too the black or white magician requires of us a certain initial fear, or at least acquiescence in the atmosphere he wishes to create.

Well, the old magician rulers of Tibet knew the power at their disposal and they used it wisely. Only when faced by the vast invading hordes from the steppes did they relinquish their control to the lower formations of kings and mere men. Once a building is painted you may decorate it beautifully with exquisite works of art. But when the building is burned down you need men with the crude strength to cut rock and wood and make caves and shelters.

The storyteller, singer of songs and magician know the danger of their art is that the openness they create latches on to them; like a newborn duckling, the 'opened soul' helplessly falls for the object of his attention. By subtle means – the content of the stories themselves, the directing of attention at self-improvement rather than adulation, the focus on creativity rather than destruction – the dangers of the lower love shown for magician or storyteller is transmuted into something useful and unharmful, until the higher love for God, of which it is a reflection, becomes clearer and clearer.

It is said that in Tibet the rulers became the ruled: the magicians became folk-remedy pedlars in the villages; the singers performed at weddings and festivals; and the storytellers earned a place by the fire and a bowl of soup in return for a good yarn. But one day, they say, when the world leaves its current upside-down state (what the Hindus name the age of Kali), then the storytellers, magicians and singers of songs shall rule again.

8

History Starts to Arrive

If a yak doesn't want to drink water,
what is the use of pressing its neck?
Tibetan proverb

I was back in Delhi for Diwali, leaving the Garwhal Himalaya under snow and sleet. I exchanged a place where people still ploughed with a wooden plough and an ox for a city with Wi-Fi, cars and ten-lane highways. It seemed that history was spreading out in space rather than time. As more and more material is made available on the Web there is a sense that history is standing still. I watch the same programmes I watched as a child, comfort viewing, on YouTube. It is less the end of history, than history riding the long tail of a flat curve. Once it was steep, lots of change that changed everything. Now there is just accumulation, mirroring the accumulation of stuff on the internet, its infinite storage capacity.

When cities have their centres laid out it is like restarting the clock; the new design of the streets is a new year zero. The sense of history sharpens, by which I mean the sense of meaningful change is suddenly increased. But after a while, we tend to build suburbs rather than redesign the centre. Delhi spreads ever south, magnetically drawn to the environs of Sector 23 and the Indira Gandhi International Airport. We lose control of our creation, the city doesn't so much grow, it sprawls. The old centre remains firmly in the present, albeit as a reminder of times past, alongside all the new additions. History flattens out, taking up more and more space as the population goes through the roof. No one wants to read about the past because they sense it is already all around them.

Paradoxically, nomads are like this too. They have too much space and nothing much to remind them of times past, but no writing, not much religion and their preferred form of warfare is raiding, skirmishing and running away to fight another day. Material for myth, but nothing substantial to document and no cities. History comes into being with the creation of the city, not with written language, though they may coincide. You can't get away from the evidence of stones; it dampens enthusiasm for making things up. You start to document, record, develop a fetish for facts.

The Tibetans were almost exclusively nomadic until King Songtsen Gampo came on the throne in the seventh century AD.

Mani wall with Buddhist prayer stones:
walls of prayer stones can be several kilometres long.

Though Buddhism had been creeping slowly over the Himalayas for centuries, it made little impact until the king, after winning a great victory in Burma, China and Nepal, decided to marry two queens from Buddhist countries – one from the palace of the Emperor of China and the other from Nepal. From this, one can date the conversion of Tibet from the Bon religion to Buddhism, a process that is still going on. It says a lot for Tibetans that both the Bonpa and the Buddhists live and let live. That they have influenced each other is clear, yet neither side has tried to exterminate the other – which seems the common occidental way of settling a religious difference of opinion.

We will see later the way Buddhism changed from its early beginnings as a personal code for a penitent mystic to a state religion covering half of Asia. In Tibet, influenced by ancient monasteries, a new theocratic state took hold. Buddhist missionaries arrived from China and Nepal and brought with them the great intellectual inheritance of those countries. King Songtsen Gampo built himself a great palace overlooking what is now Lhasa, on the site where the Potala stands today.

The early kings of Tibet were unusual in that they seem to have had a deep belief in equality and fairness. One went so far as to decree that every Tibetan should have an equal share of the country's wealth. Being a sparsely populated country possessed of some wealth, this was possible. But the poor, it is reported, finding themselves suddenly rich, behaved like lottery winners and became irresponsible and indolent; before long they had lost all they had and more (it is a fact that, five years after a big win, the majority of lottery winners are financially less well off than before). The king was a little disappointed, but his idealism remained undented. Again he deputed that the wealth of the nation should be fairly distributed, an equal share to all. And again the people let him down. For a third time – and by now the nation's coffers were running rather low – a great redistribution of wealth occurred. This time the poor, having had a few sudden handouts in the past, were more feckless than before. They believed such bail-outs would continue for ever. But the lamas had other ideas; they announced the scheme had failed because of the previous lives each of the populace had lived. It stood to reason that if everyone was at a different stage on their path to religious enlightenment, however many lives that would take, it was foolish to expect that those who were on their first span of existence would have the same financial acuity and work ethic as those who were further along the path of enlightenment. A much more compelling argument was supplied by the king's mother; fed up with seeing her own wealth dwindle alarmingly, the queen dowager had her son poisoned. And so, after some years, inequalities returned: the feckless and idle sold their land and possessions to the crafty and hardworking, and life carried on as it does to this day.

By the eighth and ninth centuries, Tibet was at the zenith of her power. Buddhism had become stronger and more widespread, which led to a steady flow of Tibetans travelling to India and Nepal to study the religion further; they brought back new developments and sophistications. The seventh to the ninth centuries

2013 in the Garwhal Himalaya

was the time of the 'three religious kings' – who were reckoned to be Gampo, Ti-Song De-tsen and Ralpa-chan – and their invasions led to the subjugation of Western China, Mongolia, Turkestan and Nepal. Only a dislike of the heat and disease of India kept them from flooding over the passes and conquering that country too.

There followed a period of kingly fratricide and then three hundred years of decentralised power, with petty chieftains ruling their fiefdoms from forts they built above the villages they dominated, the ruins of which are still visible today – though some of the more famous, such as that at Gyantse, were demolished by the modern Chinese.

The age of kings eventually gave way to a new force: the age of lamas. The old, purer forms of Buddhism, which lived on in manuscripts, were supplanted by a hybrid version. As we have seen, this was as much influenced by Bon as by the more esoteric borrowings from India and Nepal. Bon and Tibetan Buddhism influenced each other – Bon became more systematic, while Tibetan Buddhism acquired a shamanistic, magical side, supported and encouraged perhaps by the tantric elements imported from India. The lamas built monasteries which became the nucleus of cities. History had begun.

At this point I laid down my pen. I had been scribbling hard – for some reason I had given up using a laptop in India and had reverted to my old ways, using a fountain pen and a notebook. Now it was time to get on the move again, be a bit nomadic, go higher.

9

An Attitude to Altitude

A man without money is a fool.

Pashtun proverb

Shamans get high. Go higher. By travelling to altitude and breathing in a certain way, it is possible to achieve mental states – useful or not – that resemble those achieved through more conventional forms of intoxication. Everything about the Himalayas is about going higher, sometimes in all senses of the phrase. The myth of Milarepa is so central because on one level it is also a battle about who is best *at altitude*.

Being good at altitude is like being good at maths or languages; it seems you either are or you aren't. But that doesn't stop some surprising hard workers who overcome an initial disability. Generally, the top climbers find a challenge in the hypoxic state that normal people find repugnant or sickening. The desire to push on when your mind is slowing down and your body refusing to do even basic tasks with ease requires a special kind of person. It could simply be a kind of schadenfreude – you find that, although you're feeling poorly, you can disguise the effects better than the group you are climbing with; the sicker they get, the better you feel. This kind of climber always suffers when they cannot lead or strike out on their own. *Following* is a physical insult to their whole mind-body continuum. Reinhold Messner definitely falls into this category; indeed, he views this need to go at his own speed as a matter of safety – a conventional alibi for someone who needs to control every element of their progress upwards. Another realisation, perhaps unarticulated, is that rhythm, the syncopation of breathing and limb movement, has a disproportional effect on success at altitude. I suspect, though, that such people when they climb derive their will to climb by beating others. Solo climbing suits them because in one sense they are beating *everyone*. When they climb in a group, they simply have to be better than everyone in that group; the more their companions fail, the better they feel. One might reasonably speculate that the death of any member of the party is actually a disguised form of triumph for such a climber, leading to complicated feelings and possibly a disgust with the whole enterprise of high-altitude gambolling/gambling.

What becomes apparent as you gasp your way higher than 3,000 metres is that you need an attitude to altitude, otherwise you will turn back too soon or carry on when you shouldn't. Altitude effects are among the most profoundly unnatural sensations that one can experience in nature; no wonder our ancestors thought they were caused by miasmas and exhalations of poisoned ground. Altitude sickness is not only counter-intuitive (shouldn't the air be cleaner and clearer higher up?), it is also counter to the way our bodies work. Those peoples and tribes who have learned to live at altitude have evolved bodies that function differently to a lowlander's.

A further mystery of altitude sickness is that it is democratic, striking the young as readily as the old. The super-fit can be laid low at 8,000 feet while an inveterate smoker has no problems at all. Women can go just as high as men. In 1978, Roman Giutach-villi, a forty-year-old Russian with one lung, reached the summit of Everest. Immunity, like God's grace, is dispensed in a way that seems arbitrary.

My own experiences are as good a starting point as any in this highly complex area. Being basically unfit, I had only a limited interest in the athletic aspect of climbing high; and the bagging

Going higher is possible even with one lung

of peaks, though obviously addictive, seemed a bit mechanical (a bit *easy*, while at the same time monstrously difficult). Still, I was intrigued at how my body would react to going higher. It became an *idée fixe*, my own demon. Though my researches showed altitude adaptation was not a benchmark of health or fitness or youth, I'd always taken it to be strongly connected to these things. I noticed that many trekkers I came across in the Himalayas were really quite elderly; on one trek, I was the youngest – and I was fifty. The oldest man was sixty-five, very spry, fitter than me and certainly 'better' at altitude. And why not? The oldest person to climb Everest is Yuichiro Miura, an eighty-year-old Japanese man. In my mind lurked an idea, a strange transmutation of the mystical religious notion of going higher as a defence against mortality. By literally going higher, I would either accrue some kind of benefit or receive a sign that indicated I was on for a ripe old age, and could look forward to the kind of balmy later years enjoyed by such folk as Yuichiro Miura – and when you're fifty, eighty seems immortal, especially when it involves climbing 8,000-metre mountains. If you could keep going a bit longer – through such healthful activities as going high in the mountains – then maybe you would live for ever; or at least you could put off thinking about it . . .

But I found I couldn't. My first excursion above 4,000 metres told me I was certainly no natural at altitude. Intent on keeping up with the guide, I found myself feeling light-headed, queasy and lacking in any kind of stamina. We were below a pass reached by climbing up a grassy slope. I made the mistake of cutting directly upwards from one switchback to another; the sudden increase in exertion forced me to halt for several minutes of recovery. Used to being something of a mountain sprinter, the humiliation of being unable to move fast added to the discomfort of altitude sickness.

Altitude sickness is a fascinating disease – because it isn't really a disease, it is more a physical record of the body's adaptation, or lack of it, to the new conditions found at altitude. The most important of these is lack of oxygen, but, as we'll later find out, other ascenders to the heights of the Himalayas have found that dehydration, gastric illness, lack of the right food and sun blindness can create or exacerbate symptoms of altitude sickness.

The central problem the body has to solve is how to re-establish the same levels of oxygen in each cell as would be experienced at sea level. But this doesn't just mean breathing more heavily.

The brain is calibrated for sea level, and at sea level the less carbon dioxide there is in the blood, the more oxygen there must be. But at altitude it's all different. You over-breathe to get more O_2, but this strips out the CO_2. So the brain 'thinks' you actually have too much oxygen. It constricts blood vessels to reduce blood flow and minimise this imaginary excess of oxygen. Breathing deeply to get more oxygen into the system results in losing more carbon dioxide, so the brain vasoconstricts even more – causing a headache, probably. Breathing is then reduced to match the vaso-constriction (which is why the headache goes), but this means less oxygen – the opposite of what you need. Eventually, some kind of balance is reached – through reducing activity to a minimum.

Carbon dioxide diffuses much more readily in the blood than oxygen, so the rates of readjustment are different and complex – causing the wide variety of symptoms associated with altitude sickness.

One way to visualise the push-me pull-you effects of altitude on breathing is to look at sleep apnoea – very heavy snoring. At lower altitudes this condition is common among the elderly and those with lung problems, but above 2,500 metres it occurs in people with normal lung function. It's a kind of schizophrenic fluctuation mediated by a lack of CO_2 at one end and a lack of O_2 at the other. A period of rapid and increasingly deep breaths prompted by a lack of oxygen are followed by shallower breaths (because carbon dioxide levels are low) until, alarmingly, breathing almost stops. At this point oxygen levels become critical, leading to a big intake of air – and then the cycle repeats. When someone is snoring like this, it can be rather frightening to observe.

The reason for the clumsy and slow adaptation to altitude is to alert us to the new and potentially dangerous situation we find ourselves in. Pain is a message to get lower, return to the status quo. If we reacted to a lack of oxygen by simply breathing more deeply, we could effortlessly keep going higher and higher with little adverse reaction. But going higher has many corollary problems – it is colder, more dangerous, lack of oxygen dulls the brain and causes us to make stupid decisions. The higher you go, the less food there is and water tends to be frozen. The optimum settlement zones are near sources of food, like the sea; we have evolved to work best at sea level. The body wants us to stay in the safety zone.

The earliest written accounts of altitude sickness date from AD 20. Written for the benefit of Han Emperor Wu Di, the description of crossing the Karakoram speaks of climbing Mount Greater Headache and traversing Mount Lesser Headache. Around AD 400 the Chinese pilgrim Hiouen Tsang would write that the cause of altitude sickness was the mists exhaled by the mountains and mountain vegetation: 'Rhubarb is abundant there; it exhales a very strong odour which annoys the traveller very much.'

Other early theories were nearer the truth. Francis Bacon, quoting Livy and a lost manuscript by Aristotle, wrote: 'The ancients had already noted that on the summit of Mount Olympus the air was so rare that in order to climb it one must take with him sponges wet with vinegar and water and place them on the nostrils . . . the air, because of its rarity, did not suffice for respiration.' Indeed, in Europe before the eighteenth century, it was widely believed that the summits of Alpine peaks were too high for humans to survive. This despite first-hand evidence that high altitude was not *necessarily* fatal. In 1590, the Jesuit priest José de Acosta managed to climb to 5,716 metres in Peru. He wrote, 'I was surprised with such pangs of straining . . . meat, phlegm and choler (bile) both yellow and green, in the end I cast up blood with the straining of my stomach . . . If this had continued I should undoubtedly have died.'

We want to get higher, and yet something wards us off. Monasteries have often been sited at considerable height, though rarely on top of peaks. The Great Saint Bernard Monastery is the highest in Europe at 2,469 metres, above the timberline, roughly at the height that the first mild symptoms of altitude can be felt. There is 25 per cent less oxygen here. A fifth of people who get rescued by a Saint Bernard dog will be suffering from headaches, nausea and general lassitude. But for those that can adapt, a reduced oxygen intake can be mildly euphoric. This is not to say that a sharpened spiritual sense amounts to nothing but a shortage of air. It might be that, as with fasting, a reduced intake of some vital substance encourages us to re-evaluate life.

Breathing impacts on our mental state in so many ways. It is the basic method of yoga and other systems that seek an integration of mind and body. We will see later how the Tibetan system of Gumno is used to raise body temperature to a significant degree – and the two key elements in Gumno are breathing and visualisation.

Breathing affects oxygenation levels. Over time, we become used to a certain replenishment rate, a certain level of oxygen in each cell. If you inhale some pure oxygen from a tank it will make you mildly euphoric; it can also cure a hangover. It takes three molecules of oxygen to metabolise one molecule of alcohol. Your body becomes mildly hypoxic as it uses oxygen to convert the alcohol to usable products. This is why running for a bus after you have had a lot to drink is always much harder than a usual sprint – your body is depleted of oxygen. It's also why a hangover caused by smoking and drinking is always worse than one caused simply by imbibing too much alcohol. Unsurprisingly, the symptoms of altitude sickness tend to mimic those of a hangover – headache, tiredness, nausea, thick-headedness. All part of the body's response to lower levels of oxygen in every part of the organism.

So, sensibly avoiding such pain, most humans have left the mountain summits to the gods – on Olympus, Ararat, Sinai, Kailash. Indeed, it was only in the enlightened eighteenth century that Europeans began to bridle at the shadow of these giants. In 1760, Horace-Bénédict de Saussure, an aristocrat, philosopher, meteorologist, early geologist and physiologist, offered a cash reward of 20 thalers to anyone who could climb Mont Blanc. It was a sizable sum, equivalent to several months' earnings for a Chamonix local. What more fitting symbol of the dethronement of the deity? (Perhaps significantly, 'thaler', from which we get 'dollar', comes from the German *thal*, meaning 'from the valley'.) In 1776, Canon Bourrit of Geneva ascended the nearby Mont Buet on foot. Buet was 3,000 metres high, a huge achievement for the time. Bourrit believed he had reached the highest point one could safely attain: 'It would be difficult if not impossible to live long on the summit of Mont Blanc.' He reported having to stop and rest every fifty steps.

In the meantime, other ways to get high had been emerging. In

1709, the first small hot-air balloon was demonstrated in Europe. It rose about 4 metres. In 1766, Henry Cavendish published a book about a gas lighter than air: hydrogen. And then in 1783, the Montgolfier brothers, paper makers who had observed the way a fire's heat could carry paper skyward, built a two-man hot-air balloon. In the same year the world's first hydrogen balloon was constructed and powered by pouring a ton of sulphuric acid on to several tons of scrap iron and piping the ensuing gas into a silk envelope. The pilot, Jacques Charles, rose to over 2,900 metres. The following year the chemist Joseph Proust rose to 4,000 metres in a Montgolfier-designed balloon.

No one had claimed de Saussure's prize yet. Several attempts were made, but all turned back reporting 'stagnation of the air' and a great 'distaste for provisions'. And yet, fear of altitude was lessening, in part thanks to the balloon experiments. In 1786, Chamonix crystal-hunter Jacques Balmat tried to find a way to the summit. He failed and got stuck; forced to bivouac overnight at over 3,500 metres, knowing that 'the people of Chamonix believed that sleep at these great heights would be fatal'. When Balmat emerged the following day, a bit cold and stiff but other-wise fine, a psychological barrier had been broken.

Later that year, Balmat and a Dr Paccard, using several poles to bridge crevasses and a ladder for a difficult bit, climbed Mont Blanc – 4,800 metres – for the first time. They both suffered from what they believed to be the 'foul air' at that height. It would take fifty more years for the true causes of altitude sickness to emerge.

Travelling in Mexico in the mid nineteenth century, a French doctor named Denis Jourdanet noticed the effect of the high mountains on travellers. The locals seemed unaffected. He decided to test their blood, and found that reduced oxygen levels, caused by reduced atmospheric pressure, resulted in an increased red blood cell count.

After only a few days at altitude, the body releases whatever red blood cells it has in reserve and the marrow starts manufacturing more. This tends to have the effect of clogging the capillaries, slowing the circulation of oxygen. In response, blood vessels increase in diameter, some doubling in size. All of which is a stress to the system, though some people react better than others.

Jourdanet was independently wealthy, and he gave his younger friend and colleague Paul Bert financial support for further studies on the physiological effects of altitude. To this end, in 1875 Bert sponsored a balloon ride. The three balloon enthusiasts enlisted for the experiment had access to oxygen, but not enough, as Bert realised just after they took off. It was too late. The sole survivor, Tissandier, wrote:

> I now come to the fateful moments when we were overcome by the terrible action of reduced pressure. At 22,900 feet . . . torpor had seized me. Croce is panting. Sivel shuts his eyes. Croce also shuts his eyes . . . At 24,600 feet the condition of torpor that overcomes one is extraordinary. Body and mind become feebler . . . There is no suffering. On the contrary, one feels an inward joy. There is no thought of the dangerous position; one rises and is glad to be rising . . . I wished to call out that we were now at 26,000 feet, but my tongue was paralysed. All at once I shut my eyes and fell down powerless and lost all further memory.

The balloon crashed after reaching nearly the height of Everest. These tragic experiments lead to a greater understanding. Paul Bert's name lives on in several ways: one is his dicta that those who conserve energy adjust best to altitude. Hard work is penalised: in the 1968 Mexico Olympics, staged at 2,300 metres, rowers performed badly and suffered from altitude sickness owing to the massive demands made on their aerobic capacity. Those events that required only short bursts of activity (you barely need to breathe during the 100 metres) set records in the lower-pressure air.

As every doctor will tell you: the only cure for altitude sickness is to go lower, back to the humdrum valley. Some people acclimatise, some don't. There is one drug – Diamox – that does make it easier for most people. It works by altering the acidity of the blood, which, in a complicated way, allows you to breathe more freely and deeply. There is another drug, however, that has been tested recently on Mont Blanc at the Observatoire Vallot situated 305 metres below the summit at 4,350 metres. The Observatoire was built in 1890 – the world's first high-altitude laboratory. (With French attention to culinary detail, needless to say, it has a superbly equipped kitchen.) Tragedy struck early on, when, in 1891, a Dr Jacottet began to suffer the usual symptoms of altitude sickness: headache, breathlessness when doing exercise. These symptoms continued to worsen until the doctor died. The autopsy revealed the world's first scientifically recorded case of HAPE (high altitude pulmonary edema). Nowadays we know we must descend the mountain at the first sign of symptoms; once it has set in, and fluid is leaking into the lungs, there is a 44 per cent mortality rate. In the costly business of learning about altitude, Dr Jacottet was another martyr.

Yet people continue to offer themselves up as victims at the Observatoire. The basic measure is the 'exercise maximum': you are forced to pedal on an exercise bike until you can pedal no more. In 2005, a group of twelve Frenchmen were tested doing this, but half had received a drug it was hypothesised would combat altitude sickness – Viagra. Viagra dilates blood vessels so that more blood can flow, typically in blood vessels that are constricted for some reason – for example, enabling a flaccid penis to become erect. In the case of those suffering from altitude sickness, constricted blood vessels in the lungs open up to allow more blood, and therefore more oxygen, to reach the brain. In other words, it makes you more like a Tibetan.

At first the entire group – Viagra- and placebo-takers – suffered from altitude sickness. Blood pressure, which is a fairly good measure of how well you are acclimatising, rose 29 per cent. But by the sixth day, something interesting happened. While the placebo group's blood pressure remained 21 per cent higher than normal, the Viagra group's blood pressure was 6 per cent *lower* than during earlier low-altitude testing. Although both groups got breathless during exercise, the Viagra group had faster recovery rates during exercise than the placebo group.

Ancient and modern medicine has failed to really get to grips with altitude sickness. The German health service refuses to pre-scribe Diamox – a sulfa drug that most high-altitude climbers use. Dr Peter Hackett of the Institute for Altitude Medicine disagrees with the Germans. The source of this lack of a unified approach lies in the holistic nature of the illness; every part of the body suffers when oxygen levels drop, so specialists in one area can be at a loss because they cannot grasp the whole picture. My own ex-perience taught me how nuanced control of the ailment is: small adjustments made at the right time seemed to have a big effect.

Those who are 'adapted to altitude' could be marginally supe-rior in lots of areas – all of it adding up to greater efficiency overall. They could be efficient at removing water from the interstitial lung area, thus improving oxygen uptake. They could be better adapted to wet breathing, not using so much energy to warm and moisten incoming air (which takes up a lot of energy). They could be less sensitive to cold – which also takes a lot of oxygen. They could be supremely fit, so that excess work at altitude does not take such a toll – though this is by no means as crucial as it sounds; plenty of supremely fit people are bad at altitude. They are likely to be 'good breathers', meaning that in any single breath they manage to maximise the extraction of oxygen, which results in dilated rather than constricted blood and air vessels. This hinges on being relaxed as much as adequate CO_2 levels. We will later hear of Tibetan monks who can increase their skin temperature by up to 6 degrees, and plenty of biofeedback dabblers can raise hand temperature and heart rate at will. There is no question that we can interfere with autonomous bodily functions in a negative way through fear and anxiety; could we not also benefit from imposing relaxation and calm?

On each occasion that I went to altitude, my experience was different. This is far from uncommon – most of the accounts of Himalayan climbers relate occasions when they had a bad time at altitude and on other climbs were in 'perfect condition'. Certainly, Harold 'Bill' Tilman suffered at altitude at first (despite farming land in Kenya at 2,000 metres for over ten years) but later became very well adapted. I wonder if there is a parallel with diving, where beginners panic and gulp air; this results in too much of a reduction in CO_2, which leads to vasoconstriction – similar to an asthma attack – which then requires a further panicky deep breath. The cycle is broken by gradual relaxation. Divers become more efficient at breathing without really trying; they simply know they want their air to last longer. Similarly, climbers become better and more efficient at breathing at altitude – they learn not to indulge in activity that leaves them breathless because this will set off the vasoconstriction cycle.

I found that any excess exercise at altitudes above 3,000 metres was punished – unless I was already acclimatised. In my experience, the best way to acclimatise is not to exercise at all, just focus on very gently moving higher up the mountain each day. If you can sleep at only 300-metre increments each day and never get out of breath while doing it, I think the process will be as efficient as any other. Often I went over 1,000 metres in a day. What I noticed was that I would feel fine until lunchtime, but after a heavy lunch cooked by a willing Nepali, I would find the afternoon a struggle. We forget just how much energy is used in digesting food. Protein takes the most energy, then roughage, followed by fat and carbohydrates. It is interesting that the people most adapted to altitude living – Tibetans – put butter and salt in everything they can. They also tend to eat porridges and teas, which are much easier to digest than solid food. Salt is vital for remaining hydrated and melted butter is a good way to take on fats, which require less energy to digest than other foods easily available.

Those people who live year round above 4,000 metres – Tibetans and Andeans – have over time evolved to deal with altitude. Though they are not immune to altitude sickness, they are very much happier high up and crucially can do more work than an acclimatised non-native can.

Tibetans have been living on the Tibetan Plateau, which varies between 3,500 and 5,000 metres, for over 30,000 years. Andean tribes are considered to have been altitude dwellers for perhaps 11,000 years. These two groups have taken different evolutionary paths. Andeans have bigger lungs, more haemoglobin and more erythropoietin than sea-level dwellers. This means more air is processed to extract more oxygen. Tibetans don't have big lungs or more haemoglobin – actually, they have a little less than people living at sea level. What they do have is more nitric oxide. They breathe faster than others at altitude, but this doesn't result in vasoconstriction because of the high nitric oxide levels in their blood (up to 200 times higher than in the general population). Nitric oxide is a vasodilator, used as a supplement by body builders through the precursor argenine found in such foods as spinach, sesame seeds, crab and shrimp. But Tibetans have it naturally. One can read accounts online of people using nitric oxide supplements to ease altitude sickness – anecdotally, it seems to work.

The evolution of these traits probably involves a well-known aspect of living at altitude: fertility rates are lower and people don't have so many children. Those with a slight advantage – and Tibetans have two genes associated with lower haemoglobin – will tend to proliferate. Over time. It took fifty years after Spaniards moved to the Andes for the first child of Spanish-born parents to be conceived and survive childbirth. Even among natives of Tibet, fertility is lower than elsewhere. There is a reason why high mountain areas aren't overpopulated. This may explain the prevalence of polyandry in Tibet and other enclaves at altitude – it improves the chances of conceiving if a woman has three husbands instead of one. In a highly fertile population, a woman with many husbands would be exhausted by childbirth; in the mountains, she may need several lovers just to get pregnant.

So not only does going higher expose us to dangers, it also reduces the number of offspring we can produce – strong Darwinian reasons to stay in the valleys. And, mostly, we have.

Why does one feel nausea at altitude? Before eating, it is due to changing pressure in the digestive system and the many imbalances caused by a change in oxygen at the cellular level. After and during eating, nausea can result because one doesn't have enough oxygen available to digest the food properly – the body is shutting down superfluous activities to send oxygen to where it is most needed: the brain. This is one reason to eat only the food you want to at altitude. Steer clear of stodgy unpalatable food, thick candy bars, 'trail mix'; go for easy-to-digest soups and drinks. The item that runs out quickest on a trek is usually hot chocolate. Followed closely by cigarettes.

One of the curious things about altitude is the prevalence of high-altitude smokers. Stephen Venables, arguably one of the greatest high-altitude climbers ever, was still smoking the odd roll-up cigarette when he climbed Everest without oxygen. The great pre-war climbers were often photographed at base camp holding a pipe. Excessive smoking is obviously counterproductive, but smokers have higher CO_2 levels – which means less vasoconstriction and more efficient oxygen uptake. A smoker who stops smoking within a few days of starting a climb will also tend to have more haemoglobin, thus smoothing the transition to altitude. Smokers' bodies are also accustomed to running on lower amounts of oxygen – even at the cellular level – which makes getting all the body's systems into alignment easier than for someone whose body has never experienced a sustained drop in oxygen levels.

There are a number of unexplored avenues in altitude studies. One is the intriguing possibility that the way you breathe has a big effect on how you acclimatise and how you deal with altitude. The body is relatively good at dealing with low oxygen levels, once all its systems are in alignment; what it is bad at is handling high levels of CO_2 – and overreacting to low levels of CO_2. A number of breathing methods, pioneered with asthma sufferers, seek to increase CO_2 levels so that an overreaction leading to further hypoxia is avoided. Asthmatics are taught to breathe through the nose, hold the breath to the count of five or ten, then breathe in again. This helps reduce 'overbreathing', a problem whereby the asthma sufferer sucks in a lot of air through their mouth, which scrubs out all their CO_2, leading to vasoconstriction and poor oxygen intake.

Another unexplored link would be the use of certain supplements which we know work against hypoxia at sea level. These include Coenzyme Q10, typically given to heart-attack patients suffering mild hypoxia, and nitric oxide, which, as we have seen, allows Tibetans to breathe more deeply with vasoconstriction. In a way, the altitude drug Diamox, which alters blood acidity thus signalling that there is more CO_2 in the blood than there really is, fools the brain, which equates acidity with CO_2 presence; this triggers deeper breathing and more oxygen. Essentially, it performs the same function as nitric oxide – though Diamox is much more powerful.

In my subsequent visits to altitude I was much more gentle in the way I approached higher and higher levels. I spent days running around at 1,800 metres in Darjeeling – lower than the level at which altitude problems start, but still a place where the amount of oxygen available to breathe (due to lower air pressure) is 20 per cent lower than sea level. If you can exercise without generating an excessively low CO_2 response with all the bad effects of vasoconstriction, then running at lower altitudes is a very effective way to build up some immunity to mild AMS. The runners Adrian and Richard Crane, who famously ran the Himalayas at altitudes ranging from 2 to 5,000 metres, were very rarely incapacitated despite running each day.

But once I got above 2,500 metres I took it very easy, trying to establish rhythms of exercise rather than sudden bursts. Keeping going without getting out of breath is THE best way to avoid altitude problems, because you never engage in the overbreathing associated with low CO_2 and vasoconstriction.

Nepalis and Tibetans emphasise eating vasodilators such as garlic, and salt is loaded into each meal – which helps water uptake. Wearing sunglasses helps too; there may be some obscure connection yet to be discovered between vasoconstriction and bright sun glare – I know that walking fully covered in the desert one can keep going far longer than if bright sunlight gets into your eyes. There is also anecdotal evidence that hay fever sufferers benefit from wearing dark glasses. We'll see later that early Himalayan climbers thought that sun blindness contributed to mountain sickness. Perhaps it brings on vasoconstriction, which in turn exacerbates features of Acute Mountain Sickness. Being well hydrated, wearing full-cover sunglasses, eating easy-to-digest food and never over-exerting oneself is a good start to acclimatising.

Shamans go higher: the less oxygen you have, the more you focus on what is right in front of your nose. Mindfulness becomes obligatory. 'Higher' thoughts occur naturally. As you struggle to breathe, you think about your life, where it is going.

I am at 16,000 feet when I cross a huge dried-up lake. Frosted over, it looks like a snowy desert. The path I am on is cut into the rocky cliffside. It is steep and every forty paces I stop to rest. Then I go on too fast and have to rest again, after thirty paces, then twenty paces. I am still not practising the lesson of Bert's researches: *work is penalised exponentially at altitude.* For every step you go faster than you should, you are docked two steps' worth of oxygen. But within me surges something more than mere pain, more than simply wanting to show I can make it to the 'top'. I sense the benefit of the focus I am achieving. And it is all down to the fact that I am, at last, listening to my breathing.

Instead of thinking about where the others are, looking at my watch, counting my paces, I am simply listening to my breathing. I slow my pace to a point where my breathing can keep up. Some sort of inner regulator kicks in. I know instinctively what speed I can walk at and seemingly keep it up for ever. Every time I scramble over a rock, I slow right down. You can only maintain this level of activity by moving very slowly.

Listening to my breathing, I am reminded of the great noise the air makes going in and out when one is diving with a regulator and compressed air bottle. Acting coaches claim that the single key way to improve performance when on stage or interacting with others is to be aware of your breathing. It is the mainstay of many spiritual exercises. Listening to your breathing is not just good for presenting, it's good for being present. Your 'centre' goes from being up in the abstract world of your head to firmly within your body. You shift to living in the now.

As you get higher, your senses make less sense, and you pay less attention to them. Sight becomes less crucial as you fix your eyes on the ground a mere three feet ahead. That's partly for safety – to see where you should tread – and partly because it is too painful to see how far you have to go. But you listen to your breathing. Maybe you are getting into alignment with something beyond the petty confines of the body. I remember when I wanted to help my children sleep when they were tiny I used to synchronise my breathing with theirs and very quickly they would drop off. So would I, if I wasn't careful.

Near the summit, I do not rest. Instead, I ditch all my gear – heavy camera, coat, water bottle – and head off, unencumbered, up the rocky slope. I am rewarded handsomely for shedding weight. I am moving more easily despite the fact the slope has grown steeper. There is snow here and I inwardly rejoice. I am at last truly in the mountains. As a child, I loved snow and looked forward to playing in the stuff, no matter how thin the layer. But this snow is deep; sometimes I sink in up to my knees. Then it is past and I am back on the rocky path. This time I vow to never stop. If this means slowing to a virtual halt and walking like a slow-motion puppet, I'll do that rather than race ahead and rest. The strategy works. The others up ahead are resting. I catch them up just before the final push to the pass. I can feel the burn in my legs but my breathing is fine. I can keep going like this for as long as I have to.

At the top, prayer flags flap. Printed on cheap polyester, the flags adorn every pass and summit in the Himalayas like bunting. Higher peaks are seemingly very close. They look like starched white sheets folded into peaks. I bow to the mountain and follow the guide's prayer. Now we are no longer moving, it's easy to breathe. I give thanks to all the gods.

10

A Cure for Altitude Sickness
That Will Cost You

An eagle with clipped wings is not a dove.

Afghan proverb

As we've seen, there are natural cures for altitude sickness that are practised by Himalayan local people. Eating garlic, drinking a lot and walking at a steady pace can help lowlanders acclimatise to the high passes. But there are also drugs – which conveniently only grow in the place where they are most needed. *Ophiocordyceps sinensis*, or caterpillar fungus, is prized as a cure for altitude problems as it functions like nitric oxide (and Viagra) to maintain blood-vessel diameter as one went higher. But that same functionality also makes Cordyceps a natural form of Viagra – and for that reason, it is highly sought after in China.

In fact, it is so sought after, some are willing to kill in order to get their hands on it. In 2009 some Nepalese Gurkhas, trying to prove themselves and make a bit of money, targeted the Cordyceps fields of their neighbours – the more passive Buddhist Narpa people. Hindu Gurkhas are known for their fighting prowess as mercenaries, but they also provided support for the Maoist insurgency that dominated the late 1990s and 2000s. The Narpa tended to favour the monarchy and the status quo, living as they

80

did in an isolated spot that did not have a jail, so rare was crime in their area.

The Gurkha lads were not expert Cordyceps thieves. They were spotted loitering – all seven of them – by a herder from the village of Nar. There was already bad blood between the two tribes – several years earlier a Nar elder had been beaten to death and the Narpa believed Gurkhas were responsible. It was a case of finally having a real reason for bashing their neighbours. The herder rushed into the village and something very ancient and atavistic happened: every household had to give up one member – not only to defend their land and the valuable crop, but also to ensure that all would be implicated in the crime they knew they were about to commit. The conversations were all in the Ng language, the almost secret tongue of the Narpa, which no other Nepalis speak. The Narpa had much to defend – most houses now had a solar panel capable of running a hot plate and three lightbulbs, which meant a much lower requirement for firewood or yak dung. The village made upwards of $65,000 a year from the fungus; take that away and you have a huge hole in the local economy.

Ophiocordyceps sinensis is the most expensive herbal supplement in the world – or it was in 2008, when this wild fungus that grows in only one place in the world fetched the astronomical price of $75,000 a kilogram. In other parts of the Himalayas – rural Tibet – 40 per cent of all cash income is estimated to come from the fungus, something over $225 million. Between 85–185 tons a year are harvested, which, for a very lightweight piece of dry fungus, is an awful lot of picking. Indeed, in Tibet, the bribe of choice isn't cash, it's a piece of Cordyceps fungus (or preferably several pieces). You have to be careful buying the wild product though; local collectors traditionally used sticks to hold the fruit of the mushroom in bundles, but in recent years they've taken to using a piece of solder wire instead. This adds to the weight, but also imparts a lead toxicity to the product.

Nepalese, Bhutanese, Tibetans and Chinese all search for Cordyceps in the high places of the Himalayas – it grows best above 4,000 metres, wherever the ghost moth, of the *Thitarodes* genus, also lives. Excavation must be careful – the tool of choice is often a spoon. A harvest of twelve to fifteen pieces a day is not unusual. Yaks are watched – where they are unusually lively, eating caterpillar fungus is generally the cause.

Known as *yartsa gunbu* in Tibetan – the name means 'summer grass, winter bug' – it was long believed to be a genuine mix of the two. Cordyceps sinensis was first written about in AD 620 in the time of the Tang dynasty. A fifteenth-century Tibetan poem entitled 'An Ocean of Aphrodisiacal Qualities' credited the fungus with the power to 'remove prana diseases and cure bile diseases without raising the phlegm; a marvellous medicine, in particular it increases semen'. It was poetically described as an almost myth-ical beast that transformed from animal to plant in summer and from plant to animal in winter. Until very recently, we reserved the usual sneering attitude to such ancient botanising: we knew better – Cordyceps was simply a parasitic fungus that fed off the hibernating larvae of the ghost moth. But more detailed studies have revealed that there is much more of a symbiotic relationship than the one-sided parasitic kind. The fungus inhabits the moth larva and draws nutrition from it, while the larva in turn derives energy from the fungus. Despite killing many of the larvae, the presence of the fungus may enable the few survivors to be strong enough to thrive.

Like some horror film alien, *Ophiocordyceps sinensis* eventually sprouts from the head of the subterranean-dwelling caterpil-lar that ultimately becomes the ghost moth. The spores of the fungus, or perhaps the filaments of non-fruiting fungus, invade

the breathing pores of the larvae – which spends five years bur-
rowed 15 centimetres underground, before it hatches as a moth.
Or not, if the fungus gets there first.

Environmentally, Bhutan is still the favoured haunt for this
moth. Pressure on habitat in Nepal and Tibet may have driven
its numbers down in the last two decades, along with the milder
weather this region has been experiencing. At the same time,
owing to increasing publicity about its miracle effects, demand
continues to rise sharply. In the early 1990s you could buy a
kilogram of Cordyceps in Tibet for $10; now it will set you back
thousands of dollars – depending how close you are to its source.

For many years it was considered impossible to make the Cordyceps fruit in the laboratory. Now, driven by price rises, much more
sophisticated growing techniques are being used. The hypoxic
environment of 4,000+ metres is replicated in special growing
tents where oxygen levels are only two-thirds that of normal air.
The acidic quality of the soil, the low temperatures of the high
Himalayas – all this is now replicated in the commercial growing
labs producing Cordyceps. However, one quality still eludes the
cultivar as opposed to the wild version – cultivated Cordyceps has
uncontrollable variations in its mineral content, something the
wild version stabilises naturally.

To look at, the caterpillar fungus is nothing special. The fruiting part looks like a rather dark and insubstantial sausage or a
somewhat charred tuber (when fresh, it is yellower in colour). The
fruiting stalk of the fungus is about 4–10 centimetres longer than
the caterpillar (which is itself quite big at 10–15 centimetres).

We have known about caterpillar fungus in the West for a long
time. Jesuit missionaries first brought it back from China in 1726
and introduced it in Paris as an aphrodisiac and general life tonic.
In 1843, the obsessive cryptogamist (cryptogamy is the study of
plants that reproduce by asexual spores rather than seeds: lichens,

fungi, mosses, ferns and slime moulds) Miles Berkeley described the caterpillar scientifically for the first time. Yet it was only in 1993 that Cordyceps went mainstream. At the Chinese national games that year nine world records were broken in distance-running events. Then at the 1994 World Championships in athletics held in Stuttgart two more world records were broken. Controversial running coach Ma Junren declared that no steroids had been used, only infusions of turtle blood and *Ophiocordyceps sinensis*. Though later tests on athletes have not been conclusive in show-ing the benefit of the mushroom (partly as a result of the design of the tests and the kind of athletic event concerned), there has been overwhelming evidence from more widespread testing on ordinary people – and mice – that demonstrates that this fungus is far from being a figment of the quack medicinal mind.

Research has shown that imbibing Cordyceps through a tea infusion increases cellular ATP levels, which in turn increases energy output at the cellular level. One's overall energy is raised but there is no deficit later, as is the case with caffeine and other stimulants.

In one test where elderly patients were administered Cordy-ceps or a placebo, none of those who received the placebo showed any benefits (a rare result in itself; the placebo effect occurs with almost all drugs) but those who imbibed Cordyceps all showed significant improvements in chronic fatigue reduction, as well as improvements in breathing, amnesia and other symptoms of hypoxia. This is not so surprising. The Tibetans have always claimed that a major use for Cordyceps is to reduce altitude sick-ness – hypoxia – and it seems that it does.

Another group of elderly volunteers – all over sixty-five – took Cordyceps for six weeks. They showed significant improvements in stationary bicycle performance, increased energy and oxygen capacity when compared to the placebo group.

More fiendish testing is possible with mice, poor things. When placed in an oxygen-deprived vivarium (perhaps not the best word), so lacking in the gas that death was inevitable for all participants, those mice that had partaken of Cordyceps lasted an astonishing *three times* longer than those with no such fungal assistance.

In the equally desperate environment of the *terminal swimming tank*, mice were tested for their endurance and will to live. In this test, mice were tipped into a tank with slippery steep sides from which no escape was possible. The mice kept swimming until they drowned from utter exhaustion (or were pulled out by a soft-hearted technician). Those mice given Cordyceps lasted significantly longer, swam for longer and suffered less exhaustion than the mice not given Cordyceps.

Switching back to humans, the Beijing Medical University dosed fifty asthma patients with Cordyceps. It was found that not only was ATP production boosted, but auto-immune tracheal contractions were reduced. Both effects benefit asthmatics; they experienced an 81.3 per cent reduction in symptoms in only five days. Those given the more usual antihistamines found only a 61 per cent decrease in symptoms, and this took nine rather than five days.

Another Chinese study confirmed what many researchers merely hint at: Cordyceps has a sex-steroid effect – at least on mice. Are you a man or a mouse, one might ask. Stanford University followed this up and concluded that Cordyceps does indeed boost human androgen and other sex hormones found in the adrenal glands and the testicles.

It was this use of Cordyceps – as a Chinese sex drug – that led the Gurkha lads into their losing battle with sixty-five very angry Narpa villagers. They ran – and one account (the official account is considered unreliable) has it that two boys fell into a crevasse, where they died. The Narpa claim that they had only intended to give the Gurkhas a good scare. But with two dead, they feared the others would betray them to the police. With sticks, stones and farm implements the five were killed and chopped into pieces; the parts were then disposed of in the fast-flowing river.

Women from the Gurkha village went calling a month later on the police chief of Chama, the nearest town. When writer Eric Hansen interviewed him two years after the murders, he was drunk on local home brew and openly boastful: 'This was my most successful mission – we arrested 70 people!'

Since there was no jail in Chama, a stockade was improvised and most of the male populace of Nar were interned – between sixty-five and seventy male suspects, depending on whose version you read.

Meanwhile the Gurkha people demanded blood money from the Annapurna Conservation Area project. This – perceived as rich – organisation fills its coffers from the thousands of tourists who trog round the Annapurna Circuit each year. The Gurkha appeal was successful: $14,000 was awarded to the family of each victim.

Their suspected killers were not faring so well. While most were released on parole fairly quickly, twenty-seven were interned for over two years. After many prevarications and delays – some of which smacked of sheer idleness on the part of the authorities – the Narpa were sentenced. That month the people of Nar held a week-long puja. They prayed that their men be set free. Six men – said to be the murderers – were sentenced to life imprisonment. Thirteen accomplices were set free, with the two years already spent in jail serving as their sentence. The eight remaining went free, without a stain on their character maybe, but having served the same sentence as the accomplices.

That a fungus which was claimed to prolong life and supply

life-giving energy should be the cause of death is just what we should expect. As I have already noted, Hindus claim we are living in *Kali Yarg* – the age of Kali – when everything is upside down, good is bad and bad is perceived as good. Clearly, the mushroom that grows from the head of a caterpillar has driven some people mad . . .

Alexandra David-Néel and the Dawn Runners of Tibet

The mouse is the head in a house without a cat.
Balti proverb

I was in Kalimpong and feeling low. It didn't help that I was staying in a very cheap hotel, a hovel really. The manager was friendly, but it was not enough to overcome the depressing windowless bedroom. The broken window in my 'en suite' bathroom provided the only outlook: over a cracked and dribbling sewage pipe and a steel exterior staircase (on to which it dripped). All night there was a whiff of sewage and the constant passage of ringing footsteps, even with the flimsy bathroom door closed. My room had that deeply grimy look that only years of half-arsed cleaning can achieve; a line of grime highlighted every place a little awkward for mop, broom, or duster to reach. You begin to resent walking barefoot on such a floor . . .

It was time to play the luxury card. As Bruce Chatwin rightly wrote: 'luxury is only luxurious in adverse conditions'. I wanted to save money – hence hovelling – but I needed to stay cheerful. I called the Himalayan Hotel and they had one vacancy – I was over in a shot.

Kalimpong was a hill station, a sort of Mussoorie to Darjeeling's Simla; it was smaller and easier to get around but had less

The Himalayan Hotel, where many famous travellers have stayed

going for it. The Lepcha Museum of indigenous people was shut. So were the ruins of the Damsang Dzong, where the Lepcha kings were soundly beaten by the Bhutanese. Shy and retiring by nature, the Lepcha legacy was upheld by a collection of proverbs and folktales I bought in a stationer's shop (where I also found Peter Goullart's excellent *Forgotten Kingdom*). So I had high hopes for the Himalayan Hotel – a colonial-style place where everyone who was famous who had ever visited this part of the Himalayas had stayed: Hillary and Tenzing, Heinrich Harrer, Alexandra David-Néel, Joseph Rock. The hotel's founder had been David Macdonald, interpreter on the 1904 Younghusband expedition. Already I was finding that 1904/5 was a key date for my researches. It was the year Halford Mackinder proposed the 'Heartland' Theory (he suggested that whoever controls the supercontinent of Eurasia controls the world – a theoretical backup to the Great Game), and the year the West finally burst open the inner fastness and mystery of Tibet. It was also the year Aleister Crowley attempted Kanchenjunga using newly invented metal climbing aids known as crampons.

I was lucky enough to get the Alexandra David-Néel room. She seemed a saner version of Madame Blavatsky, and though there is some quibbling about the exact geography of her travels, she definitely had real experience of travelling extensively in the Himalayas. Her room was large, old-fashioned, spick and span and perfect. I imagined Alexandra lying on the bed, writing up her memoirs of mystical experiences in Sikkim and Tibet. She'd spent the first two years of the First World War in a cave in Sikkim, studying Tibetan spirituality with a fifteen-year-old monk who became her lifelong companion. Before that she'd been an opera singer in Indochina, playing Carmen in Hanoi. She met the thirteenth Dalai Lama twice – once in Kalimpong, where I was now. She wore trousers to travel when they weren't fashionable, visited Lhasa, and spent part of the Second World War in the Soviet Union.

Reading her work, I was agreeably surprised to discover she doesn't come across like a New Age nut; which is what I had been expecting. She does tend towards the fey. Often, in an ordinary situation but faced by someone who looks strange or exotic, she fantasises a *what if* situation and the *what if* is her interlocutor disappearing in a puff of genii smoke or instantly reading a mind. Her reality, from the moment she arrived in the Himalayas, was not exactly one of credulity, but it is oriented heavily towards potential invisible forces.

Her style reminds me of David Hatcher Childress, whose *Lost Cities* series of travel memoirs is equal parts intriguing and oddly pedestrian. One reason for reading both is not just for the uncensored interesting information but also the kind of vicarious travel thrill they supply; that indefinable combination of credulousness and savvy needed to make a good trip.

One invisible, possibly demonic, force, which sounds more plausible than others, is that of super endurance, which she observes among the mountain-dwelling monks. As we've seen, Tibetan monks can raise and lower their temperature at will, so it doesn't seem too unlikely that they would encourage their bodies to other feats of extreme endurance. The police report that people resisting arrest while on the drug PCP can appear to have the strength of six – easily throwing bigger and bulkier policemen out of their way. There is considerable anecdotal evidence of elderly, infirm or slight women lifting cars or other super-heavy machinery* off injured loved ones. No one really denies these situations happen – the thing is, they require immense and life-threatening situations; you can't just dial up superman's strength when you need it.

Alexandra David-Néel was travelling with a caravan in the Himalayas. She relates a small black moving dot that quickly became apparent as a human being moving with great rhythmic and elastic steps. He did not reply when spoken to. Members of her group thought he must be lost or a survivor of some mountain accident. He was almost running and yet seemed without any tiredness, despite carrying bags on his back. She compared the impression of seeing him with that of watching a slow motion film at the cinema, such was the ease and fluidity of the man's movement. No one could keep up with him on foot. One of the party followed on horseback, but turned back when the extraordinary runner took off up a steep and rocky slope impassable to equines.

Instead of focusing on wealth creation and making labour-saving inventions, the people of the Himalayas, David-Néel writes, have concentrated on psychic development. In special monasteries – the suggestively named 'powerhouses' – mastery over breathing and mind is developed using symbols, mantras and long periods of concentration. And long periods of walking.

I know of Bedouin who, in exceptional circumstances, will travel all night and day with camels, covering 70–80 kilometres in a twelve-hour period, and some of them will be walking much of

---

* To cite one recent example: Kirstie McCrum, 'Teen girl uses "superhuman strength" to lift burning truck off dad and save family', *Daily Mirror*, 11 January 2016.

the time. Masai will happily run 80 kilometres if their cattle are threatened and they need to move fast. Humans are long-distance running machines, as Arthur Newton showed in the 1920s when he started, aged forty, as an ultra-long-distance runner, shattering records of the time for fifty, seventy and one hundred mile races by times of up to an hour less than previous winners. His method was simple and evolved by himself with an eye on super endurance. Most long-distance runners evolve from marathon running and are used to a faster pace than can be sustained for seventy or more miles. They therefore run like hares with frequent rests. Newton focused instead on breathing, maintaining a pace that he knew he could keep up for the entire race – without stopping. He theorised that when the many systems of the body work together, they need to be in some kind of rhythm or syncopation to perform at peak efficiency. This feeds back to the runner as a 'second wind' – and Newton wrote about how to achieve a 'third, fourth and fifth wind'.

Newton believed that, while interval training built strength, stamina rested on getting into a rhythm dictated by breathing. Had he stumbled, or perhaps, elegantly jogged, across the same information as the Himalayan runners mentioned by Alexandra David-Néel?

What is emphasised by David-Néel is the need for the mind to dominate the body, for a mental picture of the destination to be so powerful that it almost takes over the runner's own volition.

Tell people there is buried treasure if you want them to dig their fields; they will get wealthy just the same.

Himalayan proverb

12

Release Your Fiery Inner Demons

Canals are large in a waterless land,
measures for grain are large in a land without grain.
Balti proverb

The Cordyceps fungus allows you to function better at altitude, but breathing control – conscious breathing – helps you to go higher too, and to get higher. By messing with the amount of oxygen the brain receives, all kinds of states can be triggered. The body, too, can be fooled into changing its default settings. This helps you cope with other aspects associated with altitude – namely cold.

For many years stories came from the Himalayas of monks who had absolute control over their body's autonomic systems. This is something no conventionally trained doctor can possibly agree is true. As a result, these stories remained part of the imaginary journey of many people.

Alexandra David-Néel talks about the incredible ability of certain Tibetan monks reputedly able to raise their body temperature at will.* Draped in wet sheets at minus 35 degrees Celsius, their bodies naked beneath, great gouts of steam rose from the wet cloths as their superheated torsos turned the icy garments

---

* Alexandra David-Néel, *Magic and Mystery in Tibet*

into steaming pudding cloth. Other travellers made mention of this technique, but it wasn't until the 1980s that Western science was able to catch up with Eastern expertise.

Greater knowledge of Tibet and her monks – whether they live on the Indian side or the Tibetan side of the border, the monks involved were practitioners of gTum-mo (pronounced 'dumo') – a combination of breathing exercises and meditative concentration that is mentioned in the teachings of the Tibetan Vajrayana, which itself stems from Indian Buddhist Vajrayana tradition.

The basic form involves performing 'the vase', a breathing technique where air is brought deep into the lower abdominal region and held there, making a pot belly or 'vase' of the stomach. There is a forceful version of this where the air is sucked in, held and then expelled with great vigour. There is also a gentler version where the transitions are far less marked and the intake and exhalation of breath, though deep, is gentle.

Accompanying the breathing are two varieties of meditation. For the forceful breathing (which is used to ramp up body temperature quickly from 'cold', so to speak) the meditation is to picture internally an inner flame, something like a Bunsen burner flame, roaring hot, that starts at the navel and shoots up to the crown of the head. You have to imagine that flame in all its heat, roaring noise and light, burning up through the core of the body.

For the more gentle variant of body temperature manipulation, the mental image is of a surging sensation of bliss and rising warmth throughout the body.

Nature magazine has published a scientific investigation of gTum-mo yoga conducted in the Dharamsala Monastery of the Dalai Lama's government in exile, during which three monks were able to raise the temperature of their fingers and toes by a creditable 8.3 degrees Celsius. This is rather impressive; in some situations it would mean the difference between frostbite and frost-nip or merely coldness. If climbers and others who venture into highly refrigerated environs could learn these techniques, many digits might be saved.

In 2002 the *Harvard Gazette* reported on two monks – of Western origin and living in Normandy – who were able to raise their body temperature using gTum-mo techniques. But it wasn't until 2013 that a more comprehensive set of tests and a general survey of previous attempts was made. In the previous thirty years it had been found that raising peripheral temperatures – of hands and feet – could be achieved through various easily taught meditations, and, in fact, by training people to use simple biofeedback techniques. Typically, a digital thermometer would be connected to sensors on the subject's hands and feet. Through a greater *awareness* of the temperature of the hand or foot, the extremity warms up, though you have to avoid forcing it.

But complications entered the field when it was found that raising core body temperature did not accompany raising peripheral temperatures. One theory suggested that various forms of muscular contraction served to raise hand temperature.

The 2013 tests showed that, unlike biofeedback results, gTum-mo genuinely raised core body temperatures – so much so that the wet sheet dried by body heat alone was shown to be fact not fiction.

The scientists involved located one of the very few nunneries where a body temperature-raising ceremony exists. This was at the 4,200-metre-high Gebchak convent, close to Nangchen in Qinghai province. The ceremony was held annually and the nuns participating would wear only a short skirt, shoes or sandals with a wet cotton sheet draping the rest of their body. It would be performed in winter when air temperatures would be dry but -25 to -30 degrees Celsius. Anyone who has dipped their hand in water at these temperatures will know the extreme discomfort involved, and how hard it is to regain skin warmth after drastic cooling like this has happened. Ranulph Fiennes dipped his hand in icy sea water to release a sunken sledge and did not dry and warm the hand immediately. He later remarked that these two minutes of carelessness cost him the fingertips of that hand. I've swept a frosty tent surface with a bare hand at -15 degrees Celsius and found the hand still cold ten minutes later, despite wearing a mitten. Such anecdotal evidence makes even the existence of the sheet ceremony all the more impressive.

The nuns were aged between twenty-five and fifty-two, and some performed the forceful variety of gTum-mo and some the more gentle kind. It was reported that the forceful kind could not be sustained for very long, so it was used to warm the body up, after which the gentle type would be used when walking and wearing the wet sheet.

Nuns raised their peripheral temperatures easily by 1.2 to 6.8 degrees Celsius. More importantly, the forceful type of gTum-mo raised core body temperature by over a degree. One woman was able to get it higher and only stopped because she felt uncomfortable. Another stopped because she was developing fever symptoms.

If peripheral temperature raising results in a lowering of core body temperature, then using techniques to merely warm the hands might actually hasten hypothermia. However, if, as the gTum-mo tests show, you can raise core body temperature and peripheral temperature, you have the means to withstand great cold – as the nuns show during their freezing sheet ceremony.

As a control, a group of Westerners who had some experience of yoga or meditation or kung fu were taught the gTum-mo technique. Very quickly they were able to show raised body temperature similar to that of the much more experienced Tibetan nuns. Something that appears mysterious and oriental turns out to be rather ordinary after all. I for one will certainly be using it when I next find myself shaking with cold in some Himalayan fastness.

13

Buddhism: Religion of the Himalayas

The wanderer has no land and the sulky one no food.
Ladakhi proverb

We have become diverted by the inexplicable so it is time to do some explaining. There are Hindus, Muslims, Bon worshippers, Lepchas, Mishmis and Christians all inhabiting the Himalayas. But the religion that really defines the high places is Buddhism. Just as Nepal is arguably the central Himalayan country, so Buddhism is the central Himalayan religion. And in Nepal, though Hinduism is widespread, there is a large admixture of Buddhist belief; so much so that the people see no contradiction in worshipping one day in a Hindu temple and another day in a Buddhist temple.

Buddhism was pushed out of Afghanistan by Islam and out of India by Brahmins, but it lodged in the mountains and on the 5,000-metre plateau of Tibet. It travelled to China, Japan, Thailand and Indochina, where there were no competing religions as jealous as those further west. But it was the mountains that protected Buddhism north of India.

When Tibet, the land of Bod, was also the land of Bon, there existed the odd situation of a state religion which was not only informed by folk-religious practices, but was essentially shamanistic. This is a tricky term that few can agree upon, but in the use of trance states and magical practices, Bon resembled many rites also observed among the Tungus shamans of Siberia, the origin of the term and perhaps the practices too. But the Bon religion bloated its rites with demons and masks and magical items such as ritual knives and effigies of people, that would, eventually, show up in Western black masses and witchcraft cults.

Then, in the sixth century AD, Buddhism arrived – not from its southern neighbour, India, where it had originated and grown influential over a period of a thousand years, but from Nepal and China. In this period much had changed in the original doctrine, as promulgated by the former prince turned beggar, the original Buddha or enlightened one.

The original teachings of the Buddha emphasise a turning away from both the stark asceticism of the Indian Sadhu and the pampered life of a rich princeling. The 'middle way' promises a path that hovers between attachment and detachment, wary, perhaps, of becoming too attached to the idea of being detached. There is no evidence the Buddha thought his path could become a religion that would compete with Hinduism. However, the Buddhist message that it takes many lives to reach enlightenment is rather a hard sell. That the final goal is merging with a void seems unduly pessimistic to many, though others argue there are translation problems – after all, the way of the Buddha was only written down centuries after his death.

In any case, the original teachings were never designed to be a world religion like Christianity, which was spread by the Roman empire; Buddhism was dispersed by the Indian King Ashoka.

Ashoka's grandfather was one of the great warrior kings of India. Using mass enslavement and tumultuous battles where thousands were vanquished, he wrote his will in blood and tied the vanquished kingdoms into a fledgling empire. Following the lead of his grandfather, Ashoka subdued a neighbouring state, employing the family's tried and trusted methods of axe, sword and slaughter. Instead of revelling in bloodshed – as he had been taught by his granddaddy – he was repelled by it.

To soothe his conscience, he began to meditate and follow the Dharma – the way of the Buddha. He turned his back on war and devoted his life to spreading the peaceable teachings of Buddhism. He endowed temples, had the scriptures written down in Pali – which his son took to Sri Lanka, where they remain to this day. Ashoka found that Buddhism gave a unity and meaning to the empire his grandfather had simply desired; in so doing, he created from the seedlings of the Buddha's example a world religion.

By the first century AD, Buddhism began to change. The original, rather austere version, which implied that enlightenment would take many lives to attain, remained as Theravada or Hinayana Buddhism. But a new and more hopeful version, Buddhism 2.0 so to speak, was Mahayana – the 'greater vehicle'. With Mahayana Buddhism we get the concept of the Bodhisattva, a being capable of achieving Buddhahood, who returns to Earth, is reborn in the world of suffering to help others on their way to enlightenment. By reverse reasoning, one can see that anyone helping others achieve enlightenment might well be a Bodhisattva and therefore a mere single step away from Buddhahood – which is a lot more comforting than thinking you've got several lives ahead as a stick insect or a muskrat to endure. Mahayana Buddhism opened the doors to all sorts of new concepts.

Partly this was due to its rivalry with Brahmanical Hinduism. The Brahmanist method was intellectual and the original simplicity of Buddhism became complex and rather subtle. And this complexity increased as Buddhism began to absorb the tantric traditions that probably predate Hinduism and have always been present on the fringes of Indian religion. The central tenet of tantrism is that enlightenment can be achieved in one lifetime given the right discipline and the right techniques. This injection of tantrism into Buddhism produced Vajrayana Buddhism, which was the variety that made its way to Tibet. In a way, the tantric techniques shared common ground with the folk magic

and religion of Tibetan Bon; finding this common ground, it took
root and prospered. Vajrayana is known as 'the diamond or thunderbolt' variety of Buddhism, because like a diamond bullet it can
shoot you to ultimate understanding.

Religions spread fastest when they are adopted by kings and
rulers. Gampo – the Genghis Khan, if you like, of Tibet – took
the scattered population of nomads and welded them into an efficient fighting force that enabled him to create the first Tibetan
empire, which included much of Turkestan and Nepal. In the
Kathmandu valley – an important Buddhist centre visited by
Ashoka some centuries before – Gampo requested the hand of
a Nepalese princess to seal his control over the land. The devout
Buddhist Bhrikuti at first refused his hand, then acquiesced on
condition she could bring her Buddhist retainers, tantric images
and monk instructors with her. Gampo must have been smitten
because he fell in with her plans and built a temple for her at
Ramoche in the newly established capital of Lhasa. Perhaps there
was also an element of cunning in his adoption of a new religion
– it got him away from the powerful influence of the Bon priests.
At that time, Bon had neither scripture nor much doctrine beyond
magical appeasement of the many gods of the land, but it did have
some uncomfortable rules that limited the power of kings. Once
a king had a son who had reached the age of thirteen and could
ride, he had to step aside – or risk being killed. One can see the
shadow here of the later practice of using incarnation as a way of
avoiding dynastic rule by a single family, and the practice of using
a regent to mentor an adolescent ruler. It seems the Tibetans have
always been aware of the dangers of tyranny in the institution of
kingship.

Gampo had heard of Ashoka and thought perhaps that Buddhism might bring him, too, a vaster empire. Having married a
Nepalese, he sought a bigger prize in the form of a Chinese princess. The Tang dynasty saw him as a mere frontier upstart and
ignored his overtures. To force their hand, Gampo pillaged and

slaughtered his way across half of China. This humbled the arrogant Chinese and brought them to the negotiating table with their own eligible princess, also a Buddhist. Presumably, parting with a princess seemed a small price to pay for peace. In a rather clever inversion of the truth, the current Chinese dynasty base claims to Chinese sovereignty on this piece of reverse engineering by Tibet. It is as if Italy laid claim to France because Napoleon invaded Italy and concluded long-dead treaties with them. But then colonial powers will use almost anything to justify occupation of a country.

Wen Ch'ing, the Chinese princess, did not want to share monks and images with Princess Bhrikuti, so she too brought her own entourage of monks, images and Buddhist retainers. She, too, after the manner of second wives the world over – and who can blame them – demanded her own temple. Gampo agreed, but perhaps he was a little half-hearted. The second temple kept falling down, which the Bon priests interpreted as a sign that Tibet's native demons were enraged. It was found that the temple had been sited on an ancient underground lake. Gampo was now in a tough spot – if he gave in to the Bon priests he would lose prestige in not just his own but his wife's eyes. A compromise was reached, which shows exactly how the Bon religion would impact on Tibetan Buddhism to make it the curious mix of demonology and piety we see today. Buddhist Chinese wonder-workers were employed to transport the underground lake spirit to a new location – out of Tibet (presumably because most places already had resident spirits) and into Western China, where the spirit manifested as a huge inland sea called Koko Nor. Many people drowned in the creation of the lake, which satisfied the bloodthirsty Bon priests in their demand for a suitable restitution for the disturbed underground spirit.

The site of the Chinese princess's temple was called Jokhang and faced towards Nepal; the Nepalese princess's temple, known as Ramoche, faces China. Nevertheless, Jokhang became the

main temple in Lhasa – central to Tibetan Buddhism and standing in the old centre of Lhasa.

Through the impact of the two Buddhist princesses, artists, ar-
tisans, builders, monks and scholars came from Nepal and Tibet
to create the first flowerings of Tibetan Buddhist culture. After
a while, Tibet produced its own scholars who travelled to the
world's first universities in India. It is interesting to note that these
universities are also of accidental origin. Monks who saw their
main task as living on the road, teaching, preaching and tending
to the sick, had nowhere to stay during the wettest months of the
monsoon. The first universities were hostels for such men, who,
gathered together and with nothing to do except watch the drips
fall from the banana-leaf roofs, started to teach each other and
share what they knew. Most importantly, it was found that books
could be centralised and more efficiently used and lectures could
disseminate knowledge much more quickly than one-to-one conversation. Soon a permanent institution took root – as they usually
do – and the vast early universities of India appeared. Nalanda,
founded a thousand years before Oxford and Cambridge, had
over 10,000 students (about the size of Oxford's undergraduate
population today), eight colleges and three vast libraries. The
monasteries of Tibet were founded in imitation of these universities and retain the same focus and interest in knowledge. Even
today, anyone who has met a Tibetan monk usually remarks on
their curiosity and thirst for information. The then North Indian
alphabet was adapted to writing Tibetan, which wasn't an easy
job, but this marked the beginning of Tibetan history in a way,
as events could at last be recorded. It also meant that the great
Sanskrit sutras could be translated and the Bon religion could at
last get its own liturgical canon and vie on an equal footing with
the upstart Buddhist religion.

It has been remarked – in this book and elsewhere – that here
began the strange process of symbiosis between Bon and Tibetan
Buddhism. Indeed, an uninitiated stranger can enter one of the

few remaining Bon temples and see no huge differences between that and a Buddhist temple. But whereas Bon gained a scripture and some Buddhistic teachings, Buddhism gained demons, oracles and numerous other borrowings that derived from the folk religion of the country. Interestingly, many of these are similar to the folk religious rites we have in Europe, namely:

- Scapegoat rituals
- Maypole dancing
- Fear of witches and witchcraft
- Festival welcoming the first cuckoo of the year

Many other elements of present-day Tibetan Buddhist practice derive from folk religious origins. In addition to the above, these include:

- The wind horse prayer flag symbolising a mystic journey (shamanistic flying), but in Buddhism tasked with transporting prayers
- Interest in numerology
- Faith placed in astrology
- Luck ritual performed on rooftops after a wedding
- Kusang festival – burning incense barley and beer at high points and passes
- The central column placed in the Jokhang, the most sacred temple

But outside Lhasa the Dharma did not make much headway. Tibetan nomads and farmers preferred to propitiate their demons, and the Bon priests who ministered to them and the village shamans who cured all ills were not keen to give up the power they wielded. The demons who controlled the weather, the sparse rain of Tibet, the deep snows, the biting cold, the floods and misfortunes of an extreme climate provided something the well-meaning and long-suffering Buddhists could not: someone

to blame other than one's own crappy former lives, and someone
to get help from.

Instead of going head to head with the demons and driving
them out, as Christianity did in the West, Buddhism absorbed
them as 'awesome yet benevolent spirits'.* Their immense powers
were respected: Jamun, who was known as the eminent enemy,

Crappy former life? Blame demons.

specialised in crushing enemies not just between rocks but between *mountains*; the White Dakini used thunderbolts and when
that failed to inspire, moved mountains too; the, for us, oddly
named Sham-po was a great white yak from whose nostrils came
blizzards and whirlwinds – and he too was the size of a mountain.
Then there was the huge snakelike reptile as long as a chain of . . .
mountains, which could turn up anywhere and leave you lost and
stranded. These were true demons of the Himalayas – all of them
were part and parcel of their mountainous background.

---

* Scott Berry, *A Stranger in Tibet*

The demons of the Himalayas could not be ignored; after three generations of Gampo's Buddhism they rebelled. They were so displeased they let the Tibetan empire crumble and fall. With a withering of its military strength, connections to the Silk Road routes worsened and Tibet became progressively poorer. In AD 703 the Nepalis decided they had had enough of Tibetan rule and chased their invaders back over the high passes to the plateau. The Tibetans did what they usually do in times of crisis (those not caused by China, at least) and turned to China. Another marriage of convenience was arranged and another Buddhist Chinese princess, complete with entourage of monks, was shipped in. Unfortunately – tragically, in fact – she brought an epidemic of smallpox with her that killed off many Tibetans, and some Chinese including herself.

The old Bon priests struck back. Raising harum-scarum images of displeased demons, they stirred the populace into uproar and discontent. This outcry crystallised in the expulsion of all Indian and Chinese monks (the Nepalese had already fled). By this time, the Bon was replete with its own scriptures, its own canon. Buddhism in Tibet seemed to be doomed.

In the eighth century, however, King Trison Detson (there were no dalai lamas at this stage) tried one last time to get the Tibetan people back on the Dharma path. The first attempt involved a learned Indian monk who had a very hard time getting back into Tibet. While preaching on the Red Hill in Lhasa, he incurred the seeming wrath of the White Dakini of the glaciers and the Royal Palace was struck by lightning. When the people heard the sermon and saw the lightning, the mild-mannered monk Santarakshita (which was his name) was in trouble. Then he had a brilliant idea: if demons were the enemy, all he needed was someone, or something, that killed demons.

Enter Guru Rinpoche – which means 'precious teacher' in a mix of Sanskrit and Tibetan. His other name is Padmasambhava: demon-slayer. Evans-Wentz, a pioneering Tibetologist, writes:

'His [Padmasambhava's] less critical devotees generally regard the strange stories told of him . . . as being literally and historically true; the more learned interpret them symbolically . . .' Those who lack the skill or interest to see truths in a story-based format dismiss Padmasambhava as being about as real as King Arthur, but having, like Arthur, an awful lot of glamour and legend attached.

Unlike King Arthur, however, it seems beyond dispute that he actually did exist – though beyond a bit of travelling and founding monasteries, very little is known of his life. This obscurity surrounding the eighth-century Guru Rinpoche is further clouded by his roots in the tantric tradition of India. To Westerners weaned on Sting's version of Buddhism (or the tabloid reports of it – apologies, Mr Sting), tantrism means sex. But actual tantric sex is a very small part of the whole tantric tradition. The main thrust, if you will excuse the term, of tantrism is rigorous control and subjugation of pleasure – one should be able to use it, without it using you; one should not be a slave to one's pleasures. The way to bust these addictions is varied, and tantrism goes into complex Indian detail about all of them. Men are at a disadvantage, as semen loss reduces the benefit of any orgasm. They must practise holding on and having orgasms that are dry, so to speak. The training is meticulous and can only proceed at a slow pace. It involves using milk as a semen substitute and overriding autonomic muscles in order to reverse the flow, sucking instead of releasing. Have you ever started to wee and then forced yourself to stop? Well, that's only the beginning of tantric semen retention practice. No doubt there are health benefits to the prostate – perhaps there is room for a PhD here – nevertheless, the important point remains: tantrism is about ruling the body and its passions rather than being ruled by them. In this very tricky (though obviously not impossible) enterprise it runs the risk of misinterpretation and degeneration into something rather less than spiritual. Cue tantric sex party jokes. Tibetan Buddhism has always faced such gibes and only now, with the extraordinary efforts at refining Eastern concepts

for Western ears that the current Dalai Lama has managed, do we
see a form of Buddhism not hideously shackled to a misinterpret-
able past.

Guru Rinpoche, like Christ – and trumping even the Buddha
himself – was born not of womankind but of a lotus. The symbolic school naturally point to this simply indicating a level of
purity – in other words, disregard the sordid details of his birth
and ancestry and concentrate on what he has to impart. The location of his birth is disputed, Urgyan having long disappeared;
it was thought to be either a little north of Kashmir or perhaps in
the Kingdom of Swat. Urgyan was associated with miracles, so a
miraculous birth was OK. The King of Urgyan, so the narrative
unfolds, was walking by the River Indus when he espied a boy
seated on a lotus flower. The boy was about ten years old – it
was the infant Guru himself. Floating down a river – found in a
plant – there is something of the Japanese Momotaro story here
which involves a boy being found inside a peach – which Roald
Dahl modernised into *James and the Giant Peach*.

The King, realising that this was no ordinary lad, brought him
up as a young prince. But unlike the gentle Siddhartha, the youthful Padmasambhava was a more active type; in fact, he was a triple
murderer – and this was just to get out of the grips of the royal
retinue and routine. When he found himself blocked from leaving
he got himself exiled by standing on the roof of the palace and
magically zapping a passing man, woman and child, leaving them
stone dead. In a gloss on this (for the faint-hearted, one imagines)
we discover that this family, far from being innocent, had 'harmed
Buddhism' in their current or previous life.

Padmasambhava now followed the usual training for a tantric
magician – hanging around graveyards and cemeteries honing his
skills and dealing with all manner of ghosts and demons. He also
attended the great centres of learning to imbibe more mainstream
Buddhist fare.

His abilities were such that he was able to lure the incredibly beautiful Princess Mandrava away from the land of Sohor to be his partner in sexual abstinence. The guru persuaded her to swap the usual honeymoon for a period of meditation in a cremation ground – no wonder her parents were not too pleased. The couple were captured and condemned to be burned at the stake. But the guru's powers were great – the fire hosed itself out by turning into water and the stake flattened into a lotus on which the couple could be seen meditating a few feet off the ground.

The guru then put his powers to the test in India, combining magic and debating skills to defeat the Brahmins, who were jealous of Buddhism's encroaching success. At the time, such debates were serious affairs. Whole monasteries were pledged as a stake – whoever lost, their followers had to convert to the opposing religion. In anti-Muslim rhetoric we hear that the Buddhist scriptures were destroyed in India by the invading Mongols. Except, they were lost way before this: when a debate was lost the Buddhists not only had to convert, they also had to destroy their scriptures. So it was Brahminical triumph rather than Mongol destruction which left India devoid of early Buddhist manuscripts.

In a country without sporting spectacles, these debates were

something like a Super Bowl event, but over the years the intellectual Brahmins had been scoring more and more victories. Guru Rinpoche tried to counter the magic of the Brahmins and scored a last victory before heading off to Tibet. In his absence, Nalanda University succumbed to the resurging Hinduism.

The Guru had been invited by Santarakshita to help save Buddhism in Tibet from the Bon masters of magic. Rinpoche travelled through Nepal and put down demons wherever he met them, getting into practice for the big confrontations that he knew lay ahead.

When Padmasambhava arrived in Lhasa there was the usual tussle about protocol – who should bow to whom? The Guru was in a hurry so he simply sent out a mild lightning bolt that incinerated the King's clothes (not all of them, he wasn't trying to completely humiliate the man). Anyway, the King hurriedly bowed and the fire was extinguished.

The Guru then set out to quell the troublesome demons and turn them into Dharmapala – protectors of the Dharma. In Samye he stopped a rumbling earthquake and began building the first monastery in Tibet. Along with Santarakshita, he started monastery after monastery and began the work of translating the Theravada scriptures from the original Pali, as well as the Mahayana scriptures from Sanskrit. With his tantric background in magic, the Bon priests had met their match. When others accused him – as some non-Tibetan Buddhists do to this day – of being a drunk, fornicating, violent murderer he would reply:

'In as much as this man is ignorant, I should pardon him.'

It is with something approaching shock that a naïve Westerner (me) enters his or her first Tibetan Buddhist temple or monastery meditation hall. There is something very churchlike about the rows of benches despite the squarer floor plan of the temple. But there, where you might expect to see an altar – which there is, of sorts – are the biggest pictures of the grossest-looking demons and gods you could imagine. Confusion reigns: isn't Buddhism supposed to be more or less god-free? What's going on?

These demons look very like the crazy-headed gods found in Hindu temples, which I had seen all the way up the Ganges valley from Haridwar, Rishikesh, Badrinath and higher. Was the Indian tantric influence imposing its own weird gods on Buddhism?

The answer was far more subtle. Though there are tutelary deities in Tantric Buddhism, the wrathful and passionate faces depict personifications of the purified aspects of human nature. To the initiate, these highly emotional god faces are, if untransformed through meditation and other forms of self-work, capable of causing great suffering and harm to the individual. Yet, if transformed, their energy can be put to the service of wisdom. The demon heads are there to remind us of our own demons, which, as part of life, we must ride – but not necessarily over a cliff. By being aware of them, we can retain control.

14

The Strange Death of René von Nebesky-Wojkowitz

To repeat another man's word as your own makes
your own word as valueless as water.
Himalayan proverb

In Delhi I diverted myself with studying Tibet. I wasn't going there; I didn't want to, despite the attractions of bicycling from Lhasa to Kathmandu – one of many holiday breaks I saw offered. Oh no, I had more serious work to do in the coffee shop and the Midland bookstore in Aurobindo market. I bought many books from this excellent shop which, very agreeably, always gave me a discount. My obsession with Tibet had to do with the sense that up there on the great plateau, 5,000 metres high, at the centre of the largest continent, some secret was being guarded. I knew that travelling there would only be frustrating (only group tours were permitted) and would simply distract me from the journey I was making through the endless complications of Tibetan Buddhist writing.

The man who uncovered most about the secret side of Tibetan demonology was a mild, scholarly Czech: René von Nebesky-Wojkowitz (or de Nebesky-Wojkowitz, as he sometimes styled himself in order to draw distance between himself and the un-savoury wartime German interest in Tibet).

Accounts of his death vary. Some suggest he was diagnosed with pneumonia in 1958, before succumbing to the disease in 1959, the year that Tibet finally fell to its Chinese invaders. In others, it is believed that on 9 July, after just a few hours of illness, he died from thrombosis in the lungs. Some hours later, his young wife died; most sources omit how, though some agree it was suicide.

He was a thirty-six-year-old assistant professor at Vienna University. A few months before his death – which was completely unexpected – he had returned from an expedition to Nepal, where he intended to start a new research project. His final Christmas, six months before he died, was spent in Kalimpong at the Himalayan Hotel – where I was told he liked to sit on the lawn, typing on a small Olivetti and endlessly going through tape recordings of Tibetan lamas.

He had a lot to live for. His 660-page magnum opus, *Oracles and Demons of Tibet*, had been published to great acclaim three years earlier. He was energetic and had studied Lepcha culture in Sikkim, as well as every aspect of Tibetan demonology.

Some believe that he revealed too much. He had interviewed monks, Bon priests, peasants and nomads. His main sources for *Oracles* were three monks: Dardo Tulku, Tretong Rinpoche and Nyingmapa Chima Rigdzin. Many probably had no idea what academic publication meant in the West. In Tibetan culture, such knowledge as he received would have come with a warning. Telling secrets in the East to those who are unready for them has a long history of retribution and vengeance on the secret-spiller. The very success of René's book could have spelt his end.

Though fellow Tibetologist John Blofeld would joke that de Nebesky's real crime was to make these terrifying demons boring, and that was why they killed him, one look at the vast array of materials conveyed – including detailed remarks on curses and black magic – leave one uneasy about the motives of the young researcher. It could be that he was driven by an obsession to find out and reveal everything – a compulsion not unusual among the academic. But did he understand that in the mysterious (and not so mysterious) East there is a stark functionality about knowledge, which is believed to have a counterpart in the world of action? If intellectual or merely theoretical knowledge increases too much, it creates an imbalance; various forms of action must then take place to restore balance.

It might be too much to suggest that retributive forces killed Nebesky, but a curse – if believed – might have done the job. Dr Stanley Milgram experimented by picking on a random person in a cinema and having three different students successively go up to the victim and say in a compassionate voice, 'Are you OK? You don't look so good.' By the time the third person said it, the victim would either faint or rush from the theatre bathed in sweat. Very real physical symptoms can be suggested – or blocked.

René de Nebesky was fully immersed in the subject he studied. He spent three years based in Kalimpong, collecting information for his book on demonology and black magic. Is it too much to imagine some of it rubbed off? And much of the time he was accompanied by his young wife; perhaps she too imbibed the beliefs that led to her death. What drove her to take her own life mere hours after she discovered her husband dead? Granted, it is possible that she was mentally unbalanced to begin with, living in some kind of codependent relationship with the scholar. But if she believed that René had been killed by a curse, might she not also believe herself cursed? Too many questions; all that remains is the work of René de Nebesky-Wojkowitz, and from the following glimpse at the kind of content to be found therein, you can see how it might lodge deep within your mind . . .

To put a curse on someone, Nebesky lists some of the things one should load a 'spirit trap' with. A net is filled with the following to capture a destructive *tsan* or spirit: soil from charnel fields, human skulls, murder weapons, tips of noses, hearts, lips of men who died unnatural deaths, poisonous plants and deformed

Monkey gods offer much-needed protection

animals – all of these will attract the demon spirit. He can then, with suitable rituals, be turned upon an enemy. After a purifying seven-day meditation, a lama is considered free to handle such a spirit without a problem. Did René meditate to purify himself while handling all this dangerous material?

To kill someone, you make a doll or likeness – oddly, this practice is a worldwide black magic exercise. If you can incorporate real hair and bits of cloth taken from the intended victim, so much the better. This is then stuffed in a magic horn filled with the teeth of children who failed to live to be older than ten.

Sometimes it is sufficient to simply name the victim. First a red magic diagram, drawn with the blood of a 'dark-skinned Brahmin girl', must be prepared. In its centre, a piece of cotton that once covered a plague victim is used to write the name and lineage of the victim (noting the names of their relatives makes it more potent). Stab the cotton several times with a magic dagger made from the thigh bone of another plague victim (you will see magic daggers in the museums of many Tibetan monasteries – there are several in the monastery at Tawang). Now the hard part – recite the death mantra 100,000 times. Assuming you can speak it in ten seconds, you will manage six in a minute, 360 in an hour, 3,600 in ten hours and 36,000 in a hundred hours. Two hundred and seventy-seven hours will get you to the right pitch for the curse to work – if you can put in a twelve-hour day of death mantras it will take twenty-three days – manageable, I guess, if you have nothing much else on . . . Once the plague-infested cotton is charged up, you should place it where the victim sleeps or makes camp.

To induce madness, draw a white magic circle on the summit of a mountain. In it, you place another victim figurine to focus the evil intentions that could so easily just go wandering off. In this case, the tiny doll is best made from the leaves of a poisonous tree. Write with white sandalwood resin the name and lineage of the proposed victim on the doll. Hold in the smoke of burnt human fat a demon dagger made from bone or iron – it doesn't matter which. Touch the tip of the dagger *only* on the head of the doll. Now leave the doll in a place where demonesses are known to congregate – old mines and wells, dank gullies in cliff faces, stagnant ponds and houses deserted after an unexplained death.

In other rituals the details are equally nasty: the menstrual blood of a prostitute dripped over a victim figurine; a demon cake mixed in the skull of a child from an incestuous relationship, the dough made from the brains and gall of said child; a lamp lit with a wick of human hair and fat from a person who committed murder.

All these rituals are about stunning the intellect with negative or repulsive emotional force to create a morbid belief. And such beliefs may well communicate themselves. It is the stuff of horror films, designed to scare everyone involved and raise the emotional temperature so that mad belief is possible.

Years of recording such material on his early portable Grundig reel-to-reel (an expensive item in the 1950s) must have left its mark. Deep in the subconscious brain must have been a veritable charnel house of detailed information about curses. The very act of transcribing in great detail this charged information from people who actually believed it themselves must have had some kind of effect. After all, repetition creates its own reality. Take the bizarre phenomenon of Stockholm syndrome, where prisoners come to identify with their captors (when a guard is your sole source of food and attention, the natural reaction is to try and make the guard like you – and in time you end up liking the guard). Another example from the well-documented history of brainwashing occurred in communist China, when prisoners were forced to write out false autobiographies again and again. If the prisoner was able at first to be cynical, the constant rewriting eventually got to them until they ended up believing what they had copied out so many times. Did transcribing and checking and writing up page after page of secret curses and evil ritual take its toll on the keen academic mind of Nebesky? Did he believe he had been cursed?

I think at some level he knew he had given away too much. And his wife knew that too. Perhaps all that ritual fasting and meditating before using an evil curse had a real purpose – it created a stronger belief in immunity than that of the attacking evil. But a scientific scholar, not believing in the need for protection, would be vulnerable. René de Nebesky-Wojkowitz was a truly dedicated researcher – his investigations cost him his life. He wrote in *Oracles and Demons of Tibet*: 'I have often been asked by Tibetans the question what I thought of their mediums, and whether I had the impression that really some supernatural forces manifested themselves in the course of these ceremonies.' He never tells us the answer, as if this would violate his 'objectivity'.

Scholar Zeff Bjerken found that in the Tibetan Buddhist community there was a widespread belief that René Nebesky paid with his life for revealing secrets:

> [Nebesky's] untimely death . . . was thought to have been brought about by Tibet's protective deities, who were avenging his efforts to reveal their secrets and magic power. At the library of Tibetan works and archives in Dharamsala, when I tried to check out Nebesky's text I discovered it was not on the shelf with the other books but kept separate under lock and key. Only after offering the Tibetan librarian my American passport as collateral was I permitted access to the work, although not before being warned of its dangerous content.

Killed by demons? Maybe we should all tread carefully. As physicist Niels Bohr remarked when someone exclaimed over the horseshoe hanging over his door: 'I understand it works whether you believe in it or not.'

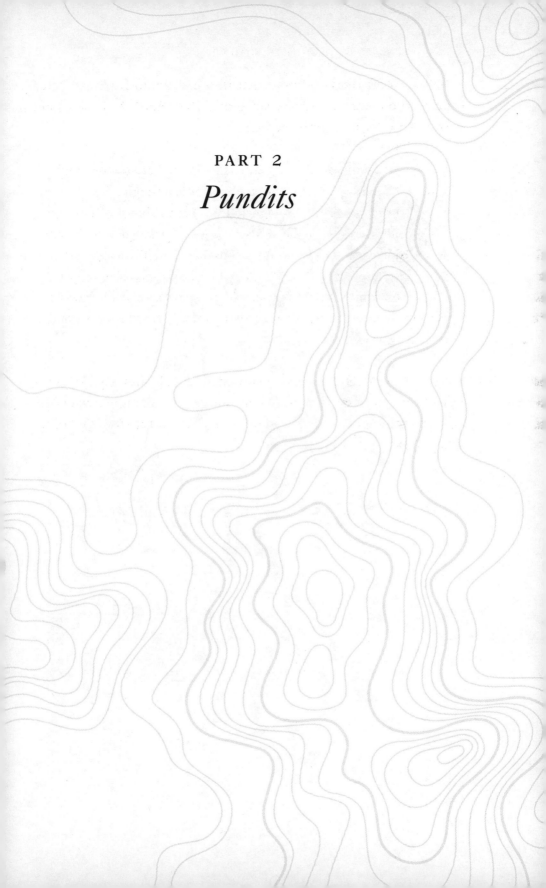

PART 2

Pundits

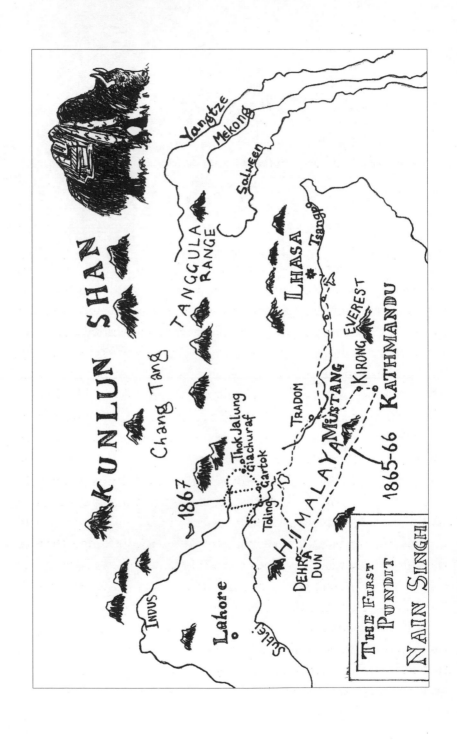

KUNLUN SHAN

Yangtze

Mekong

Salween

Chang Tang

TANGGULA RANGE

LHASA

Tsangpo

1867

Thok Jalung
Giachuraf
Gartok

Tradom

Toling

MUSTANG

EVEREST

KIRONG

HIMALAYA

DEHRA DUN

INDUS

Lahore

Sutlej

KATHMANDU

1865-66

THE FIRST PUNDIT
NAIN SINGH

I

Esoteric Invasions

If one man rides a horse, another will ride even a goat to imitate him.

Balti proverb

The Naga serpent demons may have ruled the ancient world but something new was coming to upend their world for ever. Western Europeans had been trading with the Indian subcontinent for many centuries. They knew little about its wilder and more remote extremes. As the British Empire expanded in size and ambition, it sought knowledge as well as overt power. The name for a Brahmin who was religiously learned was *pundit*. The British invaders decided to become a slightly different kind of pundit.

The Sanskrit term *pandita* means an owner of knowledge. In the traditional world, this is rather different from merely having access to knowledge, being burdened by book learning like a well-loaded mule. To own knowledge requires the fusion of experience with data from which we derive its significance in our lives and in those of others. What better way to own knowledge than to travel in its acquisition? The notion of the travelling apprentice, the *Wanderjahre* still required of German craftsmen, merges with the pilgrimage as the best way to own knowledge.

The British-inspired Industrial Revolution severed the connection between travel and wisely acquired knowledge. The British traditional craftsman became a poor second to the engineer and lathe operator, and the idea of owning knowledge in the old sense began to disappear from the Anglo-Saxon world. At the same time, in the way such things operate, the pundit arose in British India as a travelling spy who brought back secret knowledge of the hidden lands of the Himalaya. We see here an almost complete exoteric version of the esoteric impulse of those who conquered India.

This is not to say that Alexander the Great, who entered the Himalayas with his armies in 326 BC, was conscious of any mysterious reason to join with the East. It would not have been mysterious but it would have been, by today's standards, esoteric. He had been told by the oracle at Siwa that he would 'rule the world'. One of the oddities of modern history is that, though it tries hard to empathise with people from the past, it cannot do so too enthusiastically without impugning its own high standards of reason and rationality, etc. Of course, many historians look at Alexander as some kind of Greek nutter with megalomania, but more fruitful results are available if you look at him and suspend some disbelief.

Alexander, like the Semitic prophets, unites East and West – but his influence, unlike theirs, rests on the concrete (or stone) remains he has left behind in the Himalayan regions. His journey over the Khyber Pass to conquer what is now Pakistan is so audacious it is almost hard to believe – and yet we have the evidence in Greek coins and Doric columns in Afghanistan and Greek influence on Buddhist art. When Napoleon tried to emulate Alexander, he failed at the first hurdle – he couldn't get out of Egypt, which was also Alexander's first stop on his world-conquering mission. Hitler never managed to get more than a foothold in Egypt. Interestingly, all three conquered Siwa, home of the oracle, but only Alexander took the trouble to visit.

Though Alexander entered into India through the Khyber Pass and made it to the Beas River in 326 BC, his main stay in the Himalayas probably never extended much further than what is now the Swat valley. Sikandrabad is almost certainly inspired by Alexander's name – Iskander in much of the Orient; Skardu

in Pakistan also suggests some connection to the youthful conqueror, soon to be dead.

The historical fact of Alexander is exhilarating to the historian
and it is that exhilaration one feels in the grandiose plans of Napoleon. But some people have poor imaginations. Alexander was
perhaps one. In a way, the world as we see it is the construction
of people who have to make real what others manage to imagine
or dream. The world as we see it is a testament to *poor powers of
imagination* . . .

These men who would conquer entire worlds all believe in
their own story – the mythos. The mythos is linked inextricably
with the idea of destiny, an intuition from the ether, the universal
mind. The mythos is a tale, a yarn, a personal sound bite that
grows over time. It has within it some kind of growth potential
– unlike most instances of self-realisation, which hardly impact
us beyond the moment of understanding. Often we glimpse ourselves and then promptly dismiss the idea or forget it. We have to
be smacked in the face for the same shortcomings again and again
before we really start that painfully slow change that takes years
to eradicate one bad habit . . . But when the mythos takes hold,
there can be instant and incredible change on many levels all at
once. The mythos is a tale or story or image that spurs you on. It
could be an idealised and internalised image of another, an ideal,
beckoning you forward – their life (the version you have decided
is true, applicable) becomes your mythos. Richard Francis Burton
was driven to be another Byron; in the end, he outdid him in
every way except in achieving applause for his poetry. But the
mythos served to kick him majestically up the backside to skitter
through the century on journeys far and wide while writing over
forty books.

Those who subscribe to such things contend that, for the
mythos to work, it must connect in some way with the deeper
reality of things. This might be called the destiny aspect. Which
is not to say that it is inevitable, merely that a fast track has been

found – legitimate or not. One may exploit a deeper understanding of the world for wrong-headed or hate-filled purposes, which is one reason that much knowledge of a vaguely esoteric kind was well guarded. It is for good reason that many mystics are noted for their antipathy to publicising their telepathic ability – we have only to look at the Soviet and American programmes in remote viewing to see what governments will do with any esoteric information that happens to come their way.

Napoleon would later try to follow Alexander to India, as the British and Portuguese had earlier. On the surface, they sought trade goods; but the esotericist contends they sought completion with the East – the imaginary journey that would complement their Western sword power, represented as the cross, the plus sign. The Eastern sign is the zero; one beloved activity of Buddhist calligraphers is painting endless zeros. The Indians used an empty space to mean zero; Arab mathematicians – principally Ibn Musa al-Khwarijmi, who synthesised Hindu and early Greek maths – were the first to use a little circle called *sifr*, meaning empty, from which we get zero.

The zero is also the *ouroboulos* – the snake eating itself. It is yin to the sword or cross's yang. When tempered by the sword, or the staff, which morphs into the many variations of the cross, we get the dynamic cross in modified form: the Buddhist swastika and the yin-yang symbol. It is no accident that the symbol for feminine is a circle surmounting a cross, showing quite well the difference in emphasis between the sexes – the male symbol being another form of the cross, the arrow, but this time attempting to maintain, almost, dominance over the yin creativity of the circle beneath it.

Mere symbols represent the hidden forces that required Alexander to cross the mountains into India. His destiny should have been to collect and imbibe the wisdom of the Indians and cease his conquering. But what little yin energy he had left, he squandered. There was no further progress possible for his type of extreme yang adventure – so he died. Yet his mission was completed in a way by the return of Buddhists along the trade routes set up through the kingdoms he had unified.

Genghis Khan, that other extreme swordsman or archer-warrior, was also defeated by the Himalayas. He took the northern route through the top of Afghanistan, sacking the mystical centre of Balkh on his way – his grandson Timur the Lame would finish the job, turning this ancient centre of religion into a desert outpost through destruction of the vast and intricate irrigation system that had been built up over the years. The Mongols filled in the cisterns and maze of underwater posterns and tunnels that irrigated the whole region. These were never rebuilt and Balkh quietly returned to being a desert. It had not always been one: we know that four thousand years ago some of the great deserts of the world were still fertile; gradually, over the next thousand years they dried up. Balkh was thought to be such an ancient and important centre that desertification was ingeniously resisted for thousands of years; it was continually inhabited while the complex system of irrigation made life possible. But once that was destroyed, the city was lost.

With a long-standing reputation as a place for nurturing mystics of all religions, it is no surprise that Rumi – one of the world's greatest poets, and a Sufi mystic too – was also born in Balkh. With admirable foresight, he was able to escape from Balkh just before it was fully destroyed.

In more recent times, Alexandra David-Néel was among those to associate Balkh with Shambhala – Sham-i-Bala, meaning elevated candle – a classical meditation object. J. G. Bennett claimed that the name came from shams-i-Balkh, a Bactrian sun temple. We know that Rumi, its most illustrious sun/son, left, taking with him the Himalayan legacy of Zoroastrianism, Buddhism, and Islam. Not that the Sufism he developed was in any way a compote or assemblage of mismatched religious parts; rather, the very streets he walked as a child resonated with the mystical teaching of centuries.

It is a tenet of much traditional thinking (that is, the thoughts of most people of the world who have not been cornered by too much errant or arrant schooling) that certain spots in the world are propitious at certain times. These become pilgrimage spots or centres of specialisation. Balkh was undoubtedly such a spot.

The notion of the 'power spot' would become mythologised or romanticised in the notion of the 'power houses' of the Himalayas – mysterious hidden monasteries in which the monks could direct their mental force all over the world in order to intervene for good or ill. The mythical kingdom Shambhala – Shangri-la – is the power spot of power spots, deeply hidden in a valley of the Himalayas.

The dragon's back ridge: another power spot

2

Madame Blavatsky Did Not
Go to Shigatse

The man without ability shouts loudest in order to hide.
Tibetan proverb

Which brings us to the modern seekers of Shambhala: the theo-sophists. Theosophy was the invention of Madame Blavatsky, the first of the magus matriarchs, those women travellers who accomplish journeys of both body and imagination and who later get accused of telling lies ... Madame Blavatsky wrote a great deal and was highly influential, yet her influence remains slightly under the radar because she made things up.

Born in the Ukraine in 1831, Helena Petrovna von Hahn was the daughter of a highly esteemed novelist. She inherited a novelist's skill for world-building. We see what would later be combined in the person of L. Ron Hubbard, the sci-fi novelist who created a religion – the integral connection between fantasy, creativity and inner life. Blavatsky's sister wrote:

Fancy, or that which we all regarded in these days as fancy, was developed in the most extraordinary way, and from her earliest childhood, in my sister Helena. For hours at times she used to narrate to us younger children, and even to her seniors in years, the most incredible stories with the cool assurance and conviction of an eyewitness and one who knew what she was talking about. When a child, daring and fearless in everything else, she got often scared into fits through her own hallucinations. She felt certain of being persecuted by what she called 'the terrible glaring eyes' invisible to everyone else and often attributed by her to the most inoffensive inanimate objects; an idea that appeared quite ridiculous to the bystanders. As to herself, she would shut her eyes tight during such visions, and run away to hide from the ghostly glances thrown on her by pieces of furniture or articles of dress, screaming desperately, and frightening the whole household. At other times she would be seized with fits of laughter, explaining them by the amusing pranks of her invisible companions.

At seventeen she married the elderly Nikifor Blavatsky, but after two months fled with her grandmother and travelled in Greece, Turkey, Egypt and France. In London she met her first Hindu holy man. This was an exotic enough source for her to invent trips to India and Tibet.

She claimed to have crossed into Tibet in 1856, at a time when pundits rather better prepared than her would have probably been stopped. She went with a Tartar shaman and crossed over a pass from Kashmir to Shigatse, where she learned various secrets from the monks. Here she learned of the 'masters' who operate from 'powerhouse' monasteries and in a hidden way control the fortunes of the planet. Just as electricity comes from a powerhouse and enlightens the world, Blavatsky's notions appeal as some kind of mystical parallel. In order to reassert the importance of the esoteric it must be restated in modern terms – perhaps it is no accident that theosophy arises at the same time as commercially available electricity.

For those who would ignore the esoteric it is worth noting that both Gandhi and Nehru were seriously influenced by Blavatskian teachings, although, in later life, they diverted attention away from theosophical ideas. Gandhi derived his mythos from many sources, but theosophy gave him his first glimpse of the way to project Eastern ideas so that Westerners would be impressed rather than scornful. In a strange circle, Nehru would later have a huge effect in allowing the Chinese a free hand in Tibet, making it a place where Blavatskian 'powerhouses' would be outlawed and destroyed.

There is no corroborated material to suggest that Blavatsky visited India, the Himalayas or Tibet in her early life. Almost certainly she made up her early travels as even historians fairly soft on esotericism suggest there are problems with the chronology.

Yet the very fact that eventually she did go to India and the Himalayas, fact following fiction, is almost as remarkable as having made that imaginary journey in the first place. She became a guru – and then did the travelling that a guru is supposed to do . . .

Twenty-three years after her first supposed trip, when she finally arrived in Bombay in 1879 with Henry Steel Olcott, the newspaper writer who publicised the newly invented theosophy, it must have been a curious experience – all so new and yet all so familiar . . . As a child, I once told my friends I had visited the Blue John Caves in Derbyshire. When I had to do it for real in their company, no one reminded me that the key element of the journey – an exciting boat trip through a flooded tunnel – had been missing in my original narrative. I had actually made reality MORE boring than it really was in order to be believed. Madame Blavatsky certainly never made this rookie error in fabulation. I suspect she was less interested in being believed in the mundane sense and more concerned with raising the emotional pitch through narrative excess in order to overwhelm the reader's habitual and ossified defences against potential enlightenment.

But another possibility exists: to the esoterically minded, this world is but a stage and all of us, like it or not, must act various roles while reality runs a course, distinct and only sometimes overlapping, with all the acting and make-believe that we call 'reality'. To act the role of the guru requires a back story of exotic travels and strange meetings. Whether you are a fake with nothing to offer or someone with something useful to offer, this back story of exotic travel is still required. I think Blavatsky knew that – she wasn't simply a congenital liar – and once she had mastered the role she was highly productive. Her reading is vast – a true polymath – and her books contain unusual and interesting insights. *Isis Unveiled* (1877) and *The Secret Doctrine* (1888) belong to a less critical age – though it might be a useful springboard to further researches for those with much leisure time.

Gurus also have to be able to either fake, or do real, telepathic tricks.

There are many accounts of people (often Russian nobles) who claim Blavatsky could perform astounding psychic feats. I rather prefer this memory by a young American woman who provided accommodation in New York for Madame Blavatsky and had no interest in her spiritual work:

I never looked upon Madame as an ethical teacher. For one thing, she was too excitable; when things went wrong with her, she could express her opinion about them with a vigor which was very disturbing . . . In mental or physical dilemma, you would instinctively appeal to her, for you felt her fearlessness, her unconventionality, her great wisdom and wide experience and hearty good will – her sympathy with the underdog.

An instance of this kind comes to mind. Undesirable people were beginning to move into the street, and the neighborhood was changing rapidly. One evening one of our young girls, coming home late from work, was followed and greatly frightened; she flung herself breathless into a chair in the office. Madame interested herself at once, expressed her indignation in most vigorous terms, and finally drew from some fold in her dress a knife (I think she used it to cut her tobacco, but it was sufficiently large to be a formidable weapon of defense) and said she had *that* for any man who molested her.

3

The Pundit Found It

He can steal, but he can't hide.
Balti proverb

The Great Game – the name given to the scramble for influence in the Himalayan region – was played out largely between two empires: the British and the Russian. The Russians sought access to a warm-water port, the British sought to control these ambitions. The pundits were the spies who could supply the information needed to advance these claims. I've already noted that a parallel, yet real, exploration of the Himalayas was going on at the same time as the imaginary theosophical one. Each saw itself as more important than the other. Neither could really explain itself in terms the other could comprehend. Later, we'll see some figures who attempted such conjoining, most significant among them probably the nineteenth- and twentieth-century explorer and soldier, Francis Younghusband; though, in the end, he had to suffer an old age in which he became an object of affectionate ridicule for his beliefs about both the need to climb mountains and the need to connect to the greater reality behind such mountains.

Owing to the inaccessibility of Tibet to foreigners, its early exploration had to be carried out by natives or men who looked like natives – the pundits. The British, by virtue of their appearance and lack of knowledge of Tibetan, could not hope to pass as indigenes. Pundits, posing as holy men from India keen to see the places of pilgrimage in Tibet, had a much greater chance of success.

Mohamed-i-Hameed, the first pundit, set out from Ladakh in 1863 – the year Younghusband was born and only two years before Rudyard Kipling was born (it was Kipling who would immortalise the work of the pundits in his great tale of espionage, *Kim*).

Hameed was not to be as lucky as the later, better trained and equipped pundits. He managed to reach his target of Yarkand successfully, but Chinese officials had grown suspicious. Hameed managed to escape, but in hastening over the high passes of the Karakoram back into Ladakh, he died. His notes, however, survived and were eventually sent to one Captain Montgomerie stationed in the foothills of the Himalayas at Dehradun. Now a vast, sprawling, rather ugly town, it remains a centre of army training seventy years after the British left. Chastened by the mixed experience of Hameed, Montgomerie set up the 'pundit school' in Dehradun. Each new recruit was to spend two years rigorously learning the art of clandestine surveying while at the same time perfecting his cover story as a Buddhist pilgrim.

Why on earth did the pundits agree to risk their lives for this colonial power that squatted so uglily, we are led to believe, on their own land? Sir Richard Burton, himself a kind of early pundit – indeed, perhaps an inspiration for them – donned native guise and employed his unequalled mastery of Indian dialects to find out what the local Scindis thought about their British overlords. He would sanguinely comment to the effect that no Briton knew how much they were *hated* by the average Indian. I think I can interpret: what appears as hatred is nothing more than the extreme annoyance at being ignored. 'Flatter a man and he may or may not see through you, but ignore him and he will hate you forever.'* Unlike the revered pundits, most Indians did not receive their due attention from their British overlords.

* Idries Shah

Travelling to Dehradun, I had a curious encounter with a German on the train. Misunderstanding the import of having a father born in the Himalayas, he believed (and I was fairly suntanned at the time) that I was an Indian travelling to see the birthplace of his old man. He talked to me with the sort of condescending tone reserved for . . . foreigners. He slowed up his speech, in case my English was not quite up to speed. By some sort of perversity, which I recognised now in Indians I had met, I sought to use the longest words and slang expressions that could not fail to identify me as a native speaker. But he had made up his mind and so I ransacked the dictionary and appeared no doubt as a strange native fellow intent on impressing clever German tourists . . .

The pundits' reward, I hazard, was the best sort of attention – real and meaningful involvement. They would also get a pension and, if they died, their families would be cared for. In that sense, the British were fair taskmasters. But only the thought of at last being noticed, singled out, used – yes, but also trusted, rewarded with a handshake and a sincere thank-you for doing something that the mighty British man could not; to be accepted, in short, as an equal.

Therein, perhaps, lies a clue to the secret of the British conquest of the Asian subcontinent. Con/Quest or, more properly, a quest followed by a con. How a tiny minority ruled such a vast nation for so many years has always been a puzzle, yet it was no mere tyranny – had it been, the whole charade would have collapsed instantly. How do the popular kids rule? How does an otherwise repellent pick-up artist score with attractive women time and time again? They succeed by manipulating our desire for attention. Tyrants and bullies actually expend considerable attention on their victims. Indeed, it is one of the nasty facts of bullying that bully and victim are often codependent. The British con was to ration out their attention, not in terms of punishments but as a reward. This explains why the pundit schoolmaster and

*Old soldier, a fierce patriot who nevertheless
fondly remembers British military traditions*

commander, Captain Montgomerie, who obviously loved his
cohort of native-born spies, saw fit to publish not just their data,
but also their secret methods in the journal of world exploration,
the *Royal Geographical Journal*. This is where the first accounts
of Burton, Speke, Livingstone and Scott would be published. By
making the pundits' work known in the same pages, alongside
the great explorers of the day, Montgomerie was announcing their
true status – they were, indeed, the equal of any of the aforementioned men. Yet many were known only by their initials. This is
how they appeared in the *RGS* journal – the one concession to secrecy that Montgomerie made. He was gambling that no Chinese
would read the journal, which was only available to Fellows of
the Society. It was known that Russian intelligence availed themselves of its contents, but Montgomerie knew that the Russians
had as much to gain as the British when it came to discovering the

hidden topography of Tibet. It was only the Chinese, jealously guarding the gold mines and other treasures of Tibet, who would have been in a position to rumble the pundits as they plied their trade as pretend pilgrims.

How to rumble a pundit? A simple test would have been to count their rosary beads. A pundit rosary had only 100 beads instead of the required 108. Each pundit knew exactly how many of their own paces added up to a measured mile (and a pace was two steps; it is too difficult to count every step when one is speed-walking over rough terrain, but easy enough if you simply record every time the right foot hits the ground). Each man had his own secret 'pace number', usually around 1,000 – a pace being about 5 feet and there being 5,280 feet in a mile. Montgomerie would have his men walk fast, slow and then at a run around the running track at the barracks in Dehradun. One of the early pundits, Nain Singh, had mastered an exact step of 33 inches which he used for surveying smaller distances. But over time, one's natural pace evens out and once you know your 'pace number' it is an astonishingly accurate method of travel. When surveyors followed the routes of the old pundits, they found that they would be only a mile out in hundreds of miles of walking.

The rosary system allowed one bead to be moved every hundred paces. One complete circuit of the rosary would be around ten miles. A smaller string of ten beads attached to the rosary could record the total mileage per day.

Had the Chinese found out, they may have searched the staff of the pilgrim and found the top unscrewed to reveal a glass thermometer. This would be slipped into a boiling pot of water when the pundit was unobserved and the temperature recorded, thus providing an accurate measure of altitude.

The prayer wheel might also have been investigated. Inside, instead of a scroll of scripture written in the smallest hand, they would have found lists of numbers and directions. It was here the precious data was recorded. In hidden pockets within the pundits' sleeves were bits of glass and mirror, which could pass as treasures perhaps, hoarded by a poor man. But these could be swiftly assembled into a sextant which could be used at night to cross-check one's position. An artificial horizon of mercury was needed to level the sextant – the mercury was carried in a cowrie shell and tipped into a begging bowl to form the flat horizon. Larger sextants were sometimes hidden in the specially constructed false bottom of a travelling chest.

A compass was a common enough item for a Muslim to be carrying, and the first pundit was a Muslim clerk already trained in survey work, but for a Buddhist to have a brass prismatic device made in Birmingham would have been a little too suspicious. The compass, reduced to a minimum size, was hidden in a screw-top to the prayer wheel assembly.

The pundit school's first two graduates were the cousins Nain and Mani Singh. Nain was the thirty-three-year-old headmaster of a village school at Milam and had already guided with success a German expedition in the Himalayas.

In order to further protect their identity, they were forced to refer to themselves and to be referred to by their superiors as Pundit number one and Pundit number two, or G.M., which was arrived at by taking two letters from the name and reversing them for further obfuscation. Only when the pundits had long retired were their real names ever released. One realises that the apparatus of spying that appeared in Europe only in the early years of the twentieth century had its testing ground in the pundit travels of the nineteenth century in the Himalayas.

Nain Singh and Mani were extraordinarily successful in their adventurous spying. They set out in 1865 to settle many mysteries hinted at by the only existing map of Tibet – the so-called lama map instigated by Jesuits in the eighteenth century. Emperor Kang-hsi was impressed by maps of Peking made by Jesuit missionaries. He invited them to survey the whole of China, starting in 1708. He wanted Tibet included and the Jesuits trained two lamas to carry out their survey. Their data was incorporated in the finished map of 1717, which was eventually published in Paris in 1735 as part of d'Anville's atlas. Alas, the lamas most definitely were using their prayer wheels and rosaries for their intended purpose and not as surveying aids: the lama map was a fanciful illustration of mysterious Tibet and hardly a single detail was correct. The rest of China was very accurately depicted and so it was assumed Tibet was too. The truth, however, would be found out the hard way, by the pundits as they criss-crossed the Himalayas counting paces and taking covert sextant readings.

Nain Singh's disguise was one that most of the pundits would adopt – that of being a Bisahari. The Bisaharis were a Buddhist people living in British India in a valley near the hill station of Simla. They were allowed, on account of their religion, to come and go across the border with Tibet. They were also allowed to trade with Tibetans, and Nain Singh told those he met as he travelled through Nepal to the border that his aim was to travel to Lhasa and buy horses while also worshipping at the most prominent shrines along the way.

The border guards searched their belongings with great thoroughness. They assumed some sort of smuggling was going on as Bisaharis never travelled at this time of year to buy horses. They found none of the well-hidden survey instruments, but their suspicions were aroused. The Tibetan governor of that section of the border country refused them permission to travel: it was the wrong time of year and the route proposed was very unusual, not direct enough. They also had to dole out some precious funds for a poll tax that was non-refundable. There was nothing to be done but return to Kathmandu and try again. Here Nain and Mani split up to increase the chances of one getting through. Nain changed his disguise to that of a Ladakhi. Mani did not and either through want of determination or ill health failed to get over another high pass into Tibet. He returned to Dehradun to a disappointed official welcome. Nain carried on, charming a Nepalese caravan boss and making his way smoothly this time into Tibet, going in the direction of Mount Kailash and Lake Manasarovar. Crossing the Tsangpo in a dumpy leather coracle, three travelling companions were swept into the torrent and drowned. It was a reminder of the dangers ahead.

He now joined a Ladakhi caravan, which transferred their goods to coracles. He agreed to meet them 85 miles downstream at Shigatse, home of the second ruler of Tibet, the Panchen Lama. His excuse was that witnessing the deaths of his travelling companions had unnerved him; in reality, he needed to pace the entire distance to get the figures for the intended map of Tibet. Once at Shigatse, though he had no intention of getting so close to the rulers of Tibet, Nain Singh found himself forced by circumstance to be presented, along with other Buddhist pilgrims of the caravan, to the Panchen Lama, who was known for his powers of perception. Fortunately, this was a very young incarnation of the great man, a mere boy of eleven, who no doubt had other cares than unmasking fake pilgrims on mapping missions.

Nain Singh made it to Lhasa where he stayed for three months. He met the youthful Dalai Lama – the twelfth one – who was soon to die a not so mysterious death, almost certainly poisoned by the regent or possibly the Chinese Amban, the representative of the Chinese government in Tibet. Again, Nain Singh's duplicitous charade failed to be detected, though two Muslim traders he became friendly with rumbled his disguise and demanded to know who he was. Instead of turning him in, they gave him money; his own reserves were running very low, what with the additional length of the whole venture. By this time he was getting wary of being detected. A Chinese man who had visited Lhasa without the right permission had recently been beheaded – on public order from Peking – so it was high time to escape back to India with his information. By taking surreptitious night sights with the sextant, he had fixed the latitude of Lhasa and its altitude through successive measurings of boiling water. Both were very close to the current accepted figures. He thought Lhasa 3,566 metres up; in fact, it is nearer 3,656. The latitude was right to within two minutes – less than two miles out. To further eke out his money, he gave lessons in the Hindu method of keeping accounts to the Lhasa traders.

On the way back, he noted for Montgomerie the express mail service for official business in Tibet. Like the pony express in the United States, the messengers rode at high speed, changing horses at very short intervals to maintain this. To further incentivise their progress, their clothes were sealed shut with an official seal. Only the reader of the message was allowed to break it. The messengers were forbidden to undress en route, so each hard ride was a battle with accumulated grime and sweat, their skin usually raw from flea and lice bites.

For Nain Singh a more leisurely pace was needed – literally – as he had to walk every single step. When the leader of the caravan offered him a ride, he claimed that he had fallen hard as a child and this left him with a grave suspicion and fear of horses – horseshit, of course, but by all accounts the silken-tongued pundit was an excellent yarn spinner, keeping the caravan men entertained at night as they sat round the campfire on the wind-whipped plateau.

Eventually, he was able to make his way alone over a high pass into India, where he was seized by bandits. They searched his wooden chest and took his tea but failed to find the sextant. Nain Singh made his escape at night and finally got back to Dehradun and Captain Montgomerie. It had all been a glorious success.

Nain Singh's next mission was to find the famous goldfields of Tibet, which, along with their mystical reputation, had, since earliest times, been one of the major attractions of the place. This continues with twenty-first-century Chinese development and exploitation of not just gold but the plethora of mineral resources to be found in Tibet. Nain Singh penetrated the innermost sanctum of the mines by befriending the wife of the mine boss, tempting her interest with coral which he had brought along to trade (the tea with which he hoped to bribe the boss himself proved insufficiently enticing). Within four days he had all the details of the mining operation, a kind of Tibetan Klondike where any Tibetan was free to have a go – up to 6,000 would travel there in winter, the frozen ground being much safer from cave-ins than in summer, when only 300 miners could be found in the place. Despite this activity, the extent of the mines was regulated. The Tibetans believed, along with most indigenous peoples throughout the world, that there was a cost to violating the Earth; prayer offerings and rituals and restraint on certain mining practices all helped contain the wholesale desecration of the planet's surface. Plants, previously thought to not feel pain, appear to; perhaps the Earth does as well.

Montgomerie died at forty-seven, worn out by his spying operations. Before he died, he managed to have Nain Singh awarded the gold medal of the Royal Geographical Society – the same medal that all the great explorers of the nineteenth century aspired to earn – and, indeed, he had earned it.

4

The Mapping of It

A good marksman may miss.

Lepcha proverb

The deodars were huge, the smell of pine everywhere. Off the road, the going was tough so I went back to the road. I was reading my map and not understanding it; all I knew was that I was some way down the hill from Mussoorie. In a week where I had been co-opted into teaching aikido at a local army base, not unlike the bases I imagined that the pundits were trained in, I had hardly left this small hill town. It was winter and not too busy, but already the egregious development of tourist hotels and villas was apparent. I had discovered my dad's school was now a hotel – shut – and that George Everest's house was a ruin. Though it was bitingly cold at night, it was sunny and pleasant enough in the day, so I had gone hill walking with a map from the *Lonely Planet* guide. And now I couldn't make head nor tail of it. It looked rather accurate on the page, but it wasn't. I wasn't lost, exactly, I just didn't know where I was 'on the map'.

Which bring us to maps. Beyond a certain point, the more realistic the map the more useless it is. I remember the shock I had when I first saw aerial photographs of England in colour (this was before Google Earth) and compared them to maps of the same scale: the roads and towns were hardly visible in the photos! All I could see, the overwhelming impression, was green, shades of green from almost black to almost yellow. Maps give the impression that roads and towns rule, that man rules, that the countryside is . . . white. A green lie! But a road map needs to show the roads to be useful . . . and it doesn't really have to be that accurate, just a bit imaginary.

I've seen what is claimed to be the world's first map, etched into a rocky nub of limestone in the Egyptian desert. It looks rather like one of Tony Buzan's mind maps, showing the location of various springs and water mountains carved in the fifth dynasty as the desert dried more and more each year (perhaps a far more challenging climatic change than we are now experiencing). It wasn't an accurate map – but it was useful.

Such a map is useful without enthralling us. Such a map lacks scale, accuracy – which are only possible with precise instrumentation. The conquest of time and space begins with a theodolite and a watch. Actually, it begins with a precisely machined baseplate on which degrees of a circle are etched. At the heart of the British lead in map-making lies precision engineering skill.

The British in India wanted maps that were super accurate. And this all rested on the mystical notion of 'the spheroid'. I suggest that the slightly insane dedication of the two key Indian map-makers, Lambton and Everest, was due to an apprehension of the cosmic, an appreciation of the mystical, and this found form in an obsession with the spheroid. So what exactly is it?

Two French expeditions in the 1730s had established that the Earth is flatter at the poles and is a 'near sphere' rather than a perfect one. This imperfect sphere is the spheroid; no one knew exactly its size and dimensions until people started making accurate maps. Nor did they really know how much effect gravitational inconsistencies in the Earth's crust might have on the mapping. It was a shock to map-makers to discover that huge mountains like the Himalayas exerted their own gravitational pull – enough to affect the instruments being used to measure them. To calculate this imperfect sphere as accurately as possible required the mapping of an arc, a section, of the Earth's surface. The bigger the arc, the more accurately the spheroid could be calculated. These were huge scientific questions, but they were pursued not by men of the Academy, as in the French case, but practical employees of the Great Survey of India. Lambton 'sold' the necessity of making as large a measured arc as possible to a lucky old friend, Arthur Wellesley, the future Duke of Wellington, whose elder brother was Governor General of India. He spoke of the advantages of knowing the true width and extent of Indian possessions – he did not need to do much convincing of the need for maps to a military man. He simply insisted that the Great Arc was the only way to go. It wasn't. But here was a man in the throes of doing science, finding something out that no one knew – just what shape is the Earth exactly?

You might argue that this was in the early decades of the nineteenth century, when the Age of Reason was turning into the Age of Technology. Lambton chose to cast his project in technological and practical terms, not as the abstract pure information of science. It was just a way of 'selling' science. But I think that, like Kepler before them, Lambton and later Everest were driven by deeper things. To compute the spheroid – a symbolic 'O' – was an act of balance, a sort of communion with the planet, a way to ameliorate the takeover of India by the sword. That they remained only dimly aware of this throughout their great sacrifice is neither here nor there.

The Great Arc, from Cape Comorin through the middle of India to Mussoorie in the Himalayas, was an attempt, through multiple measurement and cross-reference, to establish the curvature of the Earth under India that most closely corresponded to the geoid, or actual shape of the Earth. The geoid is no use for map-making though, because it is all wobbly. It is the near perfection of the spheroid that makes it useful. Sometimes the spheroid is above the geoid, because of a dip in the Earth's surface or a flattened section. At other times the spheroid is below the surface

– in the Everest region it is about a hundred feet below the geoid. And the geoid here is also some thousands of feet above 'mean sea level' – a figure that can be checked at the coast, but as one moves inland it's necessary to rely on the spheroid to calculate its value. But if the spheroid is too 'spherical' then you can get absurd results with an area below 'mean sea level' but above actual sea level. You can see how complicated it gets. For this purpose, a bodge is employed, which is called calculating the geoid – the estimated difference between the spheroid and the real Earth's surface. To calculate this beneath the Himalayan plateau is quite an art, though the good news is that the geoid is never more than a few hundred feet away from the spheroid, the projection needed to make the original calculations of height.

Lambton and Everest are an example of that not uncommon combination, the starter and the completer-finisher. Everest on his own was probably too conventional to have come up with the extraordinary ambition of the Great Arc. Without Lambton's example and leadership, say, under another less ambitious soul, he might have plugged away for years doing a conventional, less accurate survey, but without the scientific benefits of increasing knowledge about the planet itself. But Lambton, from an obscure debt-ridden farm in Yorkshire, via a scholarship in mathematics at grammar school to an ensignship in 1781 in the infantry and thence to surveying, was a true original; a benign, eccentric and utterly obsessional worker for whom the Great Arc was his great idea. But Lambton had neither the health nor staying power to take the project to its logical conclusion: the entire length of India – providing the longest and most accurate spheroidal section ever to be made.

This multiplication, expansion, quantum enlargement of the project – and, just as importantly, its successful conclusion – was down to George Everest, a former artillery officer and son of a solicitor, for whom appointment to the Great Trigonometrical Survey of India was his great opportunity for advancement. He was born, appropriately enough, in Greenwich – perhaps meridians were in his blood. His path to India was less tortuous than Lambton's (the latter had served until he was thirty-nine in America and Canada, losing the sight of one eye during a solar eclipse too closely observed). Everest was in his twenties in 1819 when he started out; he worked until the Arc's completion in 1843. Shortly before his death in 1823, Lambton wrote:

> It is now upwards of twenty years since I commenced [the survey] on this great scale. These years have been devoted with unremitting zeal to the cause of science, and, if the learned world should be satisfied that I have been successful in promoting its interests THAT will constitute my greatest reward . . . I shall look back with unceasing delight on the years I have passed in India.

The apparatus used was basic; it was the care lavished over it that made for such accurate results, that and the constant checking and rechecking that Lambton and Everest insisted upon.

Initially, terracotta lamps were used to sight up upon in the darker hours, but these were dim and limited the distance you could reckon. Everest pioneered the use of massive bonfires – visible for sixty or more miles – which served to home in the telescope of the surveyor up his tower. Then, at a definite time, and at regular sixteen-minute intervals afterwards, a flare would be lit – brilliantly bright, providing a pinpoint location for the fix. The flares were like giant toxic haggis – each one a sheep's bladder containing: 'sulphur 136 parts; nitre 544; arsenic 32; indigo 20'. When lit, it needed to burn brightly rather than explode, so it was essential the recipe be followed exactly – and Everest was a stickler for people following his rules. Each flare weighed three pounds – in that way '160 will be the load of a camel'.

If there were convenient hills, then the sighting station and the flare could be situated on the summit. But large parts of India are flat plains, and here Everest had to build special towers and flare masts. A mast would be 21 metres high. The solid core of a tree trunk would be embedded deep in the ground (Lambton had been an expert on this and no doubt passed on his expertise; one of his earliest publications had the surreal title 'Observations on the Theory of Walls', which aimed to show that foundations beyond a certain depth are pointless). Attached to the core would be a ring of bamboo poles stretching high into the air. Attached to these would be another set, and then another, until the mast was the required height. The whole thing was then raised and stayed along its entire length, rather like a modern radio antennae mast. A pulley was fixed at the top; this was used to hoist a boom of an extra forty feet at whose end burned the flare; 'thus supplying', wrote Everest, 'a brilliant blue light at upwards of 90 feet above the surface of the ground'.

Thirty or more miles away the observer stood on a structure quite separate from the theodolite telescope down which he looked at the flare. The solid platform for the monstrously heavy theodolite rested on a tree trunk sunk 1.5 metres into the ground and rising some 10.5 metres. This was stayed all around using 'antagonising struts'. Around it, but not touching this rigid platform, would be a bamboo scaffold with a ladder attached. Up this, and resting his weight on it, the observer could operate the theodolite without upsetting its precise setting. Naturally, wind and rain and the ague-shaking hand of the surveyor all sought to interfere with the delicate process. To offset this, many, many observations needed to be taken. It was painstaking work indeed.

As Jorge Luis Borges noted, the suppressed desire of all map-makers is the ultimate accuracy of a 1:1 scale – a map that is as big as its subject. But the map, even on an exact 1:1 scale, is still necessarily an abstraction; a priori it is easier to deal with than life in all its contours and colours. You might argue that the subconscious desire to map India with *exactitude* is the desire to turn down the volume, reduce the colours, sights and smells to something manageable. Something controllable. As I have mentioned, the Indian Mutiny in 1857 occurred just as the survey reached the zenith of its ambition – the accurate recording of the height of the world's highest mountain. This seems entirely in keeping with the project. Its overt aims may have been benignly conceived, but the dark side of map-making is control, the subjugation of a nation that had subtly resisted the harassment and bullying first used in the subjugation of Ireland and the Scottish Highlands. Ireland was one place, however, in which military surveyors cut their teeth performing similar mapping operations that would later be applied to the far grander scale of the Indian subcontinent.

Lambton and Everest operated with small teams in remote places. In a nod at the aforementioned task of subjugation, Everest remarked on how overmanned the survey of Ireland was compared to his own incomparably greater task. As we've already seen, the British occupation of India is all about being undermanned – a tiny number of Europeans ruling by a kind of sleight of hand. And yet they must rule – and so they reach for their rulers. Everest used a series of six three-metre bars made from brass and iron to compensate for expansion in the heat. This was to provide a six-mile 'baseline' of known length from which to calculate further distances and ultimately the spheroid. And what they produced was nothing short of the most accurate possible spheroid model of the Earth's surface ever attempted.

The great problem of map-making is knowing where the bottom is. At what point do you start measuring upwards for a mountain like Everest? The spheroid model tells us where the bottom is. Of course, you can make maps without knowing the spheroid. You can fudge the figures and get away with it. But Everest believed in doing a job correctly. And without the Great Arc it would have been impossible to accurately work out the heights of Himalayan mountains, including the mountain that would ultimately take his name.

The method favoured by George Everest for completing the great survey of India shows a further movement in favour of the mechanical. Just as all sea charts are made using astronomical sightings, so, too, a land survey can be made in this way. But it requires great skill and patience, along with the construction and operation of observatories over several years. By comparison, triangulation is child's play. But child's play involving demonic amounts of work. By measuring very accurately a baseline you can then sight up from either end on a triangulation point (a 'trig' point). Knowing the two angles needed to converge on this third point allows one to calculate the exact length of the triangle's sides. This generates two more baselines from which new measurements can be made. Naturally, trig points are sited on high ground if possible – hills and mountains are perfect – though it was only late in the history of the great Indian survey that the giants of the Himalayas could be measured. In the United Kingdom, an excursion to any hill that commands a view of the surrounding lands is usually rewarded with finding a small concrete obelisk about four feet high, ideal for being photographed standing upon in a howling wind, having conquered that particular summit. In the top of the trig point is a scooped-out pattern and a small securing point – this is for stabilising the theodolite needed to sight up the exact angle to the next trig point. For the Great Indian Survey, the theodolite was huge: it weighed 1,042 pounds (the weight of five grown men) and was needed to sight up with pinpoint accuracy on signal markers twenty or more miles away. In this way, India was criss-crossed 'with bars and chains' until the map resembled one of those diamond-patterned papers used for drawing cubes on.

'Bars and chains' provides the clue: the Great Survey of India was but a thinly veiled attempt at precise measurement of a territory. In Normandy they still travel the rounds of the parish and beat a boy (symbolically now) so that he will remember the exact dimensions of the communal lands; 'beating the bounds' is something known only by name in Britain – but it is the same ritual. Before maps, knowing with exactitude the extent of your own domain was a vitally important part of hanging on to it. In order to get a baseline measure of +/– 0.028 inches (0.07 centimetres) deviation over a six-mile stretch, Everest's special measuring rods were used. This resulted in an accuracy of –/+ 12 feet (3.7 metres) in the distance between Delhi and Calcutta, or 125 feet (38 metres) over the entire globe. With the help of converging baselines and astronomical sightings, the measurement could be made tighter and more accurate.

Everest, unlike his predecessor Lambton, was no respecter of Indian customs. Though he believed that malaria was caused by miasmas rather than demons, he still claimed the populace had 'minds bowed down under the incubus of superstition'. He collected rocks as he made measurements and believed this work was as valuable as the survey since the specimens would contain the source of the fevers he and his team suffered.

And suffer they did. Because the monsoon and its immediate aftermath provide periods of exceptional haze-free conditions, it was essential to work during this most inhospitable period. No wonder the locals baulked at being forced into the jungle to take measurements. At one point early on in his career, Everest had to drive men on at gunpoint to get the survey extended. In both the manner of its completion and its conception, the survey teeters close to the obsessive end of insanity. The danger was 'greater than that encountered on a battlefield [and] the percentage of deaths larger; while the sort of courage ... required was of a far higher order.'* When a country devotes more effort to map-making than making war, you know that map-making is a more profitable business.

After all, what would have happened without it? A bit more vagueness for a little longer, but eventually astronomical measures would have solved most of the survey problems. But such lackadaisical progress would not have served the symbolic process of

* Sir Clements Markham, Royal Geographical Society

binding up India. Just as the Pyramids are the great monuments of Pharaonic times, so map-making is the great British enterprise; an abstract, yet hugely ambitious project, the Great Survey of India took much longer than the Taj Mahal to be completed.

Without the utter accuracy of the arc of the meridian it would be impossible to judge with certainty the heights of the mountains of the Himalayas. Not that the survey men like Everest and Lambton and Waugh really cared that much about the heights of mountains. This was mere frippery compared to the utter seriousness of mapping the rest of India. But by 1856 it was becoming at last apparent that a certain Peak 'b' might actually be a very high mountain. Not a capital 'B', though, which showed the perverse lack of drama so beloved by men on a serious project in those days.

The real drama was happening elsewhere. In 1857 the Indian Mutiny began with a group of soldiers who would not obey their British masters. The British, who had begun by admiring and being respectful of Indian culture, had, with the acquisition of technology superior at last to other nations, begun the long descent into despising their fellows. Lambton, when he started the survey, had no arguments with any Indians; Everest, though, had used guns to enforce his will. India woke up and finally realised, all too late, that the Bloody British had, using a purely abstract series of chains and bars . . . enchained them and debarred them from their whole country. The year that technology discovered Mount Everest – something abstract in its own way, an abstract inheritance of the abstract art of map-making – there was another inheritance implicit in that arrogant undertaking: a mutiny of people who would rather rule themselves.

5

Just Which One Is the Highest Mountain?

He's looking for the donkey even while he is riding it.

Afghan proverb

For many years Nanda Devi, with its proximity to northern India and Delhi making it easier of access, was considered the world's highest mountain at 7,766 metres. In 1847, just forty miles from Darjeeling, Kanchenjunga was measured and took the prize at 8,588 metres. But was the dull-sounding Peak 'b' on the Tibet/Nepal border higher? Peak 'a' hid it from clear view. Peak 'a' was the mountain now known as Makalu, so just how high was Peak 'b'?

Standing on a hotel roof in December in Darjeeling is the best time for making observations. The air is clear and the cloud is at its thinnest. Kanchenjunga is easily seen, and, with some difficulty, so is Peak 'b', 120 miles away on the Nepal–Tibet border. Andrew Waugh, the successor to George Everest, made his measurements of the distant peak he named 'gamma' in the winter of 1847. At the same time, another surveyor, John Armstrong, working from Muzaffarpur in Bihar, also took angles of elevation and direction for a certain summit he listed as Peak 'b'. He thought it 8,778 metres high. Waugh distrusted both his own and Armstrong's measurements. Peak 'a' was also of disputed height so the following season more sightings were taken. Again, nothing conclusive was noted, and the weather was so poor there had not been enough of a window to make fully detailed measurements.

Another surveyor, James Nicholson, approaching from the 'North East Longitudinal' got closer to what he called 'sharp peak "h"'. He realised it must have been the same as Peak 'gamma' and Peak 'b'.

But the Survey of India, though it brooked no obstacle in obtaining data, was always tardy in parting too soon with its findings. There were bureaucratic considerations, always, and Waugh asked that Himalayan peaks be given new designations. This time, Roman numerals. Peak 'b' became Peak XV.

Back at the Calcutta Headquarters of the survey, where all the number-crunching took place, one of the top 'computers' – indeed, his title was 'Chief Computer' – was the Bengali genius Radhanath Sikdar. George Everest had been so impressed by the abilities of this maths wizard to work through vast amounts of data that he had poached him to work exclusively on the Great Arc. Sikdar's calculations finally confirmed what many had suspected: Peak XV was the world's highest mountain.

This was not quite enough for the men of the survey, wedded as they were to complete and utter accuracy. Four more years needed to pass until tidal observations in Karachi could be made. Refraction coefficients needed to be checked (the amount the light bent travelling through different densities of air – obviously less the higher you go). Its height, calculated from the data of six base stations of the Great Arc and corrected, was reckoned to be 8,840 metres. Waugh sent for old records of the first surveyors just to check one last time. *And even then*, though the revelations about the world's highest mountain which were contained in official 'letter 29B' might be 'made use of', it was not for publication. Waugh wrote fourteen numbered paragraphs about Peak XV:

We have for some years known that this mountain is higher than any hitherto measured in India and most probably it is the highest in the whole world.

I was taught by my respected chief and predecessor Colonel Sir Geo. Everest to assign to every geographical object its true local or native appellation . . . but here is a mountain, most probably the highest in the world, without any local name that we can discover . . . in conformity with what I believe to be the wish of all the members of the scientific department over which I have the honour to preside, and to perpetuate the memory of that illustrious master of accurate geographical research, I have determined to name this noble peak of the Himalayas Mont Everest.

Later Waugh changed it to Mount Everest.

In 1856 surveying in the Karakoram revealed that Everest might have a competitor. This was K2, which despite attempts to name it Mount Waugh, Mount Albert (not surprised that didn't stick), Mount Montgomerie (the man who discovered it), or Mount Godwin-Austen (the surveyor who headed the team in the Karakoram), has steadfastly retained its original survey designation. High mountains don't always have local names – or names that locals can agree upon. Often the name covers a group of peaks rather than one. Everest is often rendered as Chomolungma, but that actually refers in Tibetan to the whole mountainous region where Everest is to be found. And, depending on where you stand, Everest does not always look the highest of its sibling peaks. It makes sense that only in the age of measurement should we care about making such fine distinctions about each summit on a broad massif.

The first attempt to fix Everest's height involved using ideas about the correction for refraction extant at the time – which have since altered. Nevertheless, as we've seen, the figure of 8,840 metres was calculated. In 1906, Sir Sidney Burrard applied

everything new that had been learned about refraction and gravitational deviation and the exact position of the geoid. His revised
figure was 8,882 metres above the spheroid but he remained
unconvinced that his figure was any more transitional than the
earlier one. In 1922 the height of 8,882 was found for the height
above the spheroid, with the geoid probably being 21 metres
higher, which meant the real height of Everest was set at 8,863
metres.

You can see the problem – height above what? Height above
sea level – but where the sea level is inland depends on how
spherical or otherwise the land is – hence the need to work out
the geoidal difference. As we know from the effect of the moon
on the tides, gravity also affects sea level, so the mean sea level in
the Himalayas is affected by their bulk, which provides another
nice complication.

In 1949 Nepal opened up to foreigners and the Survey of India
was allowed to measure Everest from much closer base stations.
This enabled a truer value to be obtained for the height of the
geoid. It was found to be a considerable 33 metres, which brought
the old figures for Everest's height down to 8,849 and 8,851 metres
respectively. One last wrinkle is the depth of the snow cap on
Everest, which was more difficult to calculate from a distance.
Observations in Nepal made between March and December then
determined what the minimum thickness of the snow cap was,
and from this the Indian Director of the Geodetic Branch of the
Survey calculated a new height of 8,848 metres. During the monsoon, Everest gets higher – maybe 3–4.5 metres, it is hard to really
know. But the figure of 8,848 seems to have stood the test of time.

Kanchenjunga was calculated at 8,579 originally, and this made
it the third-highest mountain after K2 in the Karakoram at 8,611.
But later calculations of the geoid height plus better refraction
knowledge placed Kanchenjunga at 8,603 metres. K2 for a while
was thought to stand on a lower part of the geoid – something
still debated – which puts it in real danger of being demoted to

the third-highest mountain – which would please India and annoy Pakistan no end.

Sir George Everest made no comment about the matter of his mountain. He obviously didn't object, but it would have been unseemly to lobby for his own name to be applied to the world's highest mountain. Especially as he had no interest in mountains really, and had never seen Mount Everest.

He retired to Leicestershire and surprised many by marrying, at fifty-five, a woman almost thirty years younger than him. She was devoted to her husband, a freemason and a firm believer who began each day with morning prayers, who seems to have lightened up in old age. His wife bore him six children over the next decade. He rode for many years with the local hunt and liked to teach his children trigonometry and learning 'something about logarithms'. He died at seventy-six and is buried near Hove in Sussex.

6

Younghusband: the First Mountaineer

He jests at scars who never felt a wound.

Lepcha proverb

Maps cause wars. Maps define territorial ambition. The golden age of exploration is really the age in which accurate maps of the world began to be made of remote places. The British Empire produced without doubt the greatest number of explorers (if we include the humble soldiers, surveyors and administrators of its far provinces) per head of population of any nation on earth. Its attempt at subjugation was far more insidious than the simple oppression of a bullying invader; it sought, through creating a parallel imagined reality in maps, to replace the native reality with another: their own attenuated two-dimensional version that can be folded up and stored on a shelf.

To map is to be. It is a substitute for experience of another kind; it is the most curious form of abstraction. The map-maker seeks to control the world through recreating it in an abstract form. That the map has many obvious uses is just an alibi, or a number of alibis. In fact, as various countries who map little or not at all, attest, super-accurate mapping is not really necessary. France and Spain are poorly mapped in many areas when compared to Britain and British-mapped areas of the Himalayas.

To travel without maps is to make a more human journey; paradoxically, the map-making pioneer is the most reliant of all on local guides – he needs them for local names and other off-piste information. Yet his map makes future use of such helpful people redundant. The map-maker empowers future travellers at the expense of locals. Whatever his alibi, the map-maker is involved in power games and as such should be treated warily: like the cheery scientist making bombs, he makes toys that soon control their users.

Did Younghusband know this? His name is suggestive – a young man, yet one already joined to the feminine; Younghusband was a pushy young officer, 'a thruster', who kept well hidden his spiritually alert dreamer side until he had achieved such 'big yang' exploits as crossing for the first time the Mustagh Pass. He was an explorer, a map-maker, a land-grabber for Britain in terms of power and influence; he was a great believer in the British Empire and its ability to change the world for the better.

Younghusband came from an ancient English family that traced its roots back to Saxon freeholders in Northumberland. His father had been a general in the Indian army in which his four uncles had also served.

Younghusband in quizzical old age

He went to Clifton College, a redoubtable nineteenth-century public school; no scholarship factory, it turned out public servants needed to run Britain's Imperial franchises. The poet Henry Newbolt was a contemporary and wrote: 'And hold no longer Clifton even great / Save as she schooled our wills to serve the state.' By nature inclined towards the kind of patrol work performed by cavalry – far ahead of the main force, on reconnaissance, one step ahead – Younghusband joined the King's Dragoon Guards in Meerut. He had no money for polo and was unhappy at first in his failure to keep up with the smart set. He made amends by working hard and being loyal and was made adjutant at twenty-one. In 1884 came his first break: he was sent to reconnoitre the Kohat frontier. Two years later he received six months leave to go to Manchuria. He returned by making a remarkable journey alone through Inner Mongolia, Sinkiang, Kashmir and the Mustagh Pass. He was twenty-five and famous.

The Mustagh Pass is no easy walk between welcoming peaks. The fact is, since Younghusband traversed it in 1887, there have been only three repeats. This tells you a great deal. The first was by the Italian Ardito Desio in 1929 (he was later leader of the successful 1954 Italian K2 expedition), then another by a French team in 1990, the first to use skis, and then the last in 2004, also on skis, the team including David Hamilton, who wrote:

Descending from the pass took an entire day, plus an extensive reconnaissance the previous afternoon. This was arguably the most difficult part of the journey, and certainly the most dangerous. We used over 250 m of fixed rope to prepare a route down steep slopes of snow and ice constantly threatened by massive overhanging ice cliffs above. The glacier below was strewn with thousands of tons of blue and green ice blocks that had fallen across our descent route in the previous days. I held my breath as one by one the rest of the team abseiled down the frighteningly dangerous slopes encumbered by 30 kg sleds dangling from their harnesses.

The Mustagh Pass marks the riverine transition from Central Asia to India – it is the dividing line of the two watersheds. On one side rivers flow down to the Tarim Basin in China; on the other they head through Pakistan to the Indian Ocean. It was never an easy pass to cross, though it lay on the main ancient trade route from Yarkand to Skardu. In the mid nineteenth century glacier movement began to shower the pass with huge falls of ice and it gradually ceased to be used. It had been impassable for thirty years or more when a new pass was sought and found 300 metres higher up and about 16 kilometres further on. This too was blocked by icefall by the time, in 1862, that Godwin-Austen – whose name was later attached to K2 but didn't stick – turned back during his survey of the area.

To the young, impetuous and ambitious Younghusband, the chance to pass over an impassable pass was too good a chance to miss.

Younghusband had been gallivanting around Central Asia when his commanding officer Colonel Bell wrote to him: 'Don't fail to try the Mustagh, it is your shortest route and wants to be explored.'

A few Baltis, the local Himalayan inhabitants, had made sporadic crossings of the pass in the 1870s and 80s, but no European had. Younghusband found a guide called Wali who claimed to know the way. He also engaged three servants and some pony men to carry their baggage and equipment. The leader of the small caravan was a Buddhist from Ladakh who later converted to Islam, taking the name of Mahmood Isa, though at this time he was called Drogpa. It is a measure of Younghusband's ability to inspire others that Drogpa participated in most of Younghusband's further exploits in the Himalayas over the next two decades.

The equipment was basic but not inadequate: sheepskin coats, fur hats and leather boots lined with straw. They would subsist on tea, sugar, rice, ghee made from yak butter. Included for the ponies were handfuls of small horseshoes to replace those that would inevitably be struck off climbing the rock-laden way up to the pass. They carried more robes of the Turkoman style for warmth, a rope and 'a pickaxe or two, to help us over the ice and bad ground'.

Younghusband had equipped the whole effort on credit. Being English, at the time, was literally worth its weight in gold. He would later claim: 'I had only a scrap of paper to give them but that scrap of paper was worth hard cash to enable me to prosecute my journey because previous Englishmen had been honourable.'

They followed at first the Yarkand River until it narrowed into a boiling torrent in a high-sided gorge. The way went left, over a tributary stream. Already the ponies were having trouble: it was 'cruel work ... they were constantly slipping and falling back, cutting their hocks and knees to pieces'.

They then were able to follow a valley, climbing through the ever-shortening trees to the dwarf birches at 4,000 metres above sea level. He wrote, 'One could almost see the cold stealing over the mountains – a cold grey creeps over them, the running streams become coated with ice.' It reads like something by Tolkien. At night they bedded down under some large rocks. He added, 'I recollect that evening as one of those in all my life in which I have felt in the keenest spirits. I thought to myself this is really living. Now I really am alive.'

In an excellent biography of Younghusband, Patrick French discovered that Younghusband never mentioned any illness, disease or weakness that beset him – at least, not in his published works. On one occasion, a short while before crossing the Mustagh Pass, he trod on some open scissors that punctured an inch into his foot. One of his party mentioned later that he could not stand on the foot for a fortnight, yet nowhere does Younghusband mention this. French writes, 'He seems to have regarded physical debility as somehow improper. The very idea of immobility or illness disturbed him, and throughout his life he remained extraordinarily healthy.' He died aged seventy-nine in 1942.

The key to Younghusband's character was that he was a mystic. The world was *not* meaningless, its beauty was conjoined to a real and intriguing existence beyond. This sense of the noumenal would later lead him to promote the notion of fundamental religious unity on the point of experience and establish the World Congress of Faiths. Standing at the foot of the Mustagh Pass and seeing K2, the second highest mountain in the world, he wrote, 'This world was more wonderful far than I had ever known before. And I seemed to grow greater myself from the mere fact of having seen it. Having once seen that, how could I ever be little again?'

This is a precise account of the effect of high mountains on the sensitive. The experience is one that both humbles *and* enlarges the soul. A vast city can make a man feel small, a vast bookshop can dent a writer's bigger ambitions, but the wilderness experience that Younghusband has – which is reportedly common in such remote places – is different. It is primarily one of connection. By being connected, perhaps through the initial experience of awe at the great sight, one feels uplifted, a part of this greatness which somehow flows into oneself too. This explains, partly, the addictive quality of such places: you feel more than fully human, almost superhuman, and yet without any sense of overweening arrogance that comes from mere worldly excellence or acts of recognised superiority.

As with almost all mountain ascents, they first trudged up the glacier. Younghusband had never seen one before; its size and depth, glimpsed through crevasses, astonished him. The ponies had an increasingly hard time of it. Their legs were bruised and cut by stumbling over the tumbled rocks carried by the glacier. On the third day, the ever resourceful Wali suggested the ponies be sent back. That night, approaching 5,800 metres, most of the men having a hard time breathing, Younghusband fell asleep, unsure whether they would be able to keep going. His beard and moustache froze to his face in the night. But the next morning, he and Wali, the slave Turgan, Drogpa and two other Baltis, headed ever upwards carrying everything they needed on their backs. After six more hours of strenuous climbing, through freshly fallen snow, every step requiring a moment or two of rest, they arrived at the crest of the pass. Younghusband took a few steps forward and his dreams were shattered – the route down was impossible. The glacier heading south, to the Indian Ocean, was utterly riven by icefalls and avalanches; it fell away, almost vertically it seemed. To a man who had never mountaineered in his life, it looked like a suicidal drop and nothing more. This was the dividing line between China and India, and it seemed to have defeated him.

But in a moment perhaps too little celebrated in the annals of exploration, it was his local guide who saved the day. Wali, without crampons, ice axe or any of the other gear deemed essential for modern mountain climbing, was undeterred. Using an ordinary wood-cutting axe (which works almost as well as an ice axe, though it is more cumbersome and rather riskier), he started cutting steps down the rapidly steepening ice slope. Younghusband was impressed and gained courage from his guide's steadfast behaviour: 'I freely confess that I myself could never have attempted the descent and that I – an Englishman – was afraid to go first.'

This was a key point in Younghusband's life. He was now a real explorer – going where no other European had been. It was of inner importance because it signified any moment in an enterprise where you are about to give up, where all looks impossible, where a veritable wall is faced – and yet by inching ever forwards, chipping away to make steps, progress is made and the vast difficulties dissolve as if they had never existed.

They 'roped up' using whatever bits of rope they had extended with unwrapped turbans and bits of leather rein. It was, as the tough Swedish explorer Sven Hedin put it, 'the most difficult and dangerous achievement in these mountains so far'.

Using the axe, Wali was able to chop steps that the others could use. It is amazing how hospitable a seemingly sheer snow or ice slope looks with a few good steps lopped out of it. It is like having your own personal ledge to traverse the edge of a gorge or other precipitous feature. Younghusband observed they stood 'on a slope as steep as the roof of a house'. The roping together was a potential mixed blessing. If one fell, the others would need to react fast or be pulled to their doom. As it got steeper, Younghusband wrote that if one of them now slipped

> the whole party would have been carried away and lunged into the abyss below. Outwardly I kept as cool and cheerful as I could but inwardly shuddered at each fresh step I took. The sun was now pouring down on the ice, and just melted the surface of the steps after they were hewn, so that by the time those of us who were a few paces behind Wali reached a step, the ice just covered over with water, and this made it still more slippery for our soft leather boots, which now had become almost slimy on the surface.

Younghusband was a natural mountaineer – he improvised cloth crampons by binding handkerchiefs around the smooth insteps of his leather boots – the dampened cloth was able to much better grip the ice.

As they reached a point of no return, Drogpa panicked and lost his nerve. He began a mad scramble across the ice. Younghusband admitted he 'was in a state of cold horrible fear . . . but pretended to care a bit, and laughed it off, *pour encourager les autres.*'

But worse lay ahead. Under a protecting overhang of rock (they were now being bombarded by falling rocks and ice melting away from the face in the heat of the sun, one of the commonest causes of accident in the high mountains) Younghusband assessed the situation. Retreat was unthinkable, perhaps impossible now the ice was melting. Further descent seemed equally difficult – a vertical drop lay beneath them. But there were three protruding rocks at intervals showing out through the sheer sheet of ice below. Younghusband, very rapidly coming to terms with the mechanics of climbing, realised they could lower themselves from rock to rock using their improvised rope which had to be further lengthened by the Baltis unwinding their lengthy cummerbunds and tying them into the main length. The lightest Balti was lowered with the axe. He cut steps as he went. The others were able to use both the steps and the rope as a handhold for their descent. But then came the eternal problem of climbing: how does the last man come down without leaving the rope behind? With just a touch of imperial order about it, Turgan the slave was deputed to come last, sans rope. Slipping the last few feet he made it.

The next protruding rock was reached in the same laborious manner, and the next, Turgan again bringing up the rear: 'he reached our rock of refuge in safety . . . and finally reached a part where the slope was less steep'.

They had been descending for six hours; 'when I reached the bottom and looked back, it seemed utterly impossible that any man could have come down such a place'. They were tired now and one of the Baltis fell through the thin covering of a crevasse. Again the improvised rope of reins and belts came to the rescue and they were able to lower it down to him and pull him out. At midnight they found a piece of ground that wasn't pure ice. They lit a small fire and Younghusband deemed the moment auspicious enough to break out a bottle of brandy he had been given by Lady Walsham in Peking. It had survived all of China and the Gobi – but the descent down the Mustagh Pass had been too much – the bottle was smashed and Younghusband's sleeping bag was awash with the fumes of alcohol. But still he slept 'as if nothing could ever wake us again'.

They were now on the Baltoro, the largest mountain glacier in the world, and Younghusband's boots were falling apart: 'My native boots were now in places worn through till the bare skin of my foot was exposed, and I had to hobble along on my toes or my heels.' The following night they slept in the first clump of fir trees. They had a few dry biscuits to eat and that was all. The following day he had to be carried across a river – unfortunately his porter slipped and both men almost drowned. 'The only thing to do was to walk on hard till we could find some shelter.'

Two days later they came across their first Balti village. They were now on the fringes of British Imperial influence – but far from safe. Wali refused to leave Younghusband's side in case the villagers tried to kill him and take whatever wealth they assumed he had.

Younghusband soon recovered his strength. He reconnoitred the 'new' Mustagh Pass, but found it more impassable than the old one he had taken.

They headed now down towards Kashmir. He had a pony to ride and there were apricot trees at the roadside. They had passed the fearsome Mustagh Pass. And by this act Younghusband became the 'father of Karakoram exploration'.*

---

* Kenneth Mason

7

Tortured in Tibet

Contentment is the real form of happiness.
Lepcha proverb

One of the more interesting but perhaps risible figures to be lured by the mysteries of the Himalayas and what lies beyond was the grandson of the poet Walter Savage Landor, Arnold (sometimes Henry), a friend of Dickens and Swinburne. Arnold Henry Savage Landor still had some of the creative energy of his grandfather – Tibetan explorer Sven Hedin claimed that Landor's bulky two-volume *In the Forbidden Land* was an 'extraordinary Munchausen romance'. The mountaineer Tom Longstaff found a highest-point cairn that Landor had left behind on a mountain in Nepal. Landor wrote that he had climbed to 7,000 metres; in reality, the cairn was at 5,000 metres. A true maker of imaginary journeys!

But Landor did visit Tibet and made his way to Lake Kailash. Owing to a propensity for beating and abusing locals, he soon lost his entourage – bar two intensely loyal Indians, one of whom was a leper. When Landor was insulted by a Tibetan he deemed it 'unwise to allow it to pass unchallenged'. After a short tussle in which the Tibetan's pigtail was pulled and a number of blows landed, Landor described with relish how he made the sorry lad 'lick my shoes clean with his tongue . . . thus done, he tried to scamper away, but I caught him again by his pigtail, and kicked him down the front steps.'

Savage by name, savage by nature. But such behaviour was bound to bring some bad karma in its wake. Landor was warned repeatedly that he should turn back to India but he wouldn't be deflected from his aim to reach Lhasa. Eventually, he was captured in a village he names as 'Toxem': 'When I realised that it took the Tibetans five hundred men all counted to arrest a starved Englishman and his two half-dying servants . . . I could not restrain a smile of contempt . . .'

But the smile would soon fade: he was tightly bound and forced to ride a horse with a spiked saddle – which savaged(!) his back and nether quarters. Using their fuselock rifles, his guards amused themselves by taking random pot-shots at their captive as he squirmed on his saddle. At one point he was bound to the sharpened edge of a prism-shaped log and informed by a crazed Grand Lama (Landor's description) that his eyes were about to be put out. A red-hot iron was flourished in his face and the Englishman assumed the worst when he later had problems seeing. But his eyesight returned and the only permanent damage was a scorched nose. The butt of a rifle was placed against his forehead and discharged – but Landor forced himself to laugh, despite the nasty blow, just to show his tormentors that he was their moral superior. He was then taunted by a sword before being tied to a rack and stretched in true medieval fashion.

These tortures, though, seemed designed to scare Landor away rather than really punish him. For the cocksure Englishman was led to Taklakot and allowed to escape with his loyal servants.

Back in India, Landor sailed from Bombay to Italy, where he lived as a true English gentleman in exile.

There is a curious parallel with Younghusband – who always maintained that good manners were what enabled him to dominate the natives that he met, or at least impress them enough to help him. Those who make journeys into the wild places are usually either diplomats or ruffians – both tactics can work, though being a ruffian can sometimes get you killed whereas being a diplomat may just see you kidnapped . . . In reality the single most important factor for the traveller is his determination to not give up, his willingness to use everything at his disposal to complete his journey.

8

Nanga Parbat: the First Mountaineers

A father deserted by a wise son is like being caught
in a rainstorm without a felt to protect you.

Tibetan proverb

Younghusband is, as I've already mentioned, a key figure in any full account of the Himalayas of the last century or so. He is the first Himalayan climber, he is the man who connects to the pantheistic god while stumbling down a Himalayan mountain cliff, he forces, penetrates – no less a term is appropriate – his way into Lhasa, demonstrating the yang confusion of the West; Madame Blavatsky had already 'visited' using a yin method twenty years earlier. In a sense, they complement each other; both reflect the mighty confusion of a civilisation attempting to deal with something it doesn't understand. We laugh heartily (in private now, I imagine) at the lack of understanding Native Americans showed to technology, to the Iron Horse, the Fire Stick and other marvels. I've spent time in Haiti trying to explain that a glinting flashing flying mechanical horse does not exist. But surely it must; after all – as they slyly pointed out – you have space travel and atom bombs . . .? Eastern religions attract similarly convoluted and wishful thinking. We may have 'studied' it in our schools of anthropology and comparative religion – but that's about as useful as an American Indian laboratory of nuclear physics.

But mountain climbing is what we must look at next rather

than the hidden realms reached by the mystic. In the early twentieth century a new activity emerges in the Himalayas. A hybrid of nineteenth-century exploration and alpinism creates modern mountaineering, which reaches its ultimate form in the various assaults on Everest, the most significant being the final successful climb in 1953. Interestingly, the climbers are symbolically from East and West and yet clad in the spacesuit-like apparel of dark goggles, bulked-up down-filled climbing wear, with shining aluminium oxygen tanks in a framelike structure not unlike what would later be recognised as the engineer-naïf style of the lunar module and lunar rover.

Britain rather than America (who at that moment had already shifted attention to outer space rather than the mere Earth) was accorded full honours for finally climbing Everest. It was as if the Americans already sensed the bigger game of altitude was indeed outer space. Americans have lagged behind in the urge to conquer new and remote peaks in the Himalayas, until the current era of commercially guided climbs. The 'poor' ex-communist country of Poland has more hard Himalayan climbs to its credit than the US; indeed, Polish climbers pioneered extreme winter climbing in the Himalayas.

Mostly, there's no money in climbing – nor much glamour. It is interesting that American interest exploded with the idea of the 'seven summits' – a notion that can be commercialised, and has been; wealthy(ish) men and women paying to be guided up the highest summit on each continent. Dick Bass, a businessman, was the first to prove this 'model' worked – and many have followed in his footsteps. The second ascent, which is worthless in an exploration sense, makes complete sense when it becomes part of the athletic business success culture of the US.

But all that was a long, long way ahead.

In what follows, we'll see compared two assaults on Nanga Parbat, the 'first' mountain of the Himalayas in several senses. It is the first 8,000-metre peak in the chain of peaks that constitute the Himalayas and it is one of the most accessible – so it naturally drew the first attentions of serious climbers.

Two climbers, the earliest and one of the latest, an Englishman and a German, underestimate the mountain and treat it as if it is an extension of the Alpine excursion – their training ground. The Himalayas *are* physically an extension of the Alps – as we've seen, part of a continuous ridge of mountains through Europe, Turkey, Iran and Afghanistan onwards . . .

Such lightweight, daring, Alpine-inspired climbing has always vied, and continues to vie, with the heavy-handed methods of fixed ropes and porters. Though Everest was climbed using 'siege-gun tactics' reminiscent of a military operation like Young-husband's invasion of Tibet, there has always been a minor key of climbers – Mummery, Shipton, Tilman, and later on Messner, Gajewski, Czok and Venables – who would attack at every opportunity the big, heavily sponsored stumbling expeditions as being unworthy and uncalled for in the high mountains. They uphold that such methods of climbing desecrate the mountains. It is no accident that these climbers who tend towards Alpinism and minimalist climbing are usually mystically inclined – albeit well-hidden mystics like Bill Tilman.

Nanga Parbat, until the commercial era dawned, had more than any other the reputation of being a mankilling summit. In 1895 it was responsible for the first death of a sporting mountaineer in the Himalayas; a dubious distinction, but one that set the pattern for a series of disastrous expeditions in the 1930s. Even today, it was the scene of the first murder of climbers by extremist militants, owing to its position of relative accessibility – the same reason it was targeted as an early peak to climb.

The curse of the mountain started, perhaps, in 1841 when an enormous rockslide from the mountain created a dam across one branch of the River Indus. The ensuing lake was some 55 kilometres long, a vast quantity of backed-up water which eventually burst through the rockslide dam in a wall of water 24 metres high.

This riverine tsunami carried all before it – mainly rocks, trees and livestock, until it reached Attock where what is described as a 'Sikh army' was washed to its death. Since an army in the field is, in modern terms, taken to be over 80,000 men, one cannot be entirely sure of just how many people were killed. In the mid nineteenth century what would now be called a division – around 10,000 men – would probably also be considered in local terms an army. One thing is certain: when a 24-metre wall of water hits any sizable group of people, huge loss of life is bound to ensue.

The treachery of Nanga Parbat, which means Naked Mountain, was evident from the very first attempt to climb it by the alpinist Albert Frederick Mummery in 1895. The top climber of his day, Mummery was a pioneer of what would become standard practice later on. He was highly skilled, innovative and not dependent on alpine guides, though he worked with them at times. His ambition exceeded theirs – which is what brought him to Nanga Parbat – an incredibly audacious first peak to climb in the Himalayas (actually the Karakoram, but within the greater sense of the Himalayan range). At 8,126 metres it is one of the fourteen 8,000-metre peaks in the world and therefore not an easy target. Its proximity to Rawalpindi made getting there a little easier, but it was a more dangerous mountain than Mummery could perhaps imagine.

In a sense, he parallels Reinhold Messner, who also sought to make his name on Nanga Parbat with his brother in 1970. By the 1970s Nanga Parbat had become a 'German' mountain in the sense that Everest was a 'British' one. There had been numerous German expeditions since the 1930s, many deaths and finally a German triumph in 1953.

But Mummery came before all that. Thin and bespectacled, but with the long arms and large hands of a rock-climbing tyro, he was the son of a well-to-do wholesale merchant in Dover. Not out of the top drawer, but neither was Edward Whymper, arguably one of the most influential of early alpinists, who had been a humble draughtsman and wood engraver (just as Howard Carter the archaeologist was – is there something about graphic art that enables one to grasp other skills easily?), Mummery had upset the rather staid Alpine Club in Britain and had been blackballed when he'd tried to join – despite and perhaps because of putting up some of the hardest new climbs of the day. Seeking further challenges, he'd visited first the Caucasus and then the Himalayas.

Mummery's group included two other climbers from Britain and some Gurkha soldiers and local porters for assistance. They were shocked by the effects of altitude when they warmed up on neighbouring peaks, but Mummery was the least affected. Norman Collie, one of his fellow British climbers, wrote:

> I quoted an article I had read somewhere about paralysis and de-rangement of the nerve centres in the spinal column being the fate of all who insist on energetic action when the barometer stands at thirteen inches [i.e. is above 21,000-feet altitude, pressure being the easiest way of measuring altitude at that time]. It was no good, Mummery only laughed at me.

Like many of the fastest and most successful Himalayan climbers, he seemed less affected by altitude than most. Allied to this was a fearsome ability at rock- and ice-climbing with the basic equipment of the time: nailed boots and a long ice axe. Crampons and short ice axes, ice screws and stronger ropes would make everything somewhat easier as time went by. But nailed boots have one advantage: on mixed terrain – you save time. Crampons need to be taken off for serious rock work, whereas Tricouni nailed boots grip on ice as well as rock.

In a restless fashion, Mummery assayed the various approaches to Nanga Parbat. He was an impatient man. He hated climbing down the same route he went up – something that would bedevil the Messner brothers on their attempt on the mountain seventy-five years later. Mummery made a stab at the Rupal face – the one

Messner would climb – and decided there were easier ways up the mountain. He tried the Diamir face, but his Gurkha assistant Raghobir fell ill from altitude sickness so they had to turn back. He decided to try another approach. But instead of going all the way to the bottom he made another traverse round the mountain to the Rakhiot valley. This was where the eventual first ascent was made from, so Mummery was on the right track. But first he had to ascend the Diamir Glacier and cross a high pass to reach the Rakhiot Glacier. Years later – descending rather than ascending this glacier – the Messner brothers would meet disaster. And so did Mummery. We cannot know for sure that he died here in one of the many avalanches that sweep the slopes, but he and his companions never returned. The leading climber of his day became the first martyr in the world of Himalayan climbing.

The Germans turned their attention to Nanga Parbat in the Karakoram partly because Everest was, at that time, off limits to nationalities other than the British. In 1932 Willy Merkl reached a height of 6,950 metres. He returned two years later and lost four German climbers and six Sherpas. In 1937 the bad luck continued – seven German climbers and nine Sherpas were swept away by a huge avalanche that destroyed their advance base camp.

The mountain was finally climbed in 1953 – by a German team. At the time it was the second highest unclimbed peak after Everest, which had been summited a few weeks earlier. The summit was taken by Herman Buhl, who, without oxygen, a tent or food, took advantage of a sudden burst of perfect weather to storm the peak alone. It was perhaps this astounding lone feat, snatching glory from the Germans at the last moment, that motivated the youthful Reinhold Messner seventeen years later and on a different side of the mountain.

Messner, never a particularly imaginative pioneer, sought to simply go one better on similar terrain to those who had gone before, usually German climbers. On Nanga Parbat it would lead to a tragedy some say he never really recovered from.

Messner was twenty-five and already had fifty hard first ascents behind him in the Alps. He was invited to join the 1970 expedition to climb the notoriously difficult Rupal face of Nanga Parbat, the face that Mummery had initially been drawn to. The leader of the expedition, Dr Karl Herrligkoffer, provided a link back to the successful 1953 expedition – which had been riven by argument, as many German expeditions seemed to be, unlike the more easy-going, and successful, British ones. Messner's younger brother Gunther was also invited; the two were very close and, despite Reinhold's predilection for climbing solo (by this time he had twenty solo firsts to his credit), Gunther was one of the few he liked to climb with.

In his autobiography, Messner writes a lot about Gunther. There is even a strange passage written as if authored by Gunther; it may be Messner's way of honouring Gunther by incorporating a fragment of his writing or it may be pure imagination. Certainly Messner, always by nature a loner, never formed such a close climbing relationship again.

The account Messner has written is dreamlike and full of the regret he felt at what was to happen. Towards the end of the expedition, which had laid fixed ropes up part of the Rupal face, Messner had received the go-ahead to make a solo summit dash. But he claims his brother Gunther trailed after him. It is all rather vague. He later expresses remorse for not sending Gunther back – but already Gunther had apparently crossed several difficult parts of the climb alone and unroped – as indeed Messner had. Neither was carrying any bivvy gear, just dried fruit, drink powder and a Minox camera. Yet they made it to the top – except only Reinhold should have been there.

The series of epic failures of communication began with Reinhold believing he had arranged with Gunther and another climber that he would climb to the summit alone while they busied themselves fixing ropes in the Merkl couloir. Before dawn, at around 2.30 a.m., Reinhold left the tent; the other two were still asleep.

Were they fully clothed, like Messner? We don't know. He set off up the Merkl couloir. The route wasn't obvious and he took some time finding his way. Then he noticed someone coming towards him. His brother! According to Messner: 'I waited and soon he was standing next to me. I did not ask him why he had followed me.'

You think you're soloing a mountain and, unannounced, you are suddenly joined by your brother – who doesn't bring a rope to the party? . . . The weirdness of it all is somewhat heightened by the fact that, despite leaving at least half an hour after Reinhold, Gunther managed to catch him up – clearly he was fit enough to climb the mountain.

They made it to the top, but 'Gunther did not feel up to climbing down the difficult sections that we had overcome on the ascent.' So they decided to descend a new route – but first they needed to bivouac. Though they had nothing but a foil space blanket with them, they bedded down. Gunther 'kept trying to pick something up. But there was nothing . . . My brother's condition made me uneasy. In his state, and without a rope, the traverse from the saddle to our ascent route was risky.'

This was clearly a potential emergency – in as much as one member of the party was incapable of descending by the agreed route. Messner writes: 'I decided to call for help.' As if by magic, at 10 a.m., two climbers came towards them up the Merkl couloir, going for the summit. Messner assumed they were a rescue party. When he realised they weren't, his embarrassment made him so flustered that his response to a gesticulated 'Is everything all right?' from one of the climbers was to indicate that all was well. Within moments the climbers were out of sight. In the under-statement of the century, Messner writes, 'We had misunderstood each other.' Was it his colossal pride that had stopped him from communicating the direness of their situation – out without a rope, he needed to beg for one – and he didn't?

So instead of being rescued, they were now all alone again and without a rope. With one, they could have backtracked down the Merkl couloir.

As if realising the colossal cock-up he'd made, Messner stumbled a few times and hurt his hand – punishing himself. He writes, 'It was as if I had gone mad . . . I wept without knowing why.' Gunther told him to pull himself together and the pair of them set off down the Diamir face, which Mummery had part climbed in 1895. 'If Mummery had managed to get up there in 1895, we ought to be able to do it without belaying. I did not find this plan exciting and mad, just feasible.'

Moving off, they became aware of a violent thunderstorm below them (which was hardly surprising, as the weather reports had been unfavourable). Hail rained down on them. Messner writes: 'I went ahead to find a route in the mist.' They stopped for a while and then pushed on once the moon rose to light their way. By eight the following morning they had reached a steep slope at the foot of the face, where they decided to separate: 'Tacitly we agreed to meet at the first spring; there one would wait for the other.' There is something utterly bonkers about such a plan. It is no different from the Irish (or Belgian, etc.) joke: 'If I get there first, I'll put a stone on the wall. If you get there first, knock it off.' 'Tacitly' suggests it was a common practice when they climbed in the Alps; regardless of the difference in scale between the Alps and Himalayas, Reinhold now ploughed on without checking that Gunther was following behind. When he couldn't see him, he assumed he had taken a faster route 'so as to reach the greenery quickly. Perhaps he was already there.'

The next bit is slightly mad. Messner writes about seeing people on the glacier, 'a horseman among them'; he was convinced he could hear his brother. Then it becomes apparent by a sort of ellipsis that Gunther has been buried under an ice avalanche.

This must have been very painful for Messner to write – even twenty years after the event. That is apparent in the incoherent and fractured style (Messner claims he wasted his time on formal schooling, but some might argue he didn't get quite enough in some areas), and also the strange need to prove he did everything he could to rescue Gunther. The painful fact is, he did what we have all done as kids: looking after ourselves and forgetting about the others. Messner was only twenty-five, he had little experience except in technical climbing. He'd no experience of dealing with the complications of a high-altitude Himalayan emergency.

It is by this time too late, but Messner tries. He punishes himself by getting frostbite and losing four toes on his left foot (only the little one remains) and the first two on his right. He flails around making a desperate effort to find Gunther, who he knows with a sickening and growing certainty is dead, killed by an avalanche in much the same quick and efficient way that an avalanche probably killed Mummery. Veteran British climber Chris Bonington has written perceptively:

> A snow avalanche is such an ephemeral affair. It starts with a crack, an almost imperceptible movement of the slope, and breaks away over the first ice cliff in a great boiling cloud, that gives little hint of the colossal weight of the snow and the power of the vortices in the silent, plunging cloud. It lands on the glacier, the cloud spreads out, billowing like cumulus on a summer afternoon. The distant rumble of sound only reaches the onlooker as the cloud begins to clear. It leaves hardly a trace. The permanent avalanche cone will be a little bigger, but there is no way of measuring those thousands of tons of snow that fell through the still, silent air. Only a few minutes after the avalanche, the scene looks exactly as it did before. And yet someone perhaps is buried under that fresh mantle of snow.

As Messner dashed back and forth searching for Gunther, his feet became wet and cold from wading through so much snow. Delirious now, he made it down the mountain to a place where Himalayan people dwelled. Yet Messner, half-crazed, lacked the instinct for 'making contact'. He claims it took an hour to make 'the poor peasants' understand that he was hungry. What kind of an hour was that? They finally give him a chapatti. He swapped his overtrousers for five eggs and a hen, but couldn't trust the locals to carry him, despite the state of his frostbitten feet. His paranoia is apparent as he describes being approached by two men and wondering whether they will try to kill him rather than help him (naturally, they help him).

The regret is very real, palpable and disturbing to read. You sense that in everything there is only his way of doing things. The incredible inflexibility of the man – that 'my way or the highway' style of climbing – is both his strength and weakness. Years later, Messner would tell fellow climbers and explorers that he *had* to move at his own pace – it was dangerous to do otherwise as it would tire him and put the whole expedition at risk. There is considerable truth in this: once you find your natural pace, which could be faster rather than slower, energy seems to be conserved rather than expended. You can feel yourself getting stronger as you move onwards. However, one has a responsibility beyond self-maintenance and not becoming a burden. One also has to look out for others. An expedition has to accept it is only as fast as its slowest member. If you can't accept this, don't travel with others. And this is exactly what Messner tended to do from then on, climbing solo even when it came to the great 8,000-metre peaks in the Himalayas, crowned by his extraordinary solo, without oxygen, ascent of Everest's north face.

Messner, one of six brothers, while deeply scarred and upset by Gunther's death, felt guilty too. He writes:

The death of my brother weighed heavily on me. I had to bear the responsibility for that. He would not have died if I had not encouraged him to come on the expedition. If I had not been his brother, he would probably not have tried to catch up with me on the last part of the Rupal face. I had not sent him back. During the descent I had frequently gone on ahead. Seen in this light, I was responsible for his death . . . [but] It did not help my brother if I gave up climbing.

This admission of responsibility does not seem wholehearted. There is an implication that the real cause is the weakness of Gunther, when it is obvious that a failure of foresight and a failure in the ability to plan and communicate a plan and stick to it were the real cause. It was a classic accident with one small solvable problem piling up on another.

A year later, he was trying to get to the top of the Carstensz Pyramid in New Guinea – another German shrine of a climb, in as much as Heinrich Harrer made the first ascent. The Dani tribesmen, noticing Messner's amputated toes, assumed the injury was self-inflicted as in their culture, when a loved one died, grieving relatives would hack off a finger joint to expunge the grief. Reinhold tried to explain it was the cold that took his toes – but it wasn't. Like the primitive Dani, whom he respects and resembles in some ways, he lost his toes out of grief for his beloved brother.

9

Ekai and Maurice: Zen Buddhists and Christians in the Himalayas

A hundred male and a hundred female qualities
make a perfect human being.
Tibetan proverb

If you visit the Himalayas with a view to entering Tibet, you must cross your fair share of rivers. Many have rope- or chain-supported suspension bridges; some are crossed on logs, easily swept away in a flood. But many you must simply wade across – and this is what the Japanese timid/brave explorer/poet/priest Kawaguchi did during his successful 1902 bid to secretly visit Lhasa. His first attempt at crossing fast water was not propitious. It was a wide shallow river over a hundred metres across. He wrote:

> Oh! That plunge! It nearly killed me, the water was bitingly cold, and I saw at once that I could never survive the crossing of it. I at once turned round and crawled up the bank, but the contact with the water had already chilled me, and produced in me a sort of convulsion. What was to be done?

Despite being one of the world's most unlikely explorers, Ekai Kawaguchi was nevertheless the equal of any of them, from Burton to Stanley, exceeding in courage and intelligence such blusterers as Sven Hedin and Nicholas Roerich. Kawaguchi, though, had a different motivation; he was a devout Buddhist who wanted to gain access to original Buddhist scriptures found only in Tibet. That he would be the first Japanese (and one of very few foreigners) to visit Lhasa was of secondary importance. The son of a Japanese barrel maker, he decided, at the age of fifteen, to forswear alcohol and women and all meat and fish. This sort of dedication characterised his relentless studies: he learned enough classical and vernacular Tibetan to pass as a native scholar of the language.

Though he restricted his diet to purely vegetarian food (which is hard in Tibet), the eccentric Kawaguchi was a great believer in Japanese folk medicine. He always carried clove oil, probably for any toothache he might suffer. After falling into the freezing river, he slathered this all over his body in an attempt to protect himself from the cold. Though his legs went numb, he just about made it to the other side, 'almost a frigid body, stiff and numb in every part'. It took two hours of lying in the sun and rubbing his body to recover enough strength to walk. He managed to stumble less than two miles before meeting another river. He gave up for the day and had a good cry. This is the great thing about Kawaguchi and why he is one of my favourite explorers: he's always on the verge of being beaten, he often cries with frustration or sheer worry – but he invariably keeps going. Sometimes it is all just a matter of using Hotan – a patent remedy he brought from Japan and carried with him at all times. More than clove oil, Hotan was his miracle drug. When he first encountered high altitude – over 5,000 metres – Kawaguchi suffered a bad attack of altitude sickness. Short of breath and overcome with acute nausea, he reached for his Hotan and recovered enough to continue.

As a boy, Ekai had been addicted to study rather than following his father's trade. He became a monk at a young age but did not really fit in. After hearing that manuscripts of the purest Sanskrit were hidden in the Himalayas, he became obsessed with the idea of finding them and bringing them back to Japan to revive Buddhist studies. We have the clearest idea of why Tibet so galvanised the imagination of the world – it was where the spiritual heritage of India was able to escape the Mogul invasion from Afghanistan. The early Moguls had no truck with Buddhist monasteries and destroyed a vast number of manuscripts. Fortunately, some survived, having been hidden away in Himalayan fastnesses like Mustang and Dolpo in Nepal, while others were in Tibet.

A supporter of the Hindu Bharatiya Janata Party
squats in the high mountains

The Hindu population have long harboured a certain resentment against the Moguls who built so much of what we think of as India, from the Taj Mahal to the great parks of Delhi. Over the centuries, this resentment gave rise to a desire for the return of the original works (rather as the Greeks have come to invest great emotional value in the Elgin marbles, which, had they remained in Greece, might well have been ignored or forgotten). The British, particularly those who had anything to do with Hindu or Buddhist spiritual matters, inherited that longing for the original manuscripts. This was further enhanced by stories of Tibetan wonders and by the sheer difficulty of visiting the country – though, it must be pointed out, many non-Buddhist foreigners visited Tibet, but no non-Muslim has ever visited Mecca. If Tibet was a land of wonders alone – running monks and fire walks – it would have remained a novelty. Rather it is the fact that key scriptures of the Buddhist faith were stored there. Imagine if an original copy of the Old Testament, say the first version in Hebrew, was known to be hidden away in the Hindu Kush – wouldn't that be enough to give an air of mystery and constant spiritual beckoning to a place?

But it would take a foreign Buddhist of no little commitment to find out if these rumours of ancient wisdom transcribed into early Sanskrit were actually true. Kawaguchi's three years in Tibet were preceded by three years of study in India and Nepal. He knew no Tibetan or Hindi when he arrived from Japan, and there were no Tibetan dictionaries for him to learn from. Finding teachers in monasteries and the street, he pursued his religiously inspired quest with down-to-earth practicality. And he succeeded: he visited Lhasa, gained an interview with the thirteenth Dalai Lama, but most importantly Kawaguchi brought back many manuscripts that had never before been seen outside Tibet. On his return to Japan he gave lectures about the sex lives of the Tibetans, wrote Zen poetry and maintained his scholarly interests. Kawaguchi lived to the age of 78, dying in 1945. Right to the end he maintained his principles, refusing to divulge any geographical information about Tibet to the militarist Japanese government in the Second World War.

Though it reaches forward to the interwar period, I think it is interesting to contrast the secret journeying of Ekai (he had no permission from Britain or Tibet for his travels, relying instead on disguise and superb linguistic skills) with the secret 1933 journeying of the would-be conqueror of Everest, Maurice Wilson. Both of them had reason to sneak out of Darjeeling disguised as

Buddhist monks, and both wanted to enter Tibet. But by Wilson's day the 'forbidden' was no longer Lhasa, it was Mount Everest, which the British had no intention of letting an amateur like Wilson attempt.

Wilson had fought in the First World War at eighteen and distinguished himself bravely, winning the Military Cross for singlehandedly holding a machine-gun post. The citation for the medal read: 'It was largely owing to his pluck and determination in holding this post that the enemy attack was held up.'

After the war, Wilson travelled the world and was successful in business, though he was often ill and dispirited. This changed in 1932 when, after thirty-five days of fasting and concentrative prayer, he became physically well again. He also received a series of visions telling him what he should do next.

The 1920s saw the opening of Tibet to the British. Early Everest expeditions fuelled Wilson's imagination, as did another scheme mooted at that time: an aerial expedition over the Himalayas. Back then, flying to such high altitudes was probably as daring as climbing them. Hence Wilson's mission: to fly to Tibet, crash-land on the upper slopes of Mount Everest, and climb to the summit. His motive was to spread the good news about the power of prayer and fasting. That Wilson was driven by the desire for publicity – it is unimportant that it was for a cause rather than himself – makes him much more of an attention-seeker than Ekai.

The chances of Wilson's mission succeeding seemed slim; he knew nothing about climbing or flying. A poor student, his flying teacher claimed he would never reach India, let alone Tibet. But Wilson proved him wrong. By 1933 he had learned to fly, more or less, and bought a second-hand Gypsy Moth plane he named *Ever Wrest*. He promptly crashed it in Bradford, where the wrong kind of publicity encouraged the Air Ministry to ban him from leaving Britain by plane. He did, of course. Another ban, this time in Iran, was also ignored and eventually he was able to land, if not on Everest, at least in India.

Sneaking out of Darjeeling, he headed for the Rongbuk Monastery, which was becoming the unofficial monastery presiding over Everest attempts. The monks quickly realised his incompetence and urged him to turn back. He didn't. Using equipment left behind by the 1933 expeditions, he managed to get himself some way up the mountain's north-east side – though he was so ignorant of climbing (his sole training had been to wander around some low British hills for a mere five weeks), he threw away his crampons rather than use them as a climbing aid. Instead, he laboriously cut steps and finally exhausted himself. After eighteen days' rest at a lower altitude, he tried again – but died at 6,919 metres. An optimist to the end, his last diary entry was: 'Off again, gorgeous day.' His body and diary were recovered in 1935 by that other dreamer – though, in climbing terms, supremely practical – Eric Shipton. Imagination can only carry you so far.

Always good to see prayer flags

10

AC on K2

Don't try to wipe someone else's behind if yours is still unclean.
Tibetan proverb.

While Ekai was learning Tibetan, the 'world's wickedest man' was hoping to climb the highest mountain in the world. It was 1902 and at that time Everest was impossible to get to (Younghusband's expedition would change that) owing to Tibetan and Nepalese intransigence, so K2 was where Aleister Crowley made his ascent.

In a sense, he is the darkling twin of Younghusband. He wants everything Younghusband wants but he isn't prepared to work for it in a systematic way. As a result, he is more ambitious – he plans to climb higher than anyone else in the world – but is also less organised.

Dark mystics, those who use insights denied more worldly folk to achieve mere worldly ambitions – attention in the form of fame and fortune – are often accompanied by ill luck and misfortune, which usually attaches to those who travel with them. They can often remain unscathed while those around them are driven mad or simply die. Knowledge has no favourites; these people know something – and that protects them – but it is a stillborn form of knowledge.

Those who are attracted to dark mystics, for whatever reason, are likely drawn to power. This means they cannot acquire the street smarts of the normal power seeker, nor the insights of the mystic. They come a cropper. Plenty of such people surrounded Crowley while he – corpulent heroin addict and alcoholic – survived his three score years and ten. To gain especial attention he liked to call himself the wickedest man alive, but apart from his own wild claims there is no evidence that he killed anyone; the worst that can be said is that he led people astray. World leaders from Napoleon to Tony Blair have far more blood on their hands than funny old Aleister Crowley . . .

Crowley, born in Leamington Spa, educated at boarding school and Cambridge – where he excelled at chess and climbing – at first sought to make his name as an explorer. Here he had already intuited that the remaining goals for terrestrial exploration were fast disappearing; the North and South Poles were sure to go to some Norwegian or other. Far better to concentrate on a more British-dominated area – the unknown heights of the Himalayas. Like all mystics, he had better antennae than the average man; he knew that the twentieth century would be the one in which Western man would start to go higher in every sense.

Crowley, who, perhaps in imitation of JC, preferred to be known by the abbreviation, AC, came to an agreement with one Oscar Eckenstein, an experienced British climber and the inventor (or at least promoter) of bouldering, the short ice axe and the crampon (which later Crowley would claim to have invented). The purport of the agreement was 'that they should together climb a mountain higher than any previously ascended'. The mountain chosen was Chogo Ri, Mount Godwin Austen or Peak K2 of the survey, depending on your inclination for nomenclature. Crowley bought his way in, though he was a fine rock climber, bold and experienced in Britain and the Alps. He paid £1,000 for the privilege – by today's spending equivalent, around £75,000. Not so far off the cost of a modern expedition to the region, once permits, porters, Sherpas and oxygen have been factored in.

There was some discussion as to who would be the leader (it

was to be either of them, depending on subsequent agreement), and an interesting addendum:

> Clause 5: All members of the party pledge themselves to have nothing whatever to do with women in any way that is possibly avoidable; nor to interfere in any way whatever with native prejudices and beliefs.

There were two Austrians on the expedition. Crowley claimed they could not understand the native mind. 'It was a great mistake to bring them . . . the question of international jealousy contributed indirectly to our failure.'

But the first thing that happened was that Eckenstein was detained by His Majesty's government in India and informed most strongly that he could not enter the border territory where K2 thrusts upwards from the lengthy magnificence of the Baltoro Glacier. For three weeks he chased round India trying to find out why (it may simply have been British prejudice against his European name). Meanwhile Crowley assumed leadership of the expedition.

Unfortunately, he contracted dhobi itch – a fungal infection of the groin and 'suffered perpetually from the irritation'. In the end, painting his nether regions with stinging iodine cured it in twenty-four hours.

After beating a driver with his belt for deliberately delaying the carts, Crowley discovered the coolies feared they were to be used to make a pass to Yarkand, following Younghusband's expedition – one that had cost the lives of seventeen Indian porters. But they told him they were prepared to die on the forthcoming expedition if need be: 'they were almost disappointed when I sent them back from camp 10'. Crowley claimed that in dealing with Indians one must always be just; a traveller must be 'uniformly calm, cheerful, just, perspicacious, indulgent and inexorable. He must decline to be swindled out of the fraction of a farthing. If he once gives way, he is done for.'

Though he loved to shock, Crowley had his insights: 'Indian civilisation is far superior to our own and to enter into open competition is to invoke defeat. We won India by matching our irrational, bigoted, brutal manhood against their etiolated culture . . . the best master is a go-as-you-please generous gentleman who settles everything by rude common sense.'

The expedition proceeded through Kashmir, where 'the air is clear and exhilarating, yet an atmosphere of peace tempts the wayfarer to pass away the time in the delights of live-in-idleness'. He noted astutely that the ancient bridges of Srinagar were built on the principle of the cantilever – known since Alexander the Great and not invented with the Forth Bridge as modern prejudice might have it.

The journey to K2 passed over Zoji La – at 3,500 metres, a low pass in the Himalayas, dividing Kashmir from Ladakh. Twenty-one days of marching brought them across Ladakh to the Baltoro Glacier, now in modern Pakistan. After ten minutes without snow goggles, Crowley began to get snow-blind, underestimating a cloudy sky. Climbers trained in the Alps were often careless of snow blindness – because one can climb all day without goggles and get away with it, but not in the Himalayas. Crowley cursed the two Austrians who had gone ahead to mark a route down the snow-laden pass. He found they had set a trail that was through thigh-deep snow, unnecessarily difficult for the porters carrying loads. It did not bode well for the expedition ahead.

On the other side of the pass there is a dramatic change, one of the sudden landscape shifts that occur in the Himalayas: the western side of the pass heralds a new country of barren rockiness, far fewer flowers and sparse rough grass instead of forests and meadows. Ladakh is a country of browns, every shade is represented, so you have to adjust if you have a partiality for greens. From here, they followed the Indus to Skardu. Crowley felt the only way life could be said to exist here was in the terraced fields fed by running irrigation channels from the plunging rivers that supply the Indus – the source of which is near to Kailash in Tibet. He noted that in some places these terraces watered by the river could produce up to five harvests a year including delicious apricots. But it seemed scant reward for the hard march through arid, rocky wilderness, assailed by blasts of icy wind. Crowley was obviously more intrigued by the difficulty of climbing than the environs of mountains, or at least those that did not conform to more verdant models of beauty.

Crowley believed that some dogs had spiritual significance

The travellers were entertained by rajahs and headmen of villages: 'Travel in the East is essential for any sort of understanding of the Bible. The equivalent of the word king is constantly used to describe men who may be anything from absolute monarchs over hundreds of thousands of people, to country squires or even headmen of a tribe of gypsies.' Crowley admired the stoicism of Himalayans. He described how a boy whose leg had been gashed by a falling rock remained awake, making no comment except to ask for some water the whole time the expedition doctor was cutting away flesh in a wound laid open to the bone, and then stitching it up.

When they came across a hot spring, Crowley was entranced: 'I experienced all the ecstasy of a pilgrim who has come to the end of his hardships'. He looked at his thinning body and declared himself to be in peak physical condition. On the subject of the best age for making Himalayan expeditions, he concurred with many other climbers: 'For rock climbing and lyric poetry one is doubtless best in one's twenties. For a Himalayan expedition or dramatic composition, it is better to be forty than thirty.'

Crowley was in agonies of ecstasy when they finally cooked and ate some fresh mutton rather than the canned food they had been living on for the last two months, but his greed got the better of him: 'Never in my life have I tasted anything like that mutton. I gorged myself to the gullet, was violently sick and ordered a fresh dinner.'

Reflecting on other expeditions he had been on, he reported that canned food ten years old had nothing like the nourishment of freshly canned food. Moreover the energy derived from eating freshly killed meat – i.e. before rigor mortis has set in – was far superior to that from ordinary meat from the butcher. This led him to wonder whether food might contain some element, a 'subtle principle attached to organic substances which gradually disappears after death'. In this he was perspicacious; as we now know, vitamins and minerals rapidly deplete in ageing food.

The first confrontation, a small one, came with Eckenstein, who wanted Crowley to leave behind his extensive library that weighed over forty pounds. Crowley refused, on the very reasonable grounds that they were essential for keeping him balanced and sane. I know that the moments reading at the end of a day's hike can be the best time, when you can forget everything. He wrote:

I attributed the almost universal mental and moral instability of Europeans engaged in exploring to their lack of proper intellectual relaxation far more than to any irritations and hardships inseparable from physical conditions ... Perfectly good friends become ready to kill each other over a lump of sugar. I won't say that I couldn't have stood the Baltoro glacier in the absence of Milton ... but it is at least the case that Pfannl went actually mad, that Wessely brooded on food to the point of stealing it ...

According to Crowley, he and the doctor (who occupied his mind by taking observations of nature, writing articles for the Swiss press, and playing chess with Crowley) were the only two to stay sane.

Crossing the Biafo Glacier, Crowley remarked on the huge temperature ranges encountered in the Himalayas at these altitudes. By day the maximum shade temperature sometimes got close to 40 degrees Centigrade, and was rarely less than 25. The minimum at night was always about zero – and on the glacier sometimes -10 to -30. Thick crusts of snow could evaporate in moments, leaving a 'mass of seething crystals'. Rocks heated up and fell in situations where they would have stood 'for twenty years' in the Alps.

They crossed virulent streams of meltwater. In one, the youngest member, Knowles, was almost swept to his death. Crowley observed the truth that Himalayan mountain streams are always much faster and much more deadly than their innocuous looks would suggest.

Crowley found the native Kashmiris excellent, but here he couldn't help offending someone: 'Their character compares favourably with that of any race I have ever seen. We never heard of them coming to blows or even to really high words. Imagine the difference with European peasants!' He found the Balti natives 'simple minded' but went on: 'they were all innocence, all honesty, all good faith ... they were absolutely courageous and cheerful even in the face of what they supposed to be certain death. They had no disquietude about death and no distaste for life.'

He observed the way they made bread by heating a stone in the fire and coating it in dough, wrapping the whole in their shawl while they continued walking. By the time they reached camp, the bread would be baked.

The clever use of long hair, grown into a fringe in front of the eyes, protected the locals from snow blindness; there were no cases among the porters, but on Kanchenjunga a few years later where long hair was not worn, they had several.

Conditions on the glacier were exceptionally dry. All natural grease was stripped from the hands. Water and soap tended to strip off the skin, leaving it painful. Crowley followed the local habit of not washing, keeping his hands as greasy as possible. In all, he abstained from washing for eighty-five days: 'I found myself absolutely clean except my hands and face.' The only inconvenience was lice, which found their way into the seams of all their clothes.

Along the way, Crowley described the incredible series of peaks they passed as they trudged up the huge glacial moraines. Whatever one may think of Crowley, he nails in one sentence the effect of being in such tremendous places:

> The utterly disproportionate minuteness of man purges him of his smug belief in himself as the final cause of nature. The effect is to produce not humiliation but humility, and this feeling is only the threshold of a selfishness which restores the balance by identifying one with the universe of which one's physical basis is so imperceptibly insignificant a fraction.

He missed only that such feelings and revelations form an ever-proceeding spiral, that to indulge and search for repetitions of the same is to be stalled, eventually to lose all such connection. The effort must always be directed at perceiving more, at registering the magisterial while understanding that this is only a small glimpse of an ever-burgeoning whole.

In thirty miles of walking, past the nasty black snub nose of the Baltoro and onwards, Crowley's party only ascended a few hundred metres. But it was hard going nonetheless. He found that the local footwear, consisting of straw wrapped around the feet by leather thongs, though good on the glacier, and warm, needed large steps to be cut while going over snow.

Having made numerous sketches and plotted out a route to the summit (the one still used today), Crowley eventually established 'Camp 10' at 5,710 metres. It was exposed, but Crowley chose it specifically to be out of the way of rockfall and avalanches. He wrote about how the type of avalanche encountered in the Himalayas differed from the alpine variety. The snow did not melt unless subjected to pressure; mostly, it just evaporated – he claimed that ten feet of ordinary snow could disappear in an hour's sunshine. Avalanches that started high, where the conditions were colder, could evaporate before they reached the bottom – something that never happened in the Alps.

By this time Eckenstein's party had begun to unravel. Crowley concluded they were too mixed a bunch. In order to show there was no favouritism of one nation over another, Crowley was forbidden to cross the bergschrund at the end of the glacier and start climbing the south-eastern slopes until the Austrians arrived at Camp 10. According to Crowley, he could have sprinted up the slope to the shoulder below the pyramid and made a dash for the summit before the weather broke. Weather is always the big problem on K2. In the end they spent sixty-eight days on the mountain and only had eight days of passable climbing weather (and no three days were consecutive).

They were cold and miserable, huddling in their tents, waiting for a break in the weather. Conditions were so poor, the kangri*

---

* Kangri: a copper or iron pot in which charcoal is burned.

would not work because of lack of oxygen: 'The natives put it under their blankets and squat on it. It is alleged that this habit explains the great frequency of cancer of the testicles or scrotum in the country. The analogy is with "chimneysweep's cancer".'

Having spent too long in the 'death zone', Crowley and his team were all beginning to deteriorate mentally and physically. He supported Richard Burton in holding that altitude sickness was as much about digestion as the lungs – and there is some truth in this. Interestingly, Crowley anticipates Messner and Boukreev, who hold that a mountain should be rushed, that waiting for long periods must be below the level of Everest base camp (5,400 metres) at 4,000 metres or less. Crowley asserted that acclimatising at altitude was a waste of time – of course, he had walked in over several months and was to do so again with Kanchenjunga. He claimed to be in perfect condition, having fed himself up in Darjeeling, and then taking only three weeks to get up to 6,400 metres (where he was in 'absolutely perfect condition') from the base.

But on K2 no one was in perfect condition. The two Austrians had managed to push up to Camp 12, around 6,400 metres. Pfannl became sick and was found to have oedema on both lungs. He was also babbling, which suggests he had cerebral oedema too; he told Crowley that no one could understand that he was actually three people, but AC, as a poet, could surely understand that . . .

Pfannl was awkwardly sent down on a sledge, despite the Baltis not understanding how to use one. Then came another drama: what looked like an approaching snow bear or yeti turned out to be the doctor, who had left his accompanying porter down a crevasse. It shows that selfishly leaving people to die on high mountains is nothing new. Eckenstein and Crowley donned skis and went down to the crevasse, where they found the rope that the doctor had untied from his waist. Eckenstein used just one hand to pull the man out of the crevasse, though Crowley noted,

he looked as if he 'had made up his mind to die and rather resented our interference!'

Days later they discovered that Wessely, the second Austrian
climber, before he left the camp, had stolen the bulk of the emergency rations. They decided to court-martial him when the next
opportunity arose. But the weather simply got worse and Crowley
felt they had done enough on K2 – it was time to leave. Once they
left the high altitudes and were able to eat mulberries and melons,
Crowley's health improved a great deal. He wrote of the journey
back to the city:

> To see distant prospects to the best advantage one needs fore-
> ground. In rock climbing and travelling through mountain forests
> one sees nature in perfection. At every turn, the foreground picks
> out special bits of the background for attention, so there is a con-
> stant succession of varying pictures.

Crowley had made a serious assault on one of the world's most
difficult mountains in terms of altitude, weather and technical
problems. They had been equipped in the manner of 1904 and
had survived – it was a commendable achievement. The world of
the pundit had opened up three new possibilities: mountaineering and mystical tourism – Crowley was a pioneer of these – but in
the third new zone of activity, storming the forbidden, Younghusband was the master. To this end he employed the new-found and
overwhelming force that had created colonial power in much of
the world: the Maxim machine gun and the repeating rifle. Force
rather than skill and guile were now leading the way.

PART 3

1904

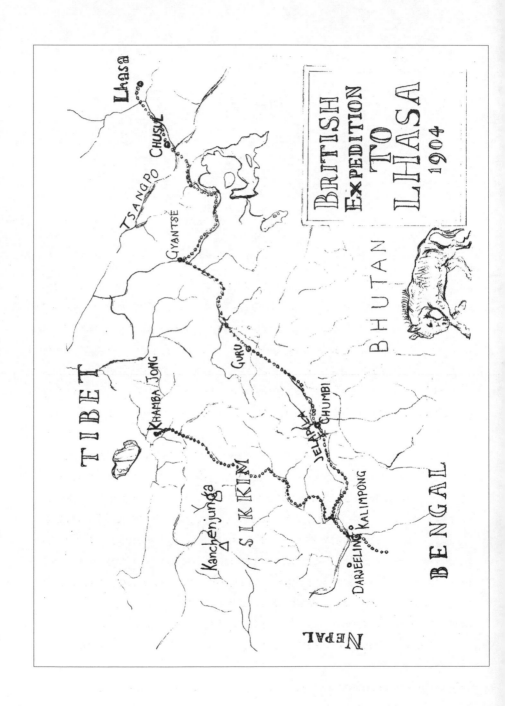

I

What of Lhasa?

At the bottom of patience, there is heaven.
Tibetan proverb

There are certain key years around which significant events seem to naturally accumulate, the innocent date bobbing along like the surfacing fin of some great hidden force not clearly in view; 1904 was such a year. Some hint of the forces at work is indicated by publication of Sir Halford Mackinder's 'Heartland' Theory coinciding with the Russo–Japanese war and the planned invasion of Tibet.* Something was in the ether – a growing realisation that once instantaneous communication exists and the sea has been conquered, the unit of defence becomes the land mass rather than the mere nation. And the largest land mass, as Halford Mackinder realised, was the Eurasian. Here, one could get further from the sea than anywhere else and therefore away from potentially aggressive sea powers. Mackinder believed that control of the Heartland of Eurasia led to control of the whole supercontinent, which in turn led to control of the world. He identified the portal to the heartland as Eastern Europe – very presciently siting the place where both world wars were to erupt so few years later. But the heart of the heartland was the inner fastness of the Himalayas and associated countries: Afghanistan, northern India and Pakistan,

---

* Mackinder was an influential English geographer and inventor of geopolitics.

Tibet. And it was here that Russia, Britain and China would compete for control. With China currently controlling the heart of the heartland as a result of the 1959 invasion and occupation of Tibet, it does not seem so surprising that despite the disparities between average wealth – in the USA, GDP per capita in 2014 was $54,000; in Europe $45–60,000; in China $7,000 – that China seems so powerful on the global stage. They control the heartland.

At the very moment that Crowley was planning to conquer the highest places on earth, Curzon and Younghusband were seeking to force their way into Tibet, the highest and one of the most inaccessible nations on the planet. We see here a two-fold attempt, a last-ditch declaration of belief in the reality of the Western journey before both endeavours collapse in the face of Oriental imagination – Crowley to espouse his own wild form of mystical endeavour and Younghusband to embrace a more socially acceptable fusion of faiths and intuitions of God's work, which would culminate in him creating the World Congress of Faiths.

The British Empire of Curzon, in the few years before the Great War, was still a place where the well adjusted could entertain ideas of real but beneficial control over the lives of others. The war changed all that; vast industrial concerns and technological progress would make men – first Western, then Eastern – the mere playthings of their self-created toys. The wisdom of Hero (and the Arabs who translated his work, which is how we know of it today), who created a steam turbine in AD 50, and never sought to harness its power, preferring to see it as a kind of executive game for Athenians, a mere bagatelle, was overthrown and lost for ever. Circumstances had overtaken man; his creations, his maps and guns and machines were now the mad master, dictating what he should do. From here on there would be no one at the controls, except nominally and destructively – it is very easy to change the world if you want to make it a worse place.

Younghusband's campaign tent

One rejection of all this is the quest to go higher. But there, at the start, Crowley and Younghusband still had the belief in the external path – the yang-style venture, though it was heavily influenced by yin intuitions – drawing them both to the abode of snow. The compromise was: invade Tibet. Why? We'll see the various paper-thin reasons for the venture. The real reason: the fumbling literalist attempt to grapple with the hidden, the invisible.

But what was the reality behind the fantasy ideas of Tibet at that time?

The clergy were the dominant feature, if not the most resilient – that must go to the nomadic Tibetans, still resisting Chinese efforts to enslave them in the sedentary life. But in 1904 the lamas were all-powerful, or seemingly so, entrenched in monasteries that took one son from every family (though for the wealthy scion, one night spent in a monastery plus a handsome contribution, a well-recognised fee, would be enough to be ordained as a lama). As in other theocracies, you had to do your time, ideally since childhood, to rise up the ranks of the ruling class.

The Tibetan aristocracy was made up of less than 300 secular families. Naturally, they had very strong connections to the elite. The families closest to the oldest kings of Tibet were highest up the pecking order. Then came members of the Dalai Lama's family, who, being plucked from anywhere, added a rogue element, a strengthening from without – outbreeding, in a sense. His family would all be ennobled once the God-King was enthroned.

Even up to the middle of the twentieth century, the majority of town and large village dwellers would be serfs, bound in a feudal relationship either to the monasteries or to the leading families. Beneath them came the lowest class, not exactly untouchables, but sharing some similarities to that Hindu caste, and also, oddly enough, with the *mizu shobai* of Japan, the 'water trade'. These were the beggars, prostitutes, fishermen, musicians, actors . . . and blacksmiths. In common with many traditional cultures – from North Africa right across Asia – metalworkers were held in low esteem. They symbolically dabbled in the work of the devil; casting metal entailed creating a miniature hell on earth. But beyond the doctrine of signatures lay a perhaps well-founded distrust of metal itself; remember, there was no word for it in Tibetan, a kind of precaution against the metalworkers taking over with their fiendish machines and weapons of war. Industrialisation entails the veneration of the metal maker and worker, and brings with it great wealth – along with pollution, satanic mills, and an escalating trade in weapons of war. It was a price we gladly paid, but the Tibetans did not.

And then there were the nomads, freest of all. They populated all of Tibet, moving across borders into the Altai or down to Nepal. Meat eaters, as most Tibetan Buddhists are (including the Dalai Lama), the nomads were armed with old matchlocks which they gladly used for hunting wild sheep and bears.

Meat eating – forbidden in some branches of Buddhism – was never outlawed in Tibet. Some people lived on vegetables, as they do in many places today, simply because of the scarcity of meat, not out of a strongly held conviction against eating it. Lamas kept animals at their monasteries and employed Muslim butchers to slaughter and prepare the meat for them.

What could wrongdoers expect? The legal system was based on that introduced by the great fifth Dalai Lama – the Ganden Podrang Codex – which in turn drew heavily on the thirteenth-century Yasa – the statute book of Genghis Khan. Punishments, as was usual in countries where there were no police, were draconian. Getting caught was hard, but if you got caught . . .

For stealing – expect the removal of limbs; for libel – tongue torn out; spying or deceit – blinding. Then there was the efficient winter technique of simply leaving the accused outside until they froze to death. Though a death sentence was strictly against Buddhist strictures, criminals would be tortured very close to death, and then it would be simply left to karma whether they would survive or not. The pillory was often in use. As were various forms of shackling, yoking and public whipping. For the very unlucky: lifelong incarceration in damp pits and monastery dungeons.

Murder was not necessarily the worst crime. As is still the case in many Gulf countries today, payment of blood money or 'life tax' to the relatives of the deceased ended the matter. It would cost thousands of dollars to buy off a high lama or monastic official's family (US$8,000–$10,000 in the 1950s) whereas a lower-caste person might cost a pound of silver.

The monasteries were economic units, selling holy images, amulets, and other paraphernalia, as well as farming and trading their surpluses. But it was the rich trading families who brought wealth into Tibet, or what wealth there was. One thoroughly Tibetan source of money was the sale of faeces and urine donated by the higher tulkus (those recognised as being of a significant former life). Pills and cakes made of lama shit and seasoned with reduced urine were popular cures for all manner of ailments. According to one researcher, when the thirteenth Dalai Lama travelled, his shit would be sequestered by his chamberlain in a golden pot and sent back to Lhasa to be processed into medicinal cures.

2

Curzon's Little Invasion

─────

A nibbling rabbit can also die of overfeeding.
Tibetan proverb

There is something a little fascistic about Lord Curzon – fascism, once you strip away its love of power, being about a cult of the *hard*. It doesn't seem surprising that, of Curzon's three daughters, one had an affair with Oswald Mosley and one married him. Or was it that other strand that seems to bump along with fascism – an interest in the occult, hidden powers latent in Tibet?

Curzon had one of those faces where, one feels, each half displays accurately the inner man. The left half with its hostile eye and downturned mouth looks harsh, even cruel. The right half looks questing, open, perhaps haughty. He was an exceptionally clever and ambitious man, who had 'a tendency to approach all public questions from a personal point of view'.[*]

He had written a letter to the Dalai Lama – several letters – and received no reply. He was not just piqued, he was annoyed. Something would have to be done. It was a curious reversal of a situation Britain had endured some thirty years earlier when, in 1860, Emperor Theodore of Ethiopia, receiving no reply to his effusive missive to Queen Victoria, captured and held all the Europeans in his realm until a satisfactory apology could be made. In later years,

─────

[*] Harold Nicolson, *Curzon: The Last Phase*

George W. Bush was strongly motivated to attack Saddam Hussein because of the latter 'disrespecting' his father George Bush, Senior. Big egos have the twisted energy needed to succeed in a job most would rather not do; the downside is that they can take things too personally. And no one likes an email ignored, let alone an exquisitely crafted diplomatic letter to a world leader.

Curzon had achieved marvellous results as a young man in 1894 with an ornate seven-page vellum letter to the Amir of Afghanistan. Though the Indian government was against it, Curzon obtained an invitation to visit the Amir and was treated royally on arrival, largely due to the 'powerful and liberal minded sovereign' liking the flattery he received. A few years later, Curzon would describe the man as 'cruel, vindictive and overweeningly proud'.

In the current situation, Curzon saw Tibet as a problem that needed a solution. The British liked neat lines and clearly marked and administered borders. Tibet refused to comply. The convention signed in 1890 and the trade regulations agreed in 1893 were simply ignored. All items entering Tibet were levied with an illegal tariff. But behind all this dickering was Britain wanting to force open a new and lucrative market. When the usual tactic – securing an agreement backed by guns – failed, they needed a new strategy. Curzon wrote his letters and waited and got more and more annoyed at being ignored by the young thirteenth Dalai Lama (who nevertheless had time to ask a customs official visiting British Darjeeling to buy some artificial flowers for him).

The humiliating lack of agreement over the exact position of the frontier, the incursions and illegal tariffs, were perhaps simply not solvable. Both India and Tibet had nomadic herders who crossed into each other's territory – there was a reciprocal use of pastures both sides of the border. But no one would consider invading a country to settle such minor disputes.

Curzon then discovered a grand strategical reason to invade. Russia had made contact with Tibet and perhaps had designs on extending her ever-expanding grip on Central Asia southwards.

At this point the enigmatic Dorjiev enters the story. A Buddhist monk from Mongolia but educated in Tibet, Dorjiev understood the ways of the East rather better than Curzon. Dorjiev left Tibet as a penniless monk, albeit one who had been the instructor of the Dalai Lama; he returned as a wealthy man – backed by the government of Russia. He had also written a book in which the Czar would be the ruler of a new Buddhist empire called Shambhala, whose centre would be the Czar's palace. The Czar had sent the Dalai Lama a set of Orthodox episcopal robes – it is often underestimated by the unreligious that religious leaders like being admitted into religions other than their own. Curzon quite forgot to send a set of cassocks from the Archbishop of Canterbury . . . and so his letters, unlike the Czar's, went ignored.

The evidence of Russian intrigue was circumstantial at best. It was an alibi, an excuse. Curzon knew what he wanted, and like a lot of clever but deluded men he reasoned backwards to convince both himself and, more dangerously, his masters.

View across Sikkim, the start of the Younghusband expedition

3

The War of the Yaks and the Zebrules

Beat a Chinese long enough and he will talk Tibetan.
Tibetan proverb

In order to push the button on the invasion of Tibet, Curzon needed a *casus belli*. He used the capture by the Tibetans of some Indian traders to try and hasten action. He needed something more. It came with the unexpected sound of a Tibetan rattle. And a few yaks. Curzon actually wrote, 'An overt act of hostility has taken place, Tibetan troops having, as we are now informed, attacked Nepalese yaks on the frontier and carried off many of them.'

What really happened is that Nepalese herders entering Tibetan territory met a strong party of armed men. These men proceeded to disperse the yaks of the Nepalese using rattles. Not a very friendly thing to do, but hardly a just precursor to war.

It tipped the balance – this telegram followed from London:

In view of the recent conduct of the Tibetans, His Majesty's Government feel that it would be impossible not to take action, and they accordingly sanction an advance of the Mission to Gyantse. They are clearly of opinion however that this step should not be allowed to lead to occupation or permanent intervention in Tibetan affairs in any form. The advance should be made for the sole purpose of obtaining satisfaction and as soon as reparation is obtained a withdrawal should be effected ... His Majesty's Government are not prepared to establish a permanent mission in Tibet ...

It was enough. It was 1904. The invasion was on.

Yaks, having started the thing, would suffer immensely during the campaign. Of the 2,953 Nepalese yaks conscripted for service, 2,922 would die of aconite poisoning. Aconite grows everywhere in Sikkim – in Britain it's called monkshood or wolfsbane and, though deadly poisonous, is used by homeopaths in minute quantities as a cure. The 31 yaks that survived the poisoning were slaughtered for food, so none survived in the end. Tibetan yaks fared a little better – they had a 78 per cent casualty rate compared to a 100 per cent one. During the winter, when the force was immobile, grazing was poor. The Tibetan casualties were due to poor food and undernourishment.

Mules had a much higher survival rate: of 7,096 employed there were only 910 casualties. Having seen the Sikkimese yak and dzo* at first hand, as well as the mule favoured in other parts of the Himalayas, the mule comes off better. It is more sure-footed, digs up the path less and can carry 70 kilos of luggage to the yak's 100 kilos.

Bullocks, buffalo and pack ponies were always part of the baggage train, but by far the oddest beasts were the camels and the zebrules. All six camels – two-humped bactrians – perished in Tibet. History doesn't record the fate of the zebrules – half-zebra, half-donkey – which were sent by the government to be tested as a new form of gun mule, supposedly hardier than the conventional mule. The men reputedly hated them: 'They are more trouble on the march than the whole section put together. They cannot carry

* Hybrid of a cow and a yak.

any load at all, and even bareback have to have men haul them up the slopes."*

The same soldiers of the 7th Mountain Battery who despaired of the zebrules captured two kyangs or wild asses, which they rode for sport. These two were tethered alongside quiet old mules and by osmosis became quite tame. On the way home, one had a heart attack swimming the mighty and mighty cold Tsangpo River; the other found its way to London, where it was adopted by the Royal Fusiliers as a mascot and marched through the City behind a fixed-bayonet envoy.

But what of the manpower behind all these animals? Though Curzon was the moving spirit, the brains of the expedition all belonged, very appropriately, to Captain Francis Younghusband, while the brawn was supplied by Colonel James Macdonald of the Royal Engineers. Macdonald was the commander of the escort, Younghusband merely a passenger, a man with a mission who needed to be defended until it was delivered. Awkwardness was almost bound to develop in such a relationship, mainly because Macdonald had already shown his stripe in a similar situation when escorting Frederick Lugard out of Uganda to the coast. Standing on ceremony, forcing Lugard to sign an affidavit over who was in command, humiliating Lugard by forcing him to dine in his tent but then reading all the time while eating, Macdonald was a line-serving, deeply conservative rule-follower who lacked initiative. He was also a slippery customer, much given to using procedure and bureaucratic delay to his advantage. He wore, at all times when in the field, a pair of red rubber wellington boots, advanced in their own way, but surely indicative of some deep personal failing.

Younghusband by contrast was a generous-hearted, well-liked man. It wasn't until nine months into his joint expedition with

---

* A 7th Mountain Battery subaltern quoted in Peter Fleming's *Bayonets to Lhasa*.

Macdonald that he made mention of the man's faults in a letter to Curzon. This stood him in good stead, especially when Macdonald's character became apparent – everyone likes someone long-suffering, as long as it isn't themselves.

As we have already seen, Younghusband had made a name for himself as a courageous and bold explorer. Now was his chance to really enter the history books.

Sikkimese students welcome a local dignitary

But who were the mounted infantry on whom he would have to rely? Raised in Sikkim by Macdonald – one of his better ideas – there were two companies (later three), one of Sikhs and the other made up of Gurkhas. Each company was around a hundred strong. The Sikhs had no previous cavalry experience and the Gurkhas, coming from a place where horses can hardly travel, are not horsey folk at all. They were all mounted on pack ponies, twelve or thirteen hands – not far to fall and easy enough to ride, though these were tired beasts with loose mule girths and oversized bridles. Reportedly, the infantry were delighted to be upgraded to horseback (cavalry always trumps infantry in status – I once expressed admiration for the infantry to my grandfather – a former trooper in the Cavalry, a normally humorous and undemonstrative man; the expression of scorn on his face was not to be argued with). Issued with long serge trousers instead of riding breeches, the men were chafed terribly and the trousers had to be patched after every long ride. Eventually these were replaced before the march on Lhasa. Brushes, curry-combs, nose bands, hoof picks and head ropes arrived from Darjeeling. Riding ponies rather than old pack animals were secured and morale was high. Questing far ahead of the main body of the mission, patrolling out on the flanks, this group of smiling men were, unlike in most other conflicts of the twentieth century, able to discharge to the utmost the traditional tasks of a light horse contingent.

They would climb high on their horses, and the climb to the passes was horrendously steep in places:

First British soldier: I thought they told us Tibet was a fucking table-land.

Second British soldier: So it fucking well is, you silly fucker. This is one of the fucking table-legs.

Once they had ascended to the Tibetan Plateau, they knew the enemy would be watching for them. At times Younghusband made out thousands of Tibetan soldiers – falling back, falling back, waiting for the right moment to attack, or just watching?

Wild asses were mistaken for enemy attackers. The kyangs, in droves of up to twenty, 'no troop of cavalry was ever more symmetrically ranked, more precisely simultaneous in its evolutions'.[*] The kyangs executed a precise wheel round that any troop of light dragoons would have been proud of. They spread out and reformed in lines as if under orders. But it was just another

---

* Peter Fleming, *News from Tartary*

mystery of the Himalayas . . . horses but no enemies atop them.

The unopposed march ended at Tuna, where it was decided to over-winter. It was a strange choice, made perhaps because the place was deserted, and for good reason. Tuna was a hamlet with a water supply three miles out of town; it had no material advantages, no military or political significance. Macdonald didn't like it. After a few days he came to Younghusband complaining there was not enough fuel or grass to survive. He said it was too cold. Younghusband replied (and the Indian government backed him up on this): 'If fifty men die of cold then it would be better than retiring.'

Then Macdonald really started to panic. He claimed they had only seven days' rations left. Younghusband wrote,

> It was a close shave and to show what a terrible mistake it would have been to retire I may mention that a camp of 2,000 Tibetans who were six miles off our flank *themselves* retired on the very day that Macdonald wanted us to. We have found an inexhaustible supply of fuel and grass, enough for weeks yet.

Watching them were thousands of Tibetans. Yet an attack seemed to Younghusband, a connoisseur of risks, to be unlikely. Mounted infantry patrols captured a Tibetan general's cook, interrogated and then released him. A flock of Tibetan-owned sheep were taken, but handsome compensation was paid to the Tibetans. No looting would take place so long as no fighting sanctioned it, that was the message Younghusband hoped to send.

Delegates from the Tibetan side rode quite frequently to the British perimeter. The message was always the same: the Mission must retreat to Yatung on the Tibetan border before any negotiations could take place. Macdonald actually retired back towards India to rest at a more equable altitude and climate. Tuna really was an inhospitable place. At 4,572 metres the air was thin enough to cause discomfort and hacking coughs to the Sikhs, and a detail of the Madras Sappers and Miners had to be sent back down the line to Macdonald. In all, about two hundred fighting troops remained in Tuna, facing more than ten times that number of Tibetans. The oil would freeze at night in the bolts of the rifles. Hadow, the subaltern in charge of the Maxims, used to remove the mechanism and sleep with it at night under his blankets. By day the rifles of the mounted infantry would freeze in the leather bucket where the rifle hung below the saddle. The Sikhs suffered casualties: eleven out of twelve cases of pneumonia proved fatal. Since the body had to be cremated by Sikh tradition, there was much muttering about the valuable firewood used – you cannot cremate the dead using yak dung. One Indian civilian, an employee of the postal service, was not entitled to an issue of 'Gilgit boots' – quilted, wool-lined boots extending above the knees; a lifesaver in such cold conditions. Without them, he died after having both feet severely frostbitten and then amputated.

It was not all boredom and cold, however. On 13 January, the day after the first Tibetan delegation came with their message to the British, Younghusband did something that was either incredibly foolhardy or fantastically well-judged – either way, it proved

A frosty morning at 4,000 metres

he had the kind of guts, nerves and level-headedness that had allowed the British to dominate so great a part of the globe for so long. He decided to ride alone right into the Tibetan camp with only two men – a Lieutenant Sawyer and Captain O'Connor, the Tibetan translator who had parlayed the day before with the delegation. Sawyer, who was studying Tibetan, had begged to be taken along for educational purposes; Younghusband had initially thought of going alone with just his translator. O'Connor had reported that at the end of the meeting there was a hint that discussions might take place in Tuna rather than back at the border. Amplifying this hint, Younghusband had taken a chance that the time was right for a bold move. O'Connor was also a cool customer: 'I merely remarked that it was a bit risky.' Younghusband took no armed escort, no orderly to hold their horses. He knew and absolutely wanted to show the Tibetans that he came in peace as a logical extension of the deputation already initiated. His reading was justified thus: if people want to talk, and you talk, the fighting will always wait. Rarely do people give up the chance of a discussion they have initiated to steal a march on their interlocutor, unless they are exceptionally stealthy. Which of course the Tibetans could have been.

The army of Tibet, or the six hundred or so encamped in Guru, a 'miserable village' some ten miles away, was the base of the Tibetan generals. Younghusband was riding right into the lion's den.

As they approached, the garrison were all out collecting yak dung for fires. No sentries were posted and no barriers erected. As they drew closer, men turned out of their stone shelters armed with broadswords, spears and matchlock rifles. No modern weaponry was on display. Nor was any aggression shown as O'Connor asked for their commander; they were met 'not with any scowls, but laughing to each other as if we were excellent entertainment'.

In the largest house of the village they met the Tibetan general, 'a polite, well dressed and well-mannered man'. His other officers seemed equally genial. Younghusband shook hands all around but noted three lamas watching the proceedings with stony faces.

What followed was a masterpiece of negotiation where the object is to get out alive. Younghusband set the scene as he received his tea by saying he was not there in an official capacity, but that he had ridden over without escort or ceremonial pomp in order to just have a chat, that they might arrive at some kind of solution to the impasse that faced them both.

The Lhasa general spoke for the Tibetans and said that it was out of a desire to preserve their own culture and religion that they forbade foreigners from entering Tibet. Behind him, the lamas added their own more aggressive version of the same point of view. Things could only be resolved if the Mission returned to Yatung.

Younghusband had nowhere to go now and he overplayed his hand, according to Curzon. He told the Tibetans: why so hostile to Great Britain when you have so much truck with the Russians? If you are opposed to foreigners, expel Dorjiev who carries mail between Moscow and the Dalai Lama.

The general and the lamas heatedly denied any commerce with the Russians. Dorjiev was a Mongol and not a Russian in any case. Younghusband then tried the pointless gambit that the British never interfered with religion wherever they went – look at India as an example of that. The lamas laughed bitterly and spoke long against this assertion. They did not mind revealing that it was their power they feared losing, not the prospect of some emasculated form of Buddhist life being allowed to prosper under British rule.

Younghusband later wrote,

So far the conversation, in spite of occasional bursts from the monks, had been maintained with perfect good humour; but when I made a sign of moving, and said that I must be returning to Tuna, the monks, looking black as devils, shouted out 'No you won't, you'll stop here.'

Quite politely, one general said they were nothing but thieves and brigands. The monks clamoured for a date to be set for the British withdrawal. 'The atmosphere became electric . . . one of the generals left the room; trumpets outside were sounded, and the attendants closed round behind us.'

They were seconds away from absolute disaster. Captives of the Tibetans could rot for twenty years in a Lhasa prison, or perhaps be killed outright if a frenzy took hold.

'I told Captain O'Connor, though there was really no necessity to give such a warning to anyone so imperturbable, to keep his voice studiously calm, and to smile as much as he possibly could.'

Younghusband was thinking furiously of a way out. The monks were the key, it seemed – and they had demanded a date for with-drawal. Well, he couldn't lie – that would jeopardise any chance of further talks – but he could give a ray of hope . . .

I said I had to obey the orders of my government just as much as they had to obey the orders of theirs; that I would ask them to report to their Government what I had said, and I would report to my Government what they had told me . . . but if the Viceroy or-dered me back to India I should personally be only too thankful, as theirs was a barren and inhospitable country, and I had a wife and child in Darjeeling, whom I was anxious to see again as soon as I could.

It was a masterstroke that eased the situation with the generals, though the lamas continued to clamour for a date. Then one of the generals suggested a messenger come with Younghusband to Tuna, then and there, to receive the answer from the Viceroy.

Despite what civilians might think, generals only get to be generals by a marked lack of enthusiasm for unnecessary conflict (which is very different to a reluctance to fight when the fight has started); they know that any conflict has a way of throwing you off your game, confusing the issue and creating a new set of priorities.

Better to let Younghusband go with the possibility of a solution, rather than keep him and risk certain bloodshed. The monks muttered but the generals were all smiles again, conducting the British officers to the door with the same geniality and politeness they had shown when the party arrived. As for Younghusband and his companions:

> We preserved our equanimity of demeanor and the smiles on our faces till we had mounted our ponies and we were well outside the camp, and then we galloped off as hard as we could, lest the monks should get the upper hand again and send men after us. It had been a close shave but it was worth it.

4

The Incident at Guru

Credulity breeds credulity and ends in hypocrisy.
Tibetan proverb

Of course, the Viceroy said no to a retreat. All winter the Tibetans watched the British and wondered what would happen next. At Guru they built a 1.5-metre wall and waited for the enemy to arrive. The road to Gyantse and Lhasa beyond was now effectively blocked. Either the Tibetans backed off or there would be a fight. Younghusband and Macdonald (now back), one fine day in April 1904, moved off with their troops behind them. They were greeted by the same Lhasa general who had been so cordial before. He was no longer smiling. The Tibetans had been told the British had no wish to fight. Now they would be tested. After twenty minutes of wrangling with the general, Younghusband told the Tibetans that they would be dislodged by force from the road and the wall they hid behind. There were, at a guess, over a thousand of them – armed with antique broadswords and strange forked guns embossed with turquoise and coral.

Fifteen minutes passed with no sign of movement by the Tibetans. Macdonald, ever lacking in boldness, suggested they simply open fire and then attack with all force. Younghusband, revealing again his gambler's instinct, or perhaps a much greater ability to read Himalayans – he had, after all, been dealing with them for fifteen years by now – prevailed upon Macdonald instead to order an advance in which the troops would hold their fire unless fired upon.

It was a cold grey day. The mounted infantry were somewhat breathless with the effects of altitude. But they marched forward. Macdonald had wanted to use the artillery they had with them. It would have given them a decisive advantage. Instead, they were advancing on a serious barrier, a wall, with loopholes for the Tibetans to fire securely. And behind the wall massed the Tibetan troops, ready to fan out and overwhelm the British.

No shot was fired. Inch by inch the troops grew closer and closer. Right and left flanking movements by the British-positioned Maxim guns and infantry bearing down on the Tibetans from each side. In front of the wall, the impasse continued. On the escarpments either side of the wall, grey-clad Tibetan musketeers hiding in hastily built sangars were hustled out by the 8th Gurkhas and the 23rd Sikh Pioneers. This was all conducted in silence, as if the native soldiers knew that any sound might wake the Tibetans from their stunned reverie. They were disarmed 'with the good humoured severity that London policemen display on Boat Race night'.*

The men from the sangar ambled downhill – not exactly driven, but moving away from the Gurkhas. They joined the milling throng of Tibetans behind the wall. Appearing from behind it, the Lhasa general slumped down on the ground while Sikh soldiers gathered round. It was impossible to say what was going through his mind.

Already the tension seemed to have died down. Reminiscent of modern-day soldiers taking phone selfies, the British officers were busy with their folding cameras, taking snapshots. Candler, a reporter from the *Daily Mail*, penned a quick sketch about an absurd, bloodless victory. Younghusband composed a short

* Peter Fleming, *Bayonets to Lhasa*

dispatch and sent an orderly rushing to the telegraph head to send it to Calcutta.

But the Tibetans were quite unlike any other soldiers the British had battled. There is a certain etiquette to any violent encounter, and so far this seemed to be observed. But war is never over until the weapons are all on one side, and at this point the Tibetans still had theirs. What's more, they greatly outnumbered the British force and were still behind the wall. It would have marked the short path from audacity to folly to expect that they could pass the Tibetans and walk away from them, exposed from the rear, passing the obstruction as if it were inconvenient road-works. Macdonald agreed with Younghusband that they would have to disarm the Tibetans before moving on.

Again, the finer points of violence and potential violence. It is one thing to not fire your musket; it is quite another to give it up. In the mind of the Tibetans, the fact of not firing had earned them the right to keep their guns. They had proved they could be trusted . . .

Disarming men without some kind of prior agreement is always going to be difficult. The actions speak for themselves, but they generate questions too: am I going to be shot now I have given up my gun? Will I now become a prisoner?

It was a risky move. The British knew, however, that the Tibetans had no alternative. Maxims and Lee Metford rifles drove a hard bargain. The Maxim – which no Tibetan had ever seen in action – could fire 600 rounds per minute and was accurate to 550 metres. It bears repetition that the whole con trick of the British colonial presence in Africa rested largely on the Maxim machine gun and its vast superiority to native firearms. And then there was the Lee Metford rifle, forerunner of the Lee Enfield, with a 10-round magazine and a rapid-firing bolt set back and within easy reach, requiring only a 60-degree turn, unlike the slower 90-degree locking turn for a Mauser. Despite being powered by black powder and not cordite, the Lee Metford was a deadly rifle to have pointing at your face – and one group of Gurkhas were a mere twenty metres from the Tibetan mass.

Who were becoming restive. They simply did not recognise what was obvious to their antagonists: the Tibetans, relying still on charms and paper spells in tiny seashells, muttered prayers and declared their firm belief in the overwhelming power of the supernatural; they were quite unaware that resistance was not an option. And here Younghusband, for all his experience, missed a vital trick: the weapons each man carried were not army-issue, general purpose, stamped with a broad arrow courtesy of the Woolwich armoury; these were individually owned broadswords that had been in the same family for generations. They were personal possessions that had meaning beyond their destructive capabilities. The decorated and elaborate matchlock rifles were also personally owned, and would have been essential for hunting and feeding troops and family – probably not in that order. So, the wrestling started. Many hands gripped the same weapon; the holiday-picture-taking atmosphere evaporated in an instant. Everything just boiled over.

At this point, the Lhasa general, no doubt feeling the iniquity of staying on the floor, had mounted his small pony. The cacophony bothered the horse but had some enlivening effect on the general's brain. Shouting hysterically, he rammed his mount forward into the melee of sepoys and Tibetans refusing to hand over their swords and rifles. A stout Sikh barred his progress and wrenched at the bridle. The general reached inside his voluminous belted overcoat, pulled out a revolver and shot the soldier through the jaw.

In an instant, firing broke out everywhere. Candler, who had only just put his pen and notebook away, was in that brief distraction cut down by a beefy Tibetan swordsman; he was slashed seventeen times and lost his hand. But the cold air had driven him to wear a thick poshteen that day – it saved him from an otherwise certain death. An officer standing with him was also wounded.

These loci of violent attack would not turn the tide in the Tibetan favour; already the Maxims were cocked and lazily emptying into the crowd. Closer, the rapid-firing Lee Metfords cut down rank after rank of Tibetans with the utmost accuracy, leaving the Sikhs and Gurkhas unharmed. The artillery lobbed shells over the wall and let them burst in the Tibetan rear, barring their escape from the tormenting rifle fire. It was a massacre.

But the Tibetans did not flee. They did not panic and run. They simply turned and weathered a hailstorm of bullets as they walked from the wall towards a spur offering cover half a mile away. Candler wrote, 'They walked, with bowed heads, as if they had been disillusioned in their gods.' 'I hope I shall never have to shoot down men *walking* away again,' a young officer wrote home. 'It was an awful sight, the slowness of their escape was horrible and loathsome to us.'

Of the Tibetan army – around 1,500 men – 700 lay dead on the field. The Lhasa general lay among them. There were 168 Tibetan wounded. All expected to be killed. They were butchered in a different way – operated on by army surgeons. Their cheerful demeanour without anaesthetic was remarked on and much admired. They were tough and healthy and only twenty died.

The British had no fatalities; six casualties in total.

Each of the Maxims had fired for a mere ninety seconds. Enough time, though, to deliver seven hundred deadly rounds. Each rifleman had only had time to loose off twelve rounds – a couple of minutes was all they fired for.

The officers were not used to such action. They were sickened by the slaughter and debated endlessly how it could have been different. If Younghusband had advanced and fired earlier, as Macdonald had wanted, the battle would have been 'fairer' – but bar an increase in British casualties, the outcome may well have been similar. It might even have resulted in a serious reverse. No, Younghusband's gamble had been correct. The Lhasa general had been a fool, but the final analysis was that men in a hurry do not always act in the wisest way.

Candler, writing later with his one good hand, was bitter: 'To send two dozen sepoys into that sullen mob to take away their arms was to invite disaster.'

The road into Tibet was now clear. The expedition hoped that the unfortunate massacre might have one salvageable aspect: it would send a message to the Tibetans in Lhasa to capitulate. But in this they would be greatly disappointed.

5

Gyantse

―――――――

Cure the illness that is not yet an illness.
Tibetan proverb

Gyantse – Madame Blavatsky had claimed to have journeyed there, an imaginary journey that lent support to her claims to be enlightened. Now Younghusband would really go there, using all the force that such journeys require.

Younghusband called a durbar – a parley – and the Tibetans arrived an hour and a half late. They were made to wait a further two and a half hours and then faced an unspeaking Younghusband until their leader, the Te Lama, apologised. Younghusband was not a tall man but he knew how to exert the high-status authority of an unmoving head, unblinking penetrating eye. But for all this, they could not agree. Again an ultimatum: clear the fort at Gyantse by noon of 5 July or prepare to be stormed.

The British were outnumbered ten to one and the fort, ever since the amnesty which occasioned the durbar, had been steadily in the process of being rebuilt. The Bhutanese king – nicknamed Alphonse on account of his French-looking goatee beard and grey Homberg hat – was a great aid in trying to smooth negotiations with the Tibetans, but even he could not broker a peace agreement. On 5 July, Younghusband sent various last-minute warnings about women and children being removed from the firing line. A burst of Maxim fire signalled hostilities had begun.

But where was Macdonald? Dilatory and hesitant as always, he sent several heliographed messages back to Younghusband from his position, with the guns a thousand metres away suggesting, 'A little more patience and I think you have the game in your hands . . .'

It was surely an odd message to receive in the very middle of an attack. Younghusband was furious, though he allowed that 'poor old' Macdonald was not in good shape. Though only forty-one, he was universally regarded as aged. A fellow officer wrote, 'He smokes cigarettes till he is sick.' Along with the smoking-induced illness, he suffered 'the trots' almost continuously, not helped by a poor diet 'mostly of slops'.

Finally, Macdonald could prevaricate no more. At 4 a.m. three columns of infantry crawled through the dark and under sporadic fire operated as a demolition party on the hastily erected stonework that defended the base of the fort. 'Bubble', an elderly seven-pounder gun, aided them in blasting a way through. But then, as Tibetan fire died away, it dawned on all that an impasse had been reached. The fort still stood massive and inviolate on top of its unscaleable rock and Macdonald was beginning to flounder.

Had he been an influential and popular leader this might have been disastrous for the attack, but such was his reputation as a pusillanimous ditherer that a kind of reactive groundswell of initiative and desperate courage had mushroomed around him. Colonel Campbell of the 40th Pathans argued strongly for attacking the eastern corner of the fort; below it he reckoned was just nine metres of scrambling, no more than a 'moderate' or perhaps a 'diff'. Macdonald reluctantly agreed after the usual prevarication. At 3 p.m., ten-pounders armed with shells newly brought up from Darjeeling – shells that shrieked and whined as they shot with deadly precision into the stonework above the lower rockface, exploding with clouds of dust and much rockfall.

The explosive shells did their work and broke through the wall, revealing a tiny black hole into the interior of the fort. This pinprick in the skin of the beast served as a pupil point on which to focus more fire. Slowly the black hole enlarged.

From within the fort came a reverberating boom – a powder magazine had blown up deep in the bowels of the building. The almost continuous Tibetan fire fell away. It was judged propitious to attack the hole at the top of the rock slope.

Two companies of men charged across. Gurkhas led the scramble up the rocky slope. The guns were still pounding the hole to make it larger and to distract the inhabitants waiting behind it. Rocks dislodged from above fell on the attackers and took them down the slope in a heap. Men shot at them from flanking turrets and more stones were hurled from high above.

As the Gurkhas got higher and closer to the breach in the wall it became possible for only one man to climb at a time. When they were right below the hole, the ceasefire bugle sounded on the plain below them. It was time to try the final assault. A Gurkha commander, Lieutenant Grant, was first at the hole, closely followed by his havildar. Both were hit by bullets and fell and skidded nine metres back down the slope. Despite their wounds, they climbed straight back up and this time made it through the hole, followed by a stream of riflemen.

The game was up. The ancient Tibetan guns known as jingals stopped their incessant booming. Ropes unfurled from the fort as men sort to escape it. Resistance ended. Grant was awarded a VC for his efforts though years later modestly claimed that the havildar (awarded the lesser Indian Order of Merit) had really led the whole group on by the example of his fighting spirit.

Gyantse was the key to Lhasa; now it had fallen, the road was open to the heart of Tibet. There was, however, one last obstacle.

6

The Major is Drowned and to be Auctioned off Today

Goodness whispers, evil shouts.

Nepali proverb

The Tsangpo is not a slow river. North of Sikkim, south of Lhasa, it hurries past the Himalayas at 7 knots, 12 kmh. It is not nearly as wide as it will become as the Brahmaputra, but it is still a wide, deep river by any standards. And across this obstacle 3,500 men, 3,500 animals and 350 tons of equipment needed to be transported in haste.

Four huge chains, cast and hammered by hand, dipping into the torrent and out the other side, were all that remained of a fifteenth-century suspension bridge (the principles of suspended bridgework were well known in the Himalayas long before Brunel began building them). On the far side, two 45-foot lighters with high and highly carved horse-head prows lay bobbing at anchor. The fleeing Tibetans had left them – a bad error.

Major Bretherton, Royal Engineers, was in charge of supply and transport and had made a splendid job of both since leaving Sikkim. The Engineers carried with them two collapsible Berthon boats, a two-skinned canvas lifeboat said to be unsinkable (the air-space between the skins provided buoyancy). These were lashed together and Major Bretherton (unlike Macdonald, he was happy

230

Even small rivers can be hard to cross

to lead from the front) set off across the wicked current with two Gurkhas at the oars. Gurkhas are not horsemen, though they can learn. Assuredly, neither are they boatmen, and there was no time to learn. Heading for the moored ferries on the other side, the unwieldy raft was picked up by the fast current. Bretherton shouted orders but the men could not control the raft's movement. What happened next was not clear but the raft upturned, or came apart, and the men were in the water. It was a wide, fast, exceedingly cold river and all the men drowned.

The mounted infantry, forever prowling about, found two square leather coracles and their owners cowering in the reeds. With a threat and the promise of a bribe if they returned with the ferries, the coracle men were dispatched. As good as their word, they returned with the ferries.

Bretherton's replacement, a Captain Sheppard, also of the Royal Engineers, slung a steel hawser across the river to tow the barges into position (they had been swept downstream during the crossing). This then served as a guide rail for the boats going back and forth. But it was still lamentably slow. The mounted infantry found and paid for twenty-seven more coracles, some large enough to take six men. The operation got up to speed and everyone was across in five days.

Before moving off, a custom had to be followed: Major Bretherton's kit was auctioned. It was a tradition of the Indian Frontier that a dead man's kit be auctioned off so that his pack pony could be put to better use. Intimate personal belongings would be returned eventually to England via Darjeeling and Calcutta. Other stuff was all for sale. It is a measure of the conditions prevailing that a bar of soap that cost four pence would sell for four shillings and six pence.

Bretherton had been a popular officer and was much missed. 'I found,' wrote the officer who conducted the sale, 'that the adoption of the correct, breezy, business-like auctioneer's manner was uphill work.'

7

The Tibetan Book of the Dead circa 1904

If you drink the country's water, obey the country's laws.
Tibetan proverb

In 1904, in Tibet, when a man died custom dictated that he be dressed back to front, with his coat buttoned up at the back. Then he was tied with his legs crossed, or, in the villages, with his knees drawn up so that he could be placed in a large pot or cauldron. Once transported to the cemetery in the cauldron, the body was removed (no easy feat; one is reminded of removing a full bin liner from a cylindrical kitchen bin). Then, in a most unexpected turn, the cauldron, rinsed only once from the dirty stream you find in such places, would be used to make a soup, or, at poorer funerals, Tibetan tea. No one seemed to mind being served from this utensil . . .

Over a period of several days a trapa – a monk somewhat lower than a lama – would sit with the decomposing corpse and advise him on what paths he should follow and which ones to avoid in the next world. In the wooded regions of Tibet around the Himalayas but below 3,500 metres, the body was then burned. But much of Tibet is above the timber line so fuel was not easy to come by. Corpses were therefore abandoned to birds of prey, either on the high solitary cliffs or in a cemetery devoted to such practices.

For lamas and other religious notables, the body would be preserved in salt and then cooked in yak butter, which mummifies the body into what is known as a mardong. These mardongs were sometimes preserved in a monastery behind glass. Grand lamas were incinerated – again using butter, this time as a fuel – and their bones preserved. The funerary monuments, or chorten, of Tibet imitate the stupa of ancient Buddhists in India – at its simplest a pile of stones of decreasing size, one laid flat on top of another.

In a typical 'guide for the spirit of the dead' we discover:

1. The body is transported to the top of a mountain, dismembered, the four limbs cut away with a well-sharpened knife. Liver, lungs and entrails are spread across the ground for ravenous birds to descend upon, leaving the rest for wolves and foxes to eat as night falls.

2. The body is thrown into a sacred river. The blood and humours are dissolved in the glacial blue water. The fish and otters eat the hanging parts of flesh and fat, leaving the bones to sink to the bottom or be carried downstream.

3. The body is burned. Flesh, bones and skin are reduced to a heap of cinders. The Tisas are nourished by the foul, sweet, compelling odours of cremation. The Tisas are demigods who feed upon odours. Some prefer sweet fragrances; others feast on smells that are offensive to humans: excrement, rotting flesh, burning hair, eyes and vitals.

4. The body is hidden in the earth. Flesh, bones and skin are sucked by worms.

Families who could afford to pay for a monk or lama to officiate at a funeral abided by a rule that there must be a religious service held every day for the next six weeks. In Egypt, a ritual was performed every day for seven weeks; in Japan also. One wonders at the similarity here: is 40–49 days a psychological tipping point for emotionally digesting a profound loss?

After the six weeks are up, a kind of scarecrow was constructed of sticks and dressed in clothes belonging to the deceased. For a face, a crudely drawn portrait on a hard-to-come-by sheet of paper. Sometimes left blank when no one was able to draw – hard though that may seem to believe. Monasteries increasingly sold printed faces, ready made for attachment to the guy – one a generic man with a fine moustache, another a full-faced woman. There was a place to write the name of the dearly departed at the bottom.

The effigy was then carried to a final service and propped up to observe more prayers. Then the lama would remove the paper face and burn it in a butter lamp, letting the last curling grey snowflakes of ash rise up in the wind.

The dead man's clothes were given to the lama as part of his fee.

After this symbolic burning, no ties remained to link the dead person to this world. This was keenly required by Tibetans, who feared haunting by ghosts and spirits. They were frightened of too many dealings with the dead. There were no professional undertakers – no one would do such a job. When the corpse was carried at last from the house on its way to the cemetery or cliff edge or burning ground, a meal was served with a portion laid out for the dead man. The oldest and most revered member of the family would address the deceased:

> You are dead. Eat well, for this is your very last meal in this place. Eat your fill and more for you have a long road and several mountain passes to cross. Take strength and do not return . . .

Sometimes, when it was feared that the dead man was too attached to this life, the following words were added:

> And let me tell you that just after you died your house was destroyed by fire, everything you owned was burned, everything, including your yaks and milking things. Because of a debt you

had long forgotten a creditor has taken your sons away as slaves in a new country beyond the white mountains. Your wife has left you for a new husband. Never return to see all this misery!

The tale, of course, was a complete lie, but spirits were believed to be easily fooled by mere words as long as the right person, a most excellent and honoured elder, spoke them.

The lama would join in, adding his own advice about following the new road and not looking back. This was sincerely meant for the benefit of the dead man, but the ordinary folk only thought about avoiding the return of a ghost which could be most dangerous.

It was believed that the spirit, during these ceremonies, was travelling through the Bardo. This was a Dantean journey during which all manner of sights would be seen by the fleeing spirit, from strange apparitions to ghastly beings to beautiful wonderful creatures. If, while seeing such things, the deceased managed to keep his head (which might depend on what forms of concentration he had mastered in his lifetime, or what levels of natural piety he had attained), he would be able to hear the words of the officiating lama. These would lead him to the right path – a place among the gods or some other pleasant spot – where he might be reborn.

But woe betide any men or women who had learned nothing of the Bardo in their short time on earth! And pity those who enter it while still full of regret about leaving the material world. Full of fear and longing for their lost life, they would be incapable of hearing or heeding the words of the lama. Their actions on earth would have consequences – not necessarily obvious ones, but unavoidable. If they'd been deceived in life, they would be doubly deceived in death. Lost in the Bardo, they might be tempted by some pleasant-looking grotto or seeming palace – only to find themselves reborn as a dog!

Others believed that if you failed to seize the spiritual

The wind ringing a bell: does it toll for thee?

illumination you were offered at death, the fleeting vision of the near-death experience, you were doomed to join the frightened flock heading pell-mell towards Shinje, the Judge of the Dead.

Shinje would examine each individual's past actions in a mirror, adding a black stone to one pile for certain deeds, a white stone for others. Never would it be made exactly clear on earth which acts contributed to which pile – only the growth of an inner sense would tell you. Claiming 'you didn't know' would mean nothing to Shinje. Whichever pile of stones was the larger would dictate the species of being among whom your spirit would be reborn. Shinje will also determine your parents' social standing, your beauty or ugliness, your intellectual gifts.

No one could escape, as the following story illustrates:

A lama of high repute was nevertheless an idle man. He had been blessed with excellent teachers and had inherited an important library; he was constantly surrounded by men of learning – yet he had scarcely learned how to read, still less apply the wisdom contained within the writings of others. He claimed he had learned wisdom from 'life', but he hadn't done that either, for he was too busy feasting on the good vittles of the monastery and arranging his rise as a powerful man of the religious world. One day, of course, this lama died.

Dugpa Kunlegs, meanwhile, was loitering in the area. A saint to some, to the less enlightened a mere vagabond and rough-speaking 'philosopher' – many are the stories you will hear about Dugpa Kunlegs. As he sat and contemplated a waterfall, Dugpa saw a girl of comely appearance stop to draw some water. As if possessed, he grabbed the lass and without saying a word roughly tried to violate her.

This was no wilting lily; the girl was robust, yet she was surprised at the force of her blows. Having landed Dugpa a hearty kick in his exposed privates, she ran back to her village and told her mother of the assault.

Her mother was shocked. The men of that region were known as gentlemen. None would attempt such a thing – the brute had to be a wandering criminal. But as the daughter described in detail her attacker, the mother, a wise woman in her own right, recognised that it was Dugpa Kunlegs, no less, who had tried to roughly seduce her only child. The mother had observed Dugpa while on a pilgrimage and her inner sense – on which she un-failingly relied – told her he was truly a saint and endowed with much wisdom.

She knew that ordinary rules do not apply to such men. They have their reasons for what they do – and it is always in accord-ance with the ways of the universe, rather than merely to appease a vulgar and temporary observer. She said to her daughter: 'This man is Dugpa Kunlegs – a great man of insight and knowledge. Whatever he does springs from great understanding. Return and offer your maidenhood to him!'

Somewhat stunned, but of natural piety and knowing her mother's good sense, the girl returned to the brook. Dugpa

Kunlegs was looking morose, but he was at least now fully covered. She prostrated herself at his feet.

'Oh, I do not care about that!' he said with a shrug. 'Women awake no desire in me. However, the Grand Lama of the nearby monastery has died, having neglected all forms of instruction. His spirit wanders frightened and aimless in the Bardo towards an inevitable bad rebirth. Out of compassion, I wished to procure him a human body but such is the power of his evil deeds that my help is of no use. Such is the power of retribution for his sloth and heedlessness, you were given the strength to escape. And while you ran home to your good mother, the asses in yonder field began to copulate. The Grand Lama will soon be reborn as a donkey.'

Stories of death, the during and after of it, abounded as the British looked for a way to force the Tibetans into signing some kind of agreement.

8

The Signing

A hand and a foot do not clap together.

Pashtun proverb

The convention was to be signed in the great Audience Hall of the Potala Palace. The Dalai Lama refused to return, fearing the British when he should have feared the Chinese, who would, within a few years, strip him of all his official powers.

The steps to the Audience Hall were worn smooth by human traffic, a barefoot traffic that left the sloping steps slippery to all the hobnailed British officers and their bodyguards. They reportedly had to climb crabwise up the steep steps, as if 'negotiating some device at a funfair'.[*] Only Macdonald, still wearing his red rubber gumboots, retained his equilibrium and his dignity and was seen for the first time leading an advance.

Wars strengthen the position of those who seek power through the disruption of old certainties. The Chinese were the ultimate beneficiaries of the invasion of Tibet, not the British or the Tibetans. Some prisoners were released once the treaty was signed: two who had been locked up for aiding Ekai Kawaguchi, and two for helping Chandra Das, the Bengali spy sent by the Indian government in the 1880s. The latter two had been imprisoned nineteen years. 'All,' Younghusband wrote, 'were in abject fear of

---

* Peter Fleming, *Bayonets to Lhasa*

the Tibetans, bowing double before them . . . their expression un-changeably fixed in horror, and their skin white and dry as paper.' Candler, his stump now on the path to recovery, felt for them: 'We who looked on these sad relics of humanity felt that their restitution to liberty was in itself sufficient to justify our advance to Lhasa.'

But ends never justify means. In the late nineteenth century, the era of Rhodes and Kitchener, the ends increasingly were used to justify the means – be they sentimental, as in the case of Can-dler's observation, or brutally pragmatic, as in the case of Rhodes. It is no accident that Rhodes was one of the very few Englishmen that Hitler openly admired.

The only judgement that counts is the one that the future makes, the one that foresight tries to envisage. In this the whole enterprise, born of Curzon's imaginings about Russian influence and Younghusband's desire for action, resulted in quite the reverse of what was intended. The Dalai Lama was stripped of his status, setting a precedent for what would happen fifty years later. The Chinese strengthened their hand, horning in on British military success but treating the Tibetans with high-handed disdain and not the simple courtesies the British visited on them (it is only in costume dramas that British officers behave like Prussians). When the British left Lhasa, as was always intended, the Chinese stayed and put about the rumour that they had forced the British to leave, that they were the saviours of the Tibetans, their true friends and allies. No Russian rifles or real evidence of a Tibetan–Russian pact was found.

The lesson perhaps being: punitive expeditions don't work. Unless you are planning to stay and rule, with all the headaches that entails, you are better off never trying to force your way in in the first place.

Younghusband had, in order to make the Tibetans sign, agreed to a seventy-five-year period for paying off the war reparations incurred because of the various attacks on the column as they approached Lhasa. It was a sum of 75,000 rupees, and a canny move no doubt by the Tibetans to put off paying for so many years. The other side of the bargain was that the British had the right to maintain a presence in what Younghusband described as 'the key to Tibet . . . the only strategical point of value in the whole north-eastern frontier from Kashmir to Burma.'

London would later be incensed by this agreement and Younghusband would be their scapegoat. But what choice did he have at the time? The Indian government backed him up fully, but already the seeds of centralism, the desire for control that heralds the end of real enterprise in any large organisation, had begun to be sewn. A century earlier and Younghusband would have been treated very differently.

The thirteenth Dalai Lama sports a fine moustache

The thirteenth Dalai Lama spent his later years wandering. He made it first to Mongolia, where he wasn't popular, and then to Peking in 1907. Only one other Dalai Lama – the fifth – had ever deigned to visit the Chinese capital, and for him they built a ramp over the walls of the Forbidden City since it was undignified for such a man to be forced in his palanquin to go beneath a gate.

Things were different now. After eight days haggling, he was allowed to approach the Last Emperor and only kneel rather than prostrate in a full kowtow. In 1909 he went back to Lhasa and the place was in turmoil. In February 1910 he slipped out of Lhasa with Chinese troops hot on his tail. His own bodyguard fought off the Chinese pursuers at the ferry over the mighty Tsangpo at Chaksam – some seventy Chinese were reported killed. Crossing into Sikkim, a motley bunch of bedraggled horsemen (the fourteenth Dalai Lama would be riding a dzo), appeared at the Gnatong telegraph station.

The sergeant on duty, unruffled by reports that he was in the presence of a religious royalty, asked, 'Now which of you blighters is the Dalai Lama?'

The British provided him with a house in Darjeeling but gave him no satisfaction by recognising the puppet government set up in Lhasa and backed by the Chinese. As the diplomat Sir Charles Bell commented at the time, 'The Tibetans were abandoned to Chinese aggression, an aggression for which the British military expedition to Lhasa and subsequent retreat were primarily responsible.' It was a policy known on the North-West Frontier as 'Butcher and Bolt' and had led to many misguided operations.

In 1911 the Manchu dynasty was overthrown and it would be fifty years before the next dynasty – the communist one – would carry on with unfinished business in Tibet. Meanwhile, the Republic of China, under the shaky grip of Sun Yat Sen, reinstated the thirteenth Dalai Lama and bade him return to a chaotic Lhasa. Which he did. Fighting between Tibetans and Chinese troops petered out and the Chinese were repatriated through Darjeeling and back to Peking. But the moment she lost control of Tibet, China changed her claim from one of suzerainty to that of sovereignty. When the Chinese returned, they would swallow Tibet whole . . .

The last forbidden country had been stormed and found to

be . . . not so very magical after all. Another dead end had been reached. But tireless men were already exploring other aspects of the forbidden – including creatures that could not possibly exist . . .

Infant in front of Potala in early twentieth-century Lhasa

9

The Yeti: True Story with Pics

He who knows a great deal has a hundred eyes
compared to the ignorant man.

Tibetan proverb

I was descending from the foothills of Kanchenjunga when I saw
the print. I snapped the photograph and walked on.

Did I really believe? Well, one thing I have noticed is that
when you are abroad, in a strange place where strange things are
believed and treated as quite normal . . . you start believing too.
I'd been in Port-au-Prince, Haiti, and heard ghosts walking in a
haunted hotel, clanking their chains . . . or was it all the rum I

Seeing is believing

245

had consumed earlier that evening? I'd been in the Indonesian rainforest and seen a witch doctor come out of a trance and correctly predict the whereabouts of a rare giant snake some two days' journey away – an impossible feat by Western standards. So, being in yeti country, I suspended disbelief; it seemed the polite and maybe right thing to do.

Imaginary creatures transform a banal journey into an exciting one. Sometimes the imaginary creatures turn out to be real, but this is rare. Though the living fossil coelacanth was found, I doubt if the Loch Ness monster will be making an appearance anytime soon. Yet even saying that fills me with a kind of sadness, as if I know, a better part of me knows, that we must never shut the door on the imaginary, fantastical, invisible world . . .

The problem is not that people are simply credulous – if that was the case, then belief in weird creatures would have died out centuries ago – the problem is that unexplained animals are a convenient way to park our huge and sometimes barely contained awe, wonder, and of course fear of the world, especially when we face that world alone. Switch off the phone, walk away from the crowd, leave your iPad behind and ditch the GPS, take a stroll in the mountains alone. All sorts of strange impressions will crowd in: flashes of fear but also wonder, humility at the hugeness of the mountains, deep pleasure at seeing flowers in the snow, and was that a blue-tailed sheep? Accepting that the yeti *might* be true means that you have a concept shape out there, your eyesight is improved instantly, though you might start seeing things. Who hasn't had the experience of being in the hills and seeing something though you are not sure what – a human, an animal, a rock. When at last you *know*, it is as if the camera lens has suddenly achieved sharp focus. You see the details that confirm the correct identification easily now.

When you have an idea of what you are looking at, you see it more easily. Birdwatchers seem like magicians: one brief glimpse of a fluttering wing and they can reel off a species and its habits, but more impressive still is when they see a bird in a tree or far off on the wing, while you see nothing until it is pointed out. They expect birds to be there – and they are.

If enough people believe a thing is true, well, maybe . . . I have certainly had experiences where reality seems to bend to the will of the group of people whose reality I am sharing. You can always find another explanation, but the simplest one is that reality is a concept concocted by the group you are a part of.

Which is why strange beasts have to live in remote places: the human group mind is weaker here.

Kanchenjunga, and the Zemu Glacier especially, is rich in yeti lore. There is some evidence that the Lepchas – the original in-habitants of that region, somewhat displaced now by Nepalese and Tibetans – were among the earliest to worship a yeti-type creature of the snows. They refer to it in stories and parables as 'The Glacier Being', and it functions as a god of the hunt.

In the pre-Buddhist Bon religion of Tibet there is a legend-ary apelike creature who fights with a large polished stone as a weapon. Certainly, the region is predisposed to believe in the yeti's existence.

Pliny the Elder wrote in his *Natural History*: 'In the land of the Satyrs, in the mountains that lie to the east of India, live creatures that are extremely swift, as they can run both on four feet and on two. They have human-like bodies, and because of their swift-ness can only be caught when they are ill or old.'

Claudius Aelianus, who lived in AD 220, wrote in his *Animal Stories*:

If one enters the mountains neighbouring India one comes upon lush, overgrown valleys. The Indians call this region Koruda. Animals that look like the Satyrs roam these valleys. They are covered with shaggy hair and have a long horse's tail. When left to themselves, they stay in the forest and eat tree sprouts. But when they hear the din of approaching hunters and the barking of dogs, they run with incredible speed to hide in mountain caves. For they are masters of mountain climbing. They also repel approaching humans by hurling stones down at them.

When Tenzing Norgay, the Sherpa who accompanied Edmund Hillary to the summit of Everest, was asked about yetis he just laughed and said in fifty years of climbing he hadn't seen one. Hillary himself organised a famous yeti hunt in 1960. And Lord Hunt, the leader of the successful 1953 Everest expedition, saw two yeti prints near Kanchenjunga, not so far from where I had seen mine. Two more Everest veterans, Eric Shipton and Bill Tilman, also claimed to have seen yeti prints. And Reinhold Messner, the first man to climb Everest solo and without oxygen, claimed to have seen a yeti while traversing the Tibetan headwaters of the Mekong River.

The yeti – famous from the Pamirs along the whole length of the Himalayas as far as the Burmese hills – has many names: chemong, shukpa, migo, kang-mi and meti. The name yeti comes from the Sherpa people, who migrated from the Khumbu area of Nepal. For generations of climbers, the Sherpas have provided tall yeti tales as entertainment after a day's climbing. But surely there cannot be so much smoke without a little fire?

The current era of 'scientific' yeti hunting started in the nineteenth century. In 1832, B. H. Hodgson, a British scholar and civil servant resident in Nepal, reported an unknown animal that 'moved erectly, was covered in long, dark hair, and had no tail'. He concluded it was some kind of orang-utan. Naturally, a certain scepticism attended his reports, but then again, Paul du Chaillu's nineteenth-century sighting of a huge gorilla in Uganda was laughed at until a specimen was actually found. Another early Himalayan traveller and Tibetan specialist, Major L. A. Waddell, reported the first of the many strange footprints that have so fuelled yeti speculation. He wrote that they were bear prints, but that they had an apelike cast to them. He noted, as many writers on the yeti do, that no one questioned had actually seen the beast – though they all knew people who had seen it.

In 1921, during the first expedition to climb Everest from the north side, Colonel Charles Howard-Bury claimed he saw dark flitting shadows at 6,000 metres. At the precise spot that he had seen these moving shapes, he found gigantic footprints to back up his claims. He wrote that these were possibly wolf prints which had been 'double printed' – back feet overprinting a front-foot paw mark to make a larger, more human-looking print.

It was after this expedition that the name 'Abominable Snowman' was first coined by newspaper reporter Henry Newman writing for the *Statesman of Calcutta*. He had reached for the description because the yeti the Sherpas described was always filthy and produced an abominable odour.

The 'scrupulous witness' and sound Scottish climber W. H. Murray wrote of the 1951 Everest reconnaissance expedition:

> They were *yetis*' tracks. At least two of them had left spoor. Shipton and Ward followed the tracks for more than a mile down the glacier, finally losing them on the lateral moraine. Some of the prints were particularly clear. Pad marks could be seen within the footprints, which were 12 inches long, and where the creature had jumped the smaller crevasses the scrabble marks of its toes could be seen on the farther side.

But years later, Edmund Hillary, after his own yeti expeditions, explained to writer Jim Perrin that the tracks were a joke played by Eric Shipton: 'We all knew, apart from Bill Murray maybe, but none of us could say, and Eric let it run and run. He just loved to wind people up that way.'

In 1960 Edmund Hillary had a different view. He led an expedition to search for the yeti. In 1953 he and Tenzing both claimed they had seen the yeti high up on the snowy flanks of Everest. In their dotage, Tenzing changed his mind and both would become rather more sceptical. One suspects that the ridicule that is heaped on any would-be cryptozoologist, even one with a high reputation like Sir Edmund Hillary, becomes irksome after a while. He also suffered when the two samples of yeti fur he brought back in 1960 turned out to be from the very rare Tibetan blue bear.

Support for the scam explanation of the yeti comes from an unlikely quarter – the Nazi ethnologist Ernst Schäfer. Liberally quoted in Reinhold Messner's book about his own quest for the yeti, one can't help being a little sceptical about anything said by a man who willingly visited Dachau to study the results of the cruel and pointless experiments staged there – the logical conclusion of science pursued without conscience, foresight or basic humanity. Messner – who, when Schäfer died, received his collection of yeti 'scalps', or rather, fur samples from Tibetan bears: 'I had the opportunity to set out on such an expedition to the uninhabitable regions of Inner Tibet . . . there I shot a number of yetis, in the form of the mighty Tibetan bear.' – unloads the usual apologies that crypto-Nazis also offer. He claims – utterly wrongly – that 'without the support of Himmler . . . expeditions abroad would have been impossible during that era.' (Heinrich Harrer's attempt on Nanga Parbat in 1939 was without Himmler's support, revealing Messner's desire to exculpate Nazi actions. He also makes the absurd statement that Schäfer 'as a cosmopolitan man with international connections couldn't have thought much of Himmler's ideas of ancestral legacy'. In other words, he was an OK chap, even if he did wear an SS uniform.)

We will look further at the abominable Dr Schäfer and his expeditions to the Himalayas later (the nasty Nazi character in the Indiana Jones film *Raiders of the Lost Ark* was based on him).

A growing group of yeti spotters, including Messner, incline to the idea that the Abominable Snowman is in fact a species of bear. Bears move through the forest with a clumsy noise that rivals human progress through such places. Bears can run on all four legs or just two. It is conceivable that there is a species or hybrid species found in the remoter parts of the Himalayas that is able to move on both two and four legs and may be the origin of all the yeti tales.

In 1933–35, the British mountaineers Frank Smythe and Eric Shipton discovered the first 'yeti footprints', and published the pictures they'd taken in the *Illustrated London News* and *Paris Match*:

> This created a sensation. The 'Abominable Snowman' aroused the interests of journalists and opened up the financial resources for numerous Everest expeditions. In 1938, after I had uncovered the whole sham in my publications . . . and established the yeti's real identity with the pictures and pelts of my Tibetan bears, Smythe and Shipton came to me on their knees, begging me not to publish my findings in the English-speaking press. The secret had to be kept at all costs – 'Or else the press won't give us the money we need for our next Everest expedition.'

There is no evidence that Shipton and Smythe ever met Schäfer or communicated with him in any way. Perhaps Schäfer invented the story, having seen the way yeti stories galvanised interest. And these stories did seem to congregate around the most expensive mountain to climb, Everest.

During his own expedition, which entered Lhasa in 1939, Schäfer spent much of 1938 in northern Sikkim. At Green Lake, in the shadow of Kanchenjunga, he found himself at the very heart of yeti country. Green Lake is where Migyud, another appellation for the Abominable Snowman, has his lair. Schäfer found his team of Gurkhas and Sikkimese much exercised with thoughts of the yeti. He took to playing tricks on them by faking footprints. Perhaps Schäfer was projecting his own cynicism about the yeti's existence on to Shipton and Smythe.

After many visits to the Himalayas, Messner found himself alone in the eastern Tibetan forest and yearning for some company. He thought he heard a yak approaching, which would signify, also, human company:

> ... noiseless and light footed, it raced across the forest floor, disappearing, reappearing, picking up speed. Neither branches nor ditches slowed its progress. This was not a yak ... It moved upright. It was as if my own shadow had been projected on to the thicket. For one heartbeat it stood motionless, then turned away and disappeared into the dusk ... The forest remained silent: no stones rolled down the slope, no twigs snapped. I might have heard a few soft footfalls in the grayness of the underbrush.

He goes into the underbrush and finds a gigantic footprint: 'My shoes didn't sink in nearly as deeply as had the creature's bare soles.'

From this position of personal experience and credulity, Messner eventually arrives at the same position as Schäfer: the yeti is one of the various misunderstood forms of the Tibetan bear – the blue, the brown and the black. Tibetan bears can vary a great deal in colour; some brown bears can be almost white. This mirrors our experience of bears in other countries: black bears in Canada can be brown, grizzlies can hybridise with polar bears, some bears are adept at tree climbing, others less so. Tibetan black bears, in their early years, are supposed to be expert and silent tree climbers; later on, they prefer padding along the forest floor. Bears are usually noisy travellers, but only where they are common – typically the arboreal forests of the far north. Where bears are hunted and endangered – such as the Pyrenees – they very rarely appear. Indeed, if the locals have made a habit of killing bears that loiter at a certain altitude, then there would be, over time, considerable evolutionary pressure for variation within the species to produce a silent, snow-loving, high-altitude bear – a yeti.

Anyone who has seen a bear print – the black bear of North America, for example – will know how similar they look to a human footprint. There are five toes and an elongated sole print, which, depending on the surface that the print is made in, can look deceptively like the clumsy spoor of a giant humanoid. If the bear has walked in its own footprints, it can be further elongated and look more human. If the double print is made in snow the differences between the two can be erased by melting, making it resemble a single giant ape footprint.

Dr Makoto Nebuka conducted a twelve-year study of the language sources for the word yeti. He concluded (somewhat controversially) that it was a corruption of meti, a regional Himalayan dialect word for bear. Other names for the yeti include dzu-the, which means 'cattle bear' and miche or midred, which means man-bear. Bun manchi or jungle man is used in Nepal outside the Sherpa communities where yeti is a more common usage.

The bear thesis found unexpected support when Professor Bryan Sykes of Wolfson College, Oxford University, found traces of ancient polar bear DNA when he tested thirty-eight fragments of supposed yeti and bigfoot specimens submitted by museums around the world. It was an act of some courage by Sykes. A younger academic would have risked ridicule and ostracism for daring to support such a controversial idea as cryptozoology. But with a professorship and a solid reputation, he was ready to risk the backlash. And of course there was one. His claim that one specimen closely resembled an extinct form of polar bear whose DNA was extracted from a frozen jawbone found in Svalbard, Norway, was disputed. The specimen was between 40,000 and 120,000 years old. If such a bear existed in the Himalayas, it would probably predate human settlement of the region. The 'yeti' would then have been displaced by incoming man and would probably have tried to terrorise the incoming homo sapiens. Perhaps this ancestral memory was the source of so many yeti myths in so many cultures?

But the challenge held up – the 'yeti' fragment of hair Sykes tested was either from a polar bear or a brown bear. Sykes altered his claim from being that the yeti was an extinct form of polar bear, to a polar bear species that had somehow become separated and got stuck at the high altitudes of the Himalayan mountains. The critics pushed home a second complaint – that it is impossible with current DNA testing and the amount of genetic material on hand to assert whether the 'yeti' was a brown bear or a polar bear. Professor Sykes prefers the exotic suggestion of a marooned clan of polar bears. Those who follow the stricter strictures of Occam's razor claim that this is evidence for a brown bear as that would be the simplest explanation.

Professor Sykes has yet to mount an expedition in search of his yeti. Yet he has stated:

> I think this bear, which nobody has seen alive, may still be there and may have quite a lot of polar bear in it. It may be some sort of hybrid and if its behaviour is different from normal bears, which is what eye witnesses report, then I think that may well be the source of the mystery and the source of the legend.[*]

Whether a new kind of bear is found or not, the balance of the evidence does incline away from a giant primate of some description. Despite a desire to believe in the yeti, forgivable surely, Professor Bryan Sykes can only be congratulated for being a real scientist – appraising the evidence in a properly scientific manner and not avoiding a subject simply because of academic prejudice. If more scientists were as courageous, many of the odd and persistent mysteries of this planet would be on their way to being solved. Too often science returns again and again to a very narrow field of interest, deeming certain areas off limits – such as the miraculous temperature-changing monks – until, finally, someone has the nerve to test such a thing. Many of the mysteries of the Himalayas – telepathy, action at a distance, altered sense

[*] Dr Bryan Sykes, *BBC News*, 19 October 2013

of time – may well rely on physical laws we have yet to discover, simply too subtle for our current methods. One of which being the possible requirement to suspend disbelief in order for certain phenomena to flourish. Just as Pasteur had to remove bacteria from food to prove that spontaneous generation did not occur, we may have to remove certain disabling states of mind in order for subtle mental effects to appear. After all, we accept in the testable world of sport that a positive focused attitude is far more effective at generating results than a negative defeated one.

I have spoken with Himalayans from Ladakh, Nepal and Bhutan about the reality of the yeti (the Bhutanese even put a yeti image on a postage stamp in 1966). All agree there must be some truth in the legend. All agree that it is a legend. Maybe we can learn from them to hold two seemingly contradictory states in our minds at the same time . . .

10

Crowley Again

――――――――

*It is easier to put leather on the soles of your shoes
than cover the world in leather.*
Tibetan proverb

Aleister Crowley wrote in his *Confessions*: 'I was keen as ever to
capture [a world record] that of having reached a higher point on
a mountain than any other climbers.'

Three years had passed since the K2 adventure. Crowley had
travelled, got married and had a child. He repaired to his country
estate in Boleskine in the Scottish Highlands (a place of madness
and mayhem, later bought by Jimmy Page of Led Zeppelin in
1970, the interim owner having shot himself in Crowley's bedroom. Fittingly, Boleskine burned to the ground in 2015). In
Scotland he kept up his rock climbing and gully scrambling. But
as 1905 began, the lure of the big mountains would not go away.
As ever, he was in a hurry. There was no time to lose if Kanchenjunga was to be climbed that summer. Not only was it the third
highest peak, it had a forbidden summit, a microcosm of Tibet
that demanded forcible Western entry.

Crowley planned to use a heliograph to signal progress of the
climb forty-five miles as the crow flies from signal hill in Darjeeling to the peak of the mountain. Easily glimpsed through the
satellite dishes on Darjeeling's hilltop roofs is incredible range of
Kanchenjunga. It is some five peaks, all strung out with a great

folded apron of white extending downwards. It is the most astonishing mountain view, as the low point in front of the mountain
is less than 1,000 metres high. Unlike Everest, which protrudes
less than 4,000 metres from a 5,000-metre plateau, Kanchenjunga
towers 7,000 metres up from its base. There is no doubt as to
its majesty and mystery. From the sunny hilltop of Darjeeling
it seems to float like a snowy mirage, extending across the far
horizon, at this distance too high to be true. Crowley wrote:
'There, above the highest hills, at an angle for which even one's
experience of Chogo Ri (K2) has not prepared me, there stands
the mass of Kanchenjunga, faint rose, faint blue, clear white, in
the dawn.'

Eckenstein believed that many of the problems on K2 had
been caused by the doctor – Jacot Guillarmod – whose lack of
climbing experience had slowed them all down. Perhaps he was
not forgetting the incident where Jacot left the porter to die in a
crevasse. But AC is too tempted to care that the good doctor is
coming on the Kanchenjunga expedition too. Eckenstein, despite
entreaties to come, refused; he claimed that 'the vanities, inex-
perience, fatuity and folly' of Dr Jacot would end in disaster. AC
admits, 'I was still much too young to realise how much mischief
may be done indirectly by the mere presence of such a man.'

With his new training regime of feeding up and relaxing before
a single powerful push to the summit, AC lounged around on a
P&O ship from London to Bombay via the Red Sea. He crossed
India by train and took the 'toy train' up its steep rails to the
2,000-metre heights of Darjeeling. Sadly, the train only runs a
short distance now and much of the track is falling into disrepair.
It is only a 24-inch gauge and runs for much of the way alongside the vertiginous road up to the old hill station. The road is
crowded, potholed and dangerous. I looked with envy at the old
railway, surely a far more civilised way to ascend a hill.

AC stayed at what was then the best hotel, Woodlands; Mark
Twain would also stay there when he visited the Himalayas during

his 1896 tour. The hotel burned down in the 1940s and on its site stands the rather plain and workaday rest house for the circuit judge. It rained a great deal while I was in Darjeeling – which is not uncommon; it gets around 330 centimetres annually – and rains 126 days of the year. When Sir Joseph Hooker was sent to find a hill station for the sultry summer months in Calcutta he recommended the Chumbi valley, nearer the border with Tibet, which has a rainfall of only 102 centimetres a year. Darjeeling was 50 miles nearer, so there it was built, on vertiginous ridges with clouds and rain and only the views to recommend it.

Many an adventure starts in the backstreets of Darjeeling

Crowley complained of Darjeeling: 'The whole town stinks of mildew. One's room is covered with mildew afresh every morning.' With a pair of powerful field glasses he surveyed the mountains and compared the scene to photographs taken on the Freshfield expedition a few years earlier. With his usual confidence he wrote, 'I have already told of my ability to describe accurately parts of a mountain which I cannot see. I judged the snow basin accessible. My clairvoyance turned out to be exactly correct.'

The confidence was not all bluster. As with K2, Crowley had picked the route which would eventually be the one that was successfully climbed in 1955 by the English genius of rock and ice, Joe Brown. The route went from the Yarlung Glacier to the snow basin and then up a rake or couloir of sorts to a col west of the highest summit.

Though less than fifty miles from Darjeeling, the country north to Kanchenjunga is hilly in the extreme. Even today it will take more than ten hours' of Jeep travel, rarely topping 30 kmh on the winding potholed mountain roads. Crowley left Darjeeling in early August, faced with two weeks of marching to reach the mountain through leech-infested forest. The summer leeches of Sikkim are legendary – it is claimed that if a leech gets into the nose of a pony it will bleed to death. The Hindi word for leech is 'jok', and an Anglo-Indian proverb has it: 'A jok's a jok, but a jok up your nose is no jok.'

Crowley relates watching a leech on a grass stalk start swinging back and forth, using this as a kind of catapult to whang across the road. He remarks correctly that legless creatures are helplessly slow on open roads – they need something to push against. A cobra on a road is nothing to fear compared to one in the grass. (He also commented on the sheep, which were muzzled to protect them from eating wild aconite, a precaution foolishly ignored on the Younghusband expedition.)

There was some predictable trouble with the coolies – there always seemed to be with Crowley around – though he claimed that the cause was the bad management of an Italian member of the party called Righi. 'He actually threatened a disobedient coolie with his kukri and revolver, and the man, knowing he would not dare to use them, laughed in his face. The natives despised him as a weak man, which is the worst thing that can befall anyone that has anything to do with them.'

Righi was another of Crowley's famous errors of character judgement. For a professed magician, he was strangely incompetent at reading people. He often picked entirely unsuitable team members. Maybe he just didn't care.

The climb started well enough. Crowley was very fit – his time in Darjeeling and the two-week walk in had acclimatised him perfectly. He quickly led the way up to Camp 4, where his porters developed what they took to be mountain sickness. When Crowley dropped a little atropine in their eyes, the symptoms of nausea and headaches disappeared – they all had nascent snow blindness, not altitude sickness. AC surmised that what we call altitude sickness is a compound of symptoms that include dehydration and snow blindness as well as the lack of oxygen found at greater heights.

By day, the climbing was very hot, but there was little wind and the conditions were good for a successful ascent. Then the trouble began. One of the porters deserted, carrying off a sleeping valise that belonged to Pache, one of the climbers. The man, in his hurry to escape, tripped and fell and was killed.

Crowley sent the doctor to make an inquiry into the matter. He sent word that, aside from suffering the loss of his sleeping valise, Pache had complained that Righi was withholding food. Food again! Crowley was incensed. But he climbed on.

He mentions a kind of snow he had never seen before. Rain that had blown against the mountain froze as it touched the ground:

> The result is to produce a kind of network of ice; as a frozen drop serves as a nucleus from which radiate fine filaments of ice in every direction. It is like a spider's web in three dimensions. A cubic foot of network would thus be almost entirely composed of air; the ice in it, if compact, would hardly be bigger than a tennis ball, perhaps much less. With the advance of the evening, the rain turns to snow; and in the morning it may be that the network is covered to a depth of several inches. The temperature possibly rises a few degrees and the surface becomes wet. It then freezes again and forms a hard crust. Approaching a slope of this

kind it seems perfectly good névé. One strikes it with one's axe and the entire structure disintegrates. In front of one is a hole as big as a cottage and as the solid slope disappears, one hears the tinkling of falling ice . . . it is a most astonishing and disconcerting phenomenon.

Pache and AC continued climbing; they were now at around 6,400 metres and going strong, but a replacement for Pache's sleeping kit had not arrived so they were having to share AC's sleeping bag and blankets. And they had no food or petrol for the stoves either.

Righi, owing to some perceived insult, was holding back food and supplies needed further up the mountain. In response to AC's increasingly furious memos asking why, Righi eventually set out with the doctor and seventeen porters. They duly arrived at Camp 5 – but without any supplies. There was nothing for it but to send them back down to Camp 4 to shelter under the rocks. The snow was in an unsafe condition and it would be madness to attempt to descend further that day. To Crowley's horror, Pache decided to go down with the doctor and Righi and continue past Camp 4.

The porters, more sure-footed than the clumsy doctor, reached Camp 4 without a problem. But a mere fifteen minutes below Camp 5, the doctor managed to get six men, roped far too closely, well and truly entangled in a small avalanche when 'a single man could have ridden it head first without the slightest risk of hurting himself'.

Instead of taking warning from this accident and waiting with the porters at Camp 4, the climbers continued going downwards. Crowley heard strange cries and shouts during the night and the next day went to investigate. He passed the porters at Camp 4 and found:

a place where the snow had slipped off the glacier ice for some distance. The angle was decidedly steep, and though I was able to cross it easily enough in my claws [crampons], it would not do for the coolies . . . but they said they wanted to follow me, which they did . . . at the time I had no doubt that this place was the scene of the accident, if there had been one, of which I was not sure . . . on arrival at camp 3 I was able to understand what had happened . . . Pache and three of my best coolies had been killed. [The doctor] was badly bruised, and thought his spine was damaged. The accident had brought him completely to his senses. He realised I had been right all along, and was appalled by the prospects of returning to Switzerland and meeting Pache's mother . . . Righi, on the other hand, showed only what an ill-conditioned cur he was. He had not been hurt at all badly, but his ribs were slightly bruised; he claimed that he had 'rupture of the heart', and spent his time moaning and bellowing . . . but he forgot all about them directly he was engaged in conversation.

Crowley concluded the expedition had to end. 'I would not risk any man's life,' he wrote. The others wanted to carry on. Righi went so far as to claim that the five dead men would be seen as a sacrifice to the five peaks of Kanchenjunga, thus ensuring success. This appalled Crowley and his will prevailed. The expedition returned to Darjeeling.

Crowley wrote about his experience in the English press and attacked the 'fatal fatuity of putting seven men on one rope, and that without knowing the use of the rope, so that one fall of one man must inevitably drag down the others.' It was a lesson few would learn until later. In 1922 the Everest expedition would suffer a similar disastrous fall with seven porters dragged to their deaths in an avalanche.

11

What Makes Sven Tick?

Learn to stand up where one falls.
Tibetan proverb

Sven Hedin is usually left out of the roll call of great explorers these days. His achievements might be acknowledged, but his later disgrace as an unashamed supporter of Nazism has coloured opinion about this Swedish pioneer. He was, however, despite all his prejudice and belief in Nordic superiority, not an anti-Semite. He petitioned successfully for several people, including Jews, to be pardoned and released.

A small and bespectacled man, he revelled in appearing tough; the account of his crossing of the Taklamakan Desert almost seems boastful in the disregard he had for his expedition team. He claimed two died, though later explorer Bruno Bauman – who replicated the journey with camels in 2000 – claimed that at least one of those survived; he also noted that such a journey could never carry enough water for camels and people – it was doomed from the start.

Hedin claimed a doctorate and a 'von' – though he was elected to the Swedish nobility it was as someone without a title. As for his doctorate, it was based on eight months' study producing a twenty-eight-page document; he more than made up for such sparse writing with the lengthy tomes his expeditions produced, especially the three-volume *Trans-Himalaya*. It was his books, which he rewrote as popular editions for children, that captivated an omnivorous young reader living in Austria before the First World War – Adolf Hitler.

Hitler loved adventure stories – many ruthless dictators do; Lenin had Jack London, Castro had Hemingway and Hitler had Karl May and Sven Hedin. He and Sven exchanged letters of mutual appreciation and met several times. Hitler always extended considerable courtesy to the old explorer, who appeared as 'keynote' speaker at the 1936 Olympics. When Hitler complained that he felt old when he was fifty, Hedin insisted, 'Fifty is nothing at all. When you are as old as I am [75], Herr Reich Chancellor, you will feel just as fresh and energetic as I do.'

'Oh no, no, I will be exhausted long before that,' replied a slightly more prescient Adolf Hitler.

Sven wrote a book entitled *America in the Battle of the Continents* in which he exculpated Hitler of any blame for starting the Second World War (Roosevelt gets it instead). Hitler read the book in one night while up at the Wolf's Lair commanding the doomed Eastern Front in late 1942. He wrote to Hedin:

> Most Honorable Herr Doctor Sven von Hedin,
> You were kind enough to forward to me a personally inscribed copy of your book America in the Battle of the Continents, which was recently published by the FA Brockhaus Verlag Leipzig. I thank you warmly for the attention you have shown me. I have already read the book and welcome in particular that you so explicitly detailed the offers I made to Poland at the beginning of the war. When I think back on that time, it all seems so far away, and seems so unreal to me that I almost blame myself for having been so forthcoming with my proposals . . .

The fate of the habitual liar: to be condemned to believe his own lies; as the soon-to-be-dismissed General Halder put it,

Hitler practised *Selbsthypnose* before any hypnosis of others.

Sven was also comfortable with a few lies. Though he most probably went where he said he went, the details were always a little hazy. Between 1905 and 1908, Sven claimed to be the first European to accurately describe the origins of both the Indus and the Tsangpo-Brahmaputra, but though he tried hard, he never made it to Lhasa.

His accounts have been re-examined for examples of possible exaggeration or outright lying; incidents of cruelty to natives and fellow travellers have been noted. Sven had once been called the 'greatest explorer in the world' – no more. What his harshest critics will concede: at least Sven was kind to animals; there's no shooting and eating dogs as Amundsen did.

Hedin, who looks (he always removed his specs first) in photos like a robber baron in his Tibetan nomad's gear, had been turned back in 1902 after getting deep into Tibet. He returned in 1905 after the Younghusband expedition, reasoning that perhaps he would have more luck after Tibet's prestige had been somewhat dampened. In Simla he managed to impress all the big names: Minto, Kitchener, and Younghusband himself. But the India Office in London were less sure of this Swedish freebooter. They gave him permission only to visit Kashmir and Ladakh, where he might join a caravan to Turkestan. Hedin had enough backing to put together a caravan of 130 yaks, mules and dogs – which he loved more than people. He engaged thirty porters to carry his special gear – without which no bona fide explorer travels. Possibly influenced by the explorer's explorer, Stanley, Hedin brought with him a collapsible boat of oiled canvas, large-format camera and surveying equipment, and a burnished aluminium medical case full of useful drugs supplied by Burroughs and Wellcome.

Sven was driven by a belief in the heroic possibilities of exploration. Being 'first' to the source of a river or over an obscure desert or mountain range was the equivalent to him of the legendary feats of the heroes of old – Jason bringing back the Golden Fleece or Odin finding Mimir's Well. When times were bad and his spirits low, he would meditate on the Swedish hero Marcus Curtius who ended his life by spurring his horse into making an impossible leap over a vast abyss . . . suicide, yes, but suicide with bells and whistles and a go-faster stripe.

Hedin talked this heroic talk whenever he met influential men and potential sponsors. It called to their own sense of the heroic, which, in the late nineteenth century, was somewhat harder to locate in everyday life. It seems appropriate that Hedin's expeditions should be generously underwritten by that strangely conflicted dynamite millionaire Alfred Nobel. Indeed, when Sven and his team were starving during the eighty-day crossing of the Chang Tang Desert they at least had sacks of money: thousands of rupees which eventually allowed him to buy new supplies and pack animals from passing nomads.

Sven didn't believe in hobnobbing with the people he met, or with his porters. He kept himself to himself; even after perilous encounters with wolves and crazed yaks he didn't bond with his team. In his account, people do not merit much enthusiasm, whereas a funny incident involving a puppy or a mule will take up several generous sentences.

Not that there weren't adventures galore – Hedin understood that all the science in the world wasn't much use without being deeply in peril a lot of the time. Trying out his patent collapsible boat on Lake Lighten, the sail proved a liability when the wind blew up and he was forced to endure a night storm. On another lake the boat could not be used as it was frozen solid – as was the lake – so they explored on sledges. He was always off exploring, which really meant being the first European to see a new thing that had never been recorded before on a map. Because of course all of Tibet was frequented, then as now, albeit sparsely, by nomads.

Despite haggling with the Tibetan authorities, Sven never managed to get to Lhasa (years later he congratulated Heinrich

Harrer on his visit there). Instead, he turned back to the Kailash region where he discovered the sources of the Sutlej, the Indus and the Tsangpo/Brahmaputra. In a heroic but sacrilegious act, he unpacked his collapsible boat – which, two years on, was a little leaky – and ventured out on to the holy Lake Manasarovar. He upped the religious insult by paddling around on the sacred Rakshas Tal too. It was either brave or foolhardy, as such violations could be expected to meet with decapitation. In any case, the locals informed him he would surely perish as this was a dire trespass on the home of the gods. He dismissed their practical explanations too – that Manasarovar was actually a transparent dome of water – to sail on it would mean climbing up one face and then plunging dangerously down the other side. He took many soundings for depth and discovered the now dry channels that connect the lakes together and to the Sutlej. He believed that this meant the Sutlej and Tsangpo had their sources very close together. It was a theory also to be found in the eighteenth-century Chinese work on hydrography by Chi Chao Nan.

Three years had now gone by and after a quick re-equip in Ladakh, Sven went back for more. But eventually the Tibetans had had enough and deported him for good. And perhaps this was his real heroism: his ability to go for years and years all alone, devoted to the cause of exploration, beside which he held all else to be trivial. By giving himself such a grandiose task he had solved one dilemma which the pilgrims at Kailash solved in another way: how to give perspective to life so that little things do not become big things.

But unlike the pilgrims' progress, Sven Hedin's solution was temporary. The British establishment decided they didn't like the cut of his jib, even after it had been on all those uncharted lakes. Tom Longstaff suggested that the earlier British explorers Strachey and Smythe had found the Sutlej and Tsangpo sources first, grudgingly conceding that Hedin might just claim 'the distinction of being the first traveller to reach the ultimate source of the Indus'. During an RGS debate, it got so heated there had to be diplomatic intervention. His old supporter Curzon tried to make amends by awarding Sven a knighthood, but what Hedin wanted was glory, tons of it – he was, after all, the last of the real heroes. He decided to spurn Britain and supported the Kaiser in the First World War. Then he got involved in supporting people who *really* appreciated the myths of the past and the lure of conquering heroes: the Nazis. Another bad choice; after the war he was very much persona non grata, living quietly until 1952 in a modern highrise in Stockholm with his siblings inhabiting the floors above and below him.

Once you have stormed all the forbidden places on earth that really exist, what next? You go to war with the world. And when the smoke cleared, the Himalayas would still be there, but now the visions were more rarefied. After the First World War there could be no more talk of duty and honour, except in private or in speeches by hypocrites. The mountains became a source of purity, a place to escape the world and find yourself by going higher.

PART 4

Going Higher

SUMMIT 29,028 FEET

LADDER AT SECOND STEP

FIRST STEP

NORTHEAST RIDGE

CAMP

ADVANCE BASECAMP

NORTH COL CAMP IV

← YAK

BASE CAMP 17,000 FEET

NORTH FACE OF EVEREST

I

Climbing the Invisible

Cattle do not die from the jackal's curses.
Lepcha proverb

The world abounds in sacred summits. Some you are encouraged to climb, on others the summit is forbidden, but a nearby viewing point, lake or pass becomes an agreed pilgrimage spot. Indian and Tibetan sacred peaks are usually forbidden. Chinese summits are not; mostly it is a plus to climb them – the same is true in Japan with Fuji-san and countless smaller sacred peaks in that country.

Mountain meditation

Everest is not a sacred summit in the way that Kanchenjunga is. Though many – Western climbers included – believe that bad karma definitely might accrue if you were to climb it in the wrong way, disregarding local traditions and customs, perhaps.

A mountain is a rich symbol. The eye follows it upward. We refer to increase of any kind, usually positive, as a 'mountain'. A person moving upwards is a symbol of achievement, triumph over adversity. The height of the mountain symbolises its superiority over the plains, its nobility, stillness, permanence, coolness. The highest mountain is therefore the highest achievement; it is a kind of turning away from the futile barbarity of the First World War. By climbing the mountain we can forget; it also utilises the heroic – which inevitably is mocked by modern war – it is no accident that in the aftermath of both the First and Second World Wars a huge spurt in climbing took place.

Every ascent of a mountain is a passage to the beyond, to the place thought impossible. It is a symbolic entry into heaven, where all is laid out below for you to see and pass judgement upon. It is a place of temptation – didn't Satan take Jesus to the top of a mountain and show him the whole world, which could have been his? The top of the mountain is a place of transcendence – the human transcends his normal earthbound condition to climb higher. The otherworldly spacesuit-like apparatus of high altitude: the oxygen mask, the rack of cylinders, the huge overboot suggestive of a gravity boot used by a spaceman. Indeed, the more equipment the climber uses, the more we appreciate his transcendence. Super alpinists like Reinhold Messner who eschew gear as 'artificial' and climb Himalayan peaks with just boots and an ice axe are levelling and debasing those peaks; by their superhuman efforts they make them more ordinary, less sacred – in as much as any high peak is sacred by virtue of its transcendence-conferring qualities.

Even the first Everest expedition had oxygen tanks, though they were problematic and not used by everyone. And supplementary oxygen was used on the second too, which has become the quint-essential mythological climbing expedition: the 1924 failure in which Mallory and Irvine famously disappeared. Edward 'Teddy' Norton, the leader of that expedition, set a record of 8,573 metres without oxygen, a record that stood for fifty-four years. This was a few days before the mysterious disappearance of Mallory and Irvine. The fact that Norton climbed so high without oxygen helped foster the belief that Mallory and Irvine actually made it to the top before they fell. At the time, though, such thoughts mattered far less than whether the two men were alive or not. Norton wrote in his diary on the day of their summit attempt: 'Of all the truly miserable days I have spent at [Camp] III this [is] by far the worst. By now it appears almost inevitable that disaster has overtaken poor gallant Mallory & Irvine – 10 to 1 they have "fallen off" high up.'

The climber seeks to transcend his human condition, the weakness and emotion-wracked everydayness of his life. By climbing the mountain, he draws on reserves he did not know he had. He proves to himself many things. He is above other men, literally, when he is atop the mountain. Many smoke a cigarette in unconscious or conscious parody of a post-coital celebration. Climbers who are non-smokers may still smoke a symbolic cig-arette on the top of the mountain – even summits where the oxygen is rare in the extreme, like Everest. This overriding of their usual health concern is another element of the transcend-ence effect induced by climbing the mountain. The climber has reached the unreachable – especially if the peak has never been ascended before. But then there is a sort of sadness; it has been 'used up'. A common enough occurrence is a desire to not climb the last three or four metres of a climb, to leave the peak sacred. This is observed on specific sacred peaks such as Nanda Devi. The apparently agnostic Shipton and Tilman deliberately 'failed' to reach the very top, though after a Japanese team made the summit all later assault parties tended to go for the very top too.

It is interesting to speculate on why the Japanese sought to violate the traditions of the mountain; almost certainly it was a reflection of their own culture, where man is welcome at the summit and becomes less a supplicant of the gods than a welcome participant in the godly life, if only for a few moments, before lack of oxygen, bad weather, incipient fatigue, etc. draw him back down to a more ordinary existence.

When the climber dies in an attempt on the summit, and before his body appears – sometimes, as in the case of Mallory, tens of years later – on a rocky frozen mountainside (or, sometimes, emerging out of the bottom of a deep glacier), in that interregnum the stories begin to grow. These stories mimic the days after Christ's body disappeared from the tomb. Just as Christ was seen by various favoured people after his death, Odell claimed to have glimpsed Mallory going strong for the top.

The Nagas, in the far eastern continuation of the Himalayas, build totem-like 'skypoles' in favour of sacred summits, though on 12,553-metre Mount Saramati, they have a place venerated as a home of benign spirits. Skypole or mountaintop, the proximity to heaven is obvious. The winding path up a sacred mountain becomes a kind of Sulam Yaakov or Jacob's ladder. Indeed, the use of multiple ladders in the icefall sections on Everest, ladders stretching away upward to the snowy heights, is suggestive of a crude actualisation of the very ladder climbed by the prophet Jacob on his visit to heaven.

The very section which Mallory was supposed to have climbed – the second step – has been free-climbed with some difficulty by top modern climbers. Conrad Anker has climbed it twice; on the first occasion he claimed it would have been beyond Mallory, but climbing it again he said Mallory would have been able to make it. It is most usually climbed by the use of a ladder installed by the Chinese on their ascent of the north ridge in 1975.

Several Talmudic commentators suggest that the site of Jacob's ladder would have been an actual peak, such as the Temple

Mount in Jerusalem. What is important is the way a ladder is provided for the one seemingly in the wrong, but still in God's favour. The mountain rewards those willing to climb it with insights and status above those who loiter at base camp or on the plains.

Jacob, it is easy to lose sight of, is actually a trickster figure who constantly twits his older brother Esau, the hunter. Jacob uses the weaknesses of Esau against him; for example, when Esau is hungry, Jacob swaps a 'mess of pottage' – a bowl of soup – for Esau's birthright. Jacob also wears a sheepskin to make his father Isaac think he is the hairier Esau – this is symbolic trickery by its very implausibility. Jacob flees the enraged Esau, and it is during this period of indeterminacy that God provides the ladder to the heavens. Here he tells Jacob that all of the land of Israel shall be his. It is the symbolic overthrow of the hunter-gatherer life for the semi-settled pastoralist with all his claims of land and ownership – Esau, being a hunter, was unconcerned about such things.

Mallory – photographed wearing nothing but his saucy smile and a rucksack in the approach hike (probably impossible to do in the twenty-first century) – is very much the modern climber: no respecter of tradition. His famous comment – 'Because it is there' – seems to fly in the face of the po-faced statements about duty and excellence made before the war.

The mountain touches the heavens – it is the cross-over point, a sort of bridge. Again, the elaborate bridges over crevasses on the approach glaciers of Everest and other high peaks come to mind. The very existence of a super crevasse, the bergschrund, where the ice detaches from the mountain to create a chasm that must be bridged, links or leads us to the sky-bridging from summit to heaven that the mountaineer may symbolically achieve. Typically, the sighting of stars on a mountain is greeted with a proprietorial air, as if by climbing the peak one 'owns' the constellations, or the individual stars of the constellations, more than the unworthy mortals lower down. Indeed, the Sherpas are very awake to the appearance of special stars when climbing Everest. Before the disaster of 1996, a low star was seen in daylight, hovering over the western cwm. It sent the Sherpas into paroxysms of superstitious anxiety, an anxiety justified by the terrible nature of what subsequently happened.

The death of Mallory turns over in the mind with additional symbolic spin as it reminds us of Sir Thomas Malory, compiler of *Le Morte d'Arthur*. The climber Mallory becomes a knight errant with the inexperienced Irvine as his squire. The quest for the Grail is now a bid for the summit. The desire for Mallory to have succeeded in his quixotic quest now revolves around the fact that Mallory was intending to leave a photograph of his wife on the summit – and that photo was not on his body when it was found in 1999. This too mimics the obsessive dedication of Sir Lancelot, dedicating his quest for the Holy Grail to his ideal love, Guinevere.

The knightly quests of King Arthur's men are a courtly manifestation of the tasks – such as pilgrimage – set by a mystical master for his disciple. The quest, though, is not ritualised and safe like the pilgrimage. The pilgrim only makes a ritual ascension into heaven, he doesn't try to climb up there for real. The ritual nature of the event assures his safe descent. He is only a spiritual tourist, so to speak, seeing 'the heaven we show to visitors'.* His is simply one of countless ascents. We can see that a first ascent, however, is a kind of violation, though all too soon it, too, will become ritualised. Then climbers seek to make a new version. For example, on Everest we see first the south-eastern ridge (the Tibetan northern ridge, though the first to be explored, was only climbed in 1960 by the Chinese), and then the west ridge, then the south-west face, and finally the immensely hard Kangshung face being climbed.

---

* Idries Shah, 'Delights of a visit to Hell' in *Reflections*

By ascending the same peak but by different routes, the climber evades the ritual nature of the ascent and violates again the sacredness of the mountain. He makes a nihilistic compact to ascend into heaven and not return. The latent nihilism of climbing is noted by Phil Bartlett in his excellent *The Undiscovered Country*. The Sherpas perhaps understand this and force climbers to make copious ritual offerings before any attempt – and double that for a new route. Typically, new routes are punished by bigger accidents of greater severity; on one level, for entirely logical reasons, but on another level, this is the revenge of the mountain for violating the peak again. In an irreverently sexual sense, the mountain-dwelling people demand a proper marriage – the ritual ascent – whereas the climber, a Westerner typically torn loose from any established spiritual tradition, or part of one deeply alien to such high mountains, seeks, like a trickster, to get away with seducing a virgin peak. The climber as trickster – as we've seen – fits both the heroic Mallory and the controversial Messner.

The interest the Sherpas show in fixing ropes and making any route more and more permanent is not simply rooted in a financial sentiment. It is a desire to ritualise ascent and make it safer both literally and symbolically. The anger seen in 2013 when Sherpas cut the ropes of Swiss super alpinist Ueli Steck, is the anger of any ritual-minded people when an important ceremony is disturbed. Given the sacred nature of Mount Everest in so many indigenous cultures involved in its current financial exploitation, we must expect to see ever greater ritualisation of ascent. In the future it makes sense to expect fixed ropes up both the north and south ridges – from top to bottom and controlled not by Western inter-lopers but by the Sherpas themselves.

Any ascent of a mountain, sacred or otherwise, is a symbolic raid on the unreachable. It is to visit a place not possible for humans. The top of Olympus was, rightly, seen as the home of the immortals. There is a sense that to reach a truly unclimbable peak confers immortality – as indeed it has on the early ascenders of Everest, Hillary and Tenzing, albeit an immortality brokered by the materialist global/gobbling culture of the occidental world. But Hillary and Tenzing belong to the secular end of revealed religion, whereas Mallory is firmly canonised as some sort of mystical entity.

The unreachable is also a way of conceptualising the absolute. Nothing gives modern man more trouble than holding the idea of the absolute in mind *at the same time* as the obvious relative truths revealed by anthropology and sociology. Seemingly unassailable scientific theories are always by definition only relative truths. Beyond that, any man who claims the existence of absolute truths may find followers, but he will not be taught in the academy. Still the absolute remains as something we require as a backdrop to a stable existence, without which all notions of significance begin to crumble.

Do we desire unreachableness, just as we desire the absolute? There exists a tension between the unreachable and the desire to reach it, which can bring out, through stretching of human capacity, both a de-trivialising of life and a growth in real abilities, strength, singlemindedness and stamina. Mallory exists as a warning that the unreachable exacts a price, but his example remains an inspiration for all climbers. Comparing the tweed jackets and ventile hoods of the 1922 expedition with modern hi-tech clothing is a common conversation among climbers.

Sometimes the symbolic mountain is destroyed by man's greed. The sacred mountain of Gauri Shankar in Nepal was voted inviolable by the people indigenous to its lower flanks. But the government, anxious to make money from climbers wishing to ascend, overruled them. The sacred summit was violated. Many locals believed that earthquakes would follow, a demonic retribution for this violation. Reinhold Messner was asked by the Chinese to violate the summit of Mount Kailash, arguably the greatest sacred summit on the planet. He turned them down.

They could send a team of their own climbers, but interestingly they have not.

The higher mountains will always remain a refuge for mystics, hermits, the nomadic, the mad, the trickster and the outlaw. They are content to contemplate the unreachable or dwell in their secret mazy ways.

2

Those Crazy Russians

―――――

Tomorrow there will be apricots.
Proverb common in the Himalayas

The advantage of a mountain to map-makers is that it is high
– you can see it from far away. So the peaks are the first to be
labelled and lose their mystery. But what of the remaining hidden
high places? Like most explorers drawn to the Himalayas, Sven
Hedin wanted to find a hidden kingdom; it is one of the most
enduring myths of the region.

The idea of a hidden kingdom, where life is perfect, where
men live to be hundreds of years old, where wisdom has been
sought and found – this idea is a very ancient one and yet it has,
in the last 150 years or so, become both more prominent and more
powerful. Now, when we suspect the world is all explored, the
Shangri-La or Shambhala myth lives on in the form of exiled
Himalayan peoples – the Tibetans, the Afghans, the Nagas –
who, if only they could return to their homeland would restore its
most ancient and magical properties.

In the early twentieth century, dreamers from the West went
looking for Shangri-La. Those from Europe and America may
have been spiritual tourists, harmless cranks or simply over curious. Those from the newly formed USSR had more sinister plans
afoot.

It is a fact that tends to get overlooked but early Soviet Russia was a decidedly esoteric and nutty place. Ideas of the strangest sort – if they promised any sort of advantage for the promised land of the proletariat – were pursued with gusto. It was a place where nonsensical ideas about agriculture promulgated by a complete fraud – Lysenko – had the backing of the entire ruling establishment. Is it any surprise, then, that a department of OGPU – the forerunner of the KGB – was devoted to investigating the occult and using it to spread communism?

Gleb Bokii characterised this fascinating mix of the weird with the prosaic. In addition to being an efficient secret policeman – he was head of the ultra-secret OGPU department of codes and cryptography – Gleb had a collection of mummified penises. Why, you might ask. The answer isn't easy to find . . . He was a small and delicate man, remembered for his politeness and excellent manners, his interest in the occult, his womanising and his belief in the existence of a secret kingdom, a 'powerhouse' of spirituality somewhere in the Himalayas. The idea wasn't new. Notions of Shambhala and Agartha had been promoted since the nineteenth century, ancient myths propounded as real places by early scholars like Sándor Csoma Kőrösi and mystical writers such as Helena Blavatsky.

In the early twentieth century a new mystic appeared who was rather different to Madame Blavatsky. He was born in the Russian Empire, in the Caucasus, of Greek and Armenian ancestry and his name was G. I. Gurdjieff. Gurdjieff would embellish the myth of the 'powerhouse monasteries' of the Himalayas and fire up communists like Bokii and others to go searching for them.

I first came across Gurdjieff when I bought a desk he'd owned during his last days in Paris. It's a good desk but I can't say that it has given me any supernatural powers. But after reading about the man I could see why he was so influential in the early and mid twentieth century. Unlike Madame Blavatsky, Gurdjieff had a *method*. Through books written by his most prominent disciple, Peter Ouspensky (a writer who sadly curtailed novel writing when he became interested in becoming a teacher like Gurdjieff – his single novel, *Strange Life of Ivan Osokin*, is remarkably promising), Russians and later Europeans became aware of this bald-headed superman who hailed, like Stalin, from somewhere in the Caucasus.

Gurdjieff first popped up in Moscow in 1912, offering instruction in many mysteries including strange dancing and music that he claimed would ultimately lead to enlightenment. This was all of Central Asian Sufi origin, but Gurdjieff, learning from Blavatsky, sought to be obscure about where he got his material. He borrowed from the Sufis the idea of group work, pursuing a limited but nonsensical objective to build focus, the notion of the 'observing self' that watches and notes the ordinary workings of the mind and the emotions, but removed the Islamic context. He had travelled widely and had a powerful personality. He had mastered all the skills of the man of mystery: he could hypnotise, he was very persuasive, he was deeply intuitive and highly energetic. But plenty of people have all of the above and fail to attract one disciple of merit (it's rather easier to attract nutters, as Charles Manson proved). But Gurdjieff did attract people of quality – such as the writers Katherine Mansfield and Peter Ouspensky – because he didn't just talk, he actually appeared to be master of any situation he found himself in. Ouspensky was highly sceptical at first, and went along to meet Gurdjieff prepared to scoff. But the more he saw him interact with others, the more impressed he was. Most gurus Ouspensky had seen, and this included seers like Rasputin, were incompetent human beings. Gurdjieff appeared to be super competent.

It is this quality – and the fact that a reputable journalist and writer is telling you, rather than Gurdjieff himself (after Ouspensky and Gurdjieff had the inevitable falling out, Gurdjieff penned his own books – some almost unreadable, others, such as *Meetings with Remarkable Men*, both instructive and enjoyable) that makes Gurdjieff's claims – that there are 'powerhouses' of knowledge in the Himalayas – so compelling. In Gurdjieff's version, there is a secret Sarmoung Monastery somewhere in the mountains – maybe Afghanistan or Tibet or Bhutan or Mustang; this monastery, and others connected to it, are pumping out vibrations that are literally controlling the planet on some deep level. Gurdjieff claimed that the Pyramids in Egypt were an attempt to pursue, through a kind of doctrine of signatures, a similarly powerful effect by building a micro-Himalaya in a fairly flat country. Be that as it may, the reports of Gurdjieff's groups, the fact that he had Westerners progressing in these arcane areas rather than simply hanging around Tibetan Buddhists and copying them – all this was tremendously exciting to certain revolutionaries, since it also chimed in with the communist ideals of the time: communal living, group work, pursuit of the idea of a 'new man', a kind of superman, living in harmony, breaking with the past and, above all, though sympathetic to the core of all religions, rejecting the authority of any one creed over another. What the Russians took from Gurdjieff was a kind of Westernised mysticism in which personal development outshone almost everything else.

It was powerful stuff because, in short, it works; as Sufis have shown throughout the centuries in the countries where they have lived, from Morocco to India to Indonesia. Small dedicated groups of wisely chosen people who can set aside ego and pettiness can achieve great things; it is widely accepted that the Arab renaissance in science, which kickstarted the European interest in science, was due to Sufi activity.

But because Bokii and his colleagues were greedy, they forgot that the basic tenet of Sufism is service, not power. They focused on the crazy stuff: the tall tales, the mind reading and mind bending, and mythological materials whose function was certainly not intended to start a world crusade to Tibet looking for a lost paradise.

There is a comforting irony in communism – a religion which abhorred the supernatural – being so easily enticed into partnership with the most supernatural and spooky elements of mystical Islam and Buddhism. But Stalin himself sanctioned the search for Shambhala, believing, like Napoleon, that religion was a political tool that could be exploited.

A drop-out medical student called Barchenko was recruited by the penis gatherer, Bokii, to go in search of Shambhala, or the remains of its power. Bokii, like many idealistic revolutionary types, was drawn to both knowledge – which he characterised as ultimate truth – and power. It is the kind of mix that makes most seekers after truth blighted almost before they have started: they want to use the knowledge they find to achieve power. Being idealists, it is not power over others so much as power to 'do good' and establish a perfect society, the kind of society that was dreamt of by the Russian revolutionary comrades of Lenin and Trotsky. Bokii had been appointed by Lenin because of these idealistic credentials. Yet the bloodshed and horror of the red terror led him to seek for truth elsewhere. His vague interest in the East and the occult took a practical turn when he met Barchenko.

Barchenko was another power seeker – for good, of course; he believed that occult powers such as telepathy, telekinesis and remote viewing would all be explained by scientific theories; it was just that we lacked the right theory. Meanwhile, one should do what any good scientist would do and experiment. Barchenko wired up people's heads with metal helmets connected to each other via long copper wires. The idea was that one person thought of a word and wrote it down. The 'receiver' then tried to get the message. The results were problematic, but Barchenko claimed that when he switched to transmitting images it worked quite well. He also made an early study of 'arctic madness' – a kind of group hysteria found in Finland and Lapland, where sufferers have fits and see visions. (A real phenomenon, it has obvious links to the more controlled use of visions by shamans in Siberia.)

Fuelled by the lectures of Gurdjieff and meetings with Agvan Dorjiev (more of him later) Barchenko became obsessed with finding secret powers that could put communism back on track.

But though both Bokii and Barchenko enjoyed a brief period of popularity with Stalin and his gang, the powers they sought never really materialised, certainly not enough to save them. Bokii was sentenced to death on 15 November 1937 and shot the same day. Barchenko was executed the following year. But another Russian was a little luckier; his name was Nicholas Roerich.

3

St Nick the Guru

Do not base your beliefs on what you overhear.

Naga proverb

Nicholas Roerich – a painter and would-be guru – enjoys today quite a reputation as a cultural explorer of Tibet and Mongolia. Unlike Blavatsky and Gurdjieff, he kept his nuttier ideas half-hidden. Born in Petrograd in 1874 and active in pre-revolutionary Russia, Roerich read Blavatsky and was influenced by Gurdjieff and the enigmatic Dorjiev.

Dorjiev emerges as a key figure in the whole Soviet intrigue in the Himalayas. Agvan Dorjiev, as you'll recall, was the thorn in Curzon's side, the 'Russian lama' who had been a teacher of the thirteenth Dalai Lama and encouraged Tibet to draw closer to Russia. Shortly after the Younghusband expedition, Dorjiev, confirming Curzon's suspicions, took up residence in Petrograd to further his ambitions to obtain Russian backing for a vast Buddhist empire in the east. He had considerable luck with Czar Nicholas II; more so than with his father Alexander III, who wrote, 'All of this is so new, so unusual and fantastic, that it is difficult to believe in its success.'

Nicholas II was convinced. He gave the go-ahead to build a Buddhist temple and dormitory in the capital. It drew support from many places. Nicholas Roerich, as an artist, was able to design and install its stained-glass windows.

In 1919 the Bolsheviks – who had persecuted Orthodox Christianity mercilessly – sponsored an exhibition of Buddhist art. Tibetan Buddhism was treated as a religion of a formerly oppressed people; by reaching out to it, the communists hoped to spread the Buryat rebellion further south. The Buryats were Russian Buddhists who had rebelled against their Mongolian lords to establish a soviet-like state. Dorjiev, as a Buryat lama, was riding high again.

Meanwhile, Roerich was pursuing his own path that had taken him away from the Buddhist temple in Petrograd via a short stay in Finland to Paris and then London. He followed clues from his wife, who was able to channel a spirit entity into talking through her either directly or with automatic writing. At first, Roerich relied solely on his wife's connection (which had miraculously cured her of congenital headaches) but he found that with some concentration he could put himself into a trance state and then write without knowing what he was writing. The entity was the spirit of the fifth reincarnation of the Buddha. Judging by the diaries of Helena Roerich, they relied on this spirit for pretty much every decision – nothing was too trivial for the Buddhist deity to advise upon, be it food, friends or the big mission, which was to establish a new order of enlightened beings on earth starting in . . . well, not London. In London there were too many big wheels, esoterically speaking – Ouspensky (whom the spirit had bade them both to re-read) was in town, and people were popping across the Channel to see Gurdjieff all the time. Roerich was second eleven at best. It is strange that he didn't try to join those whose work inspired him – but when you want to be a guru, other gurus are there mainly as sources of material you can steal rather than for instruction, which would be a little humiliating, especially if any disciples were around. One wonders what happened to the Sufi teacher's dictate – 'You show me your wisdom, and if you want, I will show you my wisdom.'

So London was out. Which left New York – a great place for folk looking to make friends and influence people. Which the Roeriches did. Coming up with a remarkably similar stratagem to Dale Carnegie, Nicholas Roerich followed the simple formula of making himself agreeable to useful and influential people, and then listening to them talk. When they ran out of things to say he would, bit by bit, draw them into the Shambhala fold. There was an inner circle, who all received special rings (strangely, Freud did the same thing with his inner circle of students) and Tibetan names and then a slightly larger circle who received less freaky names – inspired by Arthurian legend. Then there were simply well-wishers, who were there to buy the paintings. The Roeriches were nothing if not mercenary. People were there to be used and to be useful to the great cause.

The Roeriches managed to make several journeys to Tibet and Mongolia. The first was sponsored by American money, but the later ones received their backing from the Soviet Union. Nicholas Roerich was not the first person to think he could use Bolshevism to further his own plans. But he was not a completely willing participant in Red espionage. His brother Boris had been unable to escape the Soviet Union after the Revolution. As a former White officer, he was at some risk. In 1929 his apartment was searched for signs of espionage. In an abrupt turn, he was recruited into OGPU, forerunner of the KGB. Two years later, perhaps having over-extended his brief, he was arrested for smuggling artefacts to the West. Yet after only two months in prison, he was given a deal involving a generous form of house arrest. Trained as an architect, he was eventually given the task of helping design a building for the Leningrad branch of the secret police and a dacha for Stalin himself, entitled 'The Big House'. He then began working on the enormous VIEM project building – the Stalinist successor to Gleb Bokii's secret unit dedicated to looking at strange and unexplained phenomena. He was obviously in favour, as in 1937, just when so many people were disappearing to the gulags, he moved to an upmarket neighbourhood in Moscow where he lived until his death in 1945.

By some bizarre coincidence, Nicholas had also been involved in a massive building project with esoteric overtones. 'The Master Building' was the name of the twenty-nine-storey skyscraper that he had persuaded a multimillionaire currency dealer called Horch to build on strictly esoteric Buddhist principles. It's still there, at 310 Riverside Drive, New York. Now a historic landmark and exclusive residence full of fancy apartments, few know that buried in its foundations lies a treasure chest containing Tibetan coins and a letter with a prophecy of a new golden age. Ask the doorman about it and he'll simply tell you the place was 'once owned by some weird Russian painter'.

Shambhala becomes Shangri-La in James Hilton's *Lost Horizon* – this novel was the source of revived interest in the idea. Our Zen monk explorer, Kawaguchi, suggested the Russian Czar wanted to lead a Buddhist empire based on the Shambhala myth, and it

Another valley, another bridge to cross

was visions of this that so scared Curzon and Younghusband.

Of Shambhala, the current Dalai Lama has rather beautifully commented that it is a real place but only visible to those with purified eyes. The idea is certainly powerful. It was mainly prop- agated in the West, as we have seen, by Nicholas Roerich. He had great influence in the United States, especially on Henry Wallace – Franklin D. Roosevelt's Secretary for Agriculture. And FDR was hugely influenced by Wallace, who exuded a kind of 'being there' simplicity that impressed Roosevelt. It was Wallace who fell for Stalin's lies, and no doubt this encouraged the naïve view that Roosevelt had of that tyrant. Such naïvety would dearly cost the people of Eastern Europe for the next forty years . . . Roosevelt had a country retreat built in the Maryland hills and called it Shangri-La; we know it now as Camp David.

Epilogue: Roerich's paintings continue to rise in price long after his death. *The Miracle of Madonna Laboris* sold in June 2013 for £7.9 million at Bonhams, the highest price to date in a Russian art auction.

Madonna Laboris's inspiration is an apocryphal gospel. It shows the gates of heaven guarded by St Peter. Peter is perturbed and says to the Lord: 'All day long I watch the gates of Paradise; I do not let anyone in, yet in the morning there are newcomers in Paradise.'

4

The First Interrogation of
Agvan Dorjiev: Siberia, 1938

If a crow could hunt, what need would there be for keeping a falcon?
Garwhal proverb

It was an ordinary police station. An office, some old ledgers on a shelf. The young man sent to interrogate him did not know him, even got his name wrong. But the charge sheet was long, the file, in a brown cardboard flimsy was full. The young man, prematurely and aggressively bald, was able to leaf through it like an art expert leafing through a delightful portfolio of watercolours.

'So, you started a Buddhist temple in Leningrad? In 1916. This was presumably a front for Japanese Buddhist spies.'

Agvan, the Buryat Lama, was eighty-four years old. He was aware of what would happen. He was exhausted too. All those compromises. All the things he had turned a blind eye to. He had hung on to his dream of power for so long. It was burned deep into him. Then one day he knew he would die soon and he hurried home, back to the Buryat people of his youth in Siberia. His whole mind was on leaving this world, but still he lived!

In the long summer of 1937 the dappled green of poplars and larches was overwhelming. He felt the inexorable wonder and completeness of the world he was meant to leave. Of course he would be reborn, but long years rubbing shoulders with frank and

Agvan Dorjiev, the monk who played politics

brutal materialists, like the young man in front of him, manufacturing blunt awkward lies, had sharpened doubts; not doubting the reality of reincarnation, but the details. Sometimes there was complete slippage. He got depressed for a second or two and imagined himself finished and buried under the earth floor of a police yard. As he'd come in, he had seen the turned and stamped clay along the wall, shot and buried, move on.

He had seen so much, he had met two Czars, taught the Dalai Lama. He had been the cause of the Younghusband invasion of Tibet, had dealings with Lenin and Stalin. What had it amounted to? Mere shaking of the curtain's edge. He'd long since realised that the attempt to use Bolshevism was futile. It used you. You cannot be a parasite on something that is determined to consume you. The grip always slips.

'You made contact with the Japanese spy Kawaguchi in Lhasa. Through him, you supplied information that resulted in the destruction of the Russian fleet.'

On the unending train journey from Leningrad to Siberia he had worked through day by day a familiar trope: how he had drawn the British into Tibet, how his friendship with the thirteenth Dalai Lama had worked both for and against him, resulting in stalemate. He had resented that for years, but now he saw that this had kept Tibet free of the red scourge. There were no real Russians left, only members of Stalin's cult.

He was an old man. He could hardly see well enough to read. After each day's interrogation, he had to sign papers. He did it all willingly enough. Never oppose, always turn, let the wind whip by, just as it whips by the fragile windhorse flags of a monastery.

One thing he had done right. Once he'd realised he was a pawn used by Moscow to destroy the unity of Buddhists in the Soviet Union – the very opposite of his entire life's work – he'd set about sabotaging their efforts. In formal letters sent with red agents to Tibet, whose purpose was to establish a Soviet Trojan horse in the country, Agvan extolled the virtues of his communist bosses. But he had not lost his Buryat cunning. He sent secret handwritten missives using the Lhasa dialect to the Dalai Lama. These were carried by a trusted merchant travelling from Mongolia to Tibet. He'd written:

> I am an old man and will die very soon. Mongolia is not a peaceful country as it was formerly. The government is deadly against religions and monks, and they are helpless. Please don't have anything to do with the mission. I had to write a letter at their dictation to Your Holiness for these Bolshevik agents to take with them, but please do not take any notice of that letter.

The Dalai Lama allowed the covert Bolshevik mission to wander wherever they wished – but they were spied on wherever they went. No permission was given for a permanent embassy – not even Britain was allowed one, it was pointed out. The Dalai Lama expressed his friendship in vague terms, but the price of an audience (the face-to-face meeting kept being postponed) was that they should leave the next day. So they did, empty-handed.

The foolish young man and his masters knew nothing of this letter. Instead, they insisted on constructing a false case against him. Through the high window he could see nothing except the light blue sky, with that peculiar luminescence it has in Siberia; it had been a longing to see that light for the last time that had drawn him back.

'Is it not true that the reason for your current residence in Siberia is to organise counter-revolution and oppose the closing of Buddhist monasteries here? Monasteries that will be used in the Japanese invasion of the Soviet Union as counter-revolutionary bases?'

He was uncomfortable, but he was not restrained in any way. He found hard chairs uncomfortable and he preferred to kneel any day: at eighty-four, his thighs were so thin that kneeling presented no difficulty. His friends had told him the first interview was always easy – if you confessed, they shot you straight away. If you held out, they would interview you again, this time with torture. If that failed, then the third interrogation would begin with threats to one's family and friends. No one could resist that.

'Is it not true that in 1929 you buried nine hundred thousand steel needles in the Trans-Baikal to try and stir up fascist folk religion against the Communist Party?'

He answered for the record: 'Yes, it is true that I helped establish a new prayer site for the Kalachakra tantra, that is, the wheel of time meditation.'

'And you admit the charge of dabbling in folk religion and primitive witchcraft?'

'No.'

'I read here that the nine hundred thousand needles will become the "spirits of future warriors who will create the kingdom of Shambhala – a Buddhist kingdom". These are your words, are they not?'

'At the time, Comrade Stalin himself agreed to the formation of the Baikal prayer site.'

The young man shouted, 'That is a lie!'

Agvan allowed himself the luxury of smiling; he knew he would have no such luxury when they came for him again. He would not utter lies, though.

If he straightened his stiffening back it looked as though he was paying more attention, giving more respect. He could, by stretching his spine upwards, gain a glimpse of a velvety pink branch, just about to bud into bloom. It moved in the wind outside. It would be hot soon, everyone was surprised at how hot Siberia could get on a cloudless summer day.

'Is it not true that in the summer of 1923 you used the dormitory of the Buddhist centre in Leningrad as a meeting place for fellow spies, such as Barchenko?'

'I met Barchenko several times. He was a man seeking the miraculous. He did not realise it is everywhere. Neither did I, until recently. I thought it needed its own country to thrive. But all it needs is a slight turning away. Even in Soviet Russia the miraculous cannot be extinguished.'

The young man smiled. 'Quite right. The Soviet Union is a place of miracles – economic miracles.'

Agvan also smiled. He knew that this deluded soul had some part of him that was not bad, and might yet be good.

'Will you shoot me then?' he asked.

The young man did not look up from his papers. He said, 'The revolutionary court decides all matters. Besides, it is well known, there is no death penalty in the Soviet Union. Now, is it not true that you vouched for Barchenko and in return he received one hundred thousand roubles to establish spy networks for Japan?'

'That money was all used in his travels around the Soviet Union and in his attempts to discover secret sources of knowledge.'

'Do you admit to trying to organise with him a counter-revolutionary movement, first in Mongolia and Tibet, and then in the Soviet Union . . .'

The questioning went on for three days. He was fed borscht

with small unidentifiable pieces of meat. The famines had been felt here too. He was offered vodka. In the past, he had drunk deeply with Bolsheviks of every stripe. They had been like brothers in the early days of the revolution. But one by one they had turned away, saying, 'My loyalty is always to communism, my loyalty is always to the leadership, that must always precede whatever friendship we may have had.' It had been hard to believe, that men who had saved his life at risk to their own would eventually turn against him, with reluctance, but they would turn.

Ah, it wasn't like that under the Czar. He had been sixty when the revolution happened. But the nomadic Buryats were hardy people. The oracle in Tibet had predicted he would live two lives in one lifetime. After the revolution, he had indeed lived another life. He had put his dealings with the Czar behind him and embraced the Red instead. It was purer and much closer to the truth, he felt – at first. All men were brothers it seemed in those days. With the Czar there had been so much corruption – but he now saw that it was nothing compared to the total corruption of minds that Stalin had helped bring about. He thought back to the Buddhist temple the Czar had allowed to be built, had given the land for free and encouraged donations. That was a great moment – the raising of the Kalachakra Temple in 1916. No one had any clue what would happen the following year. At least the Czar had been a human being, for all the faults of the court.

There was no doubt in his mind now that all revolutions were against the 'wheel of time', the Kalachakra itself. All things came in their own time; when man forced the pace of events he brought nothing but calamity upon himself and others. Men were not meant to 'change the world', he saw that clearly now; they were meant to accept it, obey its strictures and be joyful in heart.

There was light at the centre of everything, said the inner teaching of the Kalachakra. That light was pure joy. The emotions clouded it, veiled it. The intellect clouded and veiled it, sometimes darkened it completely. The body, in pain or pleasure, could veil it, but beyond all – and this was all you could say in words – was a shining element of joy, shimmering, burgeoning like sunrise. Why had it taken so long to understand this simple thing?

The interview ended suddenly. He felt a little ill and said so. 'All right, we postpone for today,' said the young man, slapping the file shut so that the breeze could be felt.

But he did feel ill. It was not an excuse. He could not lie on the hard plank bunk in the police prison cell. He knelt on the floor. Then he bent forward to relieve the searing pain. It was really strange that the pain suddenly ebbed away. He heard his uncle's voice, which he had not heard for sixty years.

In the morning, Agvan Dorjiev was found dead of a heart attack in his cell. His body was removed to the police mortuary, where it was photographed, then kept waiting outside, owing to the pressure of bodies there to be admitted.

5

Tilman Goes East

In my homeland I possess one hundred horses,
but if I go, I go on foot.
Bhutanese proverb

Shipton and Tilman were the kings of interwar Himalayan climbing. Forget Mallory and Irvine and the sad shenanigans on Everest, Shipton and Tilman were the kings . . .

'My choice fell upon the Assam Himalaya as being the most accessible and the least known region for exploration.' So wrote Major Harold 'Bill' Tilman, who no one seems to have called Bill; his sister called him Willy, his fellow soldiers Tilly, and to most other people, including his longtime climbing partner Eric Shipton, he was plain Tilman. When after ten or more years of climbing together Shipton suggested they might call each other by their first names, Tilman thought about it for a minute and then protested, 'It sounds so damn silly!'

Tilman wanted to climb Namche Barwa, which bookends the main stretch of the Himalayas in the East. It's a high (7,782 metres) and dangerous mountain, which, like Nanga Parbat, its western counterpart at the other end, resisted climbing for many years; in fact, it was the world's highest unclimbed peak when it finally succumbed in 1992. But Namche Barwa is firmly in Tibet and was out of bounds to Tilman in 1939. He focused instead on the peaks within British Indian borders: Kangto (7,090), Gori

Chen (6,538) and Nyegyi Kansang (7,047) – all unclimbed guardians of that river which bursts through the immense barrier of the Himalayas and turns from being the Tibetan Tsangpo into the Indian Brahmaputra. But Gori Chen, a low peak by Himalayan standards, would be no easy hike in the hills. Tough conditions always appealed to Tilman. And he loved exploring: 'I also hoped to make a map; not in the cause of pure science, but with the utilitarian notion of its possible usefulness to myself in the future.' His two fingers to science, received opinion, most forms of authority while also maintaining decorum, neatly cut hair and a dislike for bohemians is all part of his endearing Englishness – as was his love of dogs and mountain people – both of which he was able to get on with far better, it seemed, than his fellow Englanders. Tilman, who fought in both wars – in the second parachuting behind enemy lines at forty-three – was a shy, supremely tough eccentric, who, aged seventy-nine, disappeared on an expedition sailing between Chile and the Falkland Islands. Despite having a back injury that gave him pain, sustained in a climbing accident in the 1930s, he kept up his adventurous exploits to the very end of his life. Though he never married, he admitted, 'I've had my peccadilloes'.

But visiting Arunachal Pradesh in the 1939 rainy season would test his toughness to the maximum.

The upper limit of hill cultivation is around 2,000 metres. Above that lies the temperate rainforest, which begins to peter out into rhododendrons and conifers around 3,000 metres. Altitude is not the only factor in determining what grows where. The surrounding vegetation has an effect. If the mountains do not exceed 2,500 metres – in Nagaland, for example – then there will be no temperate rainforest; everything is covered in what can be called hill jungle. Only in mountains that exceed 3,500 metres can we expect to see a band of temperate rainforest existing. The line where hill jungle meets rainforest is always shifting. In gorges that run deep and damp, the jungle manages to rise high and

aggressive above the 2,500-metre line. But when there are very high mountains in the range it seems to provide the temperate rainforest with a confidence that extends its reach down into what would be usually thought of as jungle areas.

In April, Tilman started from Darjeeling. It was before the monsoon yet there were still mosquitoes and leeches to bother him as he moved up through the relentless jungle of the foothills of Arunachal Pradesh.

Temperate forests are characterised by sheer variety. While the jungle is all broad-leafed trees and the high forest belt all conifers, the temperate rainforest contains a mixture of both. It is not entirely evergreen or deciduous. In natural temperate rainforest, no two trees in contact are alike.

Tilman was not used to serious jungle travel. He had lived and worked in Kenya for fourteen years at an altitude of 2,000 metres – where the air is cool and pleasant year-round. He had crossed Africa by bicycle – though this had been on roads and tracks and not by hacking your way through slippery steaming vegetation dripping with leeches and, at night, swarmed by mosquitoes. It was also hot. Tilman wore shorts and his lightweight approach meant that mosquito nets had been left behind. He was hampered too by a strong prejudice against science – which, in this case, was right in assuming that malaria came from mosquito bites and not, as Tilman half-seriously suggested, from an 'unscientific diet'. There was not enough quinine, though he did bring ample quantities of cocaine for use against snow blindness – but the snow was not to be encountered.

After they had climbed above 500 metres (the initial foothills had been only 200 metres above sea level) the party were beset by blister flies or 'dimdams' that bit incessantly, leaving behind a tiny irritating blood blister. And at night, mosquitoes feasted upon the men. Malaria soon began to show its ugly symptoms. Managing to cross some passes over 3,500 metres they still spent days resting up, too feverish to move. Tilman took his plane table and surveying equipment to 5,000 metres, but the effort cost him a week shivering and sweating in his sleeping bag. When he recovered, he found that the Sherpas were faring just as badly, and in one case, worse. Nukku, who had been on Everest with Tilman, died of cerebral malaria. They buried him and built a cairn, as Sherpas do, over his grave. The expedition was over. The headman of the nearest mountain village helped them evacuate the area. Tilman rode on a dzo, the same beast that the Dalai Lama would escape over the Assam Himalayas upon some twenty years later. A beast of last resort.

Tilman wrote: 'It is easy to be wise after the event. There are several precautions that might have been taken . . . mosquito nets, trousers instead of shorts, bamber oil [citronella-based insect repellent] and heavier prophylactic doses of quinine would all help reduce the risks.'

The master of lightweight, fast-moving, tough expeditioning had met his match. Perhaps Tilman had underestimated the place simply because it wasn't as high as Nepal and the Karakoram. Sixty years later, top British climber Doug Scott would have a similar experience trying to climb the same mountain of

Gori Chen. His eighteen days in the jungle resulted in malaria, a twisted knee and diphtheria, and no attempt at actual climbing on snow and ice had been possible.

Travelling later on would have made things easier – though colder once you got above the snow line. I visited Arunachal Pradesh in winter and found the forests leech-free, the rains abated. I spent a few days scrambling up through the jungle and it was tough going; stray off the main path and the smaller paths are little more than game trails that fizzle out. It is steep unrelenting country and the snow line is higher than in the western end of the Himalayas. In the end, I turned back before I had cleared the trees, but not before I had heard a tiger's cough deep in the shaded interior.

6

Escape from Dehradun

The bullock disappeared while in the act of ploughing.
Garwhal proverb

Up over the Himalayas was Heinrich Harrer's plan. Fresh from
failing to ascend the dangerous mountain of Nanga Parbat in 1939
– which we've already encountered – Harrer almost made it back
to Germany before war was declared . . . but not quite. He and his
fellow climbers were locked up very politely by the British. They
even admired him when he made a break for it, but nevertheless
made strenuous efforts to get him back. He was interned in 1939.
His final break, after several false starts, was in 1944. The war
had almost ended. Harrer must have known the game was almost
finished, but he would have his adventure yet.

There is something so outlandish, unnecessary and extraordinary about the whole Harrer episode – escaping over the
mountains, where he befriends the young Dalai Lama, eventually
becoming his teacher and confidant. We must recall that only
the British had access to Tibet in the pre-war period, which
meant the most outstanding climbers in Europe – mainly Germans, at that time – could not try their hand on the world's
highest peak. They were forced to try something as difficult, if
not more difficult, but not as high. This meant Nanga Parbat. And
since Mummery, the greatest of the early climbing pioneers, had
died on this peak, Nanga Parbat, if climbed, would be a kind of

commiseration prize for not being allowed to climb Everest.

It wasn't easy. The sheer numbers of Germans who had perished trying to climb Nanga Parbat had its legacy in the sensible caution of Heinrich Harrer's failed attempt in 1939. Locked up as enemy aliens, he and his friends had plenty of time to cogitate and plan an escape. Escaping would be 'their war' – though this is never mentioned in Harrer's memoir, *Seven Years in Tibet*, with its conscious biblical overtones – getting to Tibet would be his victory over the British Empire. Symbolically, the war was to be won by his huge sacrifice and the achievement of crossing the world's highest mountain range and penetrating the most mysterious country on earth, the source of all spiritual mysteries for many.

But it would not be easy.

In the final escape from India, Harrer decides to travel alone. He is a slippery narrator. He writes as if he is a simple climber with no ambition, save to climb peaks and perhaps earn his money by teaching the children of the wealthy. He abhors the twentieth-century disease of everybody being in a rush. The Tibetans don't do this rush thing. They arrive late at the office (in Lhasa, this is) and depart early. In the 1930s when Mahjong is introduced, it becomes an epidemic. Almost all work is neglected. Servants lose their life savings in a few hours. The government decide it is bad for the country so they ban it – by buying up all the sets in existence. Once the games have been fairly bought up they are destroyed and then an edict is issued condemning any secret transgressors to terrible punishment. And Harrer observes some terribly harsh punishment: a petty thief who stole a golden butter lamp from a temple had his hands publicly amputated, then he was sewn up into a wet yak skin and hurled off a vertiginous cliff.

Every now and again he lets out a strong opinion – strong enough for us to realise he probably has many more, just better hidden. He comes across a nun and a monk who have been condemned to a hundred lashes; the pair had been in a secret relationship which resulted in a child neither of them wanted, so the young mother killed the baby. Harrer can't understand the local reaction, which is, as the couple are being whipped, to beg the authorities to be lenient. He wants this woman harshly punished as a murderer, yet he fails to see that in traditional cultures children are so vulnerable to an early death that attachment to them is suspended until they pass their earliest years. He wants to see the entire hundred lashes administered.

Harrer met up with his pals when they reached Tibet. The next challenge was to get to Lhasa – this is never really explained, except HH has a vague plan that in the capital he can make a living tutoring the sons of the wealthy. The further away they were from the capital, the harder it seemed; none of the officials they met would give them a permit. So they wandered along the border with Nepal, surreptitiously getting closer all the time. Harrer and the last remaining pal – also a climber – made their way across the snowy wastes; the non-climbers, finding the going too tough, had all returned to India or Nepal. They decided to approach Lhasa from the north, an unexpected thing, and something no one in their right mind would attempt – so said all the nomads they came across and lodged with. Sometimes the nomads invited them into their tents, sometimes they seemed scared of their red beards and gaunt, bedraggled appearance, mistaking them for Kazakhs who had entered Tibet, or Indian traders. But the main fear of the nomads were Khampas: roving bands of armed brigands who parasitically lived off the unarmed nomads in their felt tents. One nomad told Harrer he paid 500 sheep to buy a modern Mannlicher rifle – it was worth it, he claimed, to keep the Khampas at bay.

Being foolhardy and brave, Harrer and his pal decided to ignore all advice and head across Khampas country. Before long they discovered that they were being followed by men on horseback. Dodging their pursuers, they came upon a nomad encampment and decided it would be a good place to hide. They were welcomed in at the tent door with such friendly politeness, their suspicions were immediately aroused. A normal nomad, fearful of the Kham-pas, would give them a hard time until it was proven they were harmless. To be taken at face value, welcomed in, could mean only one thing. The two travellers exchanged horrified glances; both men knew they had fallen right into a Khampas household.

Outside it was 40 degrees below freezing. They had no choice but to stay the night and risk being robbed and killed if they slept a wink. One Khampa wanted to use Harrer's bag as a pillow, no doubt suspecting they'd hidden a pistol inside and wanting to get it away from the two Germans. Having managed to get the bag back, Harrer handled it in such a way as to emphasise its poten-tial as a pistol pack. There was one woman Khampa who prayed all night: 'It occurred to me that she was praying in advance for forgiveness for the crime her husband intended to commit against us.'

At first light, Harrer exchanged a pocket mirror for some yak's brains, which were cooked for breakfast. They managed to get out of the tent and start walking, but Harrer's Tibetan dog did not follow them. They saw then that three men were following them. Harrer asked where the dog was and the men suggested one go back for it. Their plan was transparent – they meant to separate Harrer and his friend, then rob or kill them both. Harrer was determined not to leave without his dog, so they both turned back, speaking in such a harsh way that the men knew they were prepared to fight. Because there were two of them, the Khampas held back; like all professional robbers, they preferred violence that wasn't going to rebound on them (though Harrer mentions that their only weapons were the tent poles they carried).

Back at the tent, the praying woman appeared with the dog. Was she spoiling the plan? Or, more likely, pretending nothing was up – until it was. Turning abruptly away with the dog Harrer and his friend retraced their steps at a very hurried pace, not stop-ping until they were back with the last nomads who warned them against what they had so foolishly done. There was absolutely no question of going on – not over the Khampas territory, at least.

The nomads suggested another route and by this time it was apparent that, the nearer they got to Lhasa, the less suspicious people were about them. Using an old permit meant for another part of Tibet, they finally made their way through an unguarded gate into the Forbidden City itself.

The war had already ended, but for Harrer this was just the beginning of a new adventure.

Eventually, Harrer becomes the tutor of the fourteenth Dalai Lama – who at the time was only fourteen years old. Fascinated by the outside world, he'd had translated from English into Tibetan a recent seven-volume history of the Second World War. Mechanically inclined and very adept, despite not being able to read the English instructions, the Dalai Lama had taken apart and reassembled the film projector he enjoyed using. (It seems appropriate that Hollywood should have embraced so wholeheartedly in later years the cause of the Dalai Lama. The fourteenth Dalai Lama was fascinated by film and shot some early movies himself – along with Heinrich Harrer.)

HH threw himself wholeheartedly into teaching the Dalai Lama everything he could. A discussion of the atom bomb led to talk about elements and metals – for which there is no separate word in Tibetan. The Dalai Lama recognised all manner of different aeroplanes from his books about the war. Anything mechanical, he found fascinating, though the bulk of his training had been in philosophy and history. He gave Harrer his own lessons in the latter, for which HH seemed most grateful. In a moment of modest pride, the Dalai Lama shyly showed Harrer an exercise book where he had been attempting to copy Roman letters. Harrer agreed to teach him English.

On the flat roof of the Potala Palace, the Dalai Lama had his telescope. He admitted to sometimes spying on Harrer as he worked in the garden of a Tibetan noble. The Dalai Lama's

Harrer introduced several innovations, including ice skating, in Lhasa

brother confided to Harrer that the Dalai Lama had been lonely as a young man growing up in the Potala. Indeed, it was a kind of prison – he was unable to mingle with ordinary Tibetans or attend the parties of the fun-loving aristocrats. Harrer writes that when the glint of the Dalai Lama's telescope was seen by people at a party, they would flee indoors. It was considered rude to be having such fun when the poor boy-king could not!

When at leisure, the Dalai Lama wore a red jacket he had designed himself. He was very proud of it. Copying designs he had seen in books, he had incorporated pockets – which are not to be found in any traditional Tibetan garb. Harrer writes: 'Now like every other boy of his age he was able to carry about with him a knife, a screwdriver, sweets etc.' He also kept his coloured pencils and fountain pens in his pockets. He loved clocks and timepieces and had bought, with his own money, an Omega calendar clock. Before he attained his majority, the only money he had was that which was left at the foot of his throne. One day the treasure vaults of the Potala would be open to him and he would become one of the world's richest men.

Attracted to magic, the Dalai Lama explained to Harrer that he was making a study of all the methods by which he could be in one place while his body would be in another. This is a common magical technique – you find similar spells and references in most magical traditions. Almost certainly it refers to telepathy: the ability to know who is making that telephone call, or, by projecting the right vibe, make someone call you. Harrer was rather sceptical and declared that he would convert to Buddhism if the Dalai Lama could be in two places at once. And yet, in later life, we see him as such an inveterate traveller, and so spoken about, that it seems by Western technology he has achieved the ability to be in many places at once.

So, Harrer, having escaped the British, managed to do something that no Briton had ever managed in his wildest dreams, which was to become the personal tutor of the next ruler of Tibet.

It is the most extraordinary fable and yet it is true.

7

Public Schoolboys in Tibet

The wall that has given way will surely fall further;
the wall that is being built will surely be finished one day.

Garwhal proverb

Heinrich Harrer mentions in passing the famous four Tibetans who were sent to Rugby public school in 1913 by the thirteenth Dalai Lama in order to help Tibet modernise. Rugby was where *Tom Brown's School Days* was set. The great Thomas Arnold, reforming headmaster and father of Matthew Arnold the poet, taught there. It was in many senses the archetypal public school of the time – designed to inculcate the 'public school spirit' which manned the empire and filled the trenches of the First World War.

But just what effect did Rugby have on the Tibetans? The colonial civil servant Teddy Wakefield provides a tantalising glimpse in his diary of a visit to Tibet. Wakefield was a good public school man himself, having attended Haileybury, which had been established for the sons of the less well-off middle classes – soldiers and colonial administrators – who would then go out and rule the British Empire. Wakefield was a scholar and an athlete – he got a first in classics at Cambridge and learned to climb with Geoffrey Winthrop Young – a friend of Oscar Eckenstein, of Crowley expedition fame.

In 1929, aged just twenty-six, Wakefield, who served in the élite Indian Civil Service, was charged with inspecting the British

Trade Agency in Gartok. One of the purposes of the Younghusband invasion was to secure somewhat better trade with Tibet.
Wakefield would see how well that was developing.

He set off from the usual hill station departure point, Simla,
with a cook, bearer, four riflemen and a havildar – all Gurkhas.
His agency staff – a Dr Ram and more servants and soldiers – had
preceded him by two weeks. At Sarahan they met up and the
young Wakefield was received by the Rajah of Bashahr. He then
proceeded north to the uniquely named town of Pooh. While the
agency staff went on to Gartok, Wakefield decided to do some
exploring. This is the wonderful thing you discover about those
times – the relative freedom of young men with rather vague ad-
ministrative jobs, trusted to do their own thing and interpret their
orders.

Having struggled through trackless mountain wastes, where
one Gurkha died of altitude sickness, Wakefield came down to
the Indus valley. He arrived at the Jongpen Palace in Rudok and
was astonished when a messenger rode out of the palace with a
note written in perfect copperplate English: 'I am glad to hear
you've arrived. Please let me know what time I may come to see
you, yours sincerely, K. K. Mondo'.

Mondo was an ordained monk and the local dzongpan or
ruler, but he was also one of the Rugby School four. After Rugby,
Mondo attended Camborne School of Mines. When he returned
to his homeland, he began prospecting for gold some way north
of Lhasa. But the lamas feared he would upset the balance of life
– earth spirits do not approve of excavations – so they bade him
stop. Mining, like metalworking, has always been a spiritually
troublesome subject. And anyone who has been around old mine
workings may sense the violence expended in penetrating the
earth remains as a sort of dead atmosphere, a place of disturbed
sleep and nightmares.

So Mondo was out of a job. He hoped to become the equivalent
of an English parson with a country living, undisturbed and free

to follow his interests, but instead of retiring to a monastery he was forced to become a monk-policeman in Lhasa. He rubbed people up the wrong way. Five years at Rugby had done its work: he brought a powerful motorbike back with him and – quite a feat – manhandled it over the high passes into Lhasa. Mondo liked to roar around the Holy City on his bike, causing one highly placed lama to be pitched from his mule. For this and other obscure infractions of lama law, he was disgraced and exiled to the far west of Tibet.

Wakefield found Mondo's English a little rusty from disuse – it had been twelve years since he'd spoken the language – but 'it was perfect English when it did arrive'. The two reminisced about quadrangles, school life, perfectly mown lawns and playing fields – all absent in the dry, almost desertlike conditions in western Tibet.

Oddly enough, Mondo was regarded as the most oppressive of a series of tyrannical rulers. Wakefield wrote, 'No method by which money can be extracted from impoverished subjects has not been put into practice.' In only one way was he lenient. After being whacked at Rugby for failing to do his prep – perhaps a Flashman-style beating – he'd had his fill: corporal punishment, though common elsewhere in Tibet, was banned in his province.

En route to Gartok, the interpreter Raghu Das went down with snow blindness and 'had to be held by several men from attempting to knock his brains out against the rocks'. A cocaine solution revived and soothed him. Having saved the man, the party's doctor, Dr Kanshi Ram, who was riding ahead, managed to narrowly avoid a dacoit or bandit whose hunting mastiffs had brought down a kyang. The bandit let off a shot at the doctor, who returned fire with his revolver. This so shocked the dacoit that he gave himself up. The party delivered the miscreant to the rightful authorities, who lost no time in dealing out a rather severe 200 lashes. This was not for firing on a stranger – it was for killing the wild ass. A recent edict from Lhasa banned the killing of wild animals and smoking tobacco – both were thought injurious to the health of the Dalai Lama.

At Gartok they went to the races. The monkish viceroys or Garpons had no English-schooled sense of fairness. The big prize donated by the Lhasa government brought out foul play. Their horses were allowed to start before the others. The owners of the best horses were browbeaten into leasing their rides to the Garpons. And if that failed, their grooms and boy jockeys were given full support in waylaying and beating the opposition. Wakefield was amused rather than outraged.

A true Victorian in spirit, Wakefield was not sick once in his five-month tour. He put it down to walking not riding the 1,300 miles. He wrote that he 'suffered less than the rest of the party from colds and headaches and those bodily ailments inevitable in a country where fruit and vegetables are unobtainable'.

Frederick Spencer Chapman's views focus on the quirky. You

Ancient gate into Lhasa

can tell that he doesn't take any of the Rugby Four very seriously; he was very much a man of his time, the heyday of British influence in India shortly before the Second World War, more parochial and perhaps more arrogant than the ever-questing Victorians. Chapman would become famous as the man who stayed behind Japanese lines in Malaya after the fall of Singapore. Living on his wits for four years, he wrote the classic of guerrilla literature: *The Jungle Is Neutral*. But before this he was a mountaineer and arctic explorer. He was also a schoolmaster, and naturally when he got to Lhasa in 1937 he was interested in meeting the product of the type of school he had both attended and later taught at.

He tells us four Tibetans were sent to Rugby and four returned. Their names were Mondo, Kyipup, Ghonkar and Ringang.

One was destined to be a soldier, one an engineer, one a miner and one a monk. Ghonkar was said to be the most promising. After Rugby he went to the Woolwich 'shop' and trained with the Royal Engineers. He fell in love with an English girl, but when he asked permission to marry her the Dalai Lama refused. Instead of making use of him on his return, the lamas sent Ghonkar to the far frontiers, to the Chinese border. It was said that he died of a broken heart, pining away in the far north.

According to Chapman, Mondo was already a monk when he went in 1913 to England; it was said that he behaved always like a perfect gentleman, though he appeared to learn nothing except English and cricket. He was a very keen cricketer, but gave it up on his return. After he had served his banishment for riding his noisy motorbike through the streets of Lhasa, he was allowed to move to a village at the foot of the Potala. He was given charge of all the parklands of Lhasa. Spencer Chapman described him as 'a large genial man with a loud ringing laugh and the extraordinary consideration and politeness that is so strong a characteristic of the official class'.

Kyipup was not successful at Rugby; in fact, he liked it the least. He rose to neither games nor academe and after two years

left to study surveying. But in this he had no success either. Back
in Lhasa they saw fit to put him in charge of developing the telegraph system, the first section of which, to Gyantse, had been
laid during the Younghusband expedition. Then, under British
supervision, it was extended to Lhasa. Kyipup found that, as he
knew nothing about telegraph systems, there was little for him
to do. So he retired to his family estates. The lamas dragged him
back, made him a city magistrate and put him in charge of the
Lhasa police. Chapman asked him what would happen if there
was a smash-and-grab raid in a Lhasa shop. He replied that the
policeman would blow his whistle, on which signal others would
appear, and having restored order with their truncheons, they
would handcuff the malefactors and take them to prison. This
shut Chapman up, perhaps even stung him, because, later, he saw
fit to inquire of others whether the police had such equipment. He
discovered they had neither whistles, truncheons nor handcuffs.
Imaginary tools to solve an imaginary problem; what Chapman
failed to grasp is that smash-and-grab raids were as unknown in
Lhasa at that time as truncheons and whistles.

The last of the Rugby lads was the most successful in every
sense; he was also the youngest when he arrived in England. This
was Ringang, also known as Kusho Chango Pa. He stood in very
high favour with the Dalai Lama and spent longer in Britain than
any of the others. He spoke 'the most perfect idiomatic English'.*
At that time he was a sixth-rank official and therefore could only
wear silk in private. In his official dress as a city magistrate he
wore a scarlet broadcloth gown with a sky blue lining.

After Rugby he took additional courses in engineering. On his
return, he was given the difficult task of supplying the whole of
Lhasa, plus the Dalai Lama's summer palace, with electricity. For
a young chap just out of college, that was quite a demand. But
Ringang was a worker and he set to with tremendous gusto. Six

* Frederick Spencer Chapman, *Lhasa: The Holy City*

317

miles from Lhasa he built a hydro-electric power station driven by a fast-running mountain stream. The generator was brought in pieces from Calcutta, up to Darjeeling and then carried by yak over the Himalayas. Cables and solenoids, accumulators, condensers and insulators all had to be ordered and carried from far Calcutta. When a piece of equipment arrived that was battered and broken, Ringang would sit for hours meticulously repairing it. He laid a powerline to the city and stored the accumulators in the basement of his own house. After several months the Dalai Lama became impatient and demanded his electric light. Ringang was working as hard as he could and no one understood just how much was involved in bringing power to a place from scratch. But eventually it was finished and it all worked perfectly. By the 1930s the streets were all lit, as well as the Potala and many private houses. Except in winter, when the stream froze hard – but no one begrudged him that. After a while, Ringang was able to train some Tibetans to run the power station and the service for him. This gave him more time to be the official cabinet interpreter: to translate important items in the Indian papers and be present when any Europeans visited Lhasa.

F. S. Chapman wrote, 'Ringang is a very busy man and has every hope of one day being a Shap-pe; but he has the harassed air of one who is not quite high enough up in the scale of officialdom to feel secure from the calumnious attacks of his rivals.'

One out of four a conspicuous success. The others, certainly no worse for the experience. What if forty had been sent? Or four hundred? Going abroad was the key, perhaps rather than the nature of the establishment attended. This is what the Japanese did in 1868, and by 1904 they had transformed their country, for better or for worse, into a modern one capable of defeating Russia in a war; 1904 again.

8

How to Choose a Dalai Lama

To take revenge, give an enemy the gift of an elephant;
his greed will thank you and then will be ruined trying to feed it.

Nepalese proverb

Rather more useful in Tibet than good schooling was being of the right spiritual stock. And spiritual capabilities are notoriously egalitarian. Usually the Dalai Lama is from a peasant background. For a while though, Mongolian aristocrats or royalty supplied Dalai Lamas – when Tibet and Mongolia were going through a phase of close cooperation. (In fact, 'Dalai Lama' is a Mongolian-conferred title; in Tibet he is known as Gyalpo Rinpoche, which means Precious King. His family tend to just call him Kundun, which means 'Presence'.) There was naturally something expedient about such worldly choices as the above, but they carry risks. A Dalai Lama who represents an existing power base and carries baggage of this kind may be difficult. The peasant origin of a Dalai Lama reduces his power, initially at least, and makes for an easier distinction between secular and monastic forces. For a long run in the nineteenth century no Dalai Lama lasted much beyond his twentieth birthday. The real power, then, being in the hands of the regent. But this can change if a Dalai Lama manages, through accident or design, to exert himself successfully and shoulder aside, decorously of course, the power brokers in the monastery. The thirteenth Dalai Lama (1876–1933) was such a man – and so is the fourteenth, the current Dalai Lama, despite being absent from his country.

The Chinese representatives or Ambans sometimes had a say in choosing the Dalai Lama, but only when Chinese stock was high with the lamas. The current authoritarian-materialist government is not in favour, but they still seek to influence the choice of the next Dalai Lama some time in the twenty-first century. Naturally the Tibetans are somewhat suspicious of professed non-believers having a hand in religious matters.

There is no particular hurry to find a new Dalai Lama once the old one has died. Logically, the world beyond time and space does not conform to our clock-watching fantasies. The people have to wait until a propitious sign is observed. Meanwhile, the regent rules, and, since power (though potentially corrupting) is delightful and absolute power is absolutely delightful,* he is usually in no hurry to give up his job. It is an efficient system in its own way, with all sorts of checks and balances. The regent cannot rule for ever because then the people will become suspicious and angry. Moreover, lacking a spiritual leader, the power of the monasteries will wane in favour of the aristocratic trading families, so the regent, a lama himself, has an incentive to find a new Dalai Lama.

The signs must be propitious – actually, there must be many signs. One of the first may be observed during meditation by the regent – or perhaps another lama who has been incarnated (there are quite a few at any one time, all picked at birth as being special in some way, a unique system that seems just as efficient as inheritance, voting, favouritism or bribery – the other preferred methods of getting power). The meditation is special – it occurs while gazing out over Lake Cho Khor Gye near Lhasa. If a vision reveals where the child Dalai Lama is to be found – good. Following this, various highly placed lamas, including, in the past, the Panchen Lama, not to mention the abbots of the big monasteries,

* Idries Shah, *Reflections*

all inwardly regard their dreams and visions to get a closer picture of the date and place of birth of the new child king. The state oracle is frequently consulted to clarify matters further. More and more information comes to hand – the occupation of the parents, the topography of the country where the lad lives, the state of the local neighbourhood.

Often there are several competing locations. Monastic expeditions are dispatched to these places to check the validity of the visions and predictions. These expeditions may last several years at a time. There is no hurry, and a mistake made through hastiness would be a disaster. The travellers look for places that conform to the descriptions they have been given, but they also closely question locals about any portents or extraordinary births that may have occurred in the target area of the boy's predicted birth. Obviously there are many advantages to being the immediate family of the next Dalai Lama, so the travelling monks must be circumspect, low key and not a little crafty in their questioning. Before entering any possible house, they switch clothes with their servants, leaving the 'officials' outside. I like this move a lot. Imagine if the real power brokers in any Western negotiation were disguised as the teaboy and the cleaner, maybe the room service maid. What useful titbits they'd pick up that world leaders, insulated by all the pomp and glory, must miss! Anyway, eventually a short list of potential incarnates is drawn up; there is always a little uncertainty – indeed, there has to be until the tests of absolute authenticity are applied to find the next incarnation of the Chenrezi, another term for the Dalai Lama – which means god of grace – one of the thousand living Buddhas who have renounced Nirvana in order to help mankind, and, as such, the patron god of Tibet.

Several good signs are:

1. The next incarnation may recognise servants and officials who have served his previous incarnation.

2. He will be able to pick out a teacup used by the previous Dalai Lama.

3. He will also select the prayer wheel, bell and sacred thunderbolt.

4. He may be able to recall events that happened to him in a previous life as a Dalai Lama.

In the case of the fourteenth Dalai Lama, it went like this. When the previous Dalai Lama died in 1933 he had, just before dying, given a few cryptic clues about where his next incarnation might come from, but these were far from definitive in any sense. Then, when his body lay in state, it was noticed that his head, which had, by tradition, been laid turned to the south, was now turned towards the east. This was the first real clue and that very day the state oracle was consulted; while in a trance, he threw a white scarf towards the rising sun – confirmation. But nothing much happened for a few years. In Tibet, as in much of the ancient East, it was believed that information and time were intimately related. If too much information was uncovered at once, then a certain amount of time and living must pass before the world was in balance again and the information could be used. We are less sophisticated – though the 'data diets', 'web fasts' and 'net holidays' of the present era may be an indication that one can overdose on information just as surely as one can on sugar or other tasty but limited nutritional items.

So everyone waited a while until the regent chanced to visit Cho Khor Gye – in whose waters the future, or a fragment of it, is sometimes revealed. In the waters he saw a three-storeyed peasant monastery with a golden roof. Next to it was a Chinese peasant house with carved gables. Search groups were sent out in 1937 in an easterly direction. Each group carried a selection of sacred objects for spot testing of any infant who might be a possible candidate. In the district of Amdo, outside Tibet in the Chinese province of Chinghai, where the Tibetan population lives in amicable accord with that of the Chinese Muslims, after much wandering and speculation and trials and tribulations a three-storeyed monastery was found. Next to it, just as in the regent's vision, was a Chinese peasant house with carved gables. Though trembling with excitement, the monkish officials switched clothes with their servants and entered the house.

A cheery two-year-old who lived there ran forward and seized the skirts of one of the lamas, who, though dressed as a servant, had the thirteenth Dalai Lama's rosary around his neck. Then the child said several times, 'Sera Lama, Sera Lama' even though he couldn't have known this was a disguised lama. When the lama bent down, the boy grabbed the rosary and wouldn't let go until it was put around his own neck. Though they felt there was now no doubt, the searchers had to follow protocol so they paid their respects to the family and left.

They returned a few days later in full monkish regalia to enter into negotiations with the family and to subject the two-year-old to more tests.

It so happened that this family had already supplied one incarnation to the church (for a significant but lower kind of rebirth), so they were both informed, but also stunned, that another son was said to be divinely marked. Like winning the lottery twice, it must have been a lot to take in. Westerners get all suspicious when they hear that the searchers went back to the same house twice, but why shouldn't fate favour the same family? In the worldly sphere you get families that excel in certain areas – Venus and Serena Williams in tennis, the families of Bach and Jackson in music.

The tests were carried out in the altar room. Four rosaries were shown to the boy. The most worn was the old Dalai Lama's – he chose this without hesitation and reportedly danced round the room wearing it. He selected, from several proffered drums, one that had also been owned by the previous incarnation and used to summon his servants, no doubt a much-used item. He picked a plain walking stick – and didn't so much as glance at several competing ones with enticing silver and ivory handles. Naturally this was the right choice too.

Finally came the matter of checking for bodily signs of true Dalai Lamahood. These are reportedly

1. Marks as of a tiger skin on his legs.
2. Eyes and eyebrows that curve upwards on the outside and are rather long.
3. Large ears.
4. Two pieces of flesh near the shoulder blades indicating the two other hands of Chenrezi.
5. An imprint like a conch-shell on one of the palms of his hand.

The thirteenth Dalai Lama had scored on the last three. The choice was so certain they missed out the next stage, which is picking out the name with golden chopsticks. The fourteenth Dalai Lama only scored with (3) and (4) which still made it a certainty.

To avoid intrigues, everything now had to be done in the utmost secrecy. No one was told of the discovery and a solemn oath of silence was taken in front of a *thanka* on which a likeness of Chenrezi was embroidered. As the little lad was in Chinese territory, extra caution needed to be observed. The searchers then went off to inspect other boys in other districts as a blind.

However, the governor of the province knew something was up when they asked permission to take the young boy to Lhasa to test if he was an incarnation or not. Being canny, the governor asked for 100,000 Chinese dollars. The monks paid up straight away – which is the kind of error other-worldly monks are prone to make. The governor immediately asked for 200,000 more for the boy to be surrendered. In a compromise, some money was borrowed from Muslim moneylenders, with the rest to be paid after they had reached Lhasa. The governor finally agreed.

Once in Lhasa, the boy received an official letter confirming he was, indeed, the next Dalai Lama. His parents, who only knew at this point that he was a high incarnation, were told this – the first time they knew their son was the chosen one. Two incarnations and one a Dalai Lama – imagine!

In 1940, seven years after the old Dalai Lama died, the new one, aged five, was enthroned. Everyone was astonished at the natural dignity of the child and the gravity with which he followed the ceremony, which lasted for hours. With his predecessor's servants he was trusting and affectionate – as if he had always known them.

Which of course he had.

The God who made the mouth will provide the food.

Nepalese proverb

9

Himmler's Himalayas

<hr>

Whatever joy you seek it can be achieved by yourself,
whatever misery you seek it can be found by yourself.

Bhutanese proverb

There is no getting away from it, Nazi types seem drawn to Tibet. Whereas the Chinese communists sought to change the place and impose their own ideology, the national socialists wanted to extract its secrets to bolster their nutty ideas about race. But to enter Tibet they needed to negotiate with its British gatekeepers, some of whom were keener than others on helping the Germans. The British consul, Hugh Richardson, saw aiding the 1938 Nazi expedition as a form of appeasement. But he had been ordered by the highest authority in India – the Viceroy – to help the Germans in their 'scientific' work. To Richardson it was repellent nonsense: measuring the temple, nose width and eye height with tape and calliper, and, when lucky, making exact plaster masks of the native's head. Hadn't Franz Boas disproved the Aryan claims of craniometry in 1910?

Bruno Beger, the anthropologist on the expedition, had worked out a good routine to make his inquiries acceptable. He offered medical help wherever he went. The British had been fooled. What harm could the well-stocked German medical chest do?

Beger was a solid, well-built blond with a good sense of humour. He'd end his career in anthropology as he'd started – measuring heads and making masks – but somewhere far removed from Sikkim.

The first victim they managed to entice was Passang, a Sherpa attached to the expedition. The technique of mask making would be tested upon him. Passang had been injured in the head only a week earlier. The Germans were in a hurry and brushed aside suggestions that the process might exacerbate his injuries. Why, it was little more than a beauty treatment, like placing a mud mask on a lady's face. Passang acquiesced in the hope, no doubt, of being rewarded.

A gypsum-based plaster was worked up into a paste. Water and disinfectant were added and then the result plastered all over the face of the subject. Two straws were inserted into the nostrils to aid breathing, though one can imagine the claustrophobic feeling of depending for your air through such a fragile device. The mouth needed to remain firmly shut to take a good impression of the jaw, and when the plaster started to set it kept it shut. After the mask had set it was removed. Synthetic rubber solution was poured into the 'negative' to make a latex copy of the original face. This Beger could study endlessly back in Berlin.

Beger could find no straws that worked that day. He assured Passang he would wipe away any accumulated plaster from his nostrils. As he shut each eyelid to start plastering the eyes, he noticed that Passang was tense and fearful. He was also having difficulty breathing as small amounts of plaster had been inhaled up his nose.

Once his entire face was covered, Beger brought out his stopwatch. Now it was time to wait. He smoked a cigarette. When he turned back he saw with horror that Passang was jerking uncontrollably and the mask had begun to split. Beger's initial annoyance was fast forgotten when he realised Passang was having an epileptic fit. Breathing the wet clay into his foaming mouth, Passang fell to the floor writhing in discomfort. The wet clay further impaired his breathing. He was turning blue. Beger thrust his hands into

Passang's mouth and scooped out the clay. Passang at last began to breathe normally and his fit passed. In his own mind, he had been seized by the mountain god Kanchenjunga and been shaken violently as a warning about helping unbelievers. It was not an auspicious start.

When Schäfer, who was out hunting at the time, returned, he was furious. If Hugh Richardson learned of this, they'd be thrown out. They debated about finding a doctor to check if Passang was all right. But a doctor might talk. In the end, Beger pacified the Sherpa with the gift of his best white shirt. The other porters were threatened with instant dismissal without pay if they blabbed. Eventually, the expedition moved on to remoter places and masks were traded for quinine and other medical supplies. Beger grew adept at calming his subjects, laughing and joking with them as he measured their heads, before he slapped on the plaster.

It was training that would stand him in good stead when he continued his research in the 1940s, at first, at Himmler's request, into the links between prehistoric 'Venus' figurines, Hottentots and Jews. In 1942, following the lead of Stalin in deporting 600,000

Nazis spread their poison even in the remote mountains

Volga Germans, the Nazis realised the possibilities of massive deportations. The Jews arriving in the swampy land around Lublin in Poland to be forcibly rehoused in the new camps could be used for research.

Beger went to his death denying he ever knew where his 'research materials' came from. A report that he claimed he did not write, but most likely did, stated:

> There exist extensive collections of skulls of almost all races and peoples. Of the Jewish race, however, only so very few specimens of skulls are at the disposal of science that a study of them does not permit precise conclusions. The war in the east now presents us with the opportunity to remedy this shortage. By procuring the skulls of the Jewish-Bolshevik Commissars, who personify a repulsive yet characteristic sub-humanity, we have the opportunity of obtaining tangible scientific evidence . . .

Though Beger managed to evade punishment for what he did during the war, the evidence is clear that he had a major part in something as gruesome as anything committed by the Germans during the Second World War.

There are records of Beger travelling down to Auschwitz where he was entertained by leading SS officers and met the commandant Rudolf Hoess, who had agreed to expedite his mission to the camp. Beger wandered around looking for Asian types. Apparently he was disappointed to find only seven. He made up his numbers mainly with Jews. In all, 137 were selected. These he carefully measured, with some help from fellow prisoners (who he commended by name later). Beger would later claim that he had no knowledge of the ultimate fate of his subjects. He implied, like the people he measured in Sikkim and Tibet, that they would be free to go after he had applied the callipers and the plaster. Of course he did know what would be part two of the experiment. Beger spent eight days in Auschwitz in June 1943. He left early because of the danger of infectious diseases; his colleagues stayed on. Was he sickened by what he had seen and heard? If he was, it didn't stop him carrying on with his part in the 'experiment'.

Eighty people were shipped to Natzweiler camp in the Alsace. Records show that their fate was known from the beginning, as accommodation was requested for 'a short period only'. Here, speaking of the first of the group to arrive, the former prison commander Josef Kramer later admitted during interrogation at Nuremberg, 'I told these women that they were going into a dis-infection room, without letting them know they were going to be asphyxiated.'

The bodies were injected with preservative and stored in containers filled with ethanol. The purpose was for racial study, primarily to obtain skulls and skeletons to complement the meas-urement already done by Beger.

Beger would claim that by the time he knew of the fate of his subjects 'it was too late'. Unfortunately for him, there is a record of his trip to Natzweiler after the executions had taken place. It is an expenses claim. He also filed a complaint that the expenses were late in coming. In a letter to Schäfer he spoke of one subject he had measured in Auschwitz: 'his movements and the way he introduced himself were simply ravishing, in a word: from the Asian heartland.' His concerns – like many of the Nazis – were only aesthetic and worldly. The fates of the last people he meas-ured were marked, just as the first was, by an absence of any real human interest or sympathy.

Schäfer, paradoxically, got off less lightly than Beger. Though a member of the SS Ahnenerbe, Himmler's project in researching Aryan origins around the globe, Schäfer was less complicit in any criminal acts. Schäfer was asked to record, with the cameraman they had used in Tibet, horrific altitude experiments in Dachau. Though he did nothing to stop them, he wanted no part of it himself – and said so. This continues to be debated, even after his death in 1992. There are some, despite the lack of evidence, who believe Schäfer was a willing assistant in the murderous regime of the SS.

The official British intelligence report in 1938 on Schäfer noted:

> Dr Schäfer's chief trouble is that he is unbalanced mentally . . . an ardent Nazi who is apt to let himself go when he gets on to politics. In addition he has taken no thought to respect local prejudices in the matter of taking life etc. For all these reasons it seems highly desirable to get him back to Germany as soon as possible . . .

He had planned to take a young Nepali Gurkha back to the Fatherland with him. It is just as well he was dissuaded from doing so.

10

The Tibetan State Oracle

A person who is promiscuous steps on two boats.
Tibetan proverb

Tibet may be the only country in the world that has an official oracle (plus a few unofficial ones). It has always been so, and the current government in exile in Dharamsala sees no reason to change. Given the disastrous record of most governments in their attempts to predict the future and act with a semblance of wisdom, I can't help thinking: oracles? Why not?

Other methods of predicting the future that were used in the not so distant past in Tibet include doughball scrying, dice divination, rosary counting, bootstrap haruspication, interpretation of strange birds and other incidental phenomena, clairvoyant dreaming, ritual flame examination, observing the flickering patterns of a butter lamp, mirror divining, and – in common with the prehistoric Chinese – using the shoulder blade of a deer as a predictive knuckle bone.

The official state oracle was established, as was so much that characterises modern Tibet, by the fifth Dalai Lama in the seventeenth century AD. He combined the role of state oracle with that of the highest-ranking lama in the Nechung Monastery residence. Here the lama oracle would have his own small court and celebrate rituals and chants in a temple of his own, which would be painted black inside. This is not a colour that has the same morbid sense as it does in the West, or, rather, its morbidity is leavened by white shouldering the burden as the colour of death and mourning. So imagine a rather low-ceilinged, somewhat oppressive black-painted temple hung with dry leather masks and the likenesses of demons and terror gods. Dusty weapons – great thick broadswords and long daggers, together with more magical weaponry fashioned from bones – were displayed alongside stuffed birds, snow tigers, elephants' feet and leopards. A human ribcage, like some macabre birdhouse, dangled from the roof by a leather thong.

Bowls of incense and drumming on large tambourine-like drums, accompanied by ritual chanting, were enough to send the Nechung Lama into a trance. Once in a trance, he was transformed into a twitching, sweating demon with superhuman strength. He was known to bend iron swords, wear an 80 lb crown as if it weighed little, and could dance and leap much higher into the air than he ever could when unpossessed.

The deity that enabled this was Pedkar, or Pehar as he was sometimes known. Pehar commands five wrathful gods known as 'the protective wheel'. In pictures he has three faces of different colours and wears an ornate bamboo hat. He is armed with bow and arrows, sword, cleaver, knobbly club, and rides upon an angry snow lion. His power can, on occasion, be so strong it damages the health of the Nechung Lama. When his power is too strong, therefore, a lesser immortal takes control of the lama's body: Pehar's assistant, Dorje Drakden.

Pehar originates in the 'devil's country' – northern Tibet. In earlier times he was war god of the Hor Mongols, who were themselves described in old texts as 'red faced, flesh-eating demons'.

The Nechung Lama was observed on a number of occasions by Heinrich Harrer when he was living in Tibet. The Nechung was nineteen at the time – the late 1940s – and must have been successful as he remained the oracle until 1987, when he died. Harrer writes: 'Hollow, eerie music greeted us at the gate of the temple. Inside the spectacle was ghastly. From every wall looked down hideous, grimacing faces and the air was filled with stifling fumes of incense.' Then the young monk oracle was led into the temple to the sound of insistent drumming:

> He wore a round metal mirror on his breast . . . No sound could be heard except the hollow music. He began to concentrate. I watched him closely, never taking my eyes from his face – not the slightest movement of his features escaped me. He looked as if the life were fading out of him. Now he was perfectly motionless, his face a staring mask. Then, suddenly, as if he had been struck by lightning, his body curved upward like a bow. The onlookers gasped. The god was in possession. The medium began to tremble; his whole body shook and beads of sweat stood out on his forehead.

Harrer observed the other monks putting a heavy headdress on the oracle. He noticed the sheer physical strain on the young man and thought it might explain why so many oracles died young.

> The trembling became more violent. The medium's heavily laden head wavered from side to side, and his eyes started from their sockets. His face was swollen and covered in patches of hectic red. Hissing sounds pierced through his closed teeth . . . Now he started beating on his gleaming breastplate with a great thumb ring, making a clatter which drowned the dull rolling of the drums. Then he gyrated on one foot, erect under the weight of the giant head-dress, which just now two men could hardly carry.

The young monk was held fast by servants and a cabinet minister approached with all kinds of high-level questions. The oracle mumbled answers. Often the question was repeated several times. The oracle's answers were taken down by the secretary to the oracle, who wrote swiftly and fluently – and had been the

secretary to the previous oracle. Harrer writes, 'I could not pre-
vent myself from suspecting that perhaps the real Oracle was the
secretary.'

Harrer is sceptical but also naïve – he thinks it illogical that an
oracle who gives poor advice should be relieved of his post: 'Did
the god speak through the medium or not?'

He plays the usual game of the indignant materialist who
believes he has 'caught out' a seer or telepath. Only a moment's
reflection would surely provide a reason for an oracle failing to
deliver accurate forecasts – he is human, and of this world, and
anything that lives in this world must perforce partake of the corruption of this world, and sometimes this naturally will interfere
with the work of mediums and oracles. And if it isn't broken, why
fix it? One of the major problems for any Western researcher in
the East is to disentangle fraud and superstition from genuine
insight and reliance on methods that we only dimly appreciate in
the West. There is no 'scientific' way to distinguish between the
two – only experience and that rare but necessary combination of
an open mind and common sense can tell them apart. Harrer has
common sense but he lacks the experience to know whether he
is seeing an outright fraud or something that has a function, so he
falls back on the old chestnut of suspecting things that are not in
'his philosophy'.

He remarks that he could hardly get used to meeting the state
oracle when he was acting normally: 'his face was that of a nice-
looking young man, and bore no resemblance to the bloated,
red-flecked, grimacing visage of the ecstatic medium'.

There were several other mediums with varying functions.
One could bend long swords into a spiral. Harrer tried to do the
same thing himself – and he was strong, fit, athletic – but wrote
'I could not begin to do it'. As we have seen, humans in a trance
state are capable of gaining access to the full power of the human
frame, a power we sometimes glimpse in epileptics and those in
life-and-death situations. One of the mediums was an old woman,

the rest were men. A key medium was the rainmaker, but since the paltry fourteen inches (36 centimetres) of rain came in only one season it wasn't such a tricky task. Aufschnaiter – Harrer's fellow German escaper – installed a water-gauge on the river in Lhasa – he claimed it rose on almost the same day every year.

An example of the seriousness with which the Tibetans regarded the oracle came when the German expedition of 1939 tried to film the Tibetan New Year festival in which the oracle makes an important appearance. As the would-be cinematographers cranked their cameras, the mob suddenly caught sight of them. With a single mind, they raced after them hurling sticks, stones and anything else that came to hand. The Germans were lucky to escape with their lives, fleeing over garden walls and across low rooftops.

Pehar, who lives through the state oracle, may be dangerous but he is an old friend to successive Dalai Lamas. He was consulted before the current Dalai fled, both in 1950 and in 1959. And in 1950, as the Chinese invaded, it was the state oracle who advised, 'Make him king' – there was still a regent controlling power in Tibet at the time.

As the current fourteenth Dalai Lama writes:

> Mostly those who consider themselves 'progressive' have misgivings about my continued use of this ancient method of intelligence gathering. But I do so for the simple reason that as I look back over the many occasions when I have asked questions of the oracle, on each one of them time has proved that his answer was correct.

On 4 September 1987 a new Nechung Lama was enthroned in Dharamsala. The previous one had died three years earlier. The Dalai Lama had three minor mediums as stand-ins. Divinatory arts, astrology, the interpretation of dreams, the drawing of sanctified lots – all have a place in the Tibetan government method of proceeding. But the Dalai Lama was prepared to wait until the right person came along to fulfil the top position. With the new Nechung's arrival the Tibetan government in exile and the Dalai Lama all attended an inaugural trance session: 'We consider these spirits reliable; they have a long history without any controversy in over 1,000 years. However my relationship to Nechung is that of commander to lieutenant.'

Pehar took possession and made the following prediction: 'The shine of the wish-fulfilling jewel [the Dalai Lama] will light up in the West.' It is a prediction that has very largely come true.

11

Blame Nehru

You go on your shining path and I'll go on my single-plank bridge.
Tibetan proverb

China wanted Tibet. Mere suzerainty was not enough. China wanted full sovereignty. The British had always remained firm: China had a place in Tibet but they should not run the place and they certainly should not annex it to become a mere province of China. Two things happened to change the situation: the Korean War and Nehru's hatred of the British. True, the Brits, with the usual well-meaning bungling that characterises twentieth-century British and American foreign policy, had, in their honourable treatment of the Tibetans and their military pull-out from Lhasa, ignored a basic tenet of Eastern life, which earlier, wiser and less arrogant English diplomats had observed. This was: speak and act in the cultural language of the nation or people you wish to rule. Do not deal with them on your terms and expect them to recip-rocate as you would in their situation. Why should they? Sadly, powerful Western nations became used to getting their own way, childishly demanding instant results and insisting on 'fairness', which children always mistake for justice, though it's a rather different beast since it takes into account foresight – that subtle combination of experience, good character, objectivity, informa-tion, and, above all else, courage, that marks the higher form of intelligence. Money and power tend to insulate individuals and nations from the need to acquire courage; they certainly insulate them from the means to acquire experience of the kind that nurtures foresight: experience of not getting one's own way being rather important.

With foresight, the British should probably have left Tibet to itself. However, anxious to appear 'fair' and 'above board' to the Tibetans, yet, at the same time wanting the benefits of trade with that country, they could not leave it alone. The problem is, when you invade a country, it becomes very attractive to other vultures when you depart. Your invasion has proved the country is weak; when you leave, the implied power vacuum will be very quickly filled. We need only to look at Iraq and Afghanistan in the early twenty-first century to see evidence of this. And in Tibet's case, every invasion by a foreign power has prefigured a Chinese follow-up invasion. Mongol inroads into Tibet led to a Chinese invasion in 1720, the Nepalese incursions led to one in 1790 and British activity in the form of the Younghusband expedition and its aftermath led to the Chinese invasion of 1910 – which had special orders to capture the Dalai Lama. Luckily for him, he escaped and nine days later was licking his wounds in Darjeeling.

We tend to think of the Chinese revolution as the communist success in 1949. In reality, the Chinese revolution – like all revolutions – was a bourgeois grab for power, between 1910 and 1913, that was hijacked by those with greater ruthlessness. Mao, like Lenin, would be the ultimate inheritor of the power, once the revolutionary process had disrupted/bankrupted the country. This loss of Chinese military effectiveness with regard to Tibet during the years between the start of the revolution in 1910 and its conclusion in the dictatorship of Mao in 1949 allowed an illusion of independence to grow in Tibet. This was fostered by the benign and dull-witted attentions of the British.

Fast-forward to 1950 and another Chinese invasion was on the way, encouraged by Britain's pull-out from India. The British had yet again blundered – in Eastern political terms – by leaving India in a rush. Though morally and commercially completely under-standable, in the arena of Great Game politics that Russia and China and Britain had been playing for centuries, the withdrawal from India was bound to send a very powerful message to every country in Asia: despite winning the war, the British were defeated and were going home. What else could they have done? Employed foresight and staged the withdrawal over ten years, ending in 1957 – which had been the original plan, until Mountbatten overruled it? Maybe; it is very easy to fall prey to foresight's cheap and almost worthless companion, hindsight; however, when it came to Tibet the action of leaving India took on grave connotations and circumstances. Britain was leaving, and Britain had guaranteed Tibetans protection simply by its presence in India. If India did not offer the same assurances, then China would effectively have a green light.

Which is exactly what Nehru did. Like many intellectuals who have benefited from an education provided by an occupying power – he went to Trinity College, Cambridge – he was riven by inner conflicts all his life. India – the most discriminatory country on earth – if you are an untouchable – is extraordinarily tolerant of difference and inequality. But put an upper-class Indian like Nehru – so intoxicated by Britain's power that he never learned an Indian language to rival his preferred use of English – through an education that emphasises fairness and intrinsic merit and you are bound to have it backfire. That same person, highly educated – in a Western sense – will demand the freedom and fairness you have been teaching and preaching at him. But Nehru was still an Indian and therefore fairness could not, on nationalistic grounds, be seen to undermine India and its customs. So fairness only really applied to him and the power elite he represented. To ascribe to Nehru an inferiority complex with regard to the British is perhaps going too far; he certainly had a hang-up or two, though, and this resulted in the decision, fatal for Tibet, to support the People's

Republic of China in the United Nations and to release via the Indian ambassador this statement of 15 August 1950:

> The Indian government stated that the Government of India recognises Chinese sovereignty in Tibet. Although the newspaper claims that the Government of India is concerned about Tibet, in fact, the only concern the Government of India has towards Tibet is being afraid of tribal disturbances along the border due to military activities. Therefore [we] hope that Tibetan problems can be resolved through negotiations between China and Tibet.

Nehru would later rue these words when the implied weakness and failure to stand up to China would result in the Chinese invasion in 1962, but for the time being he was riding high on being anti-British and pro-Chinese.

As well as declining to support Tibet, Nehru refused to back the US outrage at the North Korean invasion of South Korea. Nehru had delusions of bringing the great powers to the negotiating table – little did he realise that Stalin saw him as a mere tool for advancing his own interests. Mao, too, through the cunning offices of Chou En-lai, further tricked Nehru by implying that the American support of South Korean territorial integrity justified a Chinese invasion of Tibet.

So far as the Chinese were concerned, the message was clear: India won't interfere if you invade. So they did. On 5 October 1950, Mao's 18th Army crossed into Tibet. They had managed to transport 10,000 tons of military provisions and 8,000 men to staging areas on the border. On 6 October the PLA, weighed down with backpacks of up to 40 kilos a man, marched 60 kilometres a day. By 18 October half had died along the road due to altitude-related sickness and exhaustion; 500 horses had also collapsed.

Despite this setback, Chamdo was conquered and in six days an estimated 5,700 Tibetans were killed.

The Chinese stated through Deputy Minister Zhang: 'The

problem of Tibet is a domestic problem of China. The liberation of Tibet and consolidating the border are sacred rights of the People's Republic of China, and no foreign interference shall be tolerated.'

In this act of 'liberation', China had already far surpassed the casualties of the British invasion in 1904, yet this was only the beginning.

The first town the battle-hardened PLA reached was Gartok. The Christian missionary Geoff Bull noted 'absolute confusion' reigned, 'social order' broke down and people ran around trying to save what valuables they could. The reputation for looting and destruction preceded the PLA. These were not the mounted infantry of Younghusband, who would not enter the Potala unless invited.

Bull was taken prisoner and ludicrously accused of being a 'conspirator against China'. For three years he was serially abused and mistreated in a 're-education' camp. In a form of brainwashing that became well known when employed against US prisoners in the Korean War, Bull was forced to endlessly rewrite his autobiography. Each version would then be criticised, relentlessly undermining any sense of personal history. With Bull it failed dismally; his spirit survived undimmed and unbroken by this insane attempt at mental re-wiring. Released in 1953 at the end of the Korean War, he went on to write the fascinating memoir *When Iron Gates Yield*.

Another captured Englishman was the young radio operator Robert Ford. Employed by the Tibetans, he ran the sole radio station in Chamdo. He liked to keep busy and was known for having introduced the samba to Lhasa when he worked there. In Chamdo he spent his time replying to amateur radio hams who wanted a 'QXL' card to prove they had heard one of the most distant radio stations on the planet. This harmless activity, and the letters from all over the world, sealed his fate as far as the Chinese invaders were concerned. He was sentenced to spend five years in a Chinese prison camp. He survived long periods of mental stress, and later met Heinrich Harrer in London, marked by his experiences but not broken by them.

Ford had sent the message to Lhasa advising them of the attack and desperately asking for help. The immortal message came back: 'Right now it is the period of the Kashag's picnic and they are all participating in this. Your telegrams are being decoded and then they will send you a reply.'

To this the Tibetan officer shouted, 'Shit the picnic' and hung up.

Ford later wrote, 'The Tibetans were overwhelmed; the Chinese captured over half the 10,000 Tibetan defenders. With no word from Lhasa and no possibility of stopping the PLA the Governor fled in the middle of the night, leaving the local people to fend for themselves. Panic was breaking out in the town . . . Monks were hurrying towards the monastery, gabbling their prayers . . .'

It would do little good; it was the beginning of the end of this ancient country and its ancient ways.

The British were the last to give up on Tibet; in 2008, Foreign Secretary David Milliband claimed it was 'archaic' to insist on Chinese suzerainty rather than sovereignty. It was just another deal to make money for Britain; more importantly it meant that China's invasion had succeeded – Tibet no longer existed as an independent or semi-independent nation. Wikipedia reflects this change – any 'official' document – from the United Nations or a government, anything from academia – all refer to China rather than Tibet. China is rewriting history and gradually trying to airbrush Tibet out of the picture. But rewriting history has a habit of backfiring . . .

12

Everest: Who Got There First?

He boasts about eating sweets when he actually ate a potato.

Nepalese proverb

Everest – the big one. After the Chinese invasion of Tibet in 1949/50, access to the north side, the path of all the early attempts on Everest, was denied. Attention now turned to the southern slopes on the Nepalese side, Nepal having given up barring climbers in an attempt to remain on good terms with the rest of the world now that China was at its border. In the 1950s, Everest was the last big target for explorers; the question was, had it already been climbed?

Can we discount the imaginative thesis that Irvine and Mallory climbed Everest in 1924 and fell on the way down? Perhaps not. Mallory was a good rock climber; more to the point, he was prepared to take risks. The second step on the north face has one short section now climbed using a 4.5-metre aluminium ladder left there by a Chinese expedition in 1975. There is a crack – a little too wide to fist-jam and not wide enough to fit your body into. This is the only way up if the ladder is not used. Conrad Anker, a member of the 1999 expedition that found Mallory's body, climbed it and said it wasn't easy but was certainly do-able by a competent climber from the 1920s. As this was the major technical problem facing Mallory and Irvine, it is just possible they did reach the summit. Mallory had told everyone he would

344

place a photograph of his wife on the summit; though several photographs were found on his body, the one of his wife, as we have already mentioned, was suggestively missing. In the real world it is not enough to get to the top – you have to be able to get down again. As Reinhold Messner says, 'the greatest climber is the one who is still alive'. So, as they perished in the attempt, we can discount the precocious 1924 claim – unless Irvine's body should be found beside a camera containing unequivocal shots of the summit.

For the time being, then, let us consider the real contenders: Hillary and Tenzing.

Just as it makes little sense to claim prior arrival when you simply got off the same train a fraction quicker than a fellow passenger, there is a sense in which a pair climbing together are an indivisible unit, especially when it comes to claiming a summit. Certainly, this is the usual case in mountaineering, as it is in writing academic papers, authoring books and penning pop songs.

When the pair are of vastly differing talent, where one climber is effectively hauling the other up the face, if it should happen that the lead climber is not first to set foot on the peak's very highest point, then he will generally be given the credit for the ascent. Nevertheless, the man who accompanies him will perforce share the honours.

Tenzing had been climbing as a Sherpa and sirdar for twenty years. He had been 'discovered' in Darjeeling by Tilman and Shipton and had graduated eventually to the top slot – a place on the 1953 Everest expedition led by the 'thrusting' John Hunt – after Eric Shipton was deemed to lack the necessary oomph to bag the summit. It was seen by many as a miserable return to siege-gun tactics, but for the Brits, having lost most of the empire, and firmly now in the shadow of America, this was the last chance to garner one of the top prizes in exploration. The Swiss expedition of the previous year had come close to succeeding. If the British failed, then someone else would succeed. This was the background to the momentous climb to the top led, in the final stage, by New Zealand climber Edmund Hillary (often described as a beekeeper, which, though true, is misleading – he was a professional climber in his approach, dedication and desire to succeed).

Tenzing and Hillary both knew there would be immense pressure on them to divulge who got to the top first. They decided to make a pact and tell the world they arrived together, determined that a wedge should not be driven between them. But when they descended and were on the way to Kathmandu, a kind of nationalist hysteria took over and the Nepalese decided Tenzing had been the first. A group of journalists and politicians got Tenzing – who was illiterate at the time, according to his son – to sign a document saying he had arrived first. Hillary, to his credit, did not react to this, but John Hunt announced at a press conference in Kathmandu that Tenzing was not a hero, he was an aide with little mountaineering skill, and that Hillary had led all but a small part of the climb above 8,500 metres. Later, Hunt would retract this. To settle the matter, Hillary and Tenzing met at the Prime Minister's office and signed a joint statement that they had arrived 'almost together'.

As time went by, both Hillary and Tenzing used their fame to achieve a great deal. Tenzing, however, grew weary of the attention. Often people would try to doorstep him when he was in the garden of his Darjeeling home; mistaking him for the gardener, they would ask if Sherpa Tenzing was at home. He'd reply that Tenzing was out, and then carry on weeding, happy to be thought a servant of the man they sought.

On the night before they reached the summit, Hillary removed his boots and left them outside his sleeping bag. Tenzing kept his on. Hillary's were frozen stiff the next morning and they were late leaving as Hillary and Tenzing alternated holding the boots over the stove to thaw them out. They were still immovable and stiff when they set out, so Tenzing took the lead. When Hillary had warmed up, he took over. They were able to follow and step in the footprints left by the climbers who had preceded them the day before – Bourdillon and Evans – though the wind had begun to fill the prints with snow.

Just before the south summit, the slope steepens. Tenzing had found the going difficult, as they were conserving their oxygen. But at this lower summit they retrieved fresh oxygen bottles left behind by Bourdillon and Evans, which meant they could now afford to breathe a richer mixture and push on.

The route from this point follows a narrow and potentially deadly ridge to the summit. On one side the snow flops and over-hangs the 3,000-metre drop of the Kangshung face. Sometimes unnerving holes appear in the snow, allowing a glimpse of this hugely high face. You have to walk a little way from the edge in case this cornice breaks off and takes you with it. But you can't go too far to the other side as then you might begin an unstoppable slide down into the western cwm, 2,500 metres below.

The Hillary Step – now surmounted by fixed ropes – was climbed by Hillary and Tenzing by wedging themselves between the rock and the snow of the cornice. After that, they had another half an hour of painfully slow walking – one step followed by a pause to catch their breath – until they reached the top of the mountain.

Tenzing wrote in his autobiography that Hillary reached the top a few seconds before he did. It made sense, as Hillary had led the way up the last obstacle – the Hillary Step, named after its first climber. (Some elderly Sherpas call it Tenzing's back, referring to a story that Hillary stood on Tenzing's back to get a boost – a legitimate but unconventional move.) But you can sense the ego and ambition needed to get to the top in Tenzing's words to his son on the matter. He did not refer to it as the truth; rather, he called the admission in his autobiography 'a concession in the hope of finally ridding himself of the interminable questions'.

13

The Nanda Devi Caper

The deer on a slope can be chased even by a calf.

Nepalese proverb

The new Great Game of the Himalayas was America v. Communism. At first it was the Soviet variety; Mao was seen as a sideshow. With the invasion of South Korea and Tibet in 1950, attitudes changed. But though the Chinese were a threat through the vast manpower available, they did not have what the Soviets had: nuclear weapons. Paranoid Stalin was not about to empower any nation on his doorstep – whatever their professed alignment with communism. Khrushchev thought differently – he not only sought to station Russian weapons in communist friendly countries, he allowed the Chinese to make their own.

On 16 October 1964 the evil spreading form of a mushroom cloud was observed from a spy plane in Lop Nur in Xinjiang province bordering Tibet. The explosion – a 22-kiloton device – marked a huge change in the relationship of the West to the East. It meant Tibet was no longer the logical resting place for Chinese expansionist visions; suddenly all the disputed territory they claimed on the other side of the Himalayas – large chunks of Arunachal Pradesh being among them – were all up for grabs.

The CIA's Plan A was to put some kind of spying device on a very high mountain in order to accurately observe all the time what the Chinese were up to in the field of nuclear bomb making.

A radio scanning device with five sensors would, if placed high enough, be able to directly intercept radio traffic in the Xinjiang region. But it needed to be really high.

Everest was out of the question – it was accessible from Tibet, and the Chinese had proved competent climbers when they ascended it in 1960 using the north face route that had defeated Mallory and Irvine and all the pre-war climbers.

K2 was in Pakistan – also problematic, as the CIA wanted to run this operation with India. Also K2 was harder to climb than Everest. Kanchenjunga – the third highest mountain – was the new target, but again parts of it straddled a border with Nepal. Finally, Nanda Devi was chosen; 7,816 metres high, it had American associations, having been first climbed by a party led by Dr Charles Houston, the long-lived (1913–2009) pioneer of much high-altitude medical research. Nanda Devi would also see an American Tragedy in 1976 when top American climber Willi Unsoeld took his daughter – named after the mountain, Nanda Devi Unsoeld – on an attempt on the peak that ended in her death. It was as if this peak, which was isolated and protected by a natural rock amphitheatre, and remains a sacred summit, was taking revenge after the CIA assault on its lonely integrity.

The radio tracking device needed a power source – and appropriately for something used to spy on nukes, it was nuclear-powered. Weighing 17 kilos it comprised a 'nuclear battery' – 5 kilos of plutonium 238 and 239; the bomb on Nagasaki was made of 6 kilos of the same material. The constant heat of the plutonium was converted into electricity by a surrounding bank of thermocouples – an inefficient method unless you have constant high heat – which the nuclear power pack did indeed have. Five loads were made up to carry the radio, power pack and other pieces of necessary kit. The porters, recruited from the nearest villages of Lata and Peini, competed for the right to carry the nuclear pack SNAP 19C – it kept whoever carried it toasty warm. Unfortunately, it may have had a more long-lasting effect. When

Images of gods are everywhere

Indian journalists went back to find the original thirty-three porters in 2010, apparently none were still alive. The outer case of
SNAP 19C was just 2.5 mm of nickel tungsten alloy. Though the
radioactive leakage would probably have been safe for the porters
in small bursts, no one had thought to calculate its effect during
prolonged contact. And since the device was to be planted at very
high altitude, its resistance to frost and snow was greater than its
resistance to water.

The Indian mountaineer in charge was called Kohli. The
American in charge of training was the venerable and outstanding
climber and *National Geographic* photographer Barry Bishop (who
would later die in a mysterious car crash, where he apparently just
lost control on an empty road in 1976; conspiracists reckon he
knew too much, those who believe in the curse of Nanda Devi
claim he was yet another victim).

In 1965, less than a year after the first Chinese bomb test, the Indian team were flown to Alaska for training with Barry Bishop in the placement of SNAP 19C at high altitude. Everything went swimmingly, and, after forty days, they returned to place the device on the second highest mountain in India – twenty-third highest in the world.

Following the route of British climbers Tilman and Shipton, who had been the first to breach the 'sanctuary' – the rock circle protecting Nandi Devi and its allied peaks – the Indian team established camps up the mountain. For the higher-altitude carries they employed nine Sherpas from Sikkim.

But then the weather began to get worse. Nanda Devi, which had been climbed without the use of modern equipment, was still not an easy climb. At Camp 4 on the mountain, further progress looked impossible. Kohli made the decision to leave the nuclear-powered radio scanner behind.

They found a largeish rock that formed a small semi-protective overhang. Here they covered up SNAP 19C and descended the mountain.

The following year they returned. They ascended to their old high point, yet everything looked different. The rock seemed to have moved. But when they found it, Kohli realised it was a different one. There was only one answer – there had been an avalanche and it had carried away all the equipment.

They looked everywhere, and discovered not a thing. The next year a similar device was lodged on Nanda Kot, a lower mountain in the vicinity. But they continued the search on Nanda Devi. Still nothing came up, despite using Geiger counters to scan the mountainside. It began to dawn on the Americans that SNAP 19C was no snap, that in fact it may have fallen into a crevasse and be deep inside one of the slow-moving glaciers inching their way out of the Nanda Devi sanctuary. This realisation prompted a final search in 1968, but also the decision to reclaim the device on top of Nanda Kot. It had done its work, or enough, and no one wanted to lose another nuclear battery on a mountain.

Everyone kept quiet about the debacle on Nanda Devi until 1978, when an article appeared in *Outside* magazine. This prompted embarrassing questions in the Indian parliament. A report was commissioned and ninety-four pages were filled with advice about what to do and the possible dangers involved. The main one being: what if the nuclear device should enter the Ganges? The glaciers of Nanda Devi feed the upper Ganges. It is one reason the mountain is considered sacred. Had man over-reached himself again and left a poisoned offering in the heart of sacred India?

The conclusion of the report was that very little could be done – aside from a 1982 ban on climbing Nanda Devi or entering the Sanctuary. In 1993 Indian army engineers, under the auspice of 'cleaning up the sanctuary', searched again for the nuke. They found nothing. In 2000, an expedition was sent to the Sanctuary and it recommended it be opened for climbing again – but it remains closed.

14

Messner Nearly Messes up

Whether it is upstream or downstream you'll have to toil.

Naga proverb

We've met Messner before. He is, without doubt, one of the most extraordinary climbers of the twentieth century. Perhaps not an admirable role model – his example supports well the thesis that almost anything can be achieved if you are willing to sacrifice everything and anybody, including parts of yourself, to achieve it. Reinhold Messner wanted to climb Mount Kailash. The Chinese, who decide such things nowadays (and then – it was 1985), were not so sure. On the one hand, Messner, the '*notorische Tabubrecher*' (notorious taboo breaker), was one of the world's most famous and well-regarded mountaineers, the only man to have soloed Everest without oxygen; so it would be a huge coup for materialistic communism if he could summit the peak and piss all over thousands of years of tradition and opium-like religious practice. Put like that, you can see the problem immediately. But what of the distress he would cause by violating a sacred spot for millions of Hindus, Jains, Buddhists and Bonpos, not to mention a number of Zoroastrians? His former wife, journalist Ursula Demeter, wrote that Messner believed that he should be able to climb the mountain; it was, he declared, about an individual's right to freedom. He added that taboos were only for those who create them and nobody would be insulted if they didn't *see* him climbing the mountain . . . It was a rather stupid idea, of course; clearly he was searching for feeble excuses to justify the fact that he wanted to climb this most sacred peak.

Messner and his team arrived in Tibet and waited for Chinese permission. Determined to make his mark, Messner made the 'fastest ever pilgrimage' around Kailash – 45 kilometres in twelve hours. The next day he went one better and circumnavigated the 80 kilometres around Lake Manasarovar in twenty-two-and-a-half hours. He bartered for food with nomads and for payment they accepted a lock of his hair. All was set for an assault on the summit.

The Chinese knew that the huge uproar against this insult would be directed against them, not the bearded psycho climber. Despite this, they had told Messner that when the time was 'politically propitious', he was guaranteed to have first crack at the summit.

Something intervened. Messner, as we've seen, had already lost one brother. He heard that he had lost another: Siegfried, who'd plummeted to his death in the Dolomites. The Kailash expedition decided to cut short their visit and return home.

Messner has declared he has no fear of death. He thinks the afterlife or any description of it is beyond our human thinking. He has conquered many Himalayan summits, all, in their way, sacred summits. He has lost two brothers – both while climbing. We tend to assume that punishment comes after some crime or act of folly, but there is a Tibetan belief that karma may punish you *before* the event concerned happens. You may be punished in childhood for a crime you'll commit in old age . . .

To date, Reinhold Messner has not climbed Mount Kailash.

15

Drug Trade Routes of the Himalayas

A wise man is better than a king: a king is honoured
only in his own country, a wise man everywhere.
Nepalese proverb

Walking through the western Himalayas you'll pass wild mari-
juana growing by the path. By rolling the leaves and flowers in
your hand you can accumulate small balls of resin, which can be
ingested or smoked – or sold to other backpackers. Dope is a key
attraction for some travellers and it has long been part of the hippy
trail to go to India and get stoned. The true mystic alleges dope
is correctly named – it is a soporific, a false friend, heightening
senses but dulling the intuition when sober; it mimics states that
can be made permanent only through rigorous work on the self,
including, perhaps, journeys into the mountains.

In any part of northern Nagaland, the tribal borderlands between Burma and India, you can buy old opium pipes made from
bamboo. Many will still have the sour odour of opium about them.
They were probably only given up recently. During the British
occupation, opium was tolerated: 'Opium they shoud have, but to
get it they should be made to work for it', Sir Andrew Mills wrote
in an 1854 report. The missionaries who arrived in the twentieth
century were opposed to opium, and most of Nagaland is now
Baptist country, with the huge high churches standing on every
peak where the morung longhouses used to stand. But closer

355

towards the Burmese border, opium is still being smoked. Tired old men, who look as if they have given up fighting, puff all day long and argue with their pals. But opium was only ever a minor trade good in the Himalayas; most of it went by sea after the Russians gained control of the Central Asian Khanate Khiva in 1873.

In the central Himalayas, the old trade routes, made up of endless lines of yaks going over the high passes, moved salt from

Get high on religion instead?

Tibet to India. Surplus agricultural products moved the other way. There was also a trade in carpets, furs, medicinal plants (Tibet has always been a major exporter of these), hawks, selected kinds of timber. From the earliest times, rice was shipped down from Nepal into India. Cardamom went from Sikkim and also Nepal. Most copper used in northern India came from mines in Nepal – it was used for making pots and coins, which were minted by kings as they moved from palace to palace, minting coins on the move, their own cashpoint.

Nepal, being the most dominant central Himalayan country, controlled much trade across the mountains. Rulers based in Kathmandu rarely strayed into the provinces. Instead, they were visited by their own rural agents who operated through mandis, local markets, and brought a cut to the big bosses in the capital.

In Nepal I am offered hashish, with that alluring half-heard whisper, all the time. It's funny to think of smoking, which impairs breathing, working as a substitute for the hard breathing of climbing. Of course, many climbers smoke dope, some having picked up the habit when they first visited the Himalayas in the Fifties and Sixties. In many ways, the stiff old English climbers started the hippy trail. Tilman would turn in his grave at the thought, but the example of carrying your own gear and trekking where you like started with people like Eric Shipton and him. Their contemporary Frank Smythe wrote about the Valley of the Flowers in the Himalayan foothills, which encouraged the mystic Peter Caddy to ultimately found the Findhorn New Age community in Scotland. Climbers and seekers, those who would go higher, have a real but not always obvious influence on us all.

16

The Discarded on Everest

The stolen food was eaten by the crow,
but the beak of the raven is red.
Ladakhi proverb

Years ago, driving through the Sahara Desert, I was surprised that
the tourist party I accompanied were most excited by finding the
bonnet of a 1940 Ford truck lying on a dune some 300 kilometres
from any human habitation. We had seen tektite silica glass, rock
carved with images of long-extinct giraffes and baboons, we had
found fossils and discarded flint tools including Acheulean hand
axes and elegantly fashioned harpoon tips – but none of this
compared to finding this man-made, metal, recent – within living
memory – slightly rusty artefact. Shell petrol tins that dated from
the Second World War were also found to be mesmerising . . .

Everest was as blank and clean as a desert until the early part
of the last century, yet now it is increasingly defined by what is
discarded on its slopes. Base camp has become so engorged with
its yearly fill of garbage there are now annual clean-ups to restore
it, if not to its primal pristine nature, at least making it bearable.
Everest base camp is built on a glacier, you can hear it creak and
move slowly down the hill, stretching your tent guy lines, distort-
ing the tent's shape a little each day.

Ice moves, but it moves slowly. A glacier cannot flush rubbish
away like a river. The glacier serves to slow time down as you

358

approach the mountain. The cold preserves and the slow movement of the glacier means that what is preserved, remains.

The discarded on Everest is divided into bodies and climbing
detritus.

The dead on Everest can become landmarks. 'Green boots' is
the body of an Indian climber still in a small cave high up on the
north-east ridge. He lies face down; his garish lime green plastic
boots seem absolutely new. He looks like someone resting, except
his head is buried in snow; like a child playing a game, perhaps,
his head rammed into a snow bank. There are two discarded
used oxygen cylinders; dull red and vaguely industrial-looking,
they stand in contrast to the newness of the dead Indian's boots
and clothes. The extreme difficulty of moving a body at altitude
is a large part of the problem, but not insurmountable. Think of
the ingenuity it takes to weld pipelines at five miles below the
surface of the sea . . . But perhaps I am missing the point here: the
discarded remain on Everest because we wish them to be there.

When Chris Bonington climbed Everest in 1975 'the hard way',
up the previously unclimbed south-west face, the presence of a
Chinese discarded aluminium ring flag at the top was strangely
reassuring. It proved that the Chinese had indeed climbed
Everest and by leaving behind this tethered sturdy remnant they
had somehow tamed the mountain. It is by the accumulation of
garbage that we claim the planet and render it safe for human
consumption . . . the very sight of an old shoe in the wilderness,
or a Godfather beer can on a rocky mountain path, is unwelcome
to the tourist who is already 'safe' and simply getting away from
it all for a simulated wilderness thrill, but for the real adventurer,
lost, feeling the incredible loneliness of places where you don't
count, it can be a very heartening thing to find. It means you are
less insignificant.

Of course, you only have such thoughts when you have signally
failed to connect to the oneness of the mountain, its mystico-
religious significance. On a materialist, Darwinian perspective,

the absence of anything human or human-made only serves to make one feel very small, a mere drop in the ocean. But one purpose of life is to reconcile 'dropness' with 'oceanness' in as much as the drop contains a consciousness of being both the ocean and the drop . . .

The materialist, the type who calls an ice axe an ice axe and never believes a thing that isn't right in front of his eyes (except scientific theories) is confronted by the vast wilderness of Everest, the highest mountain on earth – the supreme example of the unreachable. And then he finds . . . Edward Norton's sock. Left after the failed summit bid of 1922 (so close, and without oxygen) at a camp at 8,000 metres, found in 2001 by the party looking for the dead ones of the 1924 expedition. He or she may claim that they would prefer it to be pure and empty as the day man first set foot on its upper slopes, but they are lying. The comfort of seeing discarded oxygen bottles at the South Col, the handy ladder up the second step, the tangled cables of fixed rope . . . Some of the detritus works as an informal signpost system – 'this way', it tells you. The flapping ripped tent bases at Camp 3 may serve as a ghostly reminder of your potential fate, but they also tell you that humans have been here. Man is a track-following creature, we feel happier when we are on a well-marked trail.

When a mountain is first surveyed for climbing it is truly in a pristine state. The rock may be mossy, overgrown, dripping with water or melting ice. There may be cracks and ramps of snow – accidental ways up the mountain – but man has not left his mark. With the littering of the mountain comes its transformation into a series of 'routes'. Following another's traverse of a snow slope provides a narrow ledge in the snow to walk upon, making the whole experience seem suddenly vastly safer than heading out for the first time across a virgin slope. Climbers know that a raw mountain promises reward, but they mostly cleave to mountains that have already been processed into climbing centres, rather like the snow slopes veined with ski runs of varying difficulty. Aiming for such places – and Everest is the daddy of them all – is to aim for a kind of hybrid wilderness experience, one very much mediated by man's psychological domination of the peak. The equipment one brings to assault a mountain is less important than what one leaves behind; a siege-gun attack on an unclimbed mountain is a very different, much rawer experience than soloing a littered, much-climbed prominence like Everest. But that rawness is not what the climber is usually seeking.

The need to litter Everest extends to the leaving of human sacrifices – signpost corpses of those who lost their struggle with the mountain. The most famous, and almost most shocking, are the remains of George Mallory. His white exposed buttocks strike the po-faced as indecent. They certainly serve to memorialise the fragility of the climber – what a contrast we feel to the Zarathustra fist-shaking supermen who dare to raid the unreachable. Mallory's body – the first symbolic sacrifice to the mountain – was examined in a scientific manner in 1999 – his pockets rifled – in order to 'work out' what exactly happened. The main concern was to discover whether he and Irvine reached the summit or not. There is still a missing camera that all such detritus enthusiasts (and I include myself) longingly hope will reveal that these two did make it to the top first. This operates like the desire to prove Columbus was beaten to America by St Brendan or the Arab navigators from Spain.

If Mallory was the first, then his sacrifice will be less in vain; it will, by sleight of hand, justify his death – which is an awkward reminder to all climbers that we are in fact mortal.

The other dead include those who were ignored as they stumbled about in a hypoxic haze. Such is the difficulty of looking after yourself at high altitude, morality changes to fit the possible rather than the desired outcome. Commercial clients have neither the expertise nor inclination to help other 'customers' who have made a mistake, perhaps just a tiny miscalculation, which at 8,000 metres becomes fatal. I have read accounts where a commercial client boasts, almost, of his regret at not helping another . . . because I felt this put him in the same tragic-heroic capacity as those on earlier disaster climbs such as 1996. He was now a bona fide Everest climber, weighed down by regrets and a dose of 'real life' in seeing corpses and not helping those on their way to becoming one.

Climbing attracts all kinds, from the leftist to the fascist sympathiser: Julius Evola, Heidegger, the Nazi-sponsored attempts on the Eiger – perhaps it calls to the heartless part in all of us to see others fail and us succeed. I know that this competitive urge to overtake those weaker than oneself is always apparent on any hill or peak.

The icefall on the southern side literally eats aluminium ladders and ropes. It is the most dangerous place to be on the mountain – tottering seracs the size of a house can smash down on you at any time. The 'Icedoctors' are a team of Sherpas dedicated to fixing rope and ladders through this maze of ice. Every year there are fatalities in the icefall. The metal, crunched and fallen, the bodies of the dead swallowed by vast deep crevasses, all this slowly moves down the mountain. The glacier cannot digest these human remains; it merely preserves them, rather in the way a shark's stomach carries old number plates, life preservers and a fishing float or two – not revealed until the shark is caught and cut open. The Khumbu Glacier has its own secrets; it serves a convenient mystifying purpose, rendering vague the too horrifying end of some people.

The discarded is relied on by others. When Maurice Wilson attempted his mad solo climb of Everest in the 1930s he survived on food left behind by earlier expeditions. He found crampons but did not know how to use them . . . In 1996 a garbled message from the Moldavian team via Scott Fischer's head Sherpa was sent – the implication was that all the ropes from the south summit onwards had been fixed. The expeditions that followed were relying on the discards of others. But they over-relied. The ropes had not been fixed. The resulting time lags contributed to the disaster that followed.

If the mountain – and Everest is *the* mountain – is scarred and littered and yet is also the unreachable, we have the strange combination of a garbage-dump shrine. Russian-made oxygen bottles litter the upper reaches like syringes in a West Hollywood parking lot. The bottle, like some inflated steroidal syringe, is the 'fix' for the addicted climber. It is a mark of shame that he cannot climb unaided like the few pure ones who ascended without supplementary oxygen. A new orthodoxy claims that those who choose to climb without oxygen are 'irresponsible' and a danger to the fee-paying majority who do. Yet it is perfectly obvious that those who have only been able to ascend the heights with their bottled air account for almost all fatalities on Everest. This air, from the plains, is a sure sign of their interloper status – it allows the unreachable to be reached but also polluted in a double sense.

That the majority, who are unable to ascend to the super-athletic standards needed to make the summit unaided by oxygen, should round on the minority is a not unexpected sign of the times. In rock climbing, the use of bolts was sneered at in the past as cowardice or incompetence, but is now standard practice for high-level climbs. Soloing is used as a sort of placation of the old spirits of climbing – whereby a bolted climb will be ascended and practised using the safety of bolts and then climbed without (in a true solo rather than simply climbing alone and using the existing bolts and a self-administered belay system).

One cannot help returning again to the lonely figure of Messner, climbing Everest without oxygen, alone and with no fixed ropes. His skinny, bearded presence, the stigmata of his frost-chewed extremities – his name Messner/Messiah – gives the clue to the prophetic Christ-like role he plays in high-altitude mountaineering. His visions and temptations are set down in his hallucinatory account of his solo climb of Everest – taking nothing with him, but abandoning a tent and other gear; at one point he loses his rucksack and cries because it has become, in the hypoxic state, a dear friend. Even the chosen one cannot help but discard things on the mountain.

17

Lost for Forty-Three Days

You may find God searching for stones.
Nepalese proverb

Things are discarded or lost on the mountains. So are people.
It's very easy to get lost on a trail going downhill. When you
go uphill, say through the rhododendrons and pines and other
shrubs and bushes, you may come across forks in the trail, but
if you take the wrong turn it will either converge or branch off
considerably. This is a function of going up a mountain where
the paths tend to converge. Going downhill, the opposite
happens.

It was the middle of November and the weather was still fine.
I was coming down from the high hills, low by Himalayan standards – 3,500 metres, no more – above Yoksum, the old capital
of Sikkim. I was descending with two Germans – Susanne and
Mathias – and they were slightly ahead of me. The route was
mainly very obvious – it was an ancient pilgrimage route made
from compacted cobbles probably hundreds of years ago. Land-
slides and weather had taken their toll, so from time to time deep
cuts in the sandy, rock-laden soil marked an alternative route. But
it always joined back up with the original rocky trail.

I needed to take a piss. I did not tell them, as it was faintly
embarrassing to have them decide whether to wait or go on while
I fumbled around in the bushes looking for cover. I thought I'd be

quick and easily catch them up; Mathias had knee problems and wasn't descending very rapidly.

It was hard to find somewhere you couldn't be seen from the path. There were Indians and Sikkimese using the path. I didn't want to offend them. I roamed further through the undergrowth, past pines, prickly bushes, ferns. I found a hollow, took a piss, then, instead of heading back *up* to the path – which looked a tiring thing to do – I realised that as I was already below it I could keep going and rejoin it on the next of its snaky lower loops. The path went back and forth, winding in loops all the way down the mountain.

Eager to catch up, I charged downhill. I had both my poles, which caught in the undergrowth, but I needed at least one to keep stable on the slippery surface, made up of leaves on earth. The altitude was getting lower – maybe about 3,500 metres now – and I was feeling better and fitter all the time. Even so, I was having a hard time picking my way over boulders and rotting tree trunks.

I crossed a grassy area I didn't remember. It was criss-crossed with indistinct, undecided scuffs of sandy earth. As if giant rabbits had been making tentative attempts at burrowing. Was this part of the path? I kept going to the edge of the grass and it was a sudden steep drop.

I couldn't see anyone at all.

I had an urge to charge off to the left, but I've been lost before – on two occasions for an entire day – so I calmed down and tried to get a better sense of where I was. All I knew was that I had completely lost the path.

I wasn't in the high mountains on a proper climb, but paradoxically, there's much less chance of getting lost on such an expedition. Mountaineers are not usually alone and they are above the snow line. Wearing brightly coloured clothes, as long as the visibility is good they stand out a mile off. Lower down, beneath tree cover, among boulders, rotting tree trunks and fast-flowing glacier-fed streams, it's not so easy to be spotted.

When you're lost it all looks the same

And such mixed terrain is, as I found, difficult enough under good conditions. But imagine a heavy fall of snow and snow still falling. These were the conditions faced by James Scott, a twenty-two-year-old Australian trying to make his way back to a remote village in the Nepalese Himalayas. It was 22 December 1991 and the last hut he and his trek mate Mark had stayed at had just closed for the winter. It looked like snow, but the hut owner, a Nepali, had assured him it wouldn't snow that day. It did, heavily.

The two were trying to climb over a 4,600-metre pass – lower than the pass I had descended from that day – and down to another village. When the snow came, visibility shrank to less than ten metres. They seemed to be on the wrong side of a creek, according to the map. Snow was building up everywhere. Mark wanted to keep going, but James wanted to turn back. In such a situation you should always remain together and take the least risky option – which on the face of it was turning back. However, the situation was complicated by the usual circumstance in trekking – James and Mark had met only a few days earlier. Unlike climbing, where you are usually out with trusted fellow climbers, in trekking you may find yourself with a stranger; what is more, it is hard to verify their experience.

Mark wanted to continue ascending and looking for the path. He said that they ought to keep going until 1 p.m. and then, if they still were lost, return. He calculated that they would need no more than a few hours to get back to the last village. James thought differently. He was already thinking about Kathmandu, where he wanted to put a call through to his fiancée in Australia. By leaving it until 1 p.m. he would be that much later in getting to Kathmandu. They took the fateful decision to split up. Just like in the horror movies, it always starts going wrong when the team decide to split up. Looked at coolly, Mark's decision was the correct one if they intended to make it over the pass – he allowed for a cut-off which seemed safe. But James's decision was the classical safe option: if in doubt, turn back. If the two had turned back, it would probably have been OK. But having split up, both were now at risk.

Mark carried on climbing and found that they had indeed been way off course. At the top of the ridge where the pass lay, he was far to the west. However, he was able to make it across to the correct path and descend safely down the other side.

All James had to do was backtrack. But descending a path obscured by snow is very hard. And all he had on his feet were training shoes – 'sandshoes', he called them; his boots had seemed too heavy and cumbersome. He didn't have a cooker with him or any food. Only a sleeping bag, clothes, a water bottle and some medical supplies. James was a trainee doctor.

Wearing light shoes isn't really a problem in snow, as long as it isn't deep and it isn't steep. So up until it snowed the decision wasn't a bad one – and if he had relied on instinct and not gone over the pass instead of following the hut owner's exhortations that it wouldn't snow, then he'd have been fine. But James also had the burden of being an extremely fit young man – he had done six years of karate – and so had a more relaxed view of any physical exertion he might have to make.

It's a paradox that the fitter and stronger you are, the more likely you are to have an accident. Your confidence carries you into places you aren't prepared for, and it is lack of preparation that kills. James didn't have a lighter or any matches. He had no survival skills, such as being able to make fire with a bow drill. He wasn't a mountaineer and was unhappy with steep drops and exposed cliffs. What he did have was a strong faith in God and a fierce determination to survive.

Floundering in the snow, he was soon soaked through. He down-climbed some hairy-looking cliffs trying to find his way back to the path. For a while he followed streams that plunged downhill. This works on the plains, but not in serious mountains. Streams always end up getting into gorges or plunging over steep cliffs. It's much better to be out on a ridge when descending, where you can see some way ahead. Sure enough, James found his way blocked and had to backtrack. In the end, night fell and he had to sleep out under a large overhanging cliff face which was at least free of snow.

The next day saw him getting more lost and desperate. Unless you have been trained to deal with being lost – which means having a plan to deal with being lost before it happens – it is very hard to resist going back and forth in a more and more chaotic fashion. People regularly die on the hills of Britain, not because of any particular difficulty or danger, but because they are sufficiently high and remote to engender panic. They make mistakes like setting down their pack to move faster, only to realise they can't find their way back to their pack, leaving them lost and without resources.

Having been very lost before – once in the Indonesian rainforest and once in the Canadian Rockies – mercifully, for only a day – I knew how to judge if the situation I was in was 'serious' or not. I thought not. The weather was fine – it wasn't snowing or freezing, though at night the temperature had been -15 degrees Celsius. I was on the broad face of a mountain – I hadn't crossed any ravines or entered any new valleys. I knew that if I kept going downhill I would meet one of the several rivers I would have to cross. This river had a wire bridge, so all I would have to do is find the bridge to be back on course. I had waterproofs and a down jacket, water but no food.

Wading through snow, James's clothes were no longer frozen stiff; they soon reverted to being soaked. He was starting to get very cold. He spent another day floundering before he realised he would get hypothermia wandering around in such wet, cold conditions. He found another protected ledge which had an open area next to it. There were the remains of a campfire – years old, but still a first sign that other humans could at least reach this spot. And the open area would be visible to any helicopter, should it come searching. He decided to wait.

He had two bars of chocolate and no water – he had lost his water bottle earlier in the day, scrambling over steep rocks. He ate the chocolate in two days.

Meanwhile, the alert had been raised and his family had initiated a search for him. But they were handicapped by not really knowing what was going on. In the end, his sister Joanne flew to Kathmandu to try to find James.

The main problems had been caused by misinformation. A group of hikers had claimed they had seen James – this sent the search party off in the wrong direction. When Joanne eventually confronted the group, it was clear they hadn't been sure it was James. The hut owner claimed he hadn't seen James or Mark. But later he agreed he had – again, after a wasted search in the wrong place. And the official who had debriefed Mark had misheard the last village they had left. The search needed to get back on track.

The waiting and form-filling of embassies and official search parties didn't seem to be working. Then Joanne began a random conversation with a Nepali taxi driver who turned out to be from the very region where James was lost. She had been told one area was impassable but the taxi driver assured her that it wasn't. She now had a new area to search.

Joanne was desperate. By chance she met an American woman with an interest in Buddhism, who told her of a Buddhist temple where the monks were able to predict the future. Joanne went there, but the main monk was busy. Instead, she met the smiling and reassuring Thrangu Rinpoche, a Buddhist lama who used a simple prayer ritual to enter a different mental state in order to gain an intuition about where James was. After a pause, he told Joanne to look in the same area that the taxi driver had suggested. Without prompting, he pointed to the map. Then he smiled and said she would meet James again. Joanne at least had something reassuring to go on.

Back at the rock ledge, James had tried to break out. He managed a few hundred metres but had to turn back. He was resigned to waiting it out. He was able to melt snow in his sleeping-bag cover and then drink it. He also found that if he made a large snowball and left it in the sun (which appeared a week after the snowstorm ended), the interior turned to water and he could drink it without having to melt the snow in his mouth.

He managed at long last to dry out his clothes, which meant he was warmer at night. The first few nights, despite his sleeping bag, he was intensely cold, fearing that he would die. This was midwinter in the Himalayas – even in November walking around at 2,000 metres I have found it bitingly cold when in the shade, and at night it would be well below freezing.

James took comfort, if that's what it can be called, from the life and drawn-out death of Bobby Sands, who managed sixty-seven days without eating before he died. The alarming loss of body mass started to slow down. The first fourteen days saw the biggest amount of wasting away. He felt very weak and although his clothes were now dry, any excursion was very tiring. He realised he would either be rescued or die in this place. Not that he was scared of dying. A strong faith in God grew stronger. He prayed every night for everyone he could remember. While dreaming, he had conversations and encounters with his family and friends that seemed as if they were happening in real life; waking up on the narrow ledge was a terrible shock. At one point he was shocked by what sounded like a human howling. It was a bear. James was so hungry he believed he could kill the bear with his scissors. He shouted at the bear and it eyeballed him. Perhaps sensing his aggression, it backed away. Though he heard it howling again, it never tried to interfere with him. Unlike the crows who'd fly in every day to see whether he was still alive or not. James played dead and they got closer and closer. He tried to grab one but it was too fast. After that, they continued to check on him, but kept their distance. James tried eating various leaves and pine needles, but all seemed disgusting to him – and he didn't know which ones were poisonous. A thin caterpillar came near – and he ate it immediately, enjoying the brief respite from hunger it provided.

But he was still able to note the beauty of the world. It is worth quoting:

> Never before had I appreciated just how beautiful a small bird could appear. I'd never really taken in the majesty of a clear starry night. I had been so humbled that something as simple as a few hours of sunlight would fill me with warmth and gratitude.

Meanwhile the search was getting closer, Joanne having narrowed it down to three locations, including a huge valley right in the area predicted by the Buddhist monk.

James saw a helicopter flying over about three kilometres away. He blundered out into the clearing and waved his sleeping bag. The helicopter circled round. He could see the pilots looking straight ahead and talking. There was no way they could see him.

He decided he would make one more attempt to walk out. His pack weighed only four kilos but it felt much heavier. As he approached the thick scrub and bush, he felt nauseous from the effort. He retched and vomited. When he coughed, his spittle was bright red. He ate snow and spat it out – red snow. Should he go on, or return? By now huge storm clouds were gathering. He had no choice but to return to the ledge.

Whether to return or go on . . . I have always hated retracing my steps, and yet this is the single best way to avoid being lost. Cutting across to where you think the path might be is always very hit or miss. Some people have a natural sense of direction. I've been lost in the English hills with someone who has, and it's quite a remarkable experience to see them work out and trek their way to safety. I have a very average sense of direction, easily disturbed when in unfamiliar surroundings. Like now. Though I had a plan to descend to the river, I really wanted to find a path. Rivers in the wild can often have non-existent banks and unless the water is low it's almost impossible to ascend them.

James had to make his own decision about staying or moving. He had now reached rock bottom. Instead of making a decision, he decided to stop eating snow or drinking the water it contained. He would dehydrate himself to death. He thought that although suicide was a sin, God would forgive him, given the extreme circumstances he was in.

That night he drifted off and dreamed with incredible clarity that he was back in Brisbane with all his family and his fiancée. He thanked them all, especially his parents: 'I went on to tell the crowd how fortunate I'd been, what a good life I'd had and how much I looked forward to the many years ahead. It was all so vivid, so tangible.'

But when he awoke he was genuinely shocked to find he was still in this pitiful, cold and uninviting place. He felt anger with himself. He realised he'd been taking smug satisfaction in giving up. He realised he had a one in a million chance of being rescued and he'd given up on it.

The following morning, he started eating snow again. 'The

taste of that first mouthful, the only snow I had eaten in two days, was like heaven.' It relieved the pain of the cracks and ulcers that had developed in his mouth when he stopped drinking. Slowly he rehydrated himself with melting snow. He considered the dream to be an important lesson: never give up hope.

What he didn't know was that the helicopter *had* seen him.

The following day the search team circled overhead and waved to James. After six weeks, he had been found – the only problem now was getting him to safety. The helicopter couldn't land, so James realised he would have to survive for several more days until a ground party could get to him. He now had no strength to move. He had to urinate into a shampoo bottle, emptying it as far away as possible. Then he said his prayers and tried to sleep – except he heard someone answering him. From far off he heard voices calling – he had been found!

A year on, he had recovered except for slight balance problems and periodic flickering episodes of double vision, but these were slowly improving. He'd resumed his studies and his karate, and he'd got married.

The usual self-appointed 'survival' experts were sceptical that a man could exist on no food for forty-three days in a Himalayan winter. These reports hurt James and his sister, but he wrote, 'What does it matter what others think when I have everything I could ever want?'

In my own tiny adventure, I hoped I wasn't looking at forty-two more days on a Sikkimese mountainside. I was still blundering around looking for the path. The terrain was increasingly horrendous – rocks, tangled undergrowth, boulders, steep drops and slippery leaves lying on earth – and it wasn't snowing. Then I heard the tonk-tonk sound of yak bells. The path was behind me! Though it was only three metres away, I couldn't see it, because the cobbled stone was deeper cut than the hillside and in shade. I waited until the long line of yaks and their masters passed. The yak men were friendly, but I could tell my enthusiastic greeting startled them. Little did they know that I had thought myself lost only a few minutes earlier.

Back on the path, I raced to catch up with Mathias and Susanne. It was mostly downhill, with a few switchbacks – and about fifteen kilometres to Yoksum. After an hour I realised they must have been much further ahead than I thought, but when I reached Yoksum they weren't there. An hour later they arrived. Somehow, in all my wandering, I must have overtaken them. We both had the same question for each other – Where were you? 'I was lost,' was all I could reply.

18

Beck is Back

———

Do not start your worldly life too late;
do not start your religious life too early.
Bhutanese proverb

Lost things, lost people. But nothing could compare with the 1996 expedition – the subject of many books and now a blockbusting movie that has grossed over $200 million – when several commercial expeditions made wrong decisions during a violent storm resulting in eight deaths in a day. There were twelve deaths on the mountain in all – the worst tragedy in Everest's history until the sixteen deaths in 2014 and the eighteen deaths during the Nepal earthquake in 2015. But these later accidents had, it seems, less attributable human error and more sheer bad luck than the 1996 disaster.

The movie, of course, gets it wrong. And the most important book, by Jon Krakauer, has been contested by many. Of course, being there (Krakauer was a client climber) and being implicated does not help objectivity. I decided to read everything available on the subject in order to discover what exactly happened that terrible day. But as I did, I became more and more fascinated by the most extraordinary survivor of the whole disaster – Beck Weathers.

People have died on Everest, in large numbers. And people have survived – bivouacking like Doug Scott with no down suit

Surprisingly good views can be found on hotel roofs

or sleeping bag at 8,500 metres. But no one has been pronounced dead – not once but twice – and then risen again to tell the tale. No one except the amateur climber and doctor Beck Weathers.

Uniquely in the history of climbing, a disaster occurred on Everest that rivals the story of Scott versus Amundsen. It was also a tragedy. What is tragedy? An unavoidable disaster? Or the disastrous unfolding of the faults embedded within a character, faults that might lie undetected without the application of immense pressure? In the case of Scott, it was the ambition to reach the South Pole that revealed his weaknesses as a planner and leader. In the case of Everest in 1996, it was a huge and devastating storm that compounded follies – follies generated by character defects.

Put any man under enough pressure and he will crack. Or any woman. The trick in life is not to believe you'll never crack, rather one should become very aware of situations when one is under pressure, the sort of pressure that distorts personality and causes judgement to fail.

For those unfamiliar with the tale, it can be simply told. Two professional climbing teams with paid clients had agreed to summit Everest on 10 June. This was supposed to be a lucky day for one of the leaders, New Zealander Rob Hall. Though it had to be said, lucky was a relative term. The previous year, 1995, he had turned back a mere 180 metres below the top because he deemed there was not enough time to descend.

So here he was, exactly a year later, but this time with a top writer on board, observing everything he was doing. Perhaps acknowledging the trust extended to him, Krakauer is far from harsh on dishing out the blame. He calls the storm 'rogue' (although both teams had weather forecast data which predicted the storm coming on 11 May), and he merely suggests the Sherpas could have been faster at fixing ropes. He also went a good way to ruining the reputation of top Russian climber Anatoli Boukreev by suggesting the 'Rope Bullet' should have stayed behind to help clients down the mountain rather than shooting off ahead. Whereas, by shooting off ahead, Boukreev was in a position to make hot drinks and launch several rescue missions that succeeded in saving many members of the party.

Everest is easiest climbed by the route by which it first fell – the south-east ridge. But this is only the upper part of the climb. Everest stands on a 5,000-metre plateau which is the height at which base camp is situated. Despite its glamorous-sounding name, base camp is a flattened area of terminal moraine – gravel carried down by the Khumbu Glacier – and has the look of a rubbish-strewn quarry with bad sanitation and other problems for travellers. Tents and tarps cover the area that sits at the bottom of the famed 'icefall'. Here the glacier rises up vertically in a mass of falling blocks – some bigger than houses – runnels, chasms, and corridors that climbers squeeze through on their upward journey to the flatter section of the glacier that winds up between the peaks of Everest and neighbouring Lhotse.

To penetrate this moving mass of ice – shifting up to a metre a day sometimes – Sherpas rig a labyrinthine upward passage of fixed ropes and aluminium ladders, sometimes as many as three 3.5-metre sections lashed together to cross a seemingly bottomless crevasse. Down you look into the blue shimmering ice, which grows darker as your crampons stick and grate against the aluminium rungs. Some of the client climbers mocked Boukreev because he climbed the icefall in running spikes rather than boots and crampons, but this was a perfectly logical decision; the temperature was not high, and spiked shoes were several kilos lighter than boots.

At the top of the icefall is Camp 1 (there are three more camps before the 'high camp' in the gap between Lhotse and Everest). Much of the initial part of the climb is up the south face of Lhotse, before traversing across on to Everest and up the south-east ridge to the top. For a period of six weeks, climbers yoyo between base camp and camps 1, 2 and 3. The idea is to slowly acclimatise to higher and higher altitudes. Given that they have only walked for a week before reaching base camp, this is a necessary requirement. Compare this to the six-week walk from Darjeeling that the original attempts on Everest required and you can understand the speculation that a longer period walking in, at a less crippling – indeed, liveable – altitude, is a better way to build fitness than being choppered in and then making so many forays up the mountain. Messner's solo attempt on Everest saw him acclimatise by running 1,000 metres above and below his campsites on the walk in; the Crane brothers, too, in their celebrated 1983 running of all the main Himalayan passes, also ran comfortably up to base-camp level.

Once acclimatised, the climbers wait for 'a window in the weather'. Since Everest is so high it is plagued year-round by high winds caused by the jet stream. But just before the monsoon there is a gap – usually in May – and that is when people launch their summit attempts. In 1996, weather forecast information supplied by Denmark and the UK's Met Office, and informally shared by a team making an IMAX Everest movie with Rob Hall and Scott

Fischer (the other team leader), suggested that 11 May would be especially stormy. So 10 May was fixed upon for the summit.

The elements of the story were compelling, ramped up by the presence of media personalities. Successful author Jon Krakauer was on one team, sponsored by the world's number one outdoor magazine, *Outside*. On the opposing team was Sandy Pitman, a millionaire socialite and former fashion editor, reporting for NBC. From being a nerd's game, climbing had suddenly become super sexy.

But the presence of media reporters would be unnerving to the clients – the people who had paid up to $65,000 to be hauled up Everest by highly experienced professional guides. It would be much more unnerving than knowing that a book would be written after a 'real' expedition. Someone who pays a lot of money to get up a mountain they wouldn't be able to climb on their own, must face up to their own shame. Though it is becoming more malleable, the original climbing community lived by the unstated rule that it's OK for kids and those just starting out climbing to take a course or be guided up a peak, but after that you need to join a club and find like-minded climbers. The reason is obvious: climbing is a highly dangerous activity, and high-altitude climbing is one of the most dangerous sports around – it makes Formula One look like a race around a school playing field.

Jon Krakauer described forty-nine-year-old Beck Weathers as 'garrulous'. Weathers himself says that was just him wanting to be liked by the rest of the team. 'If someone had thrown a Frisbee I'd have caught it with my teeth to please them,' he wrote.

Weathers was certainly fit enough for the epic ascent. He'd trained hard and had considerable snow- and ice-climbing experience. His resting pulse at base camp was 'about 90' whereas Jon Krakauer's was 110, a source of some pride, perhaps; he was seven years older than the writer, after all.

But Weathers made two rookie errors before the climb started. He brought untested boots with him and he had his eyes lasered, a radial keratotomy, in order to cure his short sight. He'd assumed that boots of the same brand, style and size would be function-ally identical (I've made the same assumption and been caught out the same way, albeit in the much humbler circumstances of walking the British Columbian plateau). Manufacturers actually change lasts and tiny aspects of similar products all the time, just as perfume makers change the smell of a classic scent, but they keep quiet about it to preserve the 'brand' appeal. To take unused boots on to the world's highest mountain smacks of the kind of faith in others you need when you're working in an environment like a hospital where everything is highly controlled. If you were *too* self-reliant in such a place, you'd never get anything done, you'd spend so much time checking up on every nurse and subordinate. Beck Weathers was a successful pathologist but he had neglected to learn some basic mountain survival lessons. The boots rubbed his shins and gave him ulcers, which, at altitude, did not heal. He simply 'sucked it up', as he put it. But an open sore on your body is a source of stress, a drain on the immune system.

The second source of stress was far more pertinent: the eye operation didn't work at altitude. Doctors are so used to sceptical patients that they are often gullible when it comes to treatment for themselves – well-informed of all the options, maybe, but over-optimistic about the benefits of medical intervention. There was evidence in 1996 that lasering the eyes weakened the cornea so much it could explode if exposed to the high G forces that a fighter pilot might experience. The low pressure environment at 8,000 metres or more would simulate to some extent the effect of an external G force. Pressure on the inside would overwhelm the lower outside pressure and distort the eyeball. This is what happened to Beck. He began to go blind on the route from High Camp to the summit.

As all short-sighted people know, when the sun is bright your pupil contracts and your eyesight improves. Beck waited some way below the south summit for the sun to rise higher and for this improvement to occur. He was told by Rob Hall to wait there for thirty minutes. If his condition didn't improve, he was *not* to climb on. 'If you cannot see in thirty minutes, I don't want you climbing.'

Rob Hall and Beck were 450 metres below the summit. It was 7.30 a.m. It was not unreasonable for Hall to expect to summit at 11 a.m. as planned and be back with Beck at 12 or 1 p.m. If there were hold-ups, there was always the turnaround time of 1 p.m., meaning a return to Beck by 2 or 3 p.m.

Either way, Beck was being asked to wait with no protection, no tent or bivvy or hot drinks for five to seven hours at 8,400 metres. It was an insane suggestion. In risk-management terms, Rob Hall had just created a 'fulfilment loop': X requires Y to move to safety. Instead of X and Y having individual risk factors, they were now connected, so it was X times Y – multiplying the risk potential by a huge amount.

Any form of central control multiplies risk, unless there is a Plan C for when Plan B screws up. Because Beck worked within the high-trust and high-functioning environment of a hospital, he simply obeyed the orders of his boss, Rob Hall. Just as it didn't pay to question his superiors at work, he didn't have the mental habit of questioning Hall's judgement. He never asked himself, What if Hall is held up? What if I'm stuck here?

It's obvious that both Beck and Hall assumed that Beck would get better and climb to the top, albeit later than everyone else.

But Hall made Beck promise to wait for him. Such a promise should never have been extracted. Beck had complete faith in Hall and waited, declining offers to help him back down. He waited until noon, when the first people to turn around started descending past him. This group offered the now very cold Beck a chance to come down with them. He'd been standing still for four and a half hours. They told him they were turning back because of the logjam at the south summit, caused by delays in fixing ropes and organising oxygen supplies. The descending climbers knew that a

1 p.m. turnaround was now impossible. And Beck knew that Hall was at the back, so the likelihood of him appearing in the next two hours was very slim.

He should have gone down and saved himself. But as Beck said, 'I promised Hall I would stay put . . .'

Never give a promise you cannot keep, especially on a mountain. If Hall didn't turn up, then the implication was that he should wait there until he died – which was clearly absurd.

Of course it's easy to make judgements when you're warm and cosy at sea level. At 8,400 metres, hypoxia is a very real risk. And not altogether obvious. With less oxygen to the brain, one can become over-optimistic, over-focused, slightly euphoric – a condition known as HAS: High Altitude Stupid.

At sea level, Beck might never have made such a promise, or kept it well past the time it had any meaning. Climbers talk about the habitual actions – putting on crampons in the dark, kicking up snow slopes, using ice axes – which keep them alive. But I suggest the reason client climbing is so dangerous – or potentially dangerous, unless a guide or Sherpa is assigned to each client – is that ordinary people who live ordinary (albeit high-status and well paid) lives do not develop the right mental habits for making decisions in adverse, i.e. hypoxic, conditions. Climbers who rely on themselves know that nothing is certain in the high mountains, that a promise is something one just can't give. Every time a 'fulfilment loop' threatens to close, it should be forced open with a contingency plan.

Fellow clients agreed to leave Beck to be looked after by the guides higher up the mountain. Guides who would be dead in forty-eight hours.

Professional guiding has always had a place in Alpine climbing – and for people who just want to tell their friends they've climbed Mont Blanc or the Eiger, it works just fine. Every mountain in the Alps has a relatively easy route to the top – including the Eiger – and a guide can insist on taking a route that matches the skill of the client. The same is simply not true of Everest, or, indeed, any peaks over 8,000 metres (or 7,000 metres, for that matter). Weather and altitude make any high peak dangerous. With externally supplied oxygen, the risks of altitude are diminished somewhat. So that leaves weather as the final unalterable risk in the equation.

High-altitude climbing is a weather game. Messner may have only three toes left after his many brushes with extreme cold, but he is still alive. An expert at moving fast when the weather is right, Messner is merciless about setting his own pace. If you can't keep up with him, he'll leave you behind – because he knows that going at the wrong pace is physically much more exhausting than it ought to be 'on paper', so to speak. He needs to move at an optimum pace, because when you move fast you are less likely to be caught out by the weather.

Anatoli Boukreev had won national speed-climbing challenges in the old Soviet Union and it was known from the start that he would be climbing without oxygen. Would this slow him down? Perhaps a fraction. When he had climbed with experienced climbers wearing oxygen on another face of Everest the previous year, he had been overtaken. But this was not likely to happen on the south face of Everest with all the relatively inexperienced and elderly climbers he would be guiding to the top.

While it is true that altitude problems can affect people of any age, high-altitude climbing is an athletic activity. It's an endurance sport before anything else and the older you are, the more work you have to do to keep yourself fit. For someone who climbs professionally, perhaps that is not a problem; for an amateur who has another job, simply 'getting into shape' for Everest may not be enough if you are over forty.

There have been many accounts of the 1996 disaster – which sticks in people's imagination not just because, as I have mentioned, there were celebrity media reporters involved, nor because there was unspoken rivalry between the two main teams, led by

Rob Hall and Scott Fischer, both trying to make their names as the number one suppliers of high-altitude climbing experiences. A further reason was the ghoulish way it was repeated how climbers were left for dead and, finally, how one climber, left for dead not once but three times, finally stumbled into Camp 2 very much alive (though he would lose his nose, one arm and his fingers on the other hand to frostbite). But I suspect the real reason it became viral before viral was a term, is that Rob Hall, the most prominent leader, was able to make a final radio call to his pregnant wife a few hours before he died; it being painfully obvious to both that he was going to his death and would never see his daughter. In a heart-rending conversation, Hall and his wife agreed the name Sara for their unborn daughter. He then signed off by telling his wife 'not to worry'. Rob Hall had earlier announced it was a 'day to set records'. With excruciating irony, he was right: it was the highest number of climbers ever to perish in a single day, and the helicopter rescue of Beck Weathers was, at 5,800 metres, the highest ever successfully made. It was a tale of extraordinary dimensions, and many different viewpoints were taken after Jon Krakauer's bestselling *Into Thin Air* appeared to present a definitive case.

This turned out not to be. Which was not surprising, considering that the demands of authorship required Krakauer to find various people to blame for the mishap.

Was it the weather? Was it the failure of the Sherpas to fix ropes between the southern summit and the Hillary Step? Was it the logjam caused by people waiting for oxygen and ropes to be fixed?

Or was it simply a bad decision to not turn back?

The high camp at 8,230 metres is where the climbers wait before launching their eighteen-hour assault on the summit. Twelve hours to the top and six back to the camp. They then descend to Camp 2 the next day and head down to base camp. Eighteen hours of oxygen were to be supplied to each climber, leaving zero room for a mistake. Since each canister of oxygen costs $700 to buy and transport up the mountain, there was some explanation for this parsimonious approach. Nevertheless, with no room for error should the journey take longer than planned (bad weather or soft snow might slow things down, along with queues at the natural bottlenecks such as the Hillary Step), then the team would be out of oxygen. For the likes of Boukreev, who climbed without oxygen, this would not be a problem. But most would be relying on supplemental oxygen from Camp 1 onwards.

Oxygen mixes with the air to become an enhanced supply; the body, when suddenly deprived of this, reacts in a number of ways. For some it just slows right down, making effort supremely hard. But for some the result of a sudden drop in oxygen levels is to develop rapid altitude-sickness problems. The parallel problem is the reduction in blood circulation as the body closes off capillaries near the skin's surface to maintain oxygen levels at the core. This results in frost damage – sometimes quite terrible damage, as in the case of Beck Weathers whose entire arm would become a single frozen lump of dead meat.

At the high camp, then, the plan is to start early – ideally before midnight – climb towards the south-east ridge using head torches, to be in place for arrival at the top by 11 a.m.

Naturally, there has to be a window for errors and hold-ups. Rob Hall told his climbers this would be 1 p.m. This was emphatically stated by Lou Kasischke, one of Hall's clients. Scott Fischer, the second team leader, set no turnaround time, assuming that his clients would set their own – or, if in trouble, be turned back by the guides.

Unfortunately, such laissez-faire management doesn't work well at 8,230 metres. A feature of oxygen starvation is an increase in demented focus, monomania. You lose sight of other people, other goals. It is one reason that high places are synonymous with pilgrimage – as we have seen elsewhere – and so if an assistant guide tells you to turn back, when you've dropped $65,000 and a lot of effort to get there, you may refuse to obey them. You might listen to the boss, but both Hall and Fischer were leading from the back, focusing on helping those who were having trouble, rather than optimising the efforts of those at the front. This strategy works well on low-risk endeavours such as a school hike, where the object is for everyone to finish, but in a high-risk environment where instant decision-making is crucial, it is far more efficient to have the key decision-maker at the front.

It is interesting to note that the other commercial team on the mountain at that time was run by Scotsman Henry Todd. He really did lead from behind – taking a Lord Hunt role down at the lower camps. But this meant he gave full responsibility to his climbers higher up, who were recruited for their ability to operate at high altitude rather than their wallets. All of Todd's clients chose to turn back when they saw the way the weather was developing – but all of them had the experience to make this decision. Lou Kasischke reports that, though he and other clients expressed the desire to turn back at the high camp, Rob Hall overruled them – or rather, expressed himself thus: 'We're going.' This convinced them to carry on when they shouldn't (though in the end they turned back, unlike those who kept quiet, continued with Hall and lost their lives). Boukreev, who twice tried to get Fischer to turn back, was also overruled.

By the time all the climbers were assembled at the last camp on the South Col, nestled in the dip between the side-by-side vastnesses of Lhotse and Everest, it was quite clear the weather was not settling down. But the date had been set and the teams stumbled into action between 11 and 12 p.m.

Rob Hall and Scott Fischer knew absolutely that the Hillary Step, a twelve-metre rock climb, would be a bottleneck for climbers going to and leaving the summit. With only one set of fixed ropes, there would be single passage only, both up and down. People would have to wait their turn. Everest is a big place and thirty-four climbers – the number attempting to summit that day – would hardly look like a large number until they were all crammed into one place, waiting. The idea was to send Sherpas to fix ropes up the Hillary Step so people wouldn't have to wait.

Hall and Fischer agreed this and Fischer delegated the task to his sirdar, or head Sherpa, who told him that the Yugoslav climbers had already fixed ropes all the way to the top, a stretch between the south summit and the Hillary Step and up the Hillary Step itself. This absolved the Sherpas from making an earlier start at 10 p.m. They left with everyone else in Fischer's team.

But at the south summit, the queue of climbers stalled. Some had been waiting an hour for ropes to be fixed across an area that many climbed without fixed ropes (it was not very steep; however the wind was rising so that probably made people more nervous). Everyone was waiting for Rob Hall to make a decision – but he was down the mountain, helping the straggler Doug Hansen to come up. Hansen had already turned back once, but then changed his mind and was coming up again.

In addition to waiting for ropes to be fixed, people were waiting for Sherpas to bring up supplies of oxygen. It was obvious to some that this build-up would extend to the Hillary Step, so they turned back. Given that it was now past midday and they were still not on the summit – nor would they be by the 1 p.m. turn-around time – this was the moment Rob Hall should have done what he did at almost exactly the same time on exactly the same day one year earlier. But on 10 May 1995 there was no embedded author who would write up his ascent in a bestselling magazine. There was no TV reporter who had global media contacts. There was no precedent of having turned back a year earlier. In short, there was a lot less pressure.

So Hall did not turn back; neither did Fischer. Many of their clients therefore followed their example.

People lined up to ascend and descend the roped sections – eventually fixed quite quickly by Boukreev, once it was obvious no one else was going to do it. Some, like Krakauer, were in the lead, while others, like Doug Hansen, a US postal worker, were at the back. Rushing back down the mountain and making use of extra oxygen, Krakauer only just made it to the tents at the higher camp. And he was exhausted. Visibility was getting less and less as the wind rose and spindrift flew everywhere. As night began to fall, Rob Hall and Hansen (who was now in a very poor state) were left with no choice but to bivouac at the south summit. Hansen slipped into unconsciousness and Hall made, the next day, his last radio communication to his wife in New Zealand.

The other leader, Scott Fischer, was also exhausted and would, despite a rescue attempt, die before he could leave Everest. Japanese climber Yasuko Namba would drop and be left for dead, along with Beck Weathers.

In Jon Krakauer's account, it is obvious he is trying to do the 'right thing' and stick up for Rob Hall and everything that Rob Hall stood for – not least because there was a very real possibility of legal action against Hall's company and the other companies involved. The IMAX feature – made by the team who'd supplied their weather data to Hall – went on to gross over $100 million. Naturally the film-makers wanted to play down any kind of involvement, however tangential, in the disaster; those box-office takings might be very attractive to speculative ambulance chasing lawyers.

Then there was the culpability of Hall himself. Since he had set a turnaround time which he had stuck to in the past and survived because of it, but had failed to observe this time – then focusing on this error of judgement would show just how at fault he was. Lou Kasischke, an expert on risk assessment who owed his survival to turning back, was adamant in his account of the accident that everything that happened prior to the failure to turn back was somewhat irrelevant to the assessment of who was at fault. Yes, they had weather reports that showed the window was not perfect; yes, the Sherpas failed to start early and lay fixed rope; yes, the guide climbers showed little initiative in beating the roadblock at the southern summit; yes, oxygen supplies were inadequate . . . but if everyone had turned back at 1 p.m., no one would have been killed.

Beck Weathers and Krakauer claim the turnaround time was 2 p.m. Kasischke is adamant it was 1 p.m. By the time of the first press conferences, 2 p.m. was being bandied around – yet this could not have been accurate because it meant summiting fifteen hours into eighteen hours' worth of oxygen. It would be impossible to return before running out, which would result in all the corollary problems involved in oxygen starvation at altitude. But the 2 p.m. figure made the 4 p.m. summit time for Rob Hall and his later clients look acceptable.

It wasn't, though. Add in the fact that Hall actually waited a further hour and a half for one client to summit, and you have the makings of a disaster in that one decision alone.

Hall knew that if he went two years without getting anyone on top of Everest, while Scott Fischer managed to get *all* his team on top, then he'd look pretty silly asking $65,000 a head in 1997.

In fact, Hall was wrong-headed about the whole thing. He didn't realise that turning back was one reason many amateur climbers *chose* his outfit. He was considered *safe*. Turning back was the best advert he could have for people who wanted the kudos of standing on the world's highest peak without the risk of dying. Hall had become suckered into the internecine world of high-altitude guiding while losing sight of the bigger picture. It was a classic case of attempting to please his immediate circle of colleagues and competitors rather than the clients he relied on for money. Of course a guide would look askance if told to turn back – his capability was way higher than a client's – but that wasn't the point. Commercial guiding was about living to tell the tale, not dying and looking a hero.

Beck Weathers remained alone, somewhere below the south summit, until 5 p.m. Four hours past turnaround time. Jon

Krakauer descended past him and offered to help him back to the high camp, but Weathers gamely refused, noting a certain relief in Krakauer at this. Krakauer told him Rob Hall was at least three hours away. Half an hour later, more people descended. Finally, cold and tired, Weathers realised he had to save himself. He'd been standing or sitting for ten hours and the sun would soon go down. He knew that his eyes would cease to function properly once the light dimmed. When guide Mike Groom offered to 'tight-rope' him back, he accepted.

By now it was 6 p.m. and the wind was rising. Thanks to another small error of judgement, Beck Weathers was wearing the wrong crampons – technical ice crampons that balled up in soft snow – causing him to slide and lose his footing as they descended. Visibility got worse and worse as the wind rose, but they managed to get down to the South Col. Now all that remained was to traverse across to the tents. It should have taken less than an hour. But at that moment, in Beck's words, the storm 'detonated'. Visibility was close to zero – it was 'like being lost in a bottle of milk'. And it rapidly became very cold.

The group was lost and by some kind of instinct stopped a mere 7.5 metres from the sheer drop of the Kangshung face. Rather than face another close call, they huddled together close to the ground. The winds were terrific, so high that when Beck removed a mitt it was whipped out of his hand. He was so sure he would be blown away if he delved into his pack for a spare pair, he didn't dare try. This would result in the loss of his lower arm.

Miraculously, the clouds parted for a few minutes and the Plough was visible. One client, Klev Schoening, used this to deduce where the tents should be. He and two others set off and found the camp. With the remaining climbers too exhausted to go back, it fell to Anatoli Boukreev to go out three times with tea and oxygen to find the desperate huddled group. He brought back all of them except Beck Weathers and Yasuko Namba, both of whom he thought were beyond saving.

But Weathers was alive. And in the morning he had the great misfortune to be checked up on by another client who was also a doctor: cardiologist Stuart Hutchinson. Hutchinson claimed he had never seen someone so close to death and still breathing. And since medical orthodoxy is that you *never* recover from a hypothermic coma, it was considered safer to leave him rather than endanger others by carrying him down to the tents. The Sherpas have a rather convenient superstition that touching the dead or near dead is bad luck – so the hard work would have had to be done by the suffering clients still standing, and the hard choice was made to leave Beck Weathers.

Base camp had already called Weathers' family in Texas to inform them of his death. At that very instant (he later discovered), something flickered into life deep within the brain of the dying man. He saw his family with absolute clarity, 'in vivid focus, as if they might at any moment speak to me'. He knew then that if he didn't stand he would stay in this spot for eternity. Somehow, he got to his feet and managed to stagger over to the tents.

But his troubles were not over by a long chalk. Though he was led into Scott Fischer's tent, he was left again to die. He spent the entire day and night in the tent, drifting in and out of consciousness.

The following morning, he heard John Krakauer leaving and shouted: 'Just what do you have to do to get service around here?'

This time, he managed to get to his feet. His boots were on and he was ready to go – partly because his feet were so swollen he couldn't get them off. With the help of others, he was able to limp down the mountain. But without the use of his hands, he was dreading having to descend the icefall with its 700 lengths of ladder to climb across and down.

His wife now knew that Beck was alive. She rallied her friends to lobby everyone influential they knew in order to get him flown out in a helicopter. This worked; for the first time, a helicopter landed and picked up someone from above the icefall at Camp 1.

Flying at 6,000 metres was not easy, but in a virtuoso display of rotor control, the pilot safely removed Beck to Kathmandu hospital. Though he lost the lower arm, large parts of his face and all the fingers from the other hand, he has returned to working as a pathologist – an extraordinary recovery. He wrote: 'I learned that miracles do occur. In fact, I think they occur pretty commonly.'

The penalty for going higher is the danger of death from altitude, or attitude – that of those who disagree with you. The new stories about the mountains have changed; as we have seen, they are about the survival of greenhorns and wannabes, not the great triumphs of explorers and pioneers. Surviving is the new way of winning, since mere winning is too easy now, what with all the tech and backup and oxygen and GPS. This path is blocked and I knew I had to take another. The clue was to look at the forgotten people of the Himalayas, those who had been overlooked but still lived on, who connected to the land, yes, but also my own nebulous reasons for being here. The Naga gods and the Naga people. It would bring me back to the demons, those that are real and those that are imagined, and the journeys we make to placate them.

PART 5

Nagas

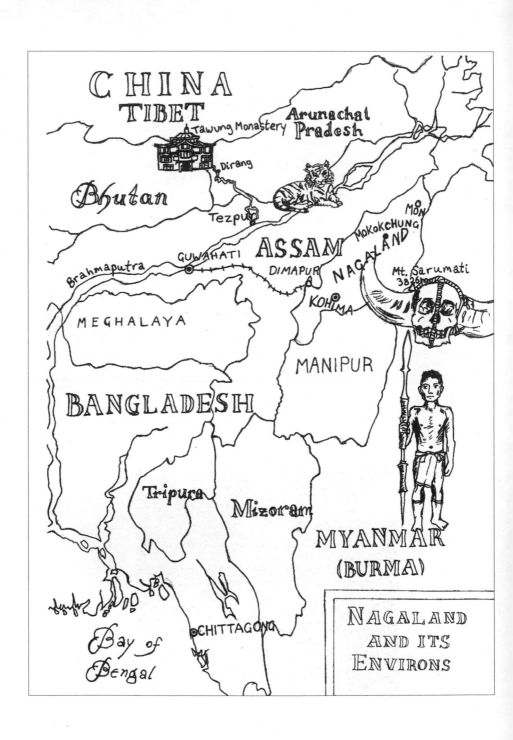

CHINA

TIBET

Tawung Monastery

Arunachal Pradesh

Dirang

Bhutan

Tezpu

Brahmaputra

GUWAHATI

ASSAM

DIMAPUR

MON

MOKOKCHUNG

NAGALAND

Mt. Sarumati 3826m

KOHIMA

MEGHALAYA

MANIPUR

BANGLADESH

MYANMAR
(BURMA)

Tripura

Mizoram

Bay of Bengal

CHITTAGONG

NAGALAND
AND ITS
ENVIRONS

I

In Nagaland

Do not teach others the way a fish teaches.

Naga proverb

Nagas, those serpent gods and ancient rulers of India, coincidentally share a name with the half-forgotten tribes living on the border with Burma. The people of Nagaland may have been called Nagas not because they are snakelike or worship snakes (they don't, though politely revering the python, they will happily eat most snakes). It was thought that the name comes either from the Sanskrit words for 'hill people' or 'naked people' – though there are plenty of both in other parts of India and they aren't called Nagas. One convincing explanation suggests the name

397

comes from Naka, meaning pierced ear in Burmese, and that they are migrant remnants of the Nakari tribe from Thailand, who were also characterised by hugely pierced ears. Certainly, the plugs and roundels you see in Hoxton and Brooklyn have nothing on the pierced ears, and noses, you see in Nagaland – among the elderly pre-Christian men, mainly. My grandfather used to give away his Players cigarette tins to Nagas, who would pierce their ears, enlarge the hole until the tins could be inserted and used as a handy metal pocket. The Naga people also use cowrie shells in their traditional costume, though they are very far from the sea; it suggests significant contact with people who were. A band of tribes who use cowrie shells runs across Burma and Thailand and Cambodia; maybe the Nagas are connected to these people.

The word and the people are getting better known. The night before I left England, I had an Indian meal with a 'dorset naga chilli' – which for a while was the world's hottest chilli, a hybrid developed from a chilli pepper that originated in Nagaland, before spreading to Bangladesh and then to England. Now I was going to where the chillis came from.

Nagaland. At long last. Nagaland was a part of my childhood – haunted it, in fact. Like most people in the current era, I put peculiar importance on my childhood. Perhaps we can thank Freud for that; he certainly instigated a wholesale restructuring in the importance of our inner lives. The Tibetans only have their past lives to worry about. When I met a Buddhist monk who had been away from his family since he was eight, he seemed so very normal – unlike a modern product of a British boarding school, wrenched away from home at the same age. But perhaps that was some innate prejudice speaking. We seem to have replaced God and the Infinite with ourselves; instead of past lives, we have our past life – our school and childhood, which, if it was a happy one, takes on the form of a sort of nirvana, except you dwell there before and not after life. What do we have to look forward to?

So, Nagaland; my father spoke about it a great deal. His own

Misty morning in the Naga hills

father had been reticent, spoke hardly at all about his childhood; my father resented this, so we were spared few details of his – to my mind – utterly idyllic years of growing up. The main and almost intoxicating fact was that he had not been sent to school until he was thirteen! Oh, there had been those few months at that prep school in Mussoorie – but he and his brother had been expelled, for loading the tablecloth with a tureen of rice pudding and trapping the huge bulge by pressing their tummies to the table. When they walked away, the whole lot splatted all over the dining hall floor. I knew I could never compete with such chutzpah. And also: how on earth did they expect to get away with that?

No school! I hated and despised school, loathed the end of the holidays, faked headaches and cold symptoms every few months just to get a break I felt I deserved. My sisters loved school and looked forward to the end of the summer holidays, which for me were dark days laden with gloom. And partly, perhaps, this was encouraged by so deeply imbibing my father's tales of building treehouses in the jungle, playing in Japanese foxholes (they lived in Kohima, site of a turning-point battle in the Second World

War), and going on hikes in the jungle with the Naga warriors who lived all around them. I could hardly imagine anything more exciting than traipsing around with a couple of dao*-wielding, head-hunting, spear-carrying warriors. My grandfather had brought many mementoes back from Nagaland, and as a child visiting his huge draughty house I could play on the stairs with the spears he kept standing in a gigantic brass shell case along with his umbrella.

My grandfather had been in Nagaland both during and after the war. He had been friends with Sir Charles Pawsey, the District Commissioner, who once came to dinner and my mischievous dad, aged seven, had pulled his chair away from under him leaving the poor DC sprawling on the floor. Much punishment followed. But Sir Charles never held it against the lad and inspired my father to go to Oxford and enter the Indian Civil Service (which he did, though the ICS had ended before he finished his studies).

It was on Charles Pawsey's tennis court that the turning-point battle of Kohima was fought. There, and the immediate surrounds of the small sleepy town in the Naga hills. The battle of Kohima and the resupply over the 'hump' of the Himalayas and the Ledo Road through what is now Arunachal Pradesh are all part of the Second World War involvement of the Himalayas. Strategically, they stood, as they always have and always will, as the supreme barrier between East and West. As weak points go, the Naga hills are remarkably resistant: hundreds of miles of jungle-infested hilltops, many over 1,800 metres, with no major rivers and certainly no roads. But the Japanese had proven they were masters of jungle warfare – indeed, until the British began experimenting with operations behind the lines, the Japanese were the pioneers and best exponents of jungle fighting in the Second World War. They travelled light – instead of cumbersome hobnailed leather boots, they wore the canvas and rubber 'two-toed' tabi that are

---

* Dao: a Naga machete used for taking heads.

worn by construction workers in Japan. They eschewed roads for travelling along jungle tracks – using local guides to show the way. Bicycles were found to make excellent vehicles: you could load a bicycle with a fifty-pound box of ammunition and still ride along a jungle track. If the going got rough, you could push the bicycle and use it like a cart as long as you pushed a stick into the handlebars to extend it so the bike could remain upright as it was pushed. Spreading out through the jungle, you could live off the land to some extent, extorting food from villages along the way. This method of fighting had beaten the British in Malaya and Burma.

Defeat in Malaya and Singapore had shocked Britain to the core, more so than the setbacks in Europe. Japan had defeated the Russians in 1904 – but it had been a rump force, far from the capital. Japan could not conceivably be a threat to Britain . . . And yet they had stormed down the Malayan peninsula and then out-bluffed the British, who had three times the number of troops as the Japanese.

By 1944, things were a little different. The Americans had gradually reoccupied the Pacific and, after the battle of Midway, had strategic control of the area. The Japanese continued their advance westwards through Burma, but their supply lines were getting longer and longer. Crucially, a special forces operation – of the kind disliked by senior army officers but beloved by Churchill – took place in Burma behind Japanese lines. The Chindit force, under wayward General Orde Wingate, failed to achieve any significant operational victories, but their role was not in vain. For the first time, it had been shown that the British soldier could fight and win in the jungle, that he could survive in the steaming inhospitable forests of Burma – that he could be dropped and re-supplied from the air, surviving disease and climate to face the seemingly invincible Japanese. They discovered the foibles of the Japanese, their preferred tactical methods. All this was of immense value when it came to fighting at Kohima and Imphal.

These places were chosen by Field Marshal William Slim to be where the decisive battles should take place.

At Imphal, the British needed a transhipment point ahead of the battle they intended to fight. This camp was built by my grandfather, who had been sent ahead with only his bearer to get the job done. Relying on hundreds of Nagas to help him, he piped in water using Naga technology – halved bamboo poles strung together to form a pipeline – that is still in use today. He dynamited limestone cliffs to get the raw material for lime, which he cooked in homemade kilns. Using this basic cement, he made concrete hut bases, essential against the mud-inducing monsoon. The Nagas helped him clear a vast area of forest, chopping the trees down with their well sharpened daos. Huts were built and thatched with palms, still used in most Naga villages to roof houses.

Building the camp achieved a sort of mythical status in my childhood. It showed that a single man could stand against a

A Naga log drum: it can be heard five miles away

whole marauding army and still achieve something – as long as he had willing native warriors to help him. It was, I suppose, the same kind of colonial fantasy so well depicted in *The Man Who Would Be King*, Kipling's yarn about two ordinary soldiers who find a hidden kingdom to rule over in the mountains of the Himalayas. Perhaps a major lure of the colonial experience is to be able to shuffle off your lowly or highly born – but nevertheless, fixed – position in the over-populated islands of Britain and arrive, like R. L. Stevenson in Samoa, as a fully fledged king with an adoring people to rule with fairness and compassion. This is what is so easily misunderstood when studying colonialism – many of the people drawn to such work desired to serve the people to the very best of their ability (while getting lots of kingly attention too, maybe).

District commissioners in Nagaland were drawn from the Indian Civil Service – as Charles Pawsey was. This was the most competitive branch of the empire's civil service; to gain entry, you needed higher marks than for the Foreign Office. The calibre of men sent out to this end-of-empire outpost is reflected in the books they wrote; previous ICS men Hutton and Mills were essentially amateurs, but their anthropologies of the Naga peoples have stood the test of time as classic works. Their value also stands in the high regard the Naga people themselves have for such tomes. When I met with Naga leaders, I was asked on more than one occasion if I could help get hold of certain ethnological works from the late nineteenth century, since some of the knowledge (admittedly largely about territory) had been lost with the steady incursion of the Indians since partition. It surprised few that not a single Naga attended the 1947 Kohima independence day parade that my grandfather was present at. The Nagas knew they would fare far worse under the Indians than under the British. The insurgency that started soon after and still bubbles away in the further reaches of the Naga borderlands is a reminder that the British once were able to rule a land without aspiring to lead it; the Indians wanted to lead the Nagas to a 'better' way of life. Which led to war.

In my grandfather's cabinet of curiosities there was a Naga headdress made of wild boar hair and a breastplate of cowrie shells. Later, I would see similar things on display in the Pitt Rivers Museum in Oxford, but these were artefacts that had been my toys.

My father spoke of one occasion when he had gone with his father hunting for jungle fowl. They had walked and walked all day, taking no food with them. The Nagas had made a fire and brewed up some wild tea – that was all they consumed, all day – and they covered, he told me, twenty miles through the jungle from dawn until dusk when they returned. 'And it was all up and down in the Naga jungle,' he added. Twenty miles and only a few cups of tea! Brilliant!

Everything about my life was so regular and planned. I had never once been without breakfast, unless I was ill – let alone lunch and tea too. It seemed a reckless but wholly attractive mark of freedom that a casual stroll out into the jungle should become an epic one-day hike. My own mother, I knew, would not have allowed such a thing. My father never went anywhere without letting her know.

It was a kind of nostalgia for a bygone age of greater wildness and freedom, a wildness enhanced by the presence of real wild men, noble savages; my father always spoke of the Naga skill at making traps and hunting, but also their quiet dignity and loyalty. He'd show me how to make a razor-sharp knife from splitting a bamboo – I'd later see Nagas using slivers of bamboo as knives to butcher meat. He and I built a trap, just as he remembered. It had a withy bent back, which acted as a spring to lift and hang any small game caught. He told me how the Nagas had scattered a poisonous plant in the streams and ponds (there were few rivers in Nagaland, he told me, mainly just streams running down the hills and along the tortuous valleys, and ponds they made themselves for fish), and this plant had stunned the fish for a while, allowing the Nagas to wade in and scoop out the lot.

I have always been intrigued by the French philosophical notion of 'the other'. That which is similarly human, but opposite and desirable, even if the desire is unconscious. The Nagas were my 'other'. They were wild and dangerous and lived at the tail end of the Himalayas. They were the eastern barrier between India and the rest of S. E. Asia. They ate dogs! And were head hunters! Human skulls adorned their long houses. And they had never been conquered by the British.

For me, as for all children brought up in the Seventies and Eighties, the Second World War continued to hang heavy on the cultural agenda. There were still a few bombsites in major towns, boys' comics featured Second World War stories and Steve McQueen jumped his motorbike (actually a disguised Triumph rather than a BMW) over the fence between Germany and Switzerland every Christmas or Easter Day afternoon – for years, it seemed. In fact, I wouldn't be surprised if the whole Seventies obsession with jumping motorbikes over big obstacles wasn't started by massive exposure to Steve McQueen . . . I digress. The fact that we had 'won the war' was part of growing up, but so was industrial decline, strikes, and the end of empire. For me, Nagaland brought end of empire and winning the war together in striking fashion. Though the British had ruled the country, they had never occupied or really exploited it. Quite the contrary; they had created a protective zone around the Nagas, insulating them from the commercial and exploitative instincts of the Assamese and Bengalis. The British administered this time-bubble, which was rudely burst when the Japanese decided Kohima would be the spot to fight the determining battle for India. Suddenly, these almost Stone Age tribesmen were in the midst of the rabid madness of twentieth-century warfare. And my father had lived there both before and after the war. His presence guaranteed me, I felt, a vicarious front seat on both war and empire.

In 1945 my grandfather returned as the garrison engineer for Kohima, overseeing some of its reconstruction. Which it needed – the town had seen some of the most vicious fighting of the Second World War, with the Japanese determined to win or fight to the death. In the post-war years, the hills around Kohima quickly recovered from the blasting they had received from British and Japanese artillery. It became for my father and his siblings the most wonderful playground you could imagine. If I had the odd bomb crater, fenced off and soon to be developed, to play in, they had foxholes, blown-up tanks, heavy artillery and discarded weapons to play with.

My uncle took it a stage further. Perhaps inspired by the Naga ritual of wearing a wild boar's tooth on a necklace, he collected the teeth of Japanese soldiers, rooted them out of skulls with a found bayonet. He kept them in a Players tin, ready to be strung as beads on a thread. When my grandmother found out, she was appalled and he had to throw them away.

2

An Encounter on the Train to Nagaland

Snake fears man. Man fears snake.

Tibetan proverb

The train took six hours, or would. I was in the station in Guwhati in Assam, waiting to get to Dimapur in Nagaland, the last stage in my journey along the Himalayas. All Indian stations are big, even the small ones. Guwhati was no exception. Confusion was everywhere. Despite my efforts to be all Zen about it, I was agitated. Though trains were rarely on time, sometimes they left a minute or two before time. I was haunted by that possibility. And there were no boards to signal what platform a train would be leaving from. The staff had only a cursory knowledge. They'd direct you to the usual platform, but all too often there had been a last-minute change and only the red-shirted and red-turbaned porters had any clue what was happening. It was miraculous how they would know exactly what platform the train would be leaving from and where to stand for the right carriage – especially when no one else could tell you this. No one. I did not begrudge handing over fifty rupees – an excessive amount, I knew – to find out such valuable data.

For a while I sat in a VIP lounge. From earlier trips to India, I knew that VIP was a nominal status. It often kept out humble backpackers, but no one would have turned them away. In reality, it meant European travellers with a bit of a brass neck and wealthy or middle-class Indians. Everyone else was out on the dark grey-shadowed dingy grubby platforms, settling down for life on a metre square of newspaper or a piece of cardboard. In the middle of a rushing thoroughfare you'd step over the tightly wrapped bundle of a man sleeping, his blue scarf encircling and cocooning his entire head. And he would be asleep – with all this cacophonous life streaming above and around him. I was reminded of the blue robe of the shaman, but somehow reversed: this man was sleeping and not flying. Or perhaps he was, in his dreams.

The countdown to the train's arrival led to crowd surges up and down bridges to other platforms. I got caught in a sort of slow lane. It was then that Chao appeared at my elbow. In careful though perfect English he said, 'Sir, the Dimapur train is more easily reached this way.' Then he sort of surged sideways across the wide metal staircase and, with no one else to follow, I followed him.

I had seen him earlier; he had a shaven head and, though not Nepali or Tibetan, he had the narrowing eyes of someone from the north. Chao was a master chef – he found me a seat next to him on the train, though my designated seat was a row or two behind. It would be sorted (I had long ago lost that paranoia of always being in the right seat; in India it was usual to bargain with families and couples so that everyone could sit together. It took out the random element when you might *not* want to sit with your travelling companion though.) Chao was travelling with a disciple chef to a town beyond Dimapur where his family lived.

How old was he? I couldn't tell. Maybe early forties, though he looked younger. He ran a restaurant and a chef school in Tezpur – about four hours from Guwhati – a place I'd been through on my way to the Tawang Monastery on the Tibetan border. Chao was full of information. He had studied both Eastern and Western cooking. He loved Gordon Ramsay and watched him on TV. He knew of Heston Blumenthal and checked recipes on his Samsung Note. He showed me how he could write down notes with the stylus. He was just showing me this enviable jotting feature when the transvestite gypsies boarded the train.

At least, that's what they looked like – rough, white-toothed, with bulging eyes, garish yellow-and-pink saris hitched up in that awkward way somehow characteristic of the cross dresser. They were coming from both ends of the carriage – eyeballing everyone. I was intrigued, yet I could see they were beggars and I didn't want to be begged from. I looked slyly but one came in under my gaze and stared right into my face. Then went on. The group of them coalesced round three middle-class Indian men in suits. They banged a tambourine – but perfunctorily. There was some excited loud talking. A silencing shout.

Chao remained staring ahead and then he relaxed. 'They are eunuchs,' he said. 'They have an uncanny sense of who to beg from – if you do not give, they curse you. Not everyone believes this curse but most do. They sometimes shame you further by exposing their genitals. That is very shameful to the average Indian.'

'I'm not surprised,' I said. 'But why did they ignore me? Surely they could have got money from me?'

'Ah, they know! They know you do not believe in their curses.'

'I've been cursed before,' I said.

'But you do not believe, even I can tell,' said Chao.

'How can they tell?' I asked (I wanted to know how Chao could tell, but settled for a general form of question).

Chao had a cheery, calm demeanour, but I sensed that he too believed in the cursing. He said with the sort of laboured intensity you have when you are explaining something you know will be discounted or ignored, 'Belief is like a web, it connects to many things. It is like superstition. Maybe we don't need it – but who is free? Many in the West put their belief in evolution and global warming, or maybe in Samsung and Vodafone—'

'Not Vodafone.'

'It is an imperfect example, but you see my meaning: it is hard to live without this kind of belief, this web that draws you into explaining the unexplainable, the things you have faith in. After all, it *might* be right. You can't be sure, so you half believe. They sense this and extort money. Look at those business chaps. In suits and such like, they are believing even more than some of these average fellows sitting here and there.'

'Is it the power of their personalities?'

'That is undoubtedly a part of it. But they are looking for a glimmer of fear. If they see this, they pounce – but not always. I have observed these eunuchs on many occasions and I can say they are intuitive people. They follow their hunches; they are not just mechanically begging like some poor fellow on the roadside.'

I wanted to know how Chao knew English so well. Had he been to an expensive international school? He waved away my question with some vagueness. 'I am from a humble background, but I have been offered a lucky break when I attend a Christian school where they speak English.' He said something to the disciple, who went to get us tea. Chao wanted to talk about cookery: 'Good Indian cooking and good European cooking start out far apart, but they are the same in the end, though we have always a more complicated way of doing things. I think this is to do with secrecy and family traditions more than anything else.'

I asked him if he knew the secret of Indian cooking. 'Green cardamom,' he said without hesitation. En passant, he told me the secret of a perfect omelette was to separate the white from the yoke and beat the white until it is like a soufflé, then recombine the two. 'Of course,' he added, 'if the egg is very fresh it may be nicer not to have to do this.'

I told Chao that I was travelling the length and breadth of the Himalayas to write a book. He got me to autograph his Samsung Note and displayed the signature to the disciple. He would find my books, he assured me. He himself had worked in Rishikesh to learn the kind of cooking they had there. In fact, he had in his youth taken jobs all over India just to increase his knowledge. 'Now I settle down,' he said, 'and pass on tips to my students. If you want to go one rung up the ladder, you must bring two up beneath you.' He paused, 'Or one, if you're stuck for good material!'

Chao believed that through cooking one could learn many things. He never actually said that, though I could see it was what he believed. I believed it too. I'd seen in Japan how martial arts could, with some students, lead to learning they could apply in their lives outside the dojo.

Chao said, 'Why do spiritual people go to the Himalayas? Because that is where the air is thin. They have to breathe, they have to listen to their breathing. This reminds them they are human after all. And they mistake this insight for something wonderful.'

I felt a little chastened, as I had experienced something similar myself.

'The Himalayas are also the source of all the great rivers – for China, Tibet, India, Vietnam, Burma – the whole of the East drinks from the Himalayas! People confuse this physical need with a spiritual one.'

'But there is something special about the Himalayas!'

'You are right. They are damned high! But seriously, people make a decision they will have an experience there or "be changed" – and sure enough, they are. But they have really changed themselves. It is like a pilgrimage – that is an excuse to make a change you already know needs to be made.'

'Then it is useful.'

'Maybe. But more useful is to make changes all your life, not just when you go on holiday. Everyday life is like water on rock, it wears away very slowly, very slowly. But over time, it changes everything about a person. Make sure you are in the right stream – one that runs all year round and not just during the monsoon. What I mean is, very few decisions are important. Who you marry, who you are friends with, what your occupation is – all these will wear you like the water on the rock. But whether you make a pilgrimage – that may be less important.'

'But a pilgrimage to some high place can serve to wake you up.'

'So can losing your job! I am not against such travel, I just think the real mystery is right in front of our very noses.'

And with that he started reading a battered James Clavell novel while I settled for Mario Puzo's *The Sicilian*, the only likely-looking thriller on the railway newsstand.

At Dimapur I was briefly detained by police; although there were no longer restrictions on entering Nagaland, old habits die hard. I had grown accustomed in Egypt to arguing strenuously with police – and it usually worked. But when I started to heat up, Chao intervened on my behalf and spoke calmly. The policemen were more like soldiers: spick and span in khaki, with Himalayan faces, blank and hard as teak. But after photocopying my passport and visa I was free to go. Chao got me a taxi rather than have me wait for the bus to Kohima.

I went looking for Chao's restaurant later in Tezpur, but when I found it I discovered there was a new owner. They rang Chao's Samsung for me, but he didn't answer. Maybe I had misunderstood and he was moving to start a new restaurant back in his hometown in eastern Assam. I recall, though, his words: 'People make things overcomplicated in India, when everything is really pretty much the same here as anywhere: your main problem is to get out of your own way!'

3

Lunch at Uncle Yong Kong's

There are two types of wise men – one who says 'I only am wise' and one who says 'I am not wise.' The one who says 'I am also wise' is not wise at all.

Tibetan proverb

Yong Kong was ready to go. On top of his sagging wardrobe was a battered cardboard suitcase, blue, scuffed, shoved up there as if Yong Kong had only just arrived and was already looking to depart. He had been in England thirty-five years.

Uncle Yong Kong was the most senior Naga nationalist then living in Britain – this was in the mid-1990s. A member of the Ao Naga tribe, he had been sent to negotiate at the United Nations in 1962, but nothing much had come of these talks except that Yong Kong stayed in London. His small one-bedroom flat was round the corner from Baker Street, and when David Ward, the founder of Naga Vigil (an NGO that campaigned for Naga human rights), was in town, Yong Kong's flat became the hub of all intrigue and gossip relating to the Naga cause. Yong Kong would cook great pots of rice and lamb curry, pass around plates and talk about the ongoing fight for Naga independence.

Later, I would see an interview in which Yong Kong made the distinction between seeking independence and seeking to expel an invader from your territory. It is a worthwhile distinction – Tibet was under Chinese suzerainty for centuries and did not chafe too much, but once they exercised sovereignty and invaded in force, the situation very quickly became intolerable (though it has been tolerated). When the Angami Nagas led a rebellion against the British invasion of Nagaland in the 1880s, they stopped fighting and waited to see what would happen. They accepted they had lost the first round to the British – but Naga tactics are some- what different from ours. To be killed in a head-taking raid is considered an ignoble death; to run away to fight another battle is a cause for celebration back at the longhouse. Hit-and-run is clearly a far saner approach to war than encouraging meaningless self-sacrifice – as long as you have hills to escape and hide out in. Which the Nagas did. They observed that the British – once they had their agreement – stayed in Kohima with a tiny force of Assam Rifles and the District commissioner. Naga life went on as usual. The unadministered area remained free – the strip of land between Burma and the regions occupied by the Ao and Angami (the two biggest and most powerful tribes). But the In- dians brought policemen, large numbers of soldiers, shopkeepers and forestry companies. The country ceased to be administered lightly; such heaviness constituted an invasion. And the Nagas fought back – hit-and-run for sixty years. When I visited in 2014, I saw little evidence of Naga separatist activity. David Ward, I know, has given up Naga Vigil – after being arrested in Nagaland and held for a year in a Delhi jail. The Khapland faction, who operate on the Burmese side of the border, are still fighting on for independence. But when I crossed into Burma in the Konyak tribal region, life seemed to be going on as normal in the villages I passed through.

I met Yong Kong and David Ward in Nepal during a clandes- tine meeting of Naga separatists in the 1990s.

The meeting was very hush-hush, but everyone knew about it. Everyone in the Nagaland Cause circle, that is. Even Susan, the Australian organiser for the Naga charity set up by David Ward would be there. She told me she'd only become interested

in Nagas by accident. She'd been looking online for dragons –
and she had found Nagas. Anyway she knew all about the secret
meeting to take place in Kathmandu of the heads of the Naga
separatist groups.

I went to Kathmandu hoping to meet the Naga separatists.
I was working as a freelance journalist at the time – writing
stories and selling pictures. Stories from a women's angle were
best, because then the story could be sold to every foreign edi-
tion of *Elle* or *Marie Claire*. Any kind of story would be tricky,
because this was in the late 1990s when it was impossible for
foreigners to visit Nagaland. Because my father had grown up
there, I had a strong desire to visit. I also thought the Nagas had
got a rough deal from both the Indians and some of their own
leaders.

Kathmandu – just before the Nepalese Maoists appeared on
the scene (and there were Naga Maoists, too; they were able to
cross from Burma into China and then down into Nepal, so they
avoided having to travel through India). The rank-and-file Naga
politicians made a show of avoiding Indian cigarettes, drinks,
food. But then I noticed the hard-core separatists, those that hid
out in the jungle and trained their guns on Indian soldiers, had
no qualms about smoking Indian bidis and drinking Indian beer
(although that was a little problematic, given that many of the
leaders were also church leaders and did not drink).

Kathmandu, with its dark, dusty streets, was then burgeoning
into a worldwide tourist destination. It had its own casino. We all
went there one day and played some blackjack. Gambling with
the guerrillas.

David Ward was fascinating to me. He was a few years older
than I was, but appeared, when he talked to the guerrilla leaders,
to be in another league of age and experience. He joked with
them in Hindi and English and told his stories of being in prison
for a year after his capture in Nagaland while publicising their
cause in 1992. I often thought about how he was captured. He was

part of a convoy heading out to eastern Nagaland. If he had made it past the checkpoints, it's unlikely he would have been caught, as the Indian army were not able to penetrate that far into the Eastern jungles. There were probably informants. A classic hero in many ways, in a tight situation, Ward had a knack for doing the right thing, the heroic thing, the stuff of mythology. Like when he was in an Indian jail, having his hands broken by a bullying guard, but never removing them from the bars like the guard wanted; when the warder heard, he wanted the guard punished and sacked from his job, but Ward intervened and said no. The guard became his best friend after that. But like all heroes, Ward had his Achilles' heel: he got migraines – very bad ones. When migraine struck, he couldn't walk, he had to lie down in a darkened space and just wait for it to pass. So the convoy was leaving for eastern Nagaland but they had to delay for him – maybe eight hours – and this delay meant that the chances of word slipping out were higher. So when they did set out, the Indian army was ready for them. When their Jeep approached the roadblock they couldn't turn back because there were roadblocks behind them too, being set up as they journeyed east. The road back went west to Kohima. So they had a choice: abandon their vehicles, or keep going. At the first roadblock, David Ward shouted in Hindi at the Indian soldiers. It was night, raining, he convinced them he was an Indian intelligence officer. They got through. The next block was harder. There was more argument. I could picture his thin, committed face, arguing in the rain. There began some kind of tussle and a doctor, who was accompanying them, was shot in the stomach at point-blank range. This was the kind of situation that Ward excelled in, though it could have no happy outcome. He had briefly been a medic in the British Army (before leaving because he refused to serve in Northern Ireland). He knew that the doctor had little chance of survival unless he was in hospital, the hospital my grandfather built in Kohima. So though this weird and tragic encounter had happened, David Ward managed to persuade the

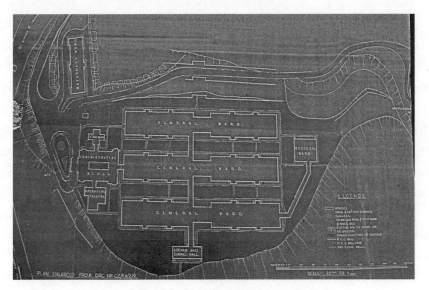

Grandad's plan of Naga Hospital, Kohima

Indian soldiers to let him go and take the doctor back to Kohima – maybe two hours' drive away.

At this point they could have left the road and gone through the jungle and escaped on foot. The doctor begged Ward to save himself. He said he would die anyway. But David Ward persisted. They drove back and got through the next checkpoint. But there were three more before Kohima. And when they got there, what would happen at the hospital? David Ward didn't care, he was so focused on getting the doctor to the hospital. You can see the hero here. A normal person would think through the consequences and get a bit confused. He'd think, OK, so we get to the hospital – then what? Or maybe we won't make it and then we all get caught. Or maybe he dies before we get to the hospital. But a hero has an intuitive grasp of the symbolic potential of all his actions. They are not pursued because they are wise or right, they are pursued because of a single-minded adherence to their symbolic worth.

In a way, a hero is like an author who considers his life less than the works it calls forth. A writer who will sacrifice health and comfort and happiness in order to produce the works that will carry his name for ever, or so he hopes. Likewise, the hero knows that symbolic acts from the past are powerful forms of motivation. They travel as images through time and space and serve to weld a people together. The hero creates his own myth. Not that for a minute am I suggesting that such a cold-blooded analysis was going through Ward's head as he drove the wounded and bleeding doctor back to Kohima (typically, Ward didn't have a driving licence). If they failed, the act would still be heroic. Whereas any other act, though potentially wiser, would not be.

And though he got through two checkpoints with bluster and guile (as Ward once told me: 'If you want to be an armed robber, you need either to be prepared to shoot someone with the intention of seriously injuring or killing them, or be a bloody good actor'), at the third they became embroiled. Word had come through on the radio. The soldiers were clear now about what had happened. Both men were arrested. Ward was beaten. The doctor was not sent to the hospital and died that night. And Ward would eventually spend a year in a tough Indian jail for his actions.

In Kathmandu, when the meetings and negotiating got too much, David would take me out to a dingy drinking den in the old part of town. He had been born in Assam, where his father had been a tea planter who stayed after the British left in 1947. The plantation was in eastern Assam, up near the Naga border, and Nagas sometimes worked on the plantation; David remembered they would arrive carrying their spears. But this idyllic life ended when he was sent to boarding school in the UK. He didn't like it. A born rebel, he left school early and joined the army, left that, and became a youth worker on a hard estate in south London. Here his moniker became 'Peace Dave', as he sought to bring warring factions together. But what goes into a salt mine becomes salt, and David Ward became a criminal. He targeted stately homes and country houses, rationalising it as part of his own 'war on the undeserving rich'. After this, he graduated to armed robbery. All along he was looking for a cause he could wholeheartedly believe in. He told me that being a gangster 'got silly' after a while. He became paranoid, worried if someone had dissed him or not, dishing out violence or threats if someone 'looked at him in the wrong way'. He was caught, sentenced, then he and two others managed to escape while in custody travelling between one prison and another, having overpowered the guards and taking the van. They left the van on the Old Kent Road and went to their local to show their faces and have a 'laugh at the old bill'. Though they hid out for several months, Ward was eventually recaptured and sentenced to six years, to be spent largely in solitary confinement, owing to his escape. It was in solitary that he became aware of the Naga separatist movement. He organised a consciousness-raising show of Naga songs and poetry and some Naga dancing – all in the prison. By now, Ward had become a poet himself, and a convinced supporter of Naga separation from Indian rule.

As soon as his sentence ended, Ward and a fellow former prisoner headed off to India and entered Nagaland illegally. Ward managed a year of activism – which included taunting authorities by sending press releases to the local paper in Kohima. The authorities decided to capture him and make an example of him.

After jail in India, Ward returned to the UK. He now had a Naga wife and worked tirelessly on managing his charity, Naga Vigil.

The purpose of the Kathmandu meeting was to achieve some measure of unity between all the different factions of the Naga separatist cause. Seventeen of them arrived in the big rented villa that David Ward had secured for the main meetings. General Moh, a veteran of the 1956 Naga war against the Indians, was residing in another villa. He was now an alcoholic and enjoying his reputation as an ex-guerrilla fighter. He liked to shock, and told me that the Nagas ate dogs. But my father had told me that years ago. 'I know,' I said.

Susan, the young Australian activist, became interested in visiting eastern Nagaland, on the Burmese side. This was also my plan. Being young, she talked about it to everyone. The representatives of the eastern Nagas grew cautious. My own visit became vaguer the more I tried to press them for concrete details. I couldn't hold it against Susan, though. I would have to get to Nagaland a different way.

I spent a lot of time hanging round the villa while the elders talked and negotiated. Eventually, they came to a big agreement. They wanted David Ward to sign the agreement too. They considered him an equal in their attempts to gain a country free from Indian domination. But he told them it was their cause; he knew that if he got too involved, people might resent such an 'imperialist' intrusion.

I spent time talking to Lucy, a young Naga whose brother had been killed in Nagaland fighting against Indian soldiers. Lucy asked me to get her French women's magazines and a Teach Yourself French book. Her English was fluent, but she had a dream to learn French and visit Paris. Every day she got up early and helped cook the immense vats of chicken curry and rice consumed by the Nagas. She was always dressed far more elegantly than seemed appropriate for a freedom fighter working in a greasy kitchen. I thought about doing a story about her as the 'women's angle' on the Naga problem, but decided it would blow her cover. I realised that, without her family connection, Lucy would never have been involved in what many would call terrorist activity. She would have been a schoolteacher or a government worker, reading her French novels in the evening. The tragedy of such a war of liberation is the way its tentacles spread everywhere, far beyond the confines of the original conflict. But I saw that life has to go on, however committed you are.

Susan and I never made it to Nagaland, not for another fifteen years anyway. Susan gave up activism and became a fashionable DJ and audio artist in Australia. David Ward went back to Nagaland in 2002, was captured again in 2003 and served another eleven

months in an Indian jail – losing twenty kilos during his imprisonment. He eventually gave up the cause in 2007 and returned
the archive of the separatist movement to Nagaland. This archive,
with its symbolic overtones, had been entrusted to Ward by Phizo,
a man who had known my grandfather in the 1940s. The architect
of the original plans for the Naga nation, Phizo had been exiled to
the London borough of Bromley of all places, and built up a vast
archive of books and material relating to the Naga cause. Some
Nagas wanted it back, but factionalism again reared its ugly head.
David Ward was seen as a neutral figure, and he looked after it for
many years before giving up solving the Naga problem.

Which is? A tragic situation involving a people caught between
modernity and traditional tribal life, riven by missionary activity
and the desire of modern India to assert its unity. Though they
had been offered Hong Kong status in 1956, Naga leaders refused
– they wanted full independence from India or they would fight.
The fighting caused much hardship and many lost lives. There
are still separatist groups way up in the hills. Most Nagas have
largely turned their backs on them. They have decided to get on
with their lives. Make the best of the situation.

In the end, the Indian government solved the 'Naga problem',
as it's called, with money. Nagaland has better roads and more
government-paid jobs than a completely 'Indian' part of the
Himalayas – the Garwhal, for example. There is a lot of evidence
of government spending in Nagaland. There are also very big
churches, funded in part by donations from Baptist associations
in America.

Nagaland has a very bizarre appearance on first acquaintance –
Western-style churches and jungle houses. There are music shops
selling electric guitars in Kohima and Mokokchung. Unlike the
rest of India, where the aim is to look like your dad, here the
young people acquire quiffs and riffs, wear leather jackets and
perform Naga rock music. There's a Naga heavy metal festival in

Kohima, which I just missed when I was there. Maybe it's better that they wield axes in this way rather than their old head-hunting daos.

I remember Yong Kong at the meeting in Kathmandu, beaming and being friendly to everyone. It was the first time I had seen diplomacy and nation-building in action. Yong Kong told me he said nothing of import to anyone. He told me that creating the right atmosphere was a slight talent he had (he was always, like most Nagas, incredibly self-effacing) that was very useful in making agreements happen. 'People can disagree because they are personally unhappy – for no other reason – I try to make them a little happy.'

He was a benign old man – or seemed to be. But I also heard him use the power of the cause to encourage young men to fight. He was quite prepared to send the next generation to die for Naga independence – he was no Dalai Lama, nor would he claim to be. I learned that any cause, when it takes up violence, is pretty ugly close up.

Uncle Yong Kong died in 2008. He still had his suitcase ready to go, sadly, no longer needed.

Yong Kong as a young man

4

Two Faces of Nagaland

Affairs cannot be handled by a two-pointed mind;
sewing cannot be done by a two-pointed needle.
Tibetan proverb

I am looking at two photographs separated by fifty years. One is of the headman of the Seangha village – a Konyak Naga from the unadministered area. It was taken in 1936. The other is the headman from Pangmi village in Burma, 1985. They could be of the same man, but they are not. Nor are they similar in any way that is crucial and significant. They merely look as if the man photographed in each one is related to the other. They are both dressed in native style.

Both have taken heads: that is the significance of the monkey skull hat and the brass heads round the Pangmi elder's neck, though he converted to Christianity in 1982.

I would rather look at their faces. The Konyak man from 1936 has a face stretched over hardened bone; there is no surplus, only watchfulness and warrior hardness, quick-fighting confidence. It is a broad face, unmarked by any signs of literacy. Everything he knows he carries with him. His intelligence lies in his mus-cled arms, heavy with a surfeit of rattan bracelets that add to his strength, or the impression of it, in the way his feathered high hat adds no doubt to the impression of height.

The other elder is broken. He looks lost, squatting like a boy;

A 1936 headman next to a 1985 headman

all that was important in his life has been changed or taken away. Maybe he is an opium addict, like some of the Nagas I met on the Burmese border. Christianity has stripped his past of any meaning. He is strung with beads, and clutches a fighting dao. He looks startled and sad.

The man from 1936 is planning something. He means business, he has somewhere to go. The poor Naga of 1985 might be his son, though by the magic of photography he looks older, and his demeanour is a thousand times older. It is someone who cannot understand the world they live in. The bottom has dropped out of everything – no morung, no head-taking raids, no drinking. What must it be like to suffer such a vast change and not want it, or to go along with it because that's what you do in a tribe, only to find you have nothing left?

The whole dilemma of 'development' can be seen in these two faces. Do we leave well alone? Or give them everything we have – from plastic bags to Jesus? Certainly, the missionaries, armed with the miracles of the West – guns mainly – wreaked the biggest changes in Nagaland. The enormous American-funded churches sit on every hilltop. It gives Nagaland a bizarre aspect – like a cross between Europe and the jungle. Christianity must have appealed to the Nagas; the idea of a father god who sends his son coincided with certain existing Naga myths. And the colonial governors of the region were, until the 1920s, active in encouraging American Baptist missionaries. After the First World War, they were less sanguine. Mills and Hutton, the district commissioners from that time, started to oppose the missionaries; they saw the disappearance of tribal customs, rituals and security as a loss, not a gain. Nagas had fought in the First World War (you can still find the odd Naga headdress fashioned from a German helmet with added horns – very Viking – brought back by Naga troops in 1918). The men who had seen Europe and the destruction of Europe formed the first pan Naga group – the Naga club. Nationalism took hold. The agitators were all Christian converts. As late as the 1980s, Naga nationalists were 'encouraging' Christian conversion among the Burmese tribes where they hid from Indian soldiers.

And yet the British are not remembered fondly, though the Indians who came later were more murderous and less just. It was the British who wanted to keep the Nagas in aspic – certainly after 1920 – to preserve their culture from the rampages of the Indian plains. Like a parent who is hated for keeping a child indoors, this was not appreciated.

What is lost when a tribe loses the old ways? I have seen in the faces of elders in the remoter parts of Nagaland that look of lostness, a cynicism, an interest in oblivion because nothing else is on offer. Old men pose for photos wearing their tribal rig and puffing on opium pipes. People complain about drugs and alcoholism among indigenous people, but if you take everything that gave meaning to their lives away, is it much of a surprise? This is where the big concrete forthright churches come in: they are the new meaning, the new life. Nagas with electric guitars playing in gospel rock groups abound.

They fought for sixty or more years for their independence

– from what? From the twentieth century? From India? From Britain? When one culture is stronger than another, is there any escape? It still seems a terrible shame that tradition, albeit a tradition of taking people's heads, should be ignored – and yet how many British people celebrate druidism, pay homage to standing stones and dance around yew trees? Folk dancing in the UK excites mockery. There are no clans, except in Scotland – perhaps a better example of cultural survival in the modern age. The Nagas still have their costumes, and you can still buy spearheads for pig-sticking in the market. Everyone carries a dao; many men are armed with ancient rifles. They are a warrior people, and that hasn't been taken completely away.

I look again at the hard bone face of yesterday. Everything such a man does has an urgency and a singing connection to the world he lives in. He is utterly self-sufficient. He is eternal and yet of the moment. The linkage to his whole world is taut; the wires are singing.

But the man fifty years on has no necessity. He could be on stage or in an old people's home. His world does not sing to him or connect to him, he is of the past, not the moment. He has become unnecessary in his own eyes.

One would desperately like to come down on one side or the other. Condemn one, say all was for the best or the worst. Softies and people who like showers and supermarkets find in their materialism excuse enough for annihilating other cultures. I cannot be so sure. But neither is it all for the bad. Nothing is ever completely lost. I think it is like death – it is another death in the Naga hills, end place of the white mountains. Emotionally, the loss must be borne. We have to wear white and go high into the hills and let the wind take away our grief for those who have passed away. We may be sure of their destination, but will always still feel a loss, a parting, a grief.

Is there anything else to say?

5

A Journey to the Burmese Border

A wise man seeing coming danger should avoid it;
on seeing it approach he should remain fearless.

Naga proverb

This was really the end of the line. I had dreamed about coming here for so long. I knew the names of villages and towns from things my father had said and from my interest in the Naga cause in the 1990s. The hills were less wooded than I imagined. Deforestation is a big problem in Nagaland – slash-and-burn agriculture breeds a casual acceptance of commercial logging – and as I pounded along dirt roads to the border, truck after truck went past loaded with logs about the diameter of telegraph poles. These were not the giant trees needed to make log drums (later I would find out that such trees still existed, but they were many miles from the road).

There are no flat places in Nagaland once you travel through the Assam hinterland where tea planting is in evidence. You start to climb quite soon. But not the horrendous hairpins of the high Himalayas; here it is gentler, but always you are going either up or down. The hills are intermittently wooded, things grow fast here, and areas that have been logged are quickly green again. The trucks loaded with logs were carting away secondary growth, a sign of a certain sustainability.

My driver was a fat laughing Konyak Naga from Mon. Mon is

a town with two hotels though not much else for the sightseer in search of more than local colour. For me it was the staging post for this relentless drive to the border.

Our vehicle was a Japanese mini-van with tiny wheels. Gamely the driver gunned it up and over muddy ruts and rubble-laden roads. Skidding and lurching up insanely steep tracks, I finally topped out at Long Wa – the village that straddles the border between India and Burma. Hill and mountain ridges are chosen as borders when the map-makers arrive – it's easier that way – but here, as on the Tibetan–Nepalese and Tibetan–Indian border, there was no real difference in landscape either side of the frontier. I was happy to see there was no fence or border crossing. There was only one official who spoke perfect English and probed why I was here, but in a very polite manner and not in the slightest with that disbelieving air so favoured by British police and immigration officials. He invited me to have a cup of tea with him in his office, but it was less like an office than his front parlour.

I was shown round by the leader of the student council in Long

Always heartening to see a thatched roof, whether in rural England or, as here, in jungle Nagaland

Wa. He was also excellent at English, but then English is the official language of Nagaland (a sort of snub to their Indian overlords). I was introduced to the King of Long Wa. He was smoking opium and having a good laugh with his pals in the longhouse. It was all a bit awkward as the student was embarrassed by the King's lack of sobriety. But he was a canny old king and he laughed mockingly at the young, rather stern lad. The King's mates wore traditional warrior kit, while His Majesty wore a necklace with several brass skulls – proof that once he had taken heads. But now he was half off his head. He offered me a blast on his pipe, but it didn't seem appropriate with my guide so disapproving.

For all his bravado, the King seemed lost, waiting for the odd tourist to show up, not at home in the new world, and the old world long gone.

6

Another Visit to Arunachal Pradesh

In the company of goats he says *goa*,
in the company of sheep he says *bea*.
Ladakhi proverb

In the Himalayas it seemed right to end by visiting a monastery. To get to the one in Tawang took the usual long, long drive over windy roads from Tezpur. I was not looking forward to it. The shared Jeeps went from the same place, the Muslim section of town. The call to prayer reminded me of Egypt; it was good to hear. The area was near the bus station. No one knew when or where the buses were going, including the staff in the station. It was very early. I had bought my ticket the night before from a youth in a kiosk who looked slightly simple. He went to another kiosk for confirmation that what he was saying was correct. He came back grinning from ear to ear. I could see he was actually a good employee; this area bounded by the kiosks and a few tin-roofed restaurants was his world, a place where he was accepted.

The next day, at 6 a.m. when it was barely dawn and chilly, he was nowhere to be seen. I went and got some puri (a fried bread), vegetable curry and instant coffee, my preferred breakfast at that time. The puri man had already made a great stack of puris and his hands were white with flour. So I accepted several freshly made, my reasoning being that if he didn't wash his hands the previous hundred puris would be the infected ones, not mine.

Then I saw the simpleton and he was very happy to see me. But he didn't know when the Jeep to the north was coming. I had my permit to visit Arunachal Pradesh; it had been less costly and time-consuming to get than the last time, but I was just as impatient to actually get there.

Then, all of a sudden, about five Jeeps arrived and my friend grabbed my bag and hurled it on top. This was the one. We were off. I had bought the window seat, second row – the least bumpy place to be – with good views out of the window. You get to be the first person out of the vehicle too.

Across the Brahmaputra into Arunachal Pradesh, we drove through flat forested areas with military camps at regular intervals. In the late 1990s this was BODO liberation territory. Then we began climbing. The hills were well covered with trees. It was almost boring to see so many completely forested hills and so few buildings and people. Arunachal Pradesh is the emptiest state in north-east India. The road passed by shacks with restaurants and a toilet in a lean-to of corrugated iron. The people were Tibetan-looking, perhaps Monpa from the north. Kids and chickens crossed in front of the slow-moving Jeeps. Hour after hour, the vehicle trudged north.

Army vehicles hogged the road in parts. Trucks turned up big plumes of dust that reduced visibility. There was something both exhilarating and irritating about having to wind up each valley in turn just to make northward progress. There was no straight road that could run directly, you had to go in and out of every valley issuing into the main valley; and then after a while you'd leap up and over some range of hills into another valley system. And all around were the conifer-forested hills.

The Jeep stopped for the night, or rather I got off, at Dirang. I had been recommended to stop here by a young Frenchman I met in Guwhati. There was something about his manner that was most earnest and convincing. Normally I am fairly wary of traveller's advice, but from him I accepted it. There was a brand-new monastery in Dirang that the Dalai Lama had visited in 2012. There was also a new nunnery on the other side of the river. Buddhism may have been pushed out of Tibet, but it is thriving here.

I stayed in a government rest house that was like a cross between a multistorey car park and a hotel. You actually entered the building up concrete stairs from the basement car park. There was one room in the basement constructed by simply fencing in some concrete roof-supporting pillars with plywood. From this enclosed hut came the sound of loud music. When I was leaving, I stuck my head round the rudimentary door. Inside it was thick with smoke. It was the cave of the taxi drivers, whose cabs I had seen outside; they had a ghetto-blaster, plenty of beer, a blue pool table and two were playing pool. They all looked up and grinned at me. The rest of the hotel was completely dead by comparison.

Like everywhere in Arunachal Pradesh, the streets were lined with beer shops. I walked out of town and on the way back in I met a local man who spoke very good English. He was weaving up the road and was completely drunk. 'I do not want you to think ill of me, so I will forget this conversation. But I welcome you to my country, I welcome you! I have been travelling myself and that is why I have been drinking, this is not what I do every day, this is not my habitual state.'

The next day I went looking for tigers in the hills. Arunachal Pradesh is probably home to more tigers than any other part of India. I went along the river, past the fluttering lines of Buddhist flags. I crossed over the flat alluvial river and walked past farms where everyone was using flails to thresh their barley on a giant tarpaulin laid out on the ground. By everyone, I mean every woman. No men were around. I watched through my zoom lens. One flailed for a while and when they were tired the daughter, or mother, took over. They had piles of cut barley waiting to be threshed.

The farms were all tiny, no more than ten or twenty acres, and they all bordered each other on the land by the river, the broad strip of green that was good, and then suddenly you were up in the forest where the tigers were supposed to be.

I had heard that tigers are rare in daylight and not at all likely to eat you unless they are man-eaters, but that was extremely unlikely. I hoped for a cough or a roar. What I mainly wanted to do was to get to the top of the hill, which was very much higher than I thought when I actually emerged from the farmland and into the forest.

There were no real paths. I followed a cut line, a kind of ditch of red earth and stones, hot in the sun and very steep. It became too strenuous, so I branched out and found another dry stream bed to climb. Every so often I clambered up what would have been small waterfalls in the rainy season. I kept an eye open for snakes and scorpions, but it was hard to keep remembering as the woods all looked like dry pine forests in Scotland. I picked up various cones to take home for my children.

It was getting steeper and lonelier and I was still no nearer the top. I had seen and heard no wildlife. Then, through a break in the canopy, I saw an eagle riding a thermal with its spread wings, fingers of feather unruffled and unmoving, still blue air behind and circling in wide lazy circles, looking down. That was the way to travel in the mountains. I carried on, but my mind was on that eagle.

It was a new place and I will never forget it, but I knew I would have to turn back. It was one of those stillborn adventures that you have to have from time to time. I took a leak against a tree and listened. It was winter and though warm there were no flies or mosquitoes. It was the best time for such walking. I then waited for long minutes in case some creature should eventually lose its shyness and emerge, but none did. It is always the way with real wilderness – usually you see nothing, sometimes for days, and then you see an abundance of wildlife in one concentrated burst. I looked for the tiger, face bars blending with the shadows, but I saw none. I turned and gratefully made my way back to the farmland and the security of the wide shallow river and the people threshing their barley.

The driving continued all the next day. We went over the pass where the Chinese came in 1962 and valiant Indian troops stopped them. It is hard to know why the Chinese are so keen to take this land. It's the other side of several very high passes. It could not be controlled from Tibet if they overran it. Perhaps they simply want to take Tawang Monastery, because that's where the Dalai Lama fled to in 1959. Symbolically home, despite being in another country.

The high pass to Tawang, above the clouds

The Jeep went ever higher; the pass is 4,500 metres and I felt fine. Maybe it would catch up with me later, but because I only got out of the Jeep and took a picture and then got back in again, I wasn't really straining myself. I had also spent a day at Dirang getting acclimatised to some extent. Tawang itself was shrouded in mist, and lower than the pass at about 3,000 metres. I made the foolish mistake of running about the town with my luggage to find the best hotel at the best price. This contradicted my self-given advice to take it easy at altitude for the first few days, even at the relatively low level of 3,000 metres. But all the hotels were similarly grim and expensive, and only with serious bargaining and asking for a new lightbulb to be thrown in as a sweetener did I get a half-decent room. Panelled with stained pine, it was like a cold ship's cabin.

I went down to the obligatory booze shops and bought some dodgy-looking rum and an extra-strong Kingfisher lager. None of the restaurants served alcohol, but no one minded if you brought your own. The best restaurant was also wood-panelled and above the ground up a flight of rickety outdoor stairs. The owner was proud of his food and it was good and also not expensive. I had been long enough in India now to have become a typical back-packing tightwad, begrudging spending more than a few hundred rupees on anything at any one time. The Himalayan parts of India are more expensive than the plains, though cheaper than the cities, and it was the memory of cheaper meals elsewhere that always drove me to find a bargain.

It was a long walk up to the monastery. The roads were not straight, nor straightforward, but all led there in the end. On the skyline to one side was an enormous Buddha, as big as a church with a high steeple. You felt far from India here.

The monastery is one of the oldest still running; it dates back to the seventeenth century. Because the style of building is square and modernistic, it doesn't look like some hoary old fantasy monastery; rather it has a freshly whitewashed, red-and-yellow-painted aspect that at first belies its great age. But away from the open central square it is ancient and labyrinthine. Dogs and chickens roam the tiny alleys where the monks live. In the main meditation hall, a cavern of polished wood and chanting monks, a bell, as big as a bucket, hung with its short tail of rope right above the entrance. As the little boy monks left, each lad gave the bell an almighty swing, trying to make the loudest noise possible.

Young monk and puppies, Tawang Monastery

Some jumped to reach it and timed their smash with aplomb. It was all tolerated, unlike school, where such obvious high jinks would have been curtailed for sure.

I went up to the museum of the monastery and an elderly monk gave me a ticket. Inside were photos of the young Dalai Lama when he arrived dressed as a Tibetan soldier in 1959. There were also pictures of him, a little later, wearing what looked like a white fedora hat and a brightly patterned robe – and why not? I once met a wealthy banker who denigrated the Dalai Lama for wearing tailored suits and Italian shoes. It was the double hypocrisy of a man guilty of his own materialism, projecting it on to another. The Dalai Lama owns nothing – in a sense – his life is spent doing his best to serve the Tibetan people. Unlike the banker, he has no wife, no kids, no fancy town house or country pad. He lives in exile and deserves all the pairs of Italian shoes he can get.

You can't nail the Dalai Lama down, he isn't one thing or the other, he's managed to twist and turn and keep the spirit of Tibet alive despite the crushing pressure of the Chinese occupation. To mention his name or to hand over a photograph of the Dalai Lama in Tibet is an arrestable offence. Even one like this.

Museum picture of the fourteenth Dalai Lama wearing hat

Leaving the Tawang Monastery, I met a young monk – only twenty – who asked me if it was true that the time in London was different to the time in India. I said it was and he marvelled at that. Then he asked me more questions. He was walking with a small boy – no more than twelve – who had a dental appointment in the town. The monk was cheerful and smiling like most Buddhist monks. And, like the Dalai Lama, full of curiosity about the outside world. It is as if, having been locked up for so long meditating and chanting, they are like prisoners tasting with joy anything on the 'outside'. We have grown decadent, have we not? I found myself thinking. Or have I simply buried my curiosity under veneers of politeness? Though I have to say, he didn't exactly answer my questions as fulsomely as I answered his. He wasn't going to waste his time with this foreigner.

In Tawang town every other shop, pretty much, is a booze shop. They certainly like drinking up there. The shops are run by Indians who trade for a living at 3,000 metres altitude, far from home, making a healthy profit on Godfather lager and super-strength Kingfisher, my preferred Himalayan tipple.

At the Swiss Cottage restaurant – a pine-panelled cosy eatery lit with a central stove – I shared a six-pack of Kingfisher with a drunken monk, as he described himself. A ruddy-faced Monpa who had learned English in the monastery school, he had left to 'get laid and see the world, but I ended up getting laid and not seeing the world!'.

'Nobody likes to think they screwed up in their life so we invent nice stories to tell ourselves – but really there is no need! It's impossible to screw up, I found that out!' He was on his third Kingfisher by now and spluttering a little, but I got the gist: we take our own paths too seriously. 'There is many many path, as many as people on the planet – no right path, wrong path. One door close, another open. All that matter is you stay alive and not get your spirit killed by worry and false thinking. Drinking is good – except it make you alcoholic like me! Smoking is good too – except it's bad for your body. But they say a man who desires tobacco is a man who desires wisdom.'

'That's a lot of people!'

'Yes – but desire is not enough, you have to do other thing.'

'What sort of thing?'

He started to laugh, filling his face with bread. 'Be like this' – he made open welcoming hands. 'And this.' Now his hand was flat, fingers pointing forwards, as if to say Don't fear to be straight-forward. Then he rocked it from side to side – 'Get good feeling for the balance in everything. And find the thing you like doing.'

'Anything else?' I may have sounded flippant. His face was suddenly stern.

'No.'

Acknowledgements

The first acknowledgement is to all the Himalayan residents and travellers I met on my various journeys, who helped me in numerous ways: they are the core of any trip. Some I have mentioned, some not, all were important.

A book is made from other books, to be sure, but it is at least as dependent on colleagues, friends and family: a thousand thanks to Dahlia Twigger for her excellent illustrated maps; Bea Hemming, Holly Harley and Elizabeth Allen at Orion; Andrew Kidd and Matthew Hamilton at Aitken Alexander; Jason Webster, Bijan Omrani, Rich Lisney, Jean and Tony Twigger, Piers Moor Ede, Adrian Turpin, Shaun Bythell, Tahir Shah, Christopher Ross, Ramsay Wood, Gill Whitworth, and John Blashford-Snell.

A special extra thanks to Tarquin and Anu Hall who put up with me over Diwali; Pete Royall at keadventure.com, who hosted me on one of their excellent treks in the Garwhal Himalaya; and Dhanraj Gurung in Yoksum, Sikkim who also did a great job in outfitting a ten-day trek with his highly recommended redpandatreks.weebly.com.

Also thanks to Rigzin Skalzang, Michael and Caroline Sterling, David Benson, Stephen Slater, Peter Holmes, Christine Stewart; Andrew Bond for maps, guides, inspiration and stimulating conversation at the Alpine Club and elsewhere.

Andrew Duff's book on Sikkim was most welcome as an introduction to this fascinating place. And Samia Hosny, as always, for being such a stalwart support.

Select Bibliography

―――――

Charles Allen, *Ashoka* (Little, Brown, 2012)

――, *A Mountain in Tibet* (Abacus, 2003)

Alexander Andreyev, *Soviet Russia and Tibet: The Debacle of Secret Diplomacy* (Brill, 2003)

Michael Aris, 'Sacred Dances of Bhutan', *National History Magazine* (March 1980), 38–48

Francis Bacon, *Novum Organum*, 1620

Phil Bartlett, *The Undiscovered Country* (Ernest Press, 1993)

C. M. Beall, D. Laskowski & S. C. Erzurum, 'Nitric oxide in adaptation to altitude', *Free Radical Biology and Medicine* 52(7) (1 April 2012), 1123–34

Charles Bell, *Portrait of a Dalai Lama: The Life and Times of the Great Thirteenth* (Wisdom Publications, 1957)

Herbert Benson, 'Body temperature changes during the practice of gTum-mo yoga', *Nature* 295 (1982), 234–6

Edwin Bernbaum, *The Way to Shambhala* (Anchor Books, 1980)

Scott Berry, *A Stranger in Tibet* (Kodansha International, 1989)

Paul Bert, *Barometric Pressure: Researches in Experimental Physiology*, trans. Mary Alice & Fred A. Hitchcock (College Book Company, 1943)

Zeff Bjerken, 'Exorcising the Illusion of Bon "Shamans": A Critical Genealogy of Shamanism in Tibetan Religions', *Revue d'Etudes Tibetaines* 6 (September 2004), 4–59

Chris Bonington, *The Climbers: History of Mountaineering* (BBC Books, 1992)

Anatoli Boukreev & G. Weston DeWalt, *The Climb: Tragic Ambitions on Everest* (St Martin's Press, 1998)

Garma Chang, *The Hundred Thousand Songs of Milarepa*, 2 vols (University Books, 1962)

Frederick Spencer Chapman, *Lhasa: The Holy City* (Chatto & Windus, 1940)

Bruce Chatwin, *Utz* (Jonathan Cape, 1988)

Clement of Alexandria, *The Stromata*, Book 1, Chapter XV

Peter D. Clift & Jerzy Blusztajn, 'Reorganization of the western Himalayan river system after five million years ago', *Nature* 438 (2005), 1001–3

Aleister Crowley, *The Confessions of Aleister Crowley: An Autohagiograhy*, eds. John Symonds & Kenneth Grant (Arkana, 1989)

Dalai Lama, *Freedom in Exile* (Little, Brown, 1993)

Alexandra David-Néel, *Magic and Mystery in Tibet* (Claude Kendall, 1932)

Andrew Duff, *Sikkim: Requiem for a Himalayan Kingdom* (Birlinn Books, 2015)

Kenneth Mason, *Abode of Snow* (E. P. Dutton & Co., 1955)

T.S. Eliot, *The Waste Land* (Faber & Faber, 1962)

Peter Fleming, *Bayonets to Lhasa* (Hart-Davis, 2012)

——, *News from Tartary* (Northwestern University Press, 1936)

Robert Ford, *Captured in Tibet* (Oxford University Press, 1957)

'Ganges receives 2,900 million litres of sewage daily', *Hindustan Times*, 14 May 2015

Richard Gombrich, 'Ancient Indian Cosmology' in *Ancient Cosmologies*, eds. Carmen Blacker & Michael Loewe (Allen & Unwin, 1975)

Nicholas Goodrick-Clarke, *Helena Blavatsky* (North Atlantic Books, 2004)

Tom Grunfeld, *The Making of Modern Tibet* (Routledge,1996)

Christopher Hale, *Himmler's Crusade* (Bantam Press, 2003)

David Hamilton, 'The Great Karakoram Ski Traverse', *Alpine Journal* (2005), 113–23

Eric Hansen, 'The Killing Fields', *Outside* (2 August 2011)

Heinrich Harrer, *Seven Years in Tibet* (Hart-Davis, 1953)

Sven Hedin, *Southern Tibet*, 14 vols (Lithographic Institute of the General Staff of the Swedish Army, 1917–22)

——, *Trans-Himalaya: Adventures in Tibet* (Macmillan, 1910)

John C. Holliday & Matt P. Cleaver, 'Medicinal value of the caterpillar fungi species of the genus *Cordyceps* (Fr.) Link (Ascomycetes). A Review', *International Journal of Medicinal Mushrooms* 10(3) (2008), 219–34

Peter Hopkirk, *The Great Game: On Secret Sevice in High Asia* (John Murray, 2006)

——, *Foreign Devils on the Silk Road: The Search for the Lost Treasures of Central Asia* (John Murray, 2006)

John Hunt, *The Ascent of Everest* (Hodder & Stoughton, 1956)

Maurice Isserman, *Fallen Giants: A History of Himalayan Mountaineering from the Age of Empire to the Age of Extremes* (Yale University Press, 2008)

Lou Kasischke, *After the Wind: 1996 Everest Tragedy – One Survivor's Story* (Good Hart Publishing, 2014)

Ekai Kawaguchi, *Three Years in Tibet* (Theosophical Society, 1909)

John Keay, *Where Men and Mountains Meet: The Explorers of the Western Himalayas 1820–75* (Century, 1977)

John Keay, *The Great Arc: The Dramatic Tale of How India was Mapped and Everest was Named* (HarperCollins, 2010)

Maria Kozhevnikov, James Elliott, Jennifer Shephard & Klaus Gramann, 'Neurocognitive and Somatic Components of Temperature Increases during g-Tummo Meditation: Legend and Reality', PloS ONE 8(3) (2013), e58244

Jon Krakauer, *Into Thin Air* (Macmillan, 2011)

Perceval Landon, *Lhasa*, 2 vols (Hurst & Blackett, 1905)

Arnold Henry Savage Landor, *In the Forbidden Land* (Long Riders Guild Press, 1898)

Philip Larkin, *Whitsun Weddings* (Faber & Faber, 1967)

Stuart Legg, *The Barbarians of Asia: The Peoples of the Steppes from 1600 BC* (Marboro Books, 1990)

Andreas Lommel, *Masks: their Meaning and Function*, trans. Nadia Fowler (McGraw-Hill, 1972)

——, *Shamanism: The Beginnings of Art*, trans. Michael Bullock (McGraw-Hill, 1967)

David MacDonald, *Twenty Years in Tibet* (Pilgrims Publishing, 1932)

Halford Mackinder, 'The Geographical Pivot of History', *Geographical Journal* 23 (1904), 421–37

Kenneth Mason, *Abode of Snow* (E. P. Dutton & Co., 1955)

Marion Meade, *Madame Blavatsky* (Putnam, 1980)

Reinhold Messner, *My Quest for the Yeti*, trans. Peter Constantine (St Martin's Press, 2000)

——, *Free Spirit: A Climber's Life* (Mountaineers Books, 1991)

A. J. Moffat Mills, *Report on the Province of Assam*, (Johns, 1854)

W. H. Murray, 'The Reconnaissance of Mount Everest, 1951', *Alpine Journal* 58, 285 (1952), 433–52

Arne Naess, 'Mountains and Mythology', *The Trumpeter* 12, 4 (1995)

Jeremy Narby, *The Cosmic Serpent* (Weidenfeld & Nicolson, 1999)

René de Nebesky-Wojkowitz, *Oracles and Demons of Tibet* (Gordon Press, 1976)

Mary Neff, *Personal Memoirs of H. P. Blavatsky* (H. P. Dutton & Co., 1937)

Harold Nicolson, *Curzon: The Last Phase, 1919–1925: A Study in Diplomacy* (Constable, 1934)

Christopher Norton, *Everest Revealed: The Private Diaries and Sketches of Edward Norton, 1922–24* (The History Press, 2014)

Michael Palin, *Himalaya* (Weidenfeld & Nicolson, 2004)

Michel Peissel, *Cavaliers of Kham: The Secret War in Tibet* (Heinemann, 1972)

Jim Perrin, *Shipton and Tilman* (Hutchinson, 2013)

Graham Ratcliffe, *A Day to Die For: 1996, Everest's Worst Disaster – One Survivor's Personal Journey to Uncover the Truth* (Mainstream Publishing, 2011)

George N. Roerich, *Trails to Inmost Asia: Five Years of Exploration with the Roerich Central Asian Expedition* (Yale University Press, 1931)

James Scott & Joanne Robertson, *Lost in the Himalayas: James Scott's 43-Day Ordeal* (Lothian, 1993)

Mike Searle, *Colliding Continents* (Oxford University Press, 2012)

Idries Shah, *Reflections* (Octagon Press, 1975)

——, *Wisdom of the Idiots* (Octagon Press, 1969)

——, *The Sufis* (W. H. Allen, 1964)

——, *Oriental Magic* (Octagon Press, 1956)

R. R. Shimray, *Origin and Culture of Nagas* (Pamleiphi Shimray, 1985)

David L. Snellgrove & Hugh Richardson, *A Cultural History of Tibet* (Prajna Press, 1968)

R. A. Stein, *Tibetan Civilization* (Faber & Faber, 1972)

H.W. Tilman, *Mount Everest 1938* (Pilgrims Publishing, 2004)

Giuseppe Tucci, *The Ancient Civilisation of Transhimalaya*, trans. James Hogarth (Barrie & Jenkins, 1973)

Beck Weathers, *Left for Dead: My Journey Home from Everest* (Sphere, 2000)

C. White, *Sikkim and Bhutan: Twenty-One Years on the North-East Frontier 1897–1908* (Arnold, 1909)

Ludwig Wittgenstein, *The Mythology in Our Language: Remarks on Frazer's* Golden Bough, ed. Giovanni da Col, trans. Stephan Palmié (University of Chicago Press, 2015)

Andrei Znamenski, *Red Shambhala* (Quest Books, 2011)

Index